Is it WRONG to try to PiCK UP GiRLS in a DUNGEON? ON THE SiDE

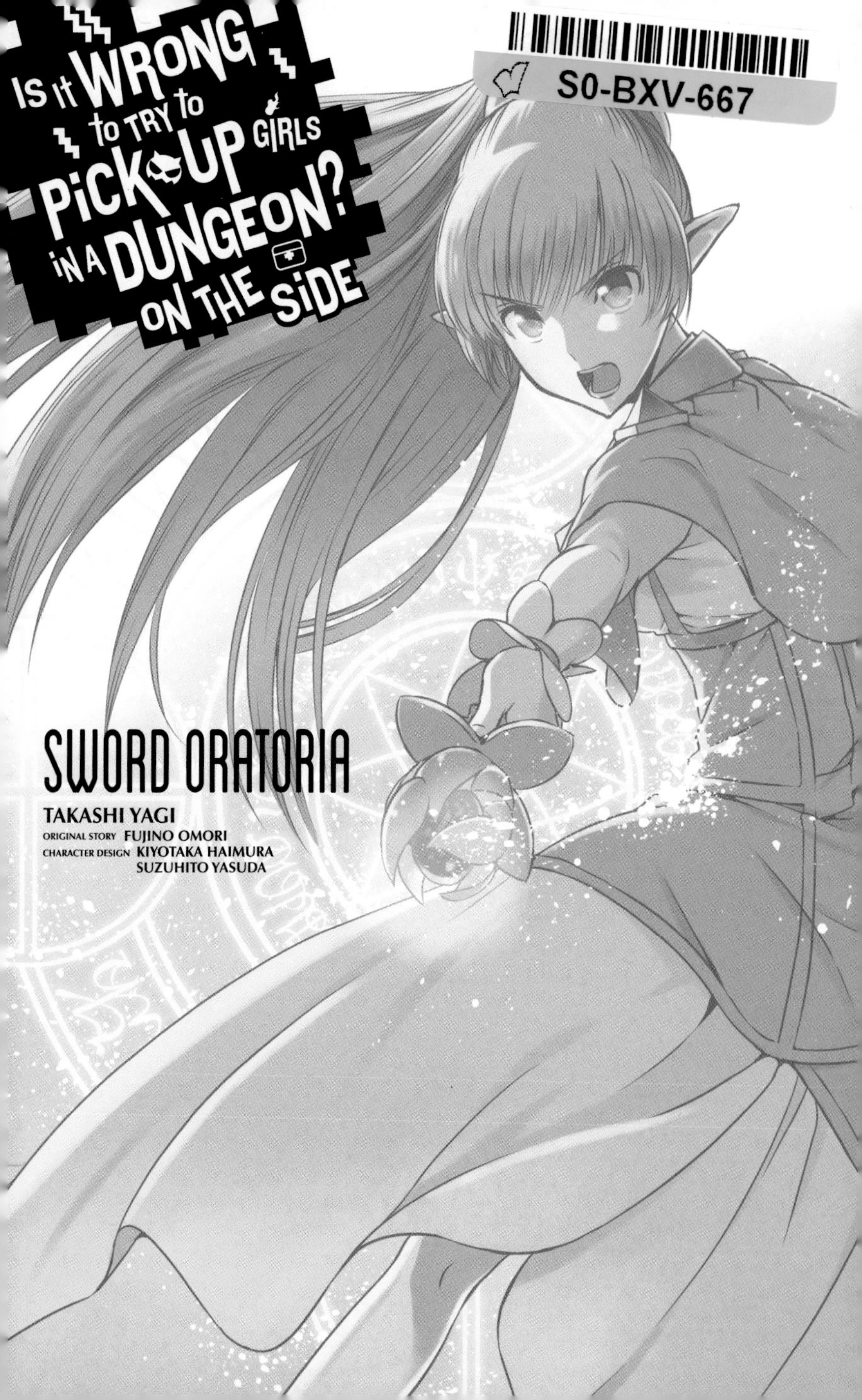

SWORD ORATORIA

TAKASHI YAGI
ORIGINAL STORY FUJINO OMORI
CHARACTER DESIGN KIYOTAKA HAIMURA
SUZUHITO YASUDA

10

SWORD ORATORIA

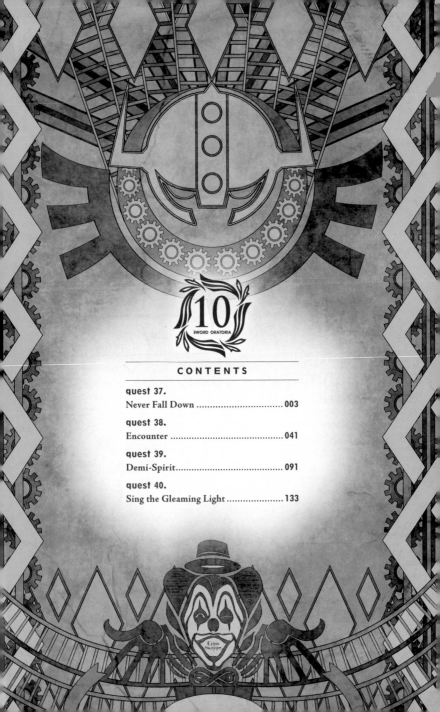

CONTENTS

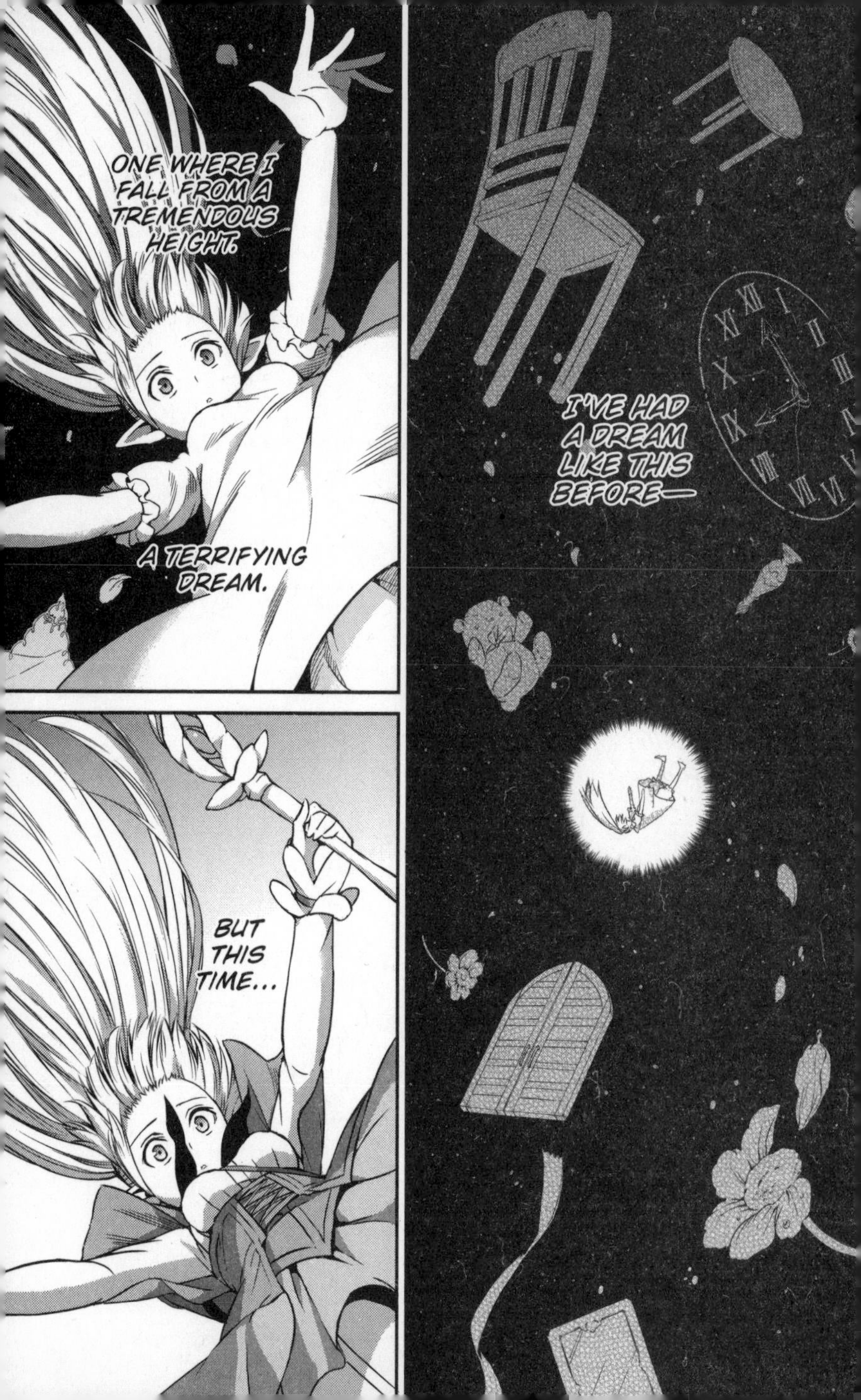
I'VE HAD A DREAM LIKE THIS BEFORE—
ONE WHERE I FALL FROM A TREMENDOUS HEIGHT.
A TERRIFYING DREAM.
BUT THIS TIME...

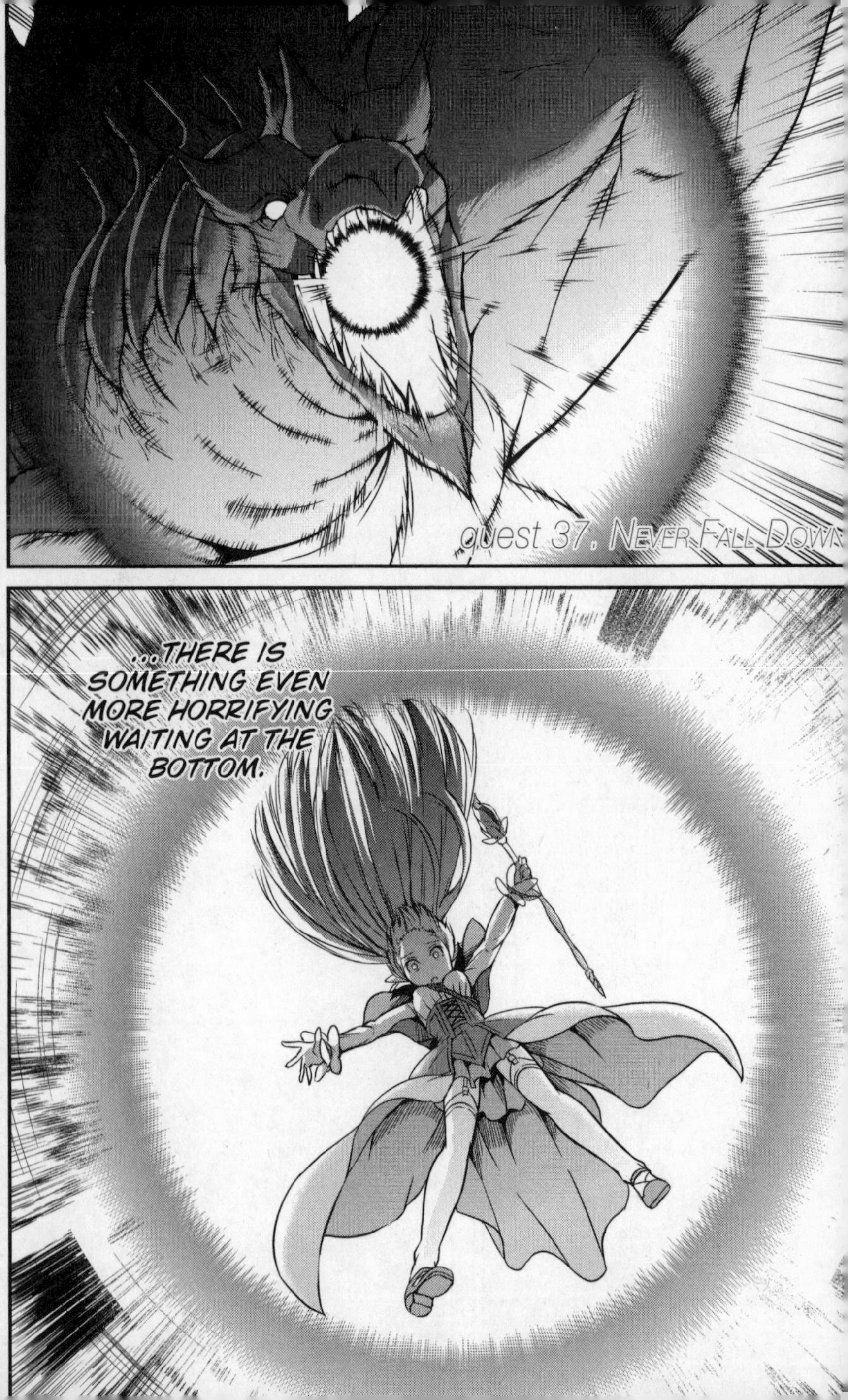
quest 37. Never Fall Down
...THERE IS SOMETHING EVEN MORE HORRIFYING WAITING AT THE BOTTOM.

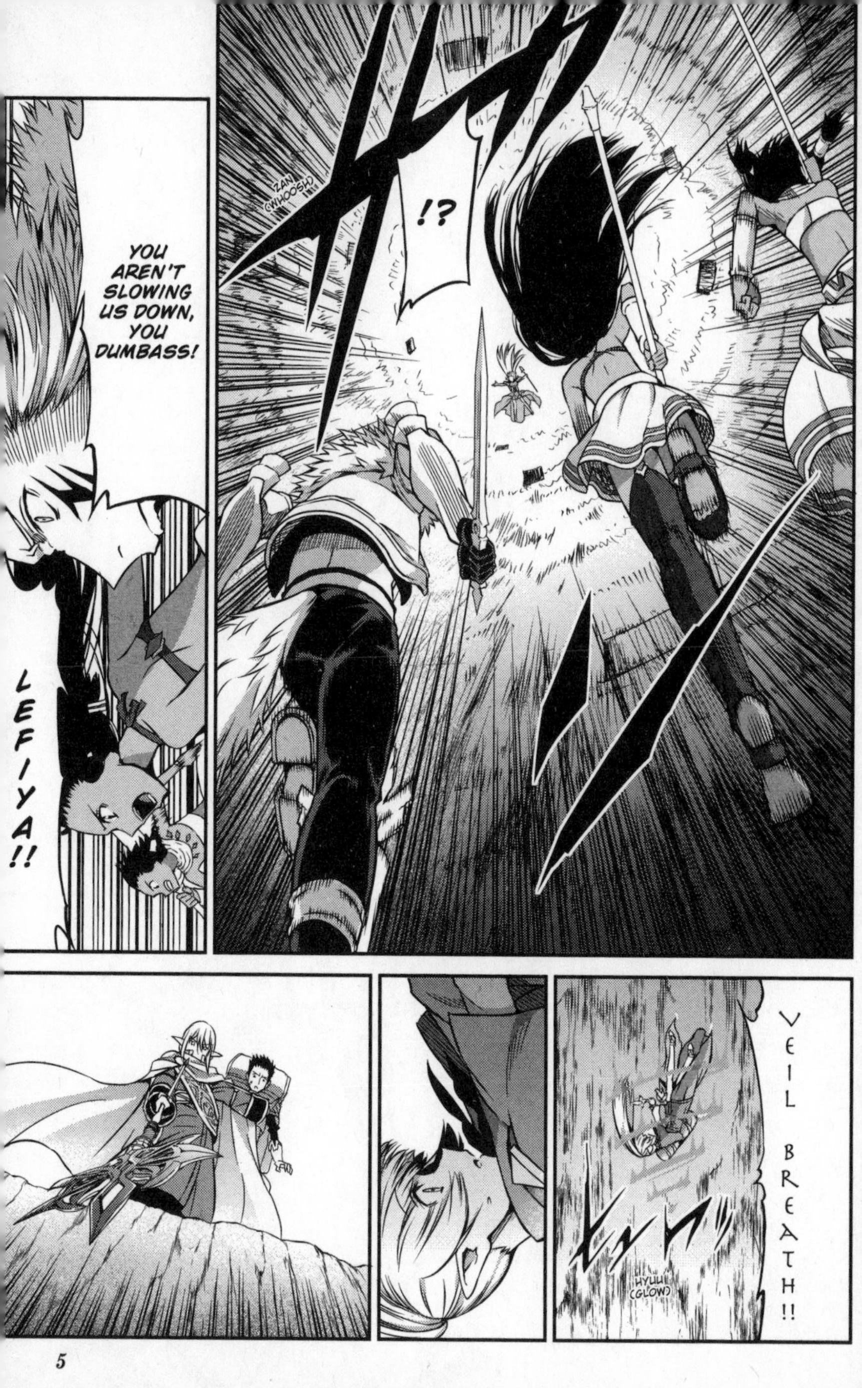
ZAN (WHOOSH)
!?
YOU AREN'T SLOWING US DOWN, YOU DUMBASS!
LEFIYA!!
VEIL BREATH!!
HYUUU (GLOW)

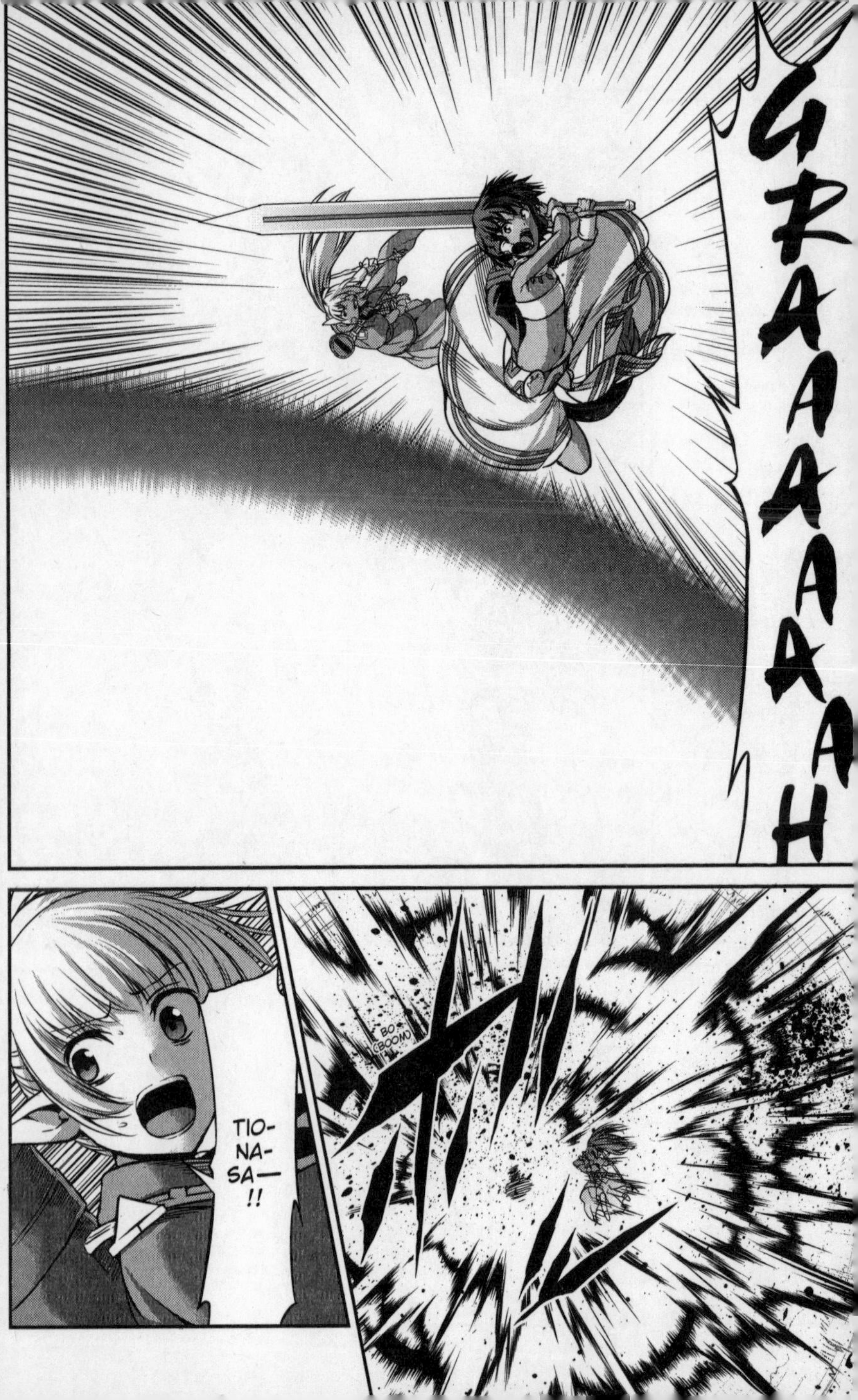
GRAAAAAAH
TIO-
NA-
SA—
!!
BO
(BOOM)

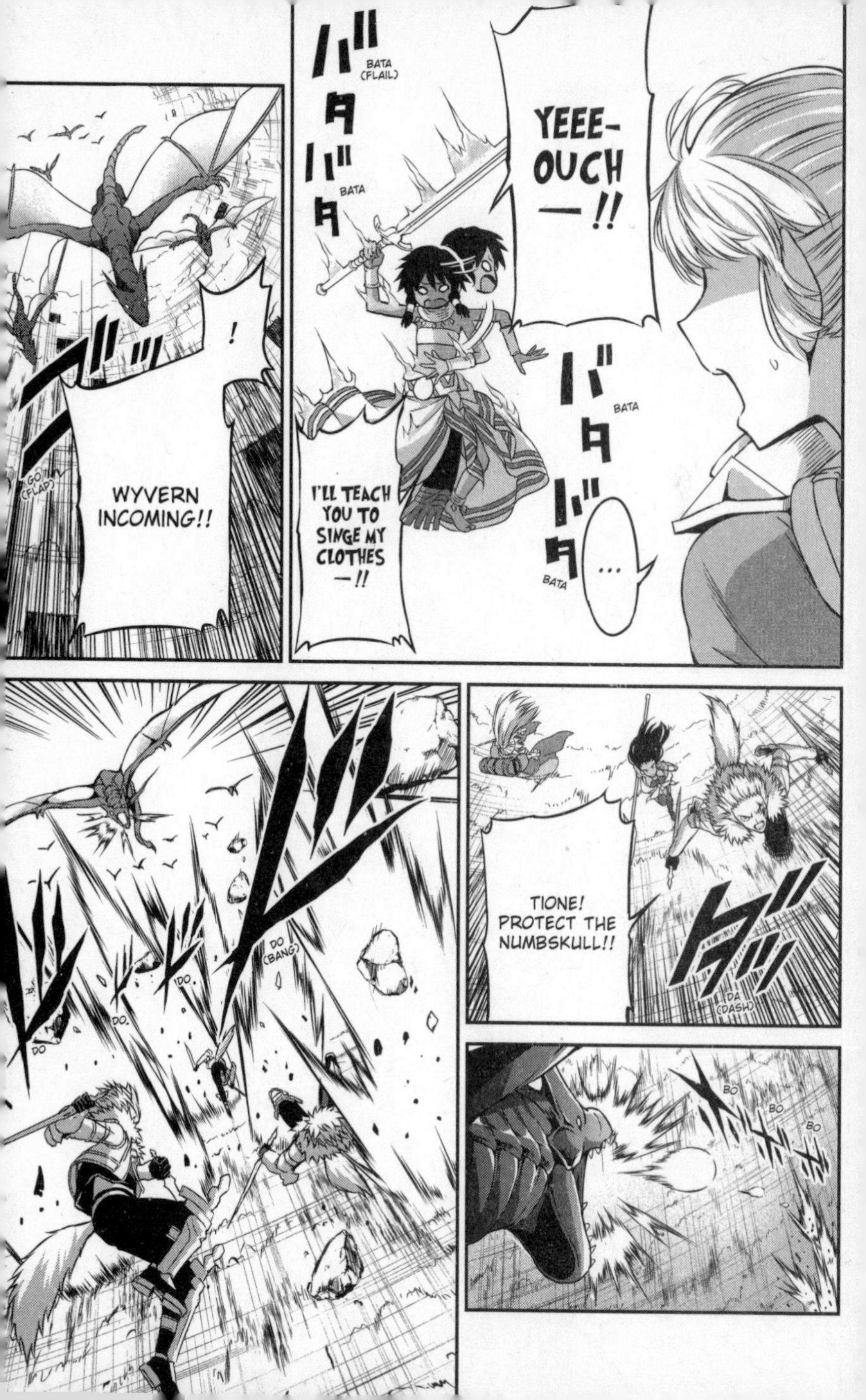
YEEE-OUCH —!!
BATA
BATA
...
BATA (FLAIL)
BATA
I'LL TEACH YOU TO SINGE MY CLOTHES —!!
GO (FLAP)
WYVERN INCOMING!!
!
TIONE! PROTECT THE NUMBSKULL!!
DA (DASH)
BO
BO
BO
DO (BANG)
DO.
DO.
DO

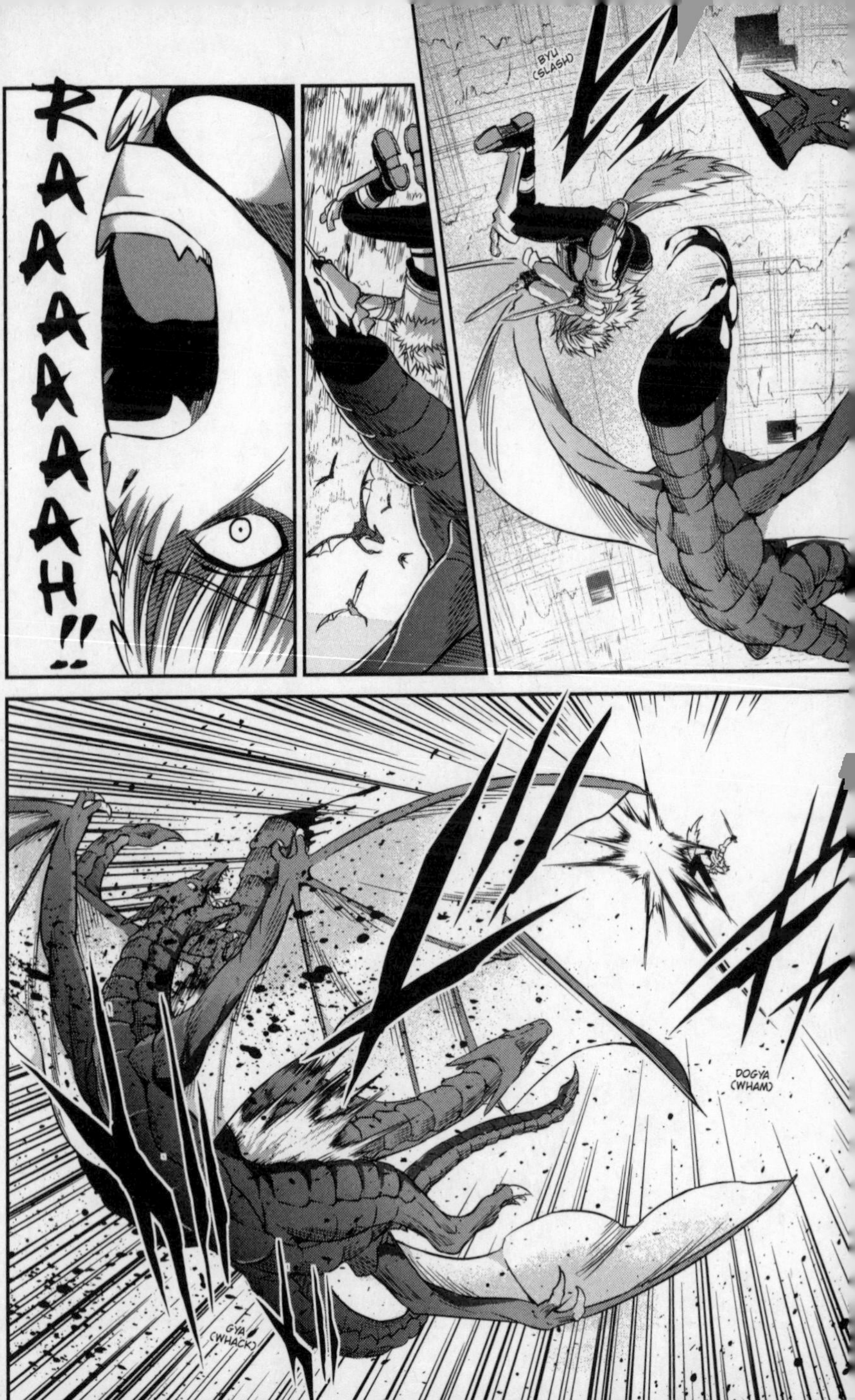
BYU (SLASH)
RAAAAAAAH!!
DOGYA (WHAM)
GYA (WHACK)

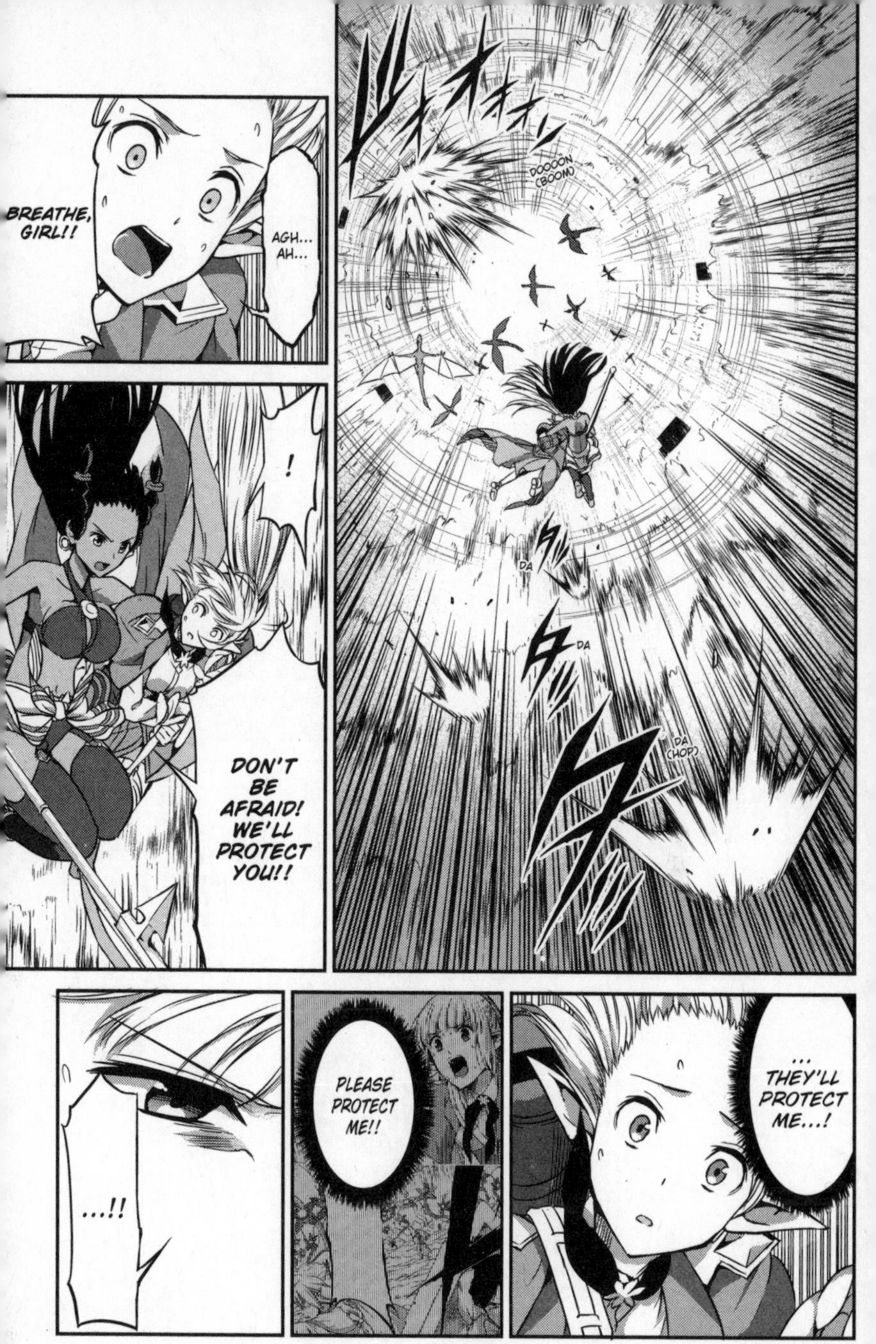
DOOOON (BOOM)
DA
DA
DA (CHOP)
AGH... AH...
BREATHE, GIRL!!
!
DON'T BE AFRAID! WE'LL PROTECT YOU!!
... THEY'LL PROTECT ME...!
PLEASE PROTECT ME!!
...!!

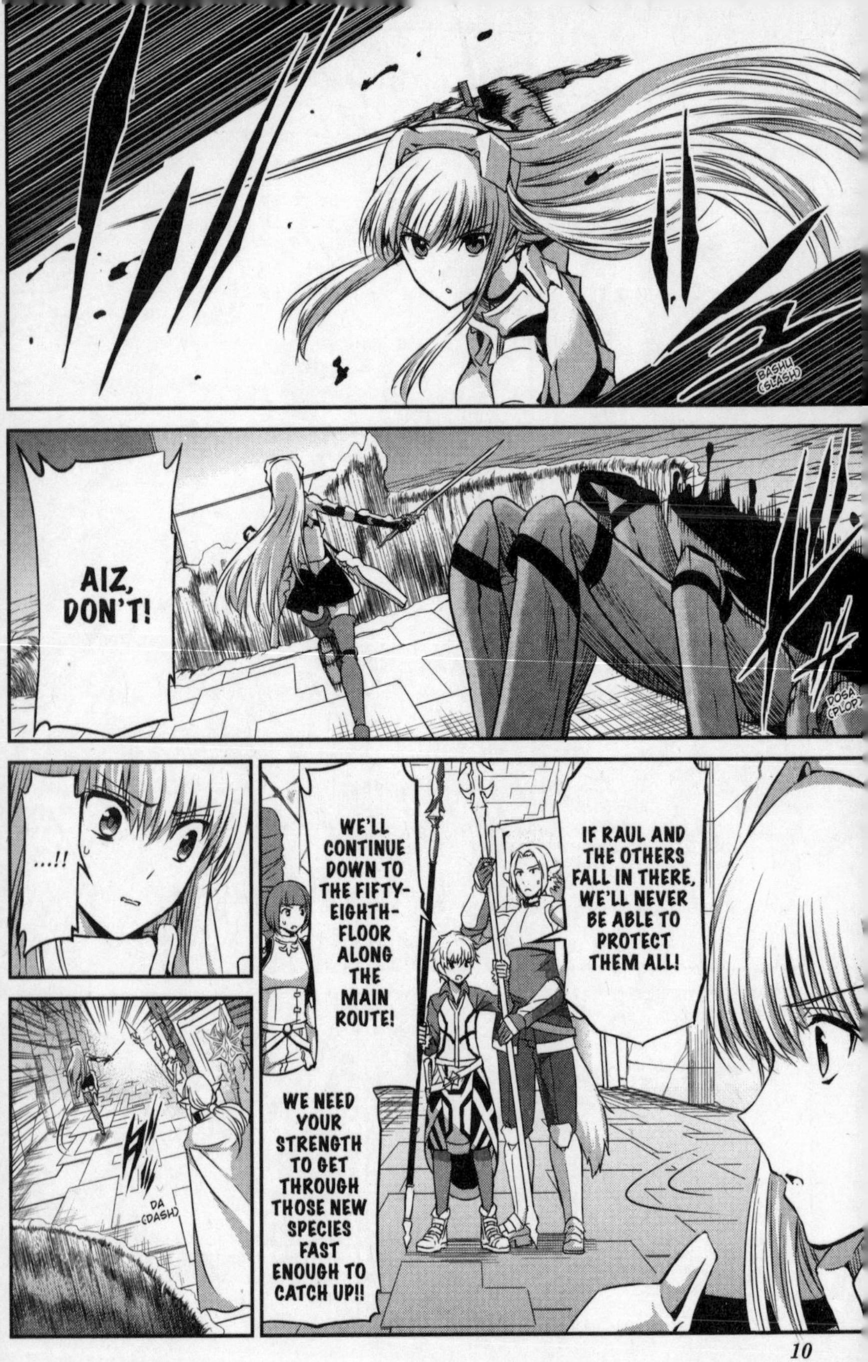
BASHU (SLASH)
DOSA (PLOP)
AIZ, DON'T!
IF RAUL AND THE OTHERS FALL IN THERE, WE'LL NEVER BE ABLE TO PROTECT THEM ALL!
WE'LL CONTINUE DOWN TO THE FIFTY-EIGHTH-FLOOR ALONG THE MAIN ROUTE!
WE NEED YOUR STRENGTH TO GET THROUGH THOSE NEW SPECIES FAST ENOUGH TO CATCH UP!!
...!!
DA (DASH)

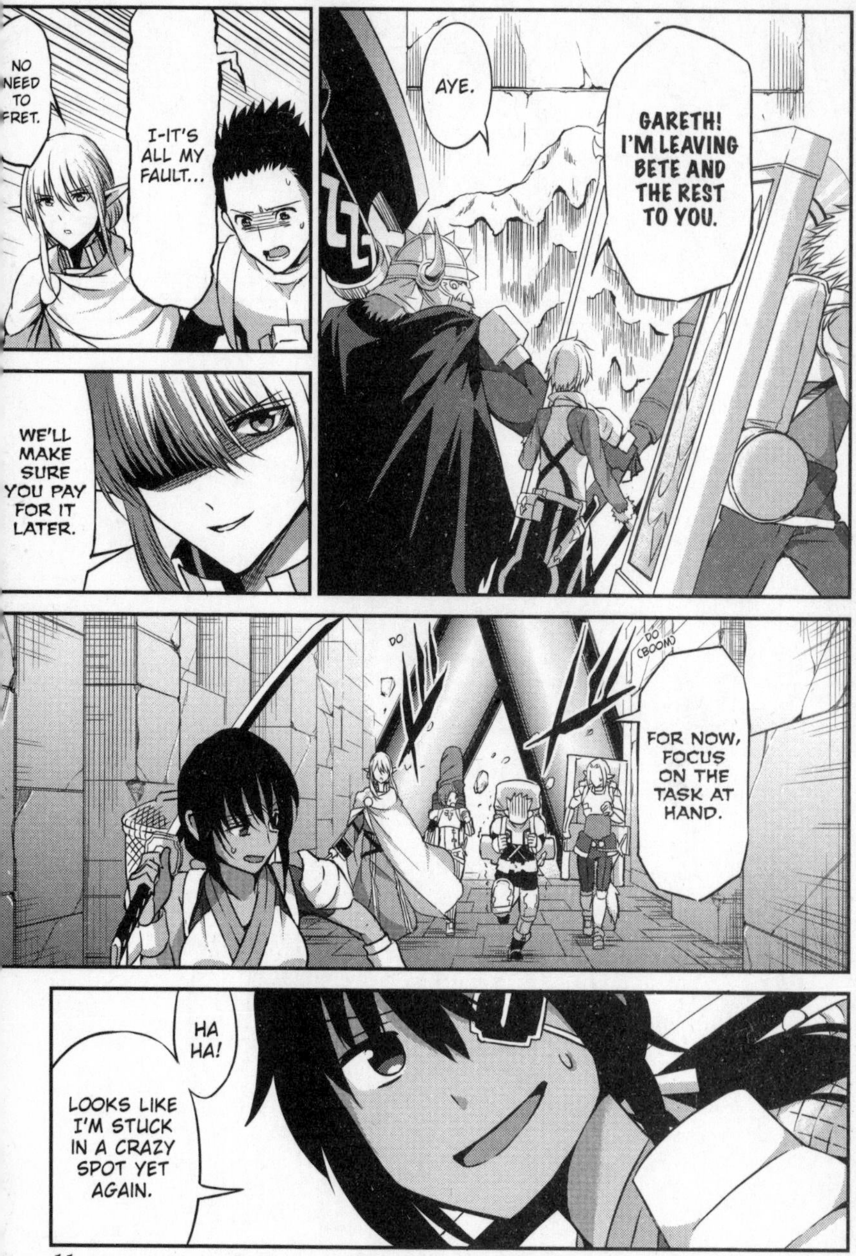
GARETH! I'M LEAVING BETE AND THE REST TO YOU.
AYE.
I-IT'S ALL MY FAULT...
NO NEED TO FRET.
WE'LL MAKE SURE YOU PAY FOR IT LATER.
DO (BOOM)
DO
FOR NOW, FOCUS ON THE TASK AT HAND.
HA HA!
LOOKS LIKE I'M STUCK IN A CRAZY SPOT YET AGAIN.

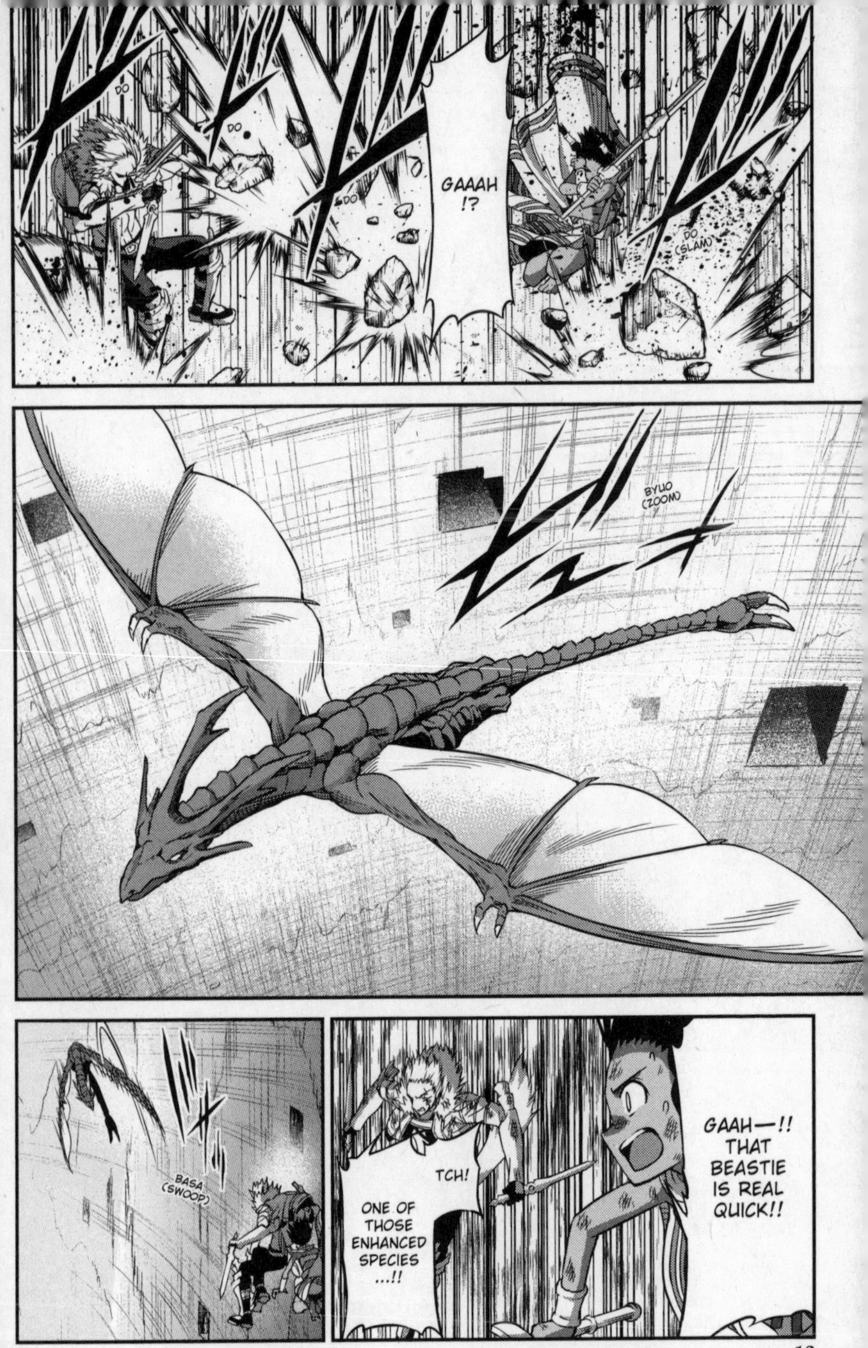
DO (SLAM)
GAAAH !?
DO
DO
DO
BYUO (ZOOM)
GAAH—!! THAT BEASTIE IS REAL QUICK!!
TCH!
ONE OF THOSE ENHANCED SPECIES ...!!
BASA (SWOOP)

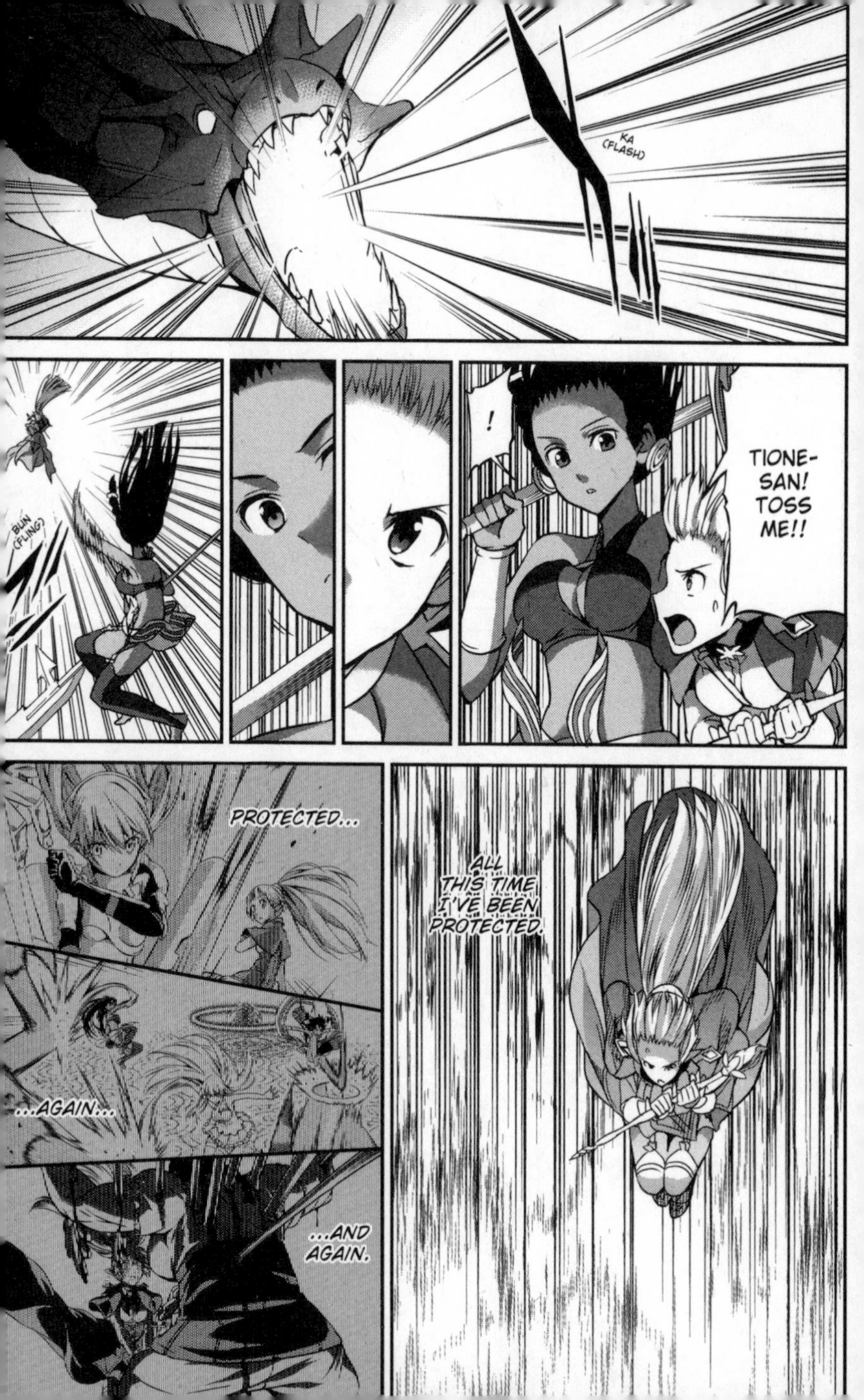
KA (FLASH)
!
TIONE-SAN! TOSS ME!!
BUN (FLING)
ALL THIS TIME I'VE BEEN PROTECTED.
PROTECTED...
...AGAIN...
...AND AGAIN.

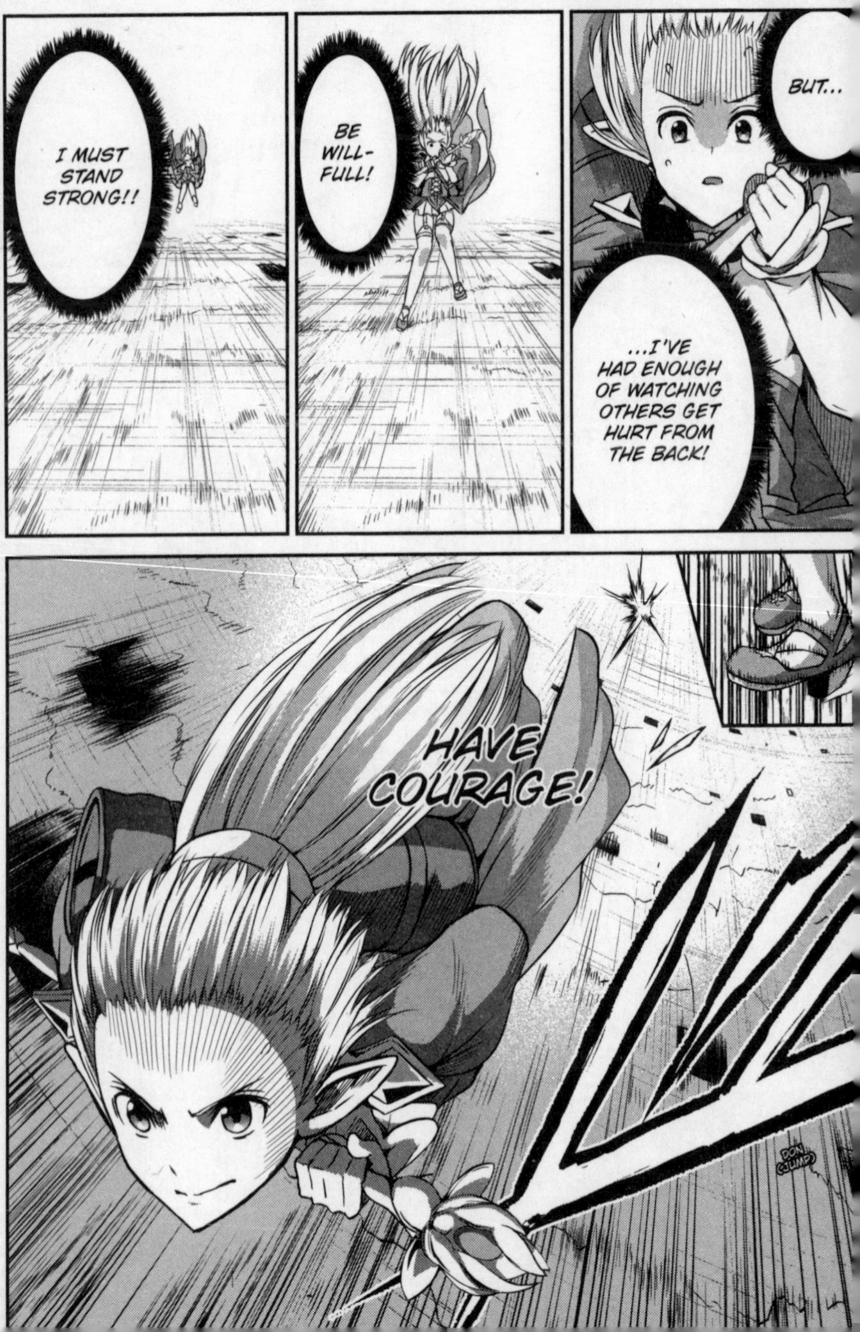
BUT...
...I'VE HAD ENOUGH OF WATCHING OTHERS GET HURT FROM THE BACK!
BE WILL-FULL!
I MUST STAND STRONG!!
HAVE COURAGE!
DON (JUMP)

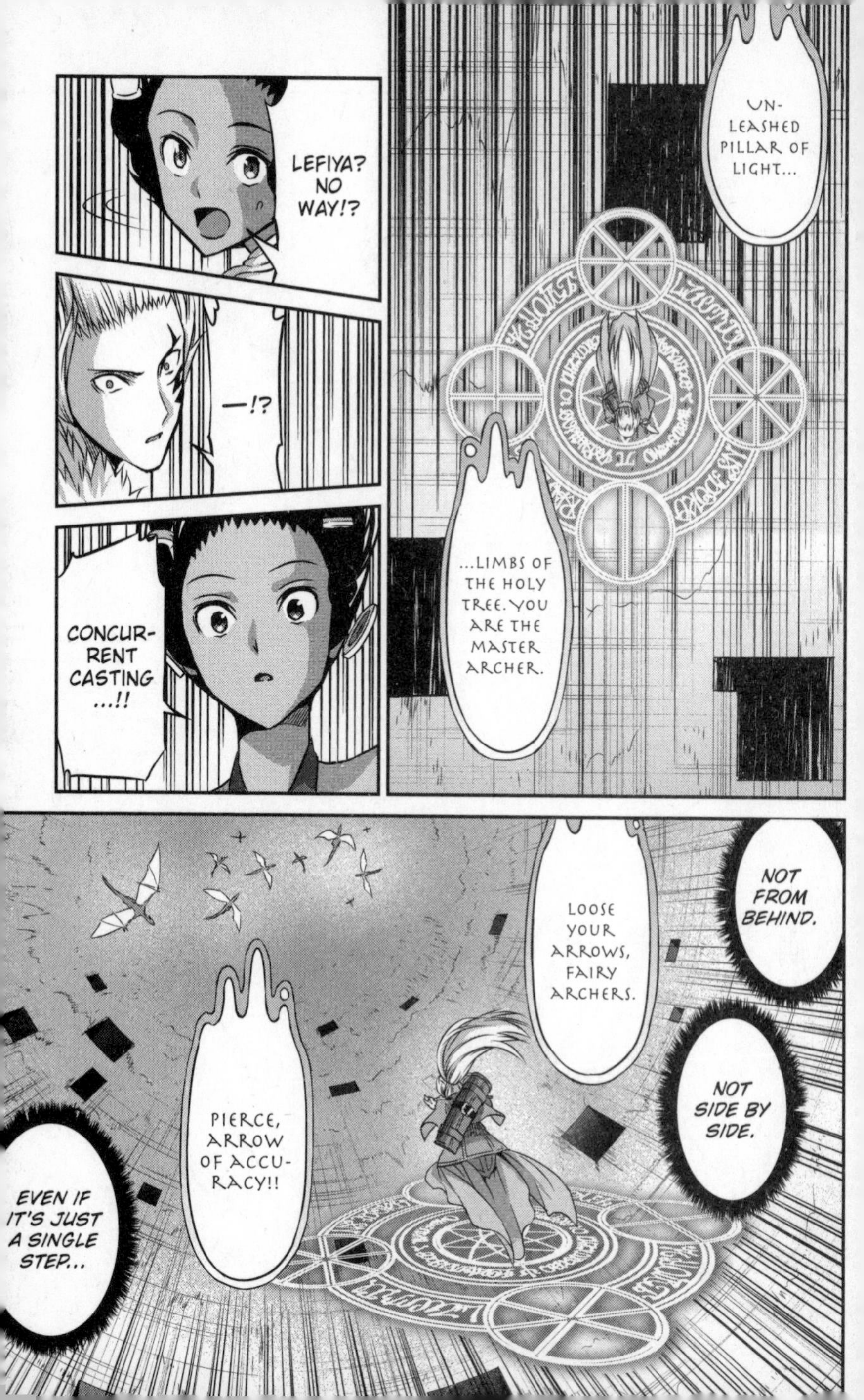
UN-LEASHED PILLAR OF LIGHT...
...LIMBS OF THE HOLY TREE. YOU ARE THE MASTER ARCHER.
LEFIYA? NO WAY!?
—!?
CONCUR-RENT CASTING ...!!
NOT FROM BEHIND.
LOOSE YOUR ARROWS, FAIRY ARCHERS.
NOT SIDE BY SIDE.
PIERCE, ARROW OF ACCU-RACY!!
EVEN IF IT'S JUST A SINGLE STEP...

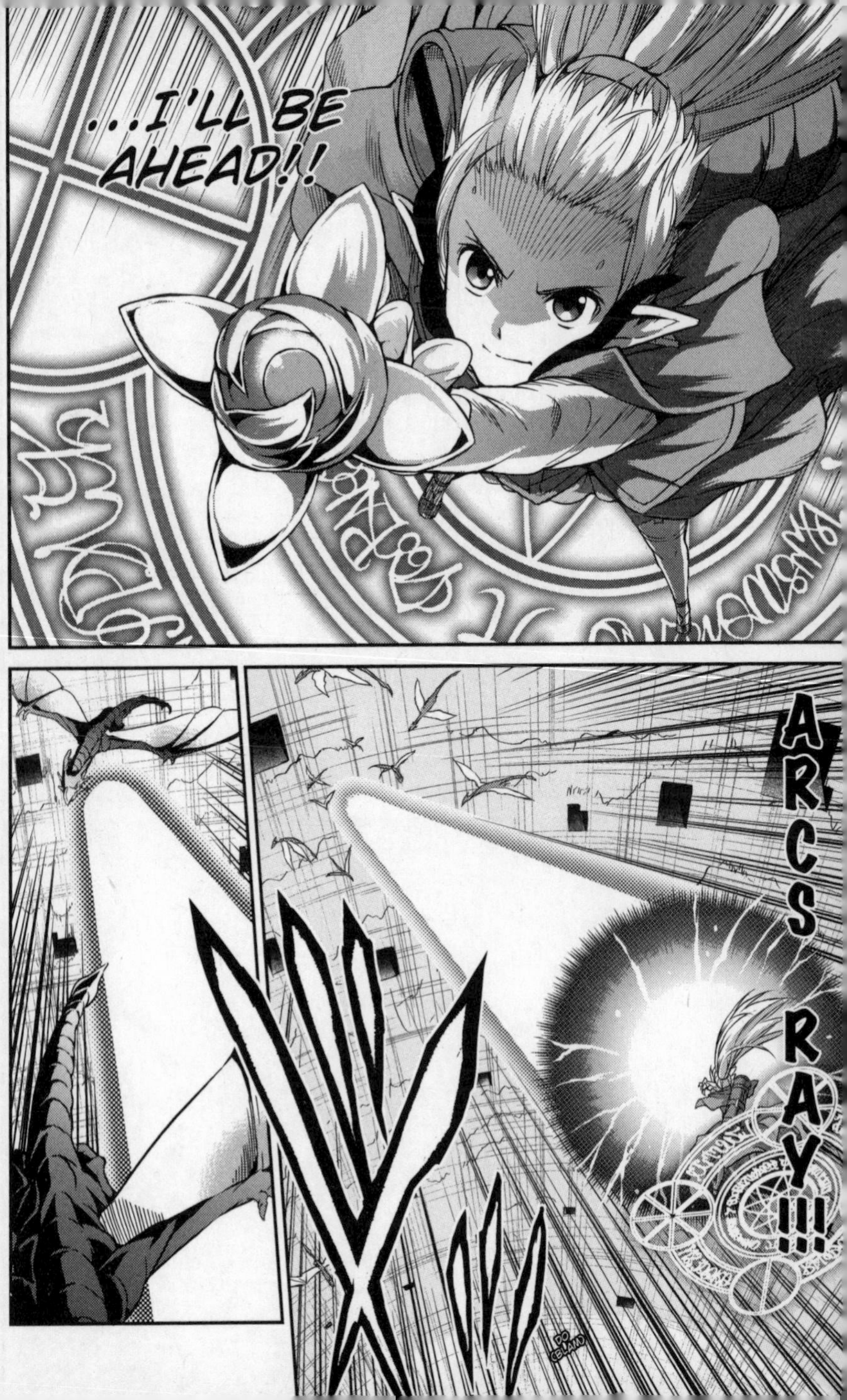
...I'LL BE AHEAD!!
ARCS RAY!!!
DO (BLAM)

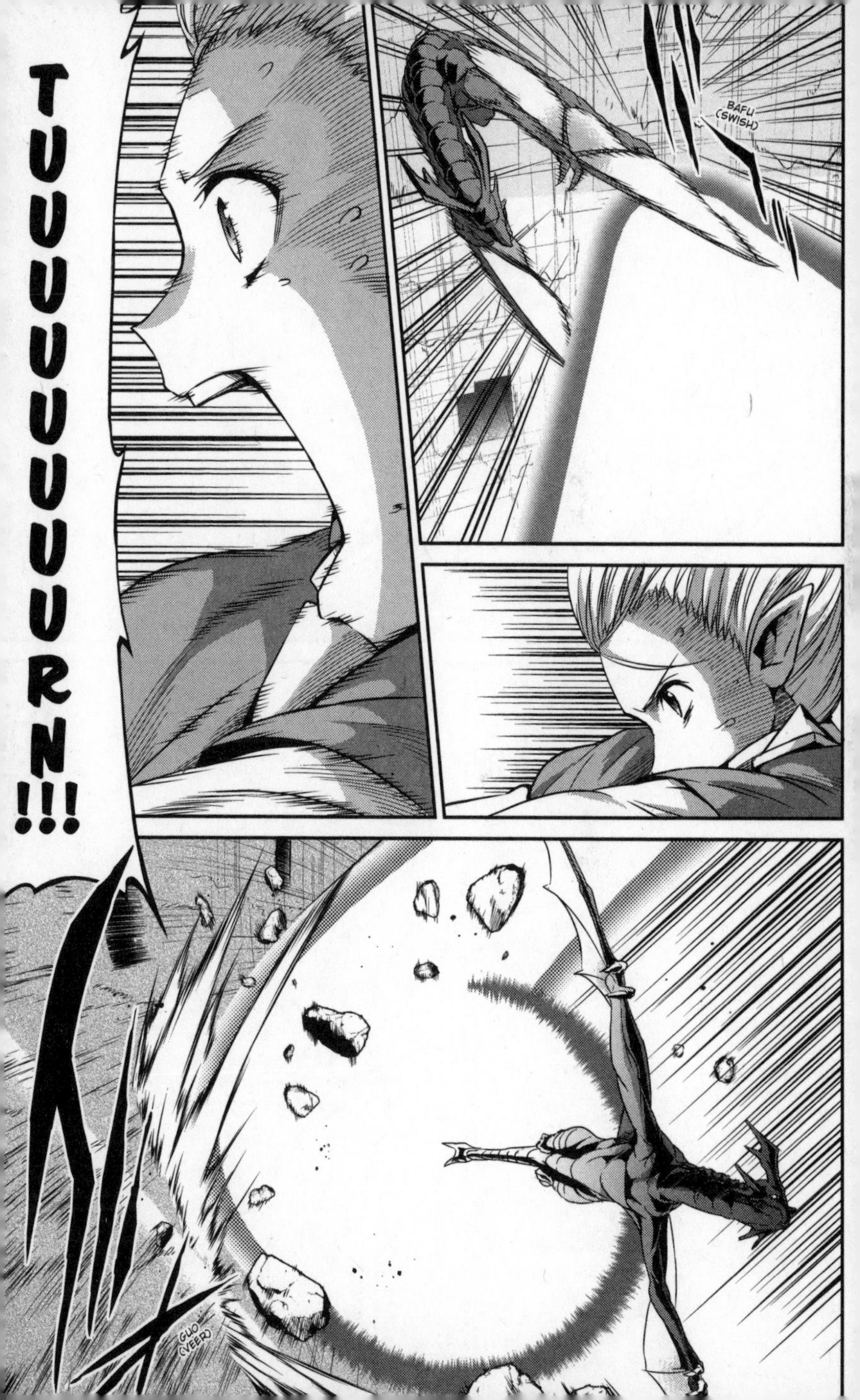
BAFU (SWISH)
TUUUUUUUUUURN!!!
GUO (VEER)

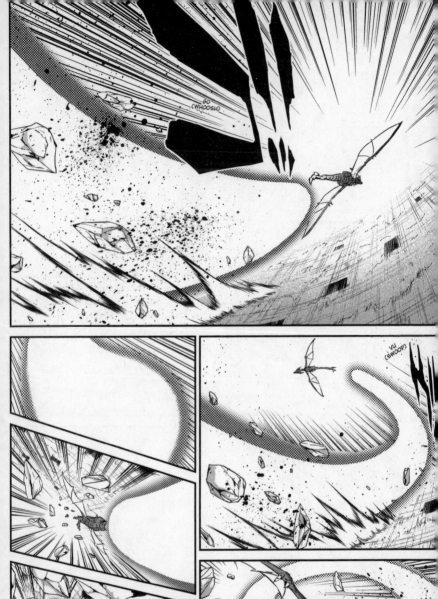

GO
(WHOOSH)

VU
(SWOOP)

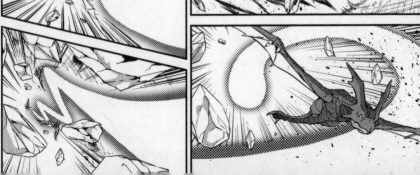

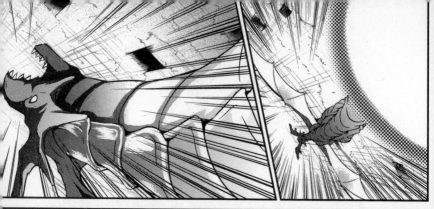

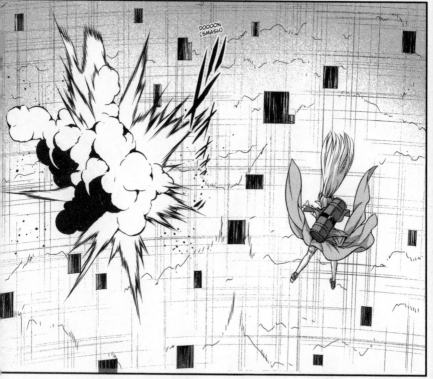

DOOOON
(SMASH)

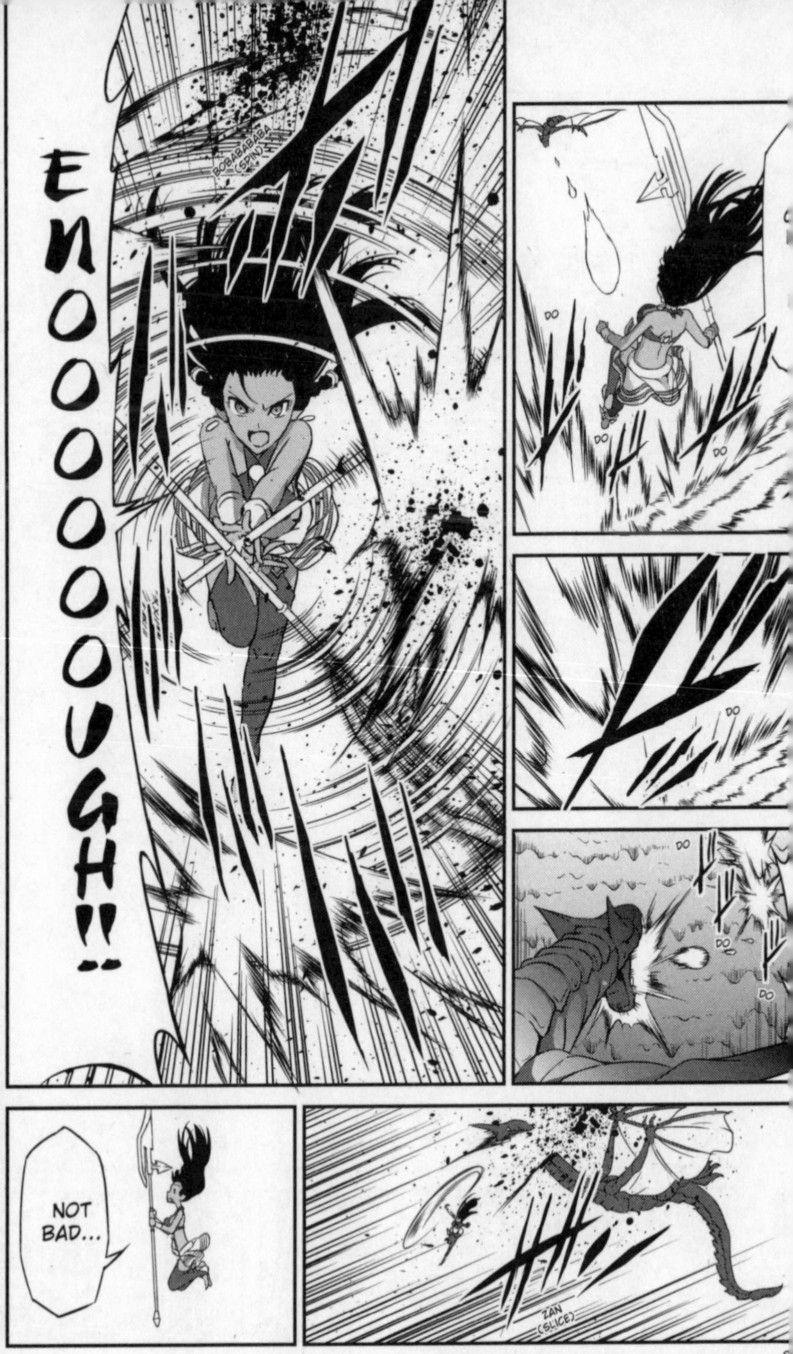
DO
DO
DO
DO
DO
DO
DO
BOBABABABA (SPIN)
ENOOOOOOUGH!!
ZAN (SLICE)
NOT BAD...

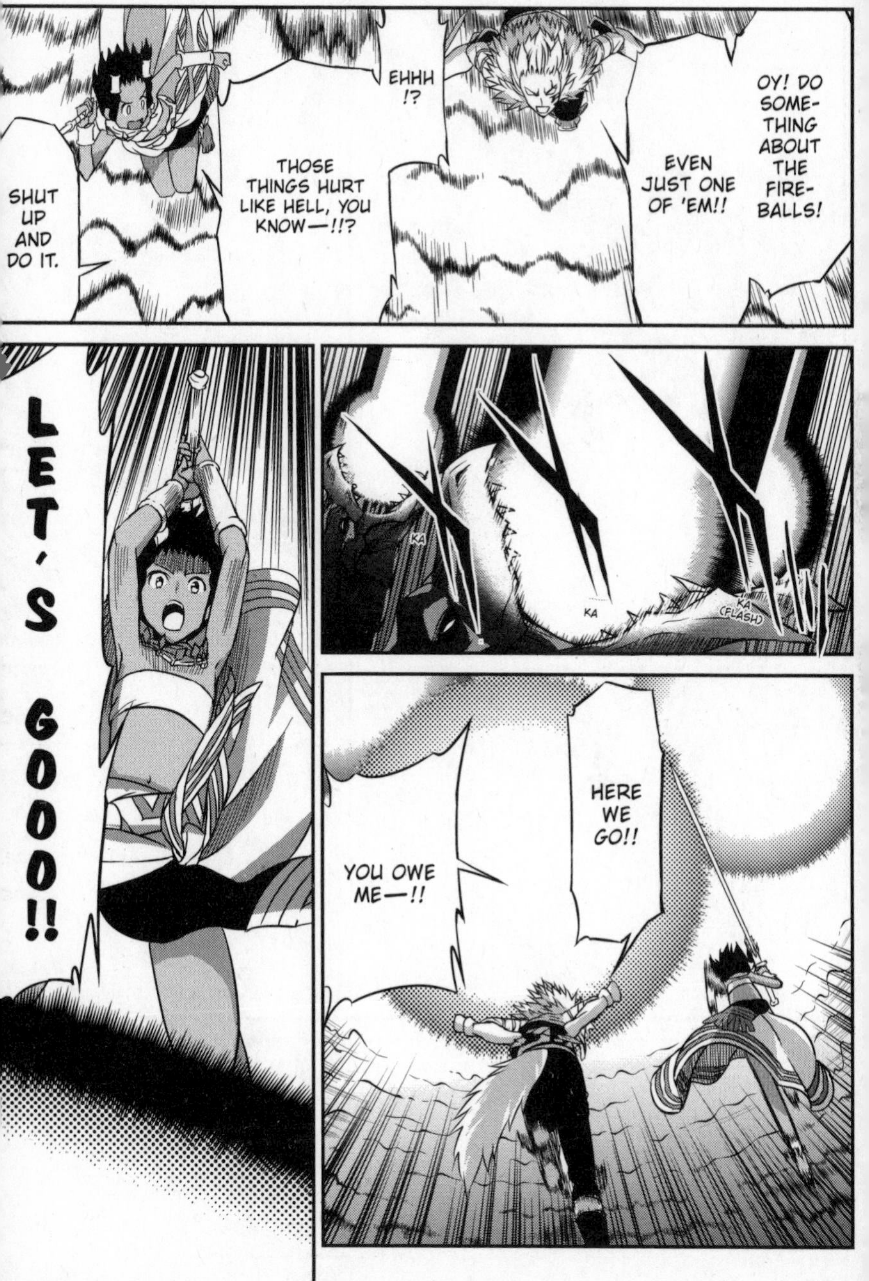
OY! DO SOME-THING ABOUT THE FIRE-BALLS!
EVEN JUST ONE OF 'EM!!
EHHH!?
THOSE THINGS HURT LIKE HELL, YOU KNOW—!!?
SHUT UP AND DO IT.
KA (FLASH)
KA
KA
HERE WE GO!!
YOU OWE ME—!!
LET'S GOOOO!!

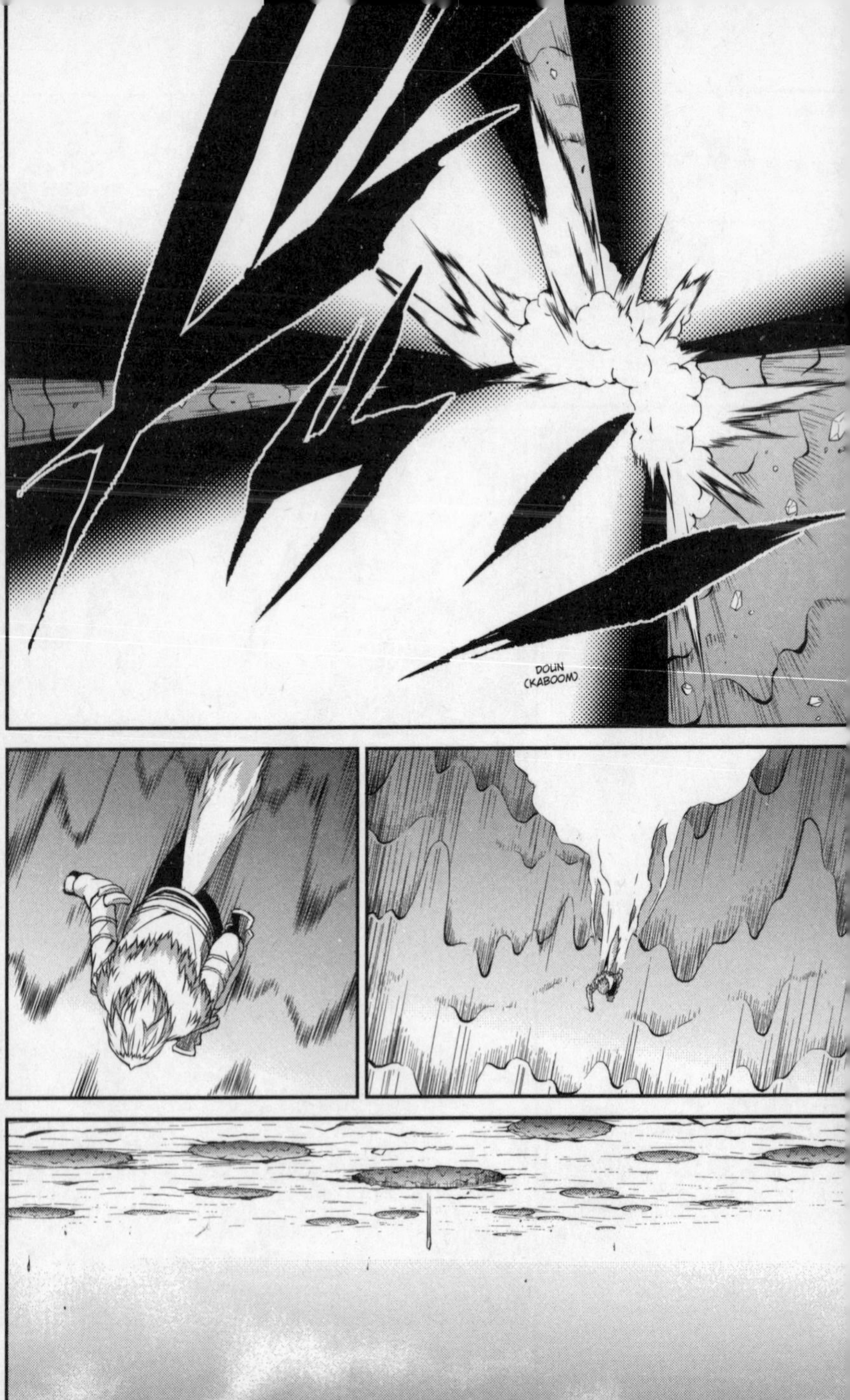
DOLIN
(KABOOM)

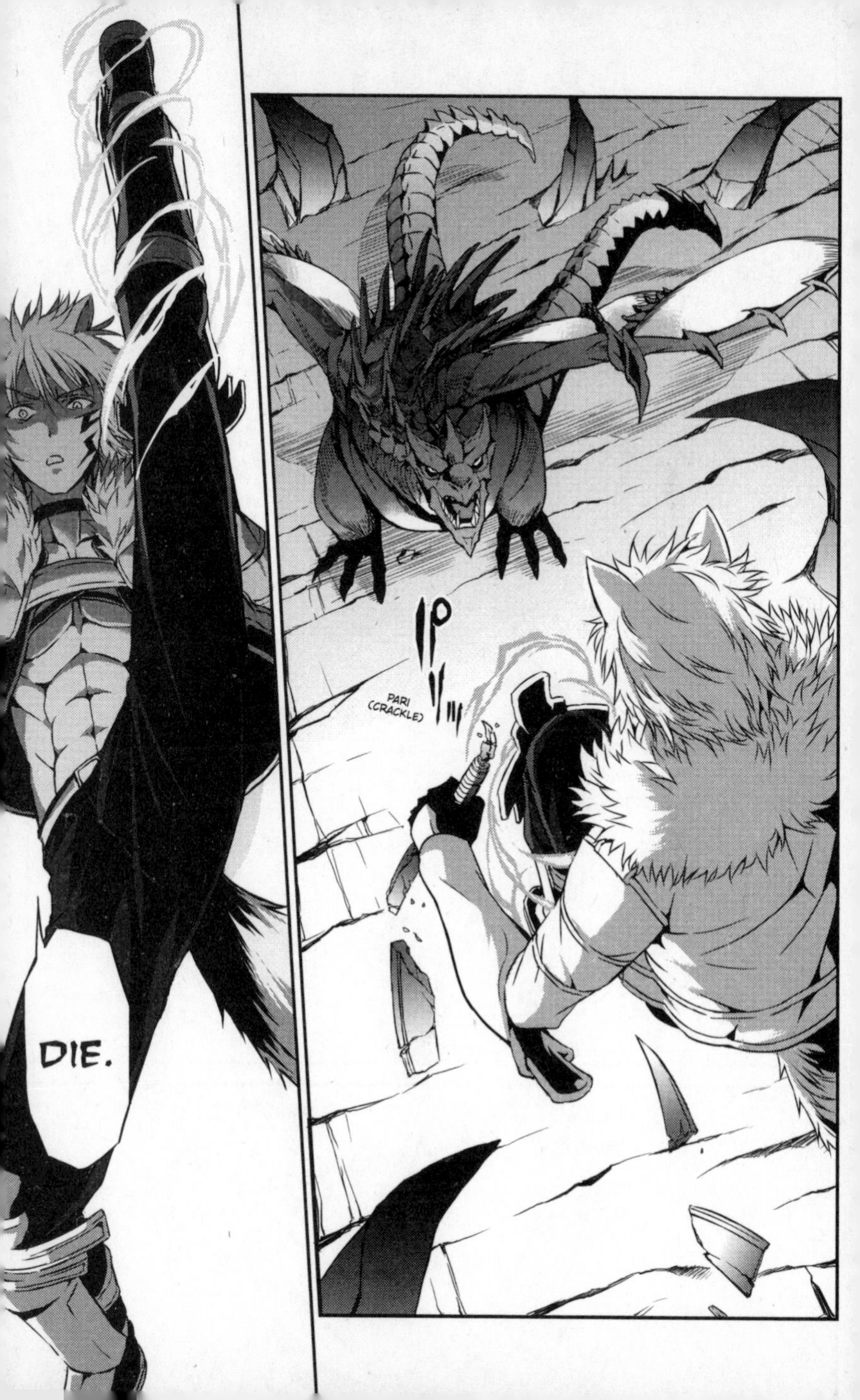
PARI
(CRACKLE)
DIE.

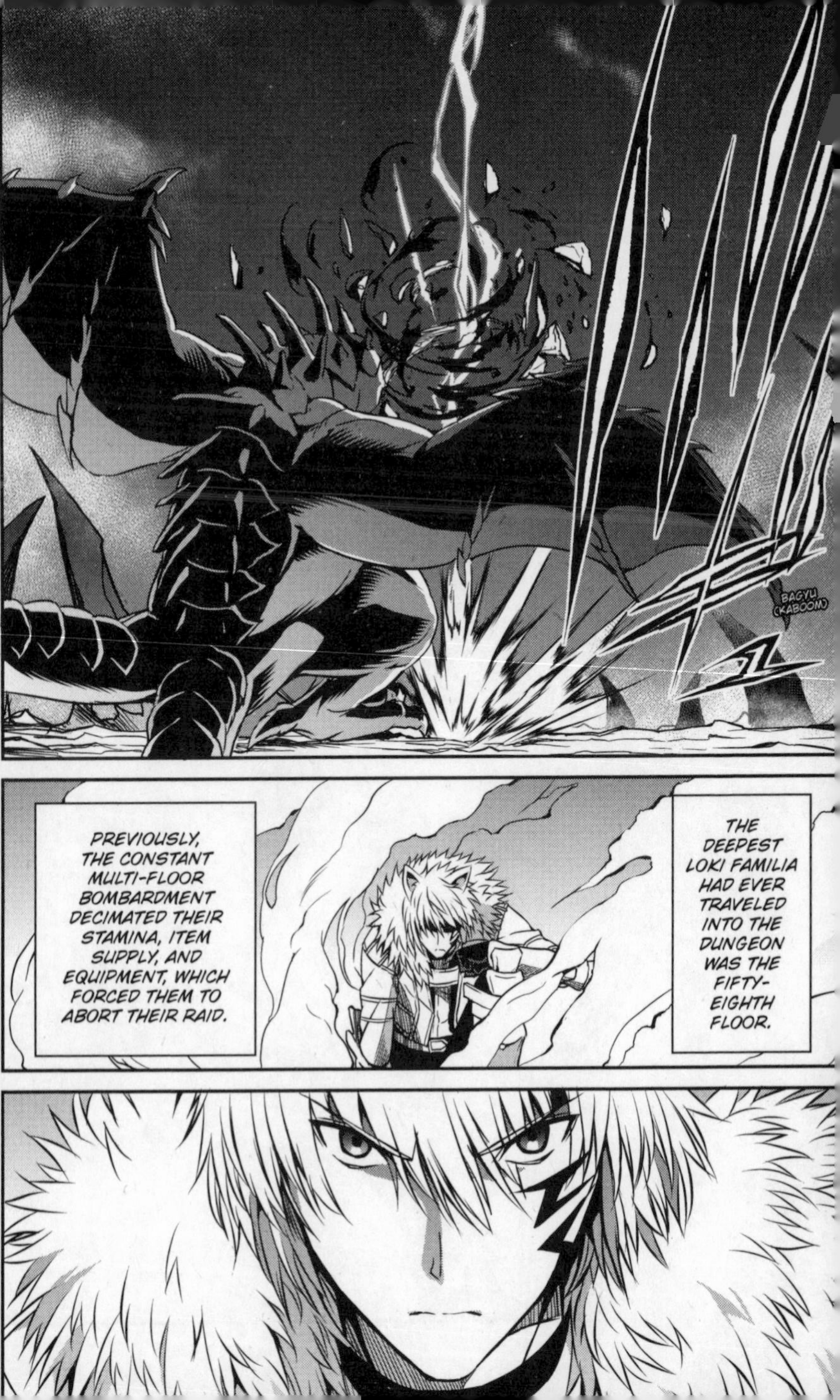
BAGYU
(KABOOM)
THE DEEPEST LOKI FAMILIA HAD EVER TRAVELED INTO THE DUNGEON WAS THE FIFTY-EIGHTH FLOOR.
PREVIOUSLY, THE CONSTANT MULTI-FLOOR BOMBARDMENT DECIMATED THEIR STAMINA, ITEM SUPPLY, AND EQUIPMENT, WHICH FORCED THEM TO ABORT THEIR RAID.

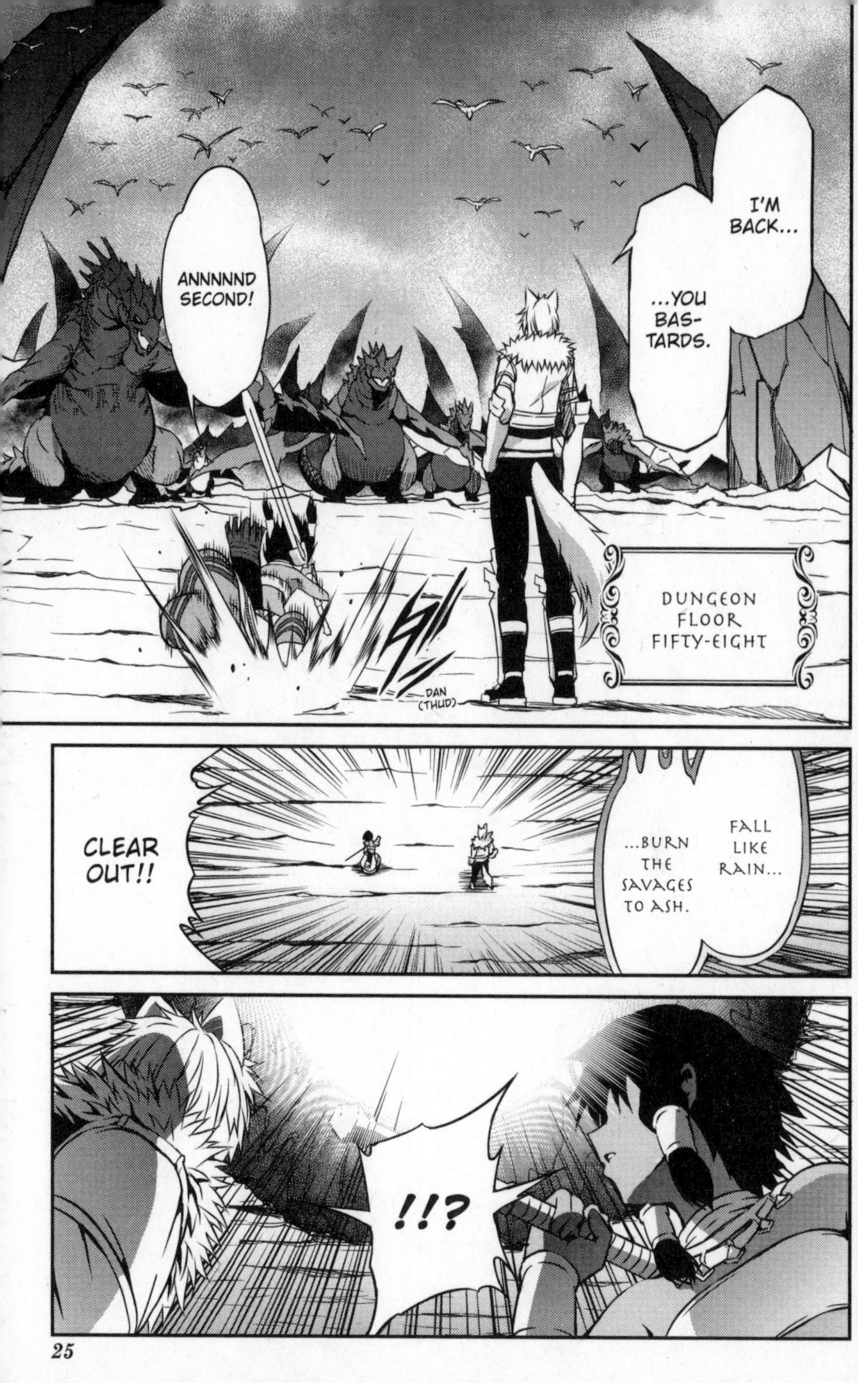
I'M BACK...
...YOU BAS-TARDS.
ANNNNND SECOND!
DUNGEON FLOOR FIFTY-EIGHT
DAN (THUD)
FALL LIKE RAIN...
...BURN THE SAVAGES TO ASH.
CLEAR OUT!!
!!?

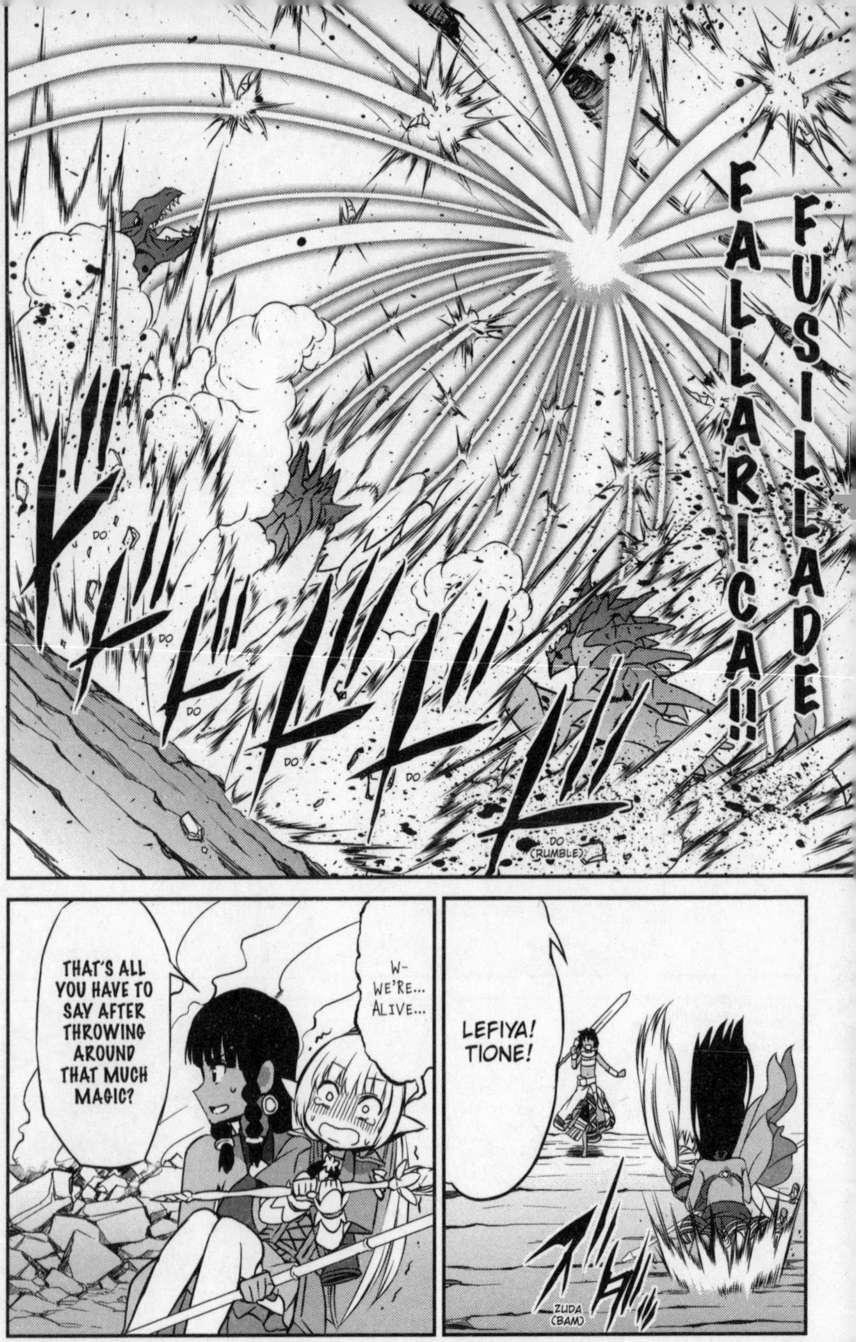
FUSILLADE
FALLARICA!!
DO
DO
DO
DO
DO
DO (RUMBLE)
LEFIYA! TIONE!
ZUDA (BAM)
W- WE'RE... ALIVE...
THAT'S ALL YOU HAVE TO SAY AFTER THROWING AROUND THAT MUCH MAGIC?

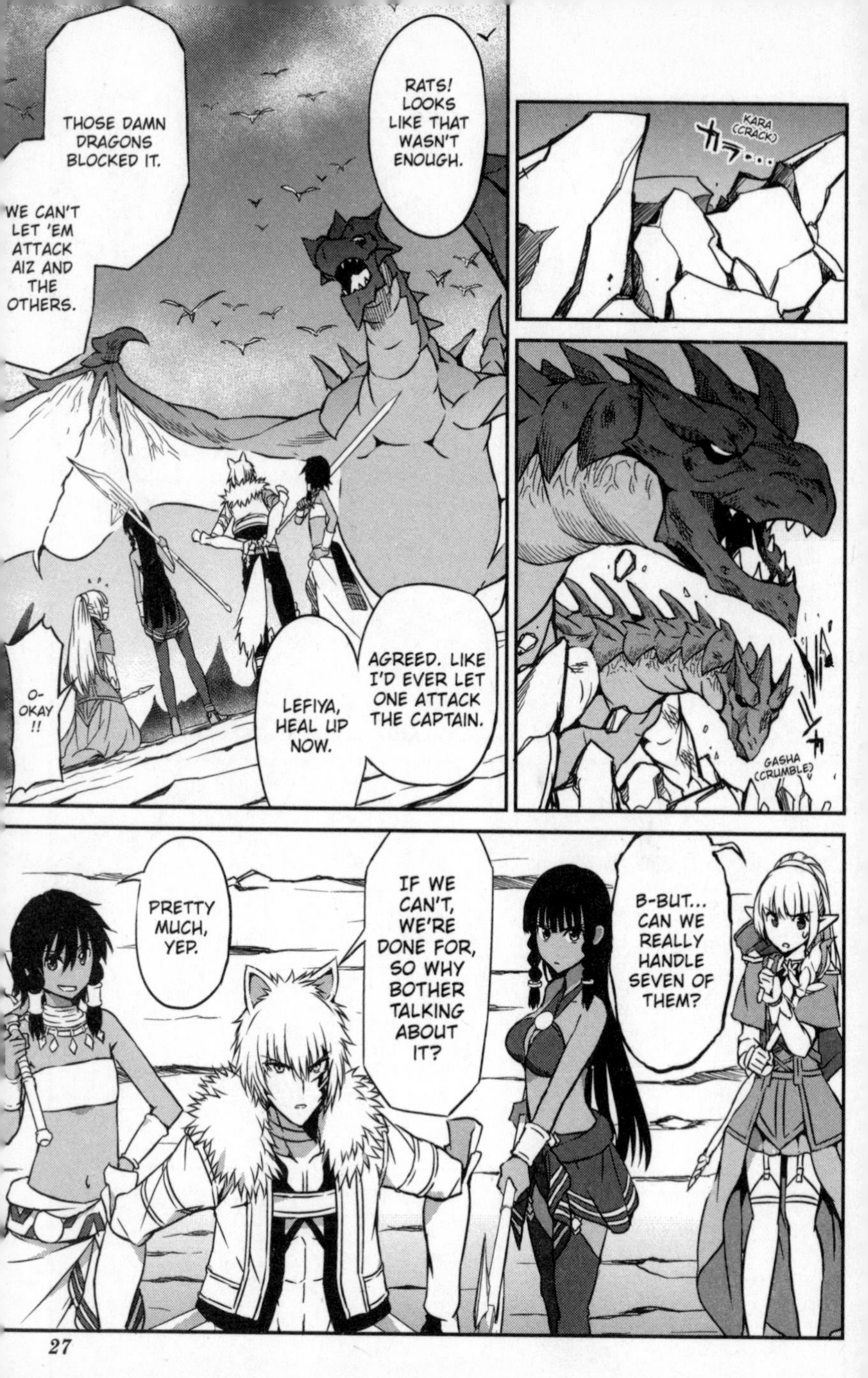
カラ…
KARA (CRACK)
GASHA (CRUMBLE)
RATS! LOOKS LIKE THAT WASN'T ENOUGH.
THOSE DAMN DRAGONS BLOCKED IT.
WE CAN'T LET 'EM ATTACK AIZ AND THE OTHERS.
AGREED. LIKE I'D EVER LET ONE ATTACK THE CAPTAIN.
LEFIYA, HEAL UP NOW.
O-OKAY!!
B-BUT... CAN WE REALLY HANDLE SEVEN OF THEM?
IF WE CAN'T, WE'RE DONE FOR, SO WHY BOTHER TALKING ABOUT IT?
PRETTY MUCH, YEP.

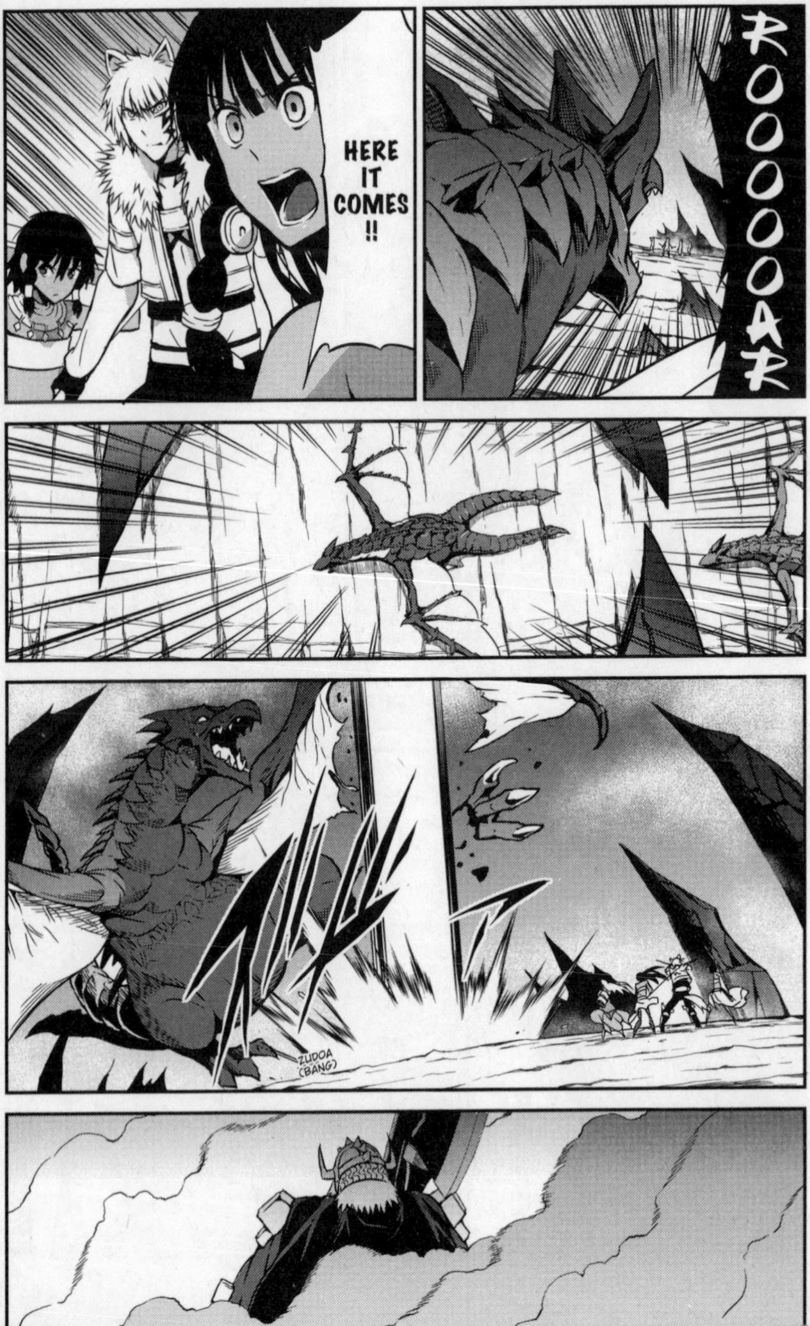
ROOOOOAR
HERE IT COMES!!
ZUDOA (BANG)

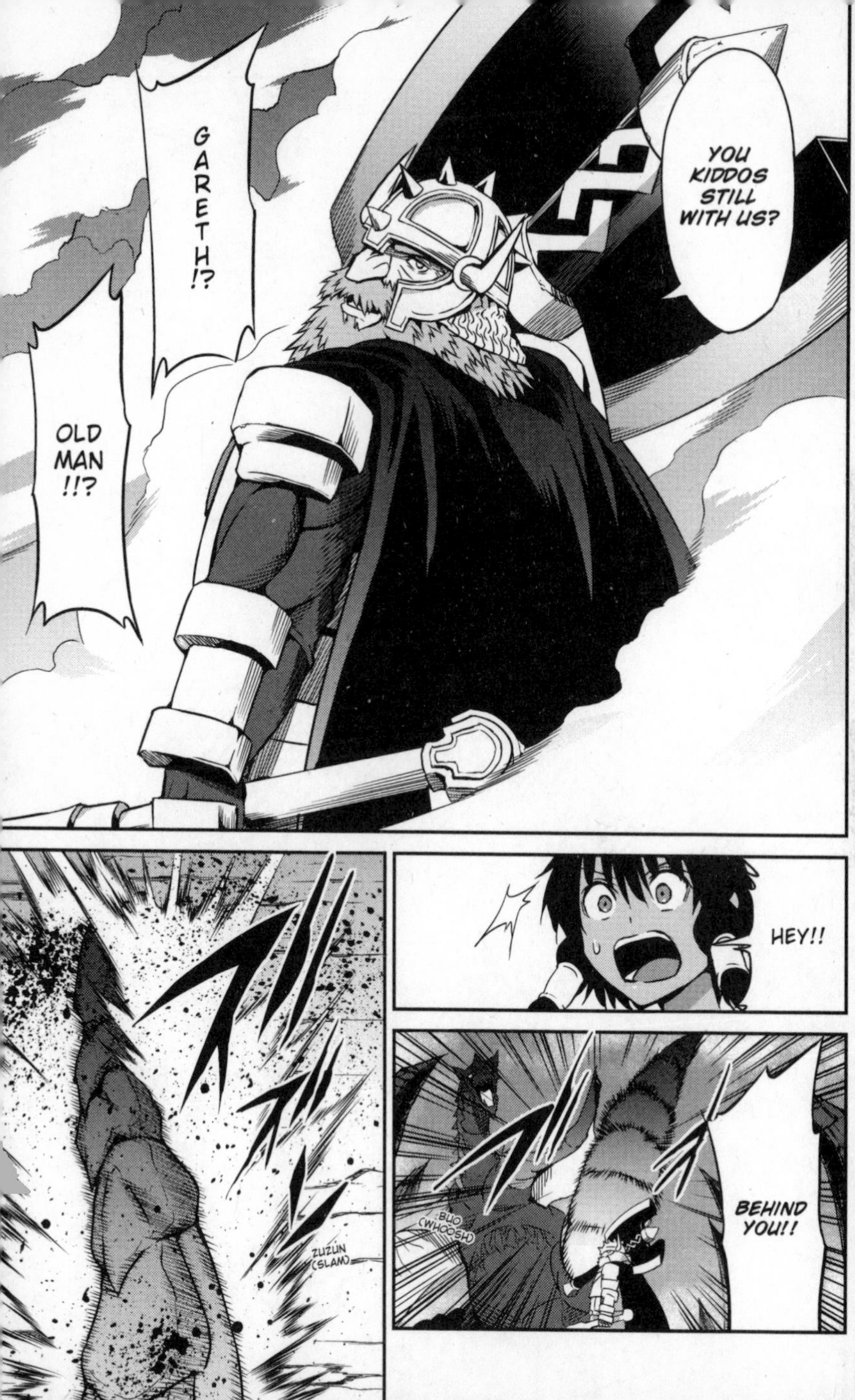
YOU KIDDOS STILL WITH US?
GARETH!?
OLD MAN!!?
HEY!!
BEHIND YOU!!
BUO (WHOOSH)
ZUZUN (SLAM)

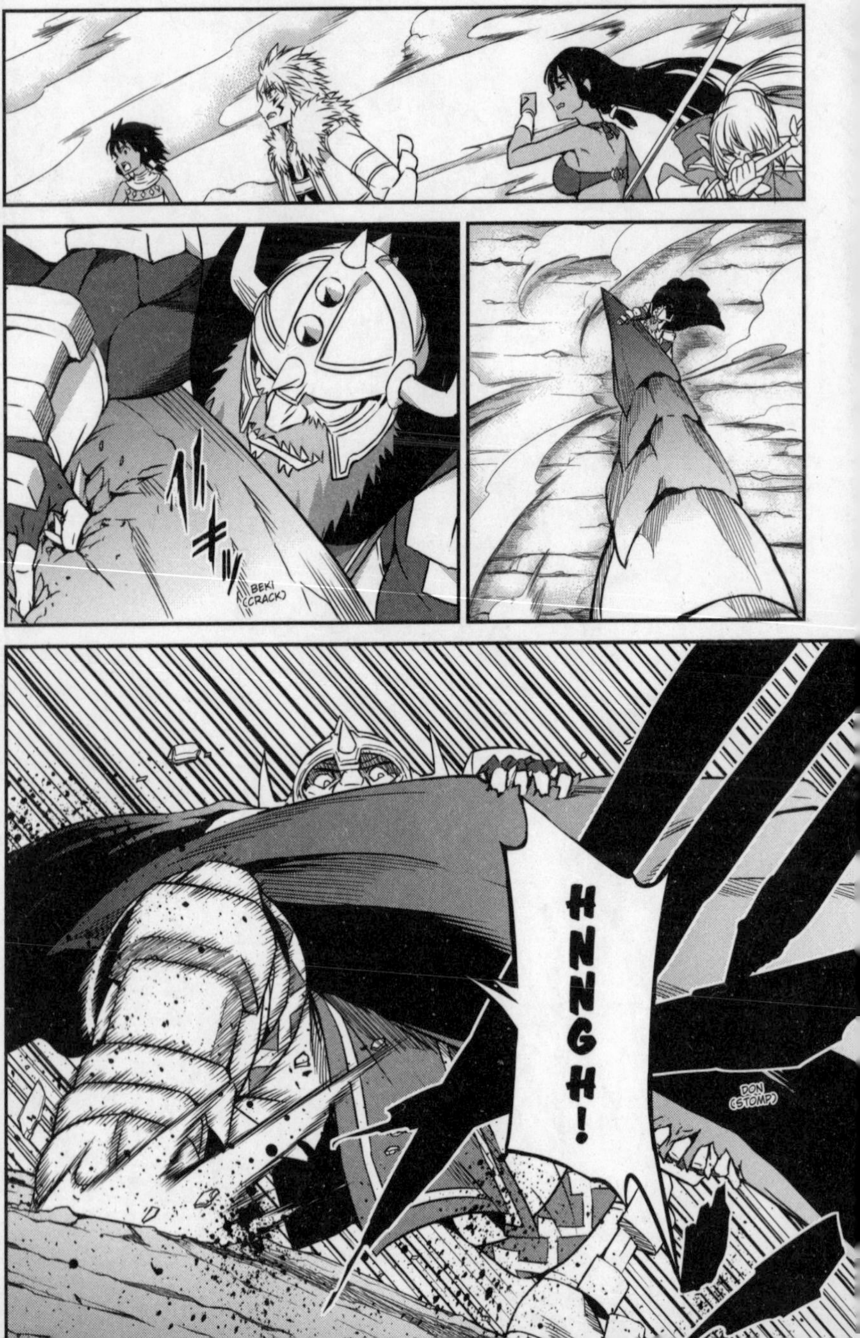
BEKI (CRACK)
HNNGH!
DON (STOMP)

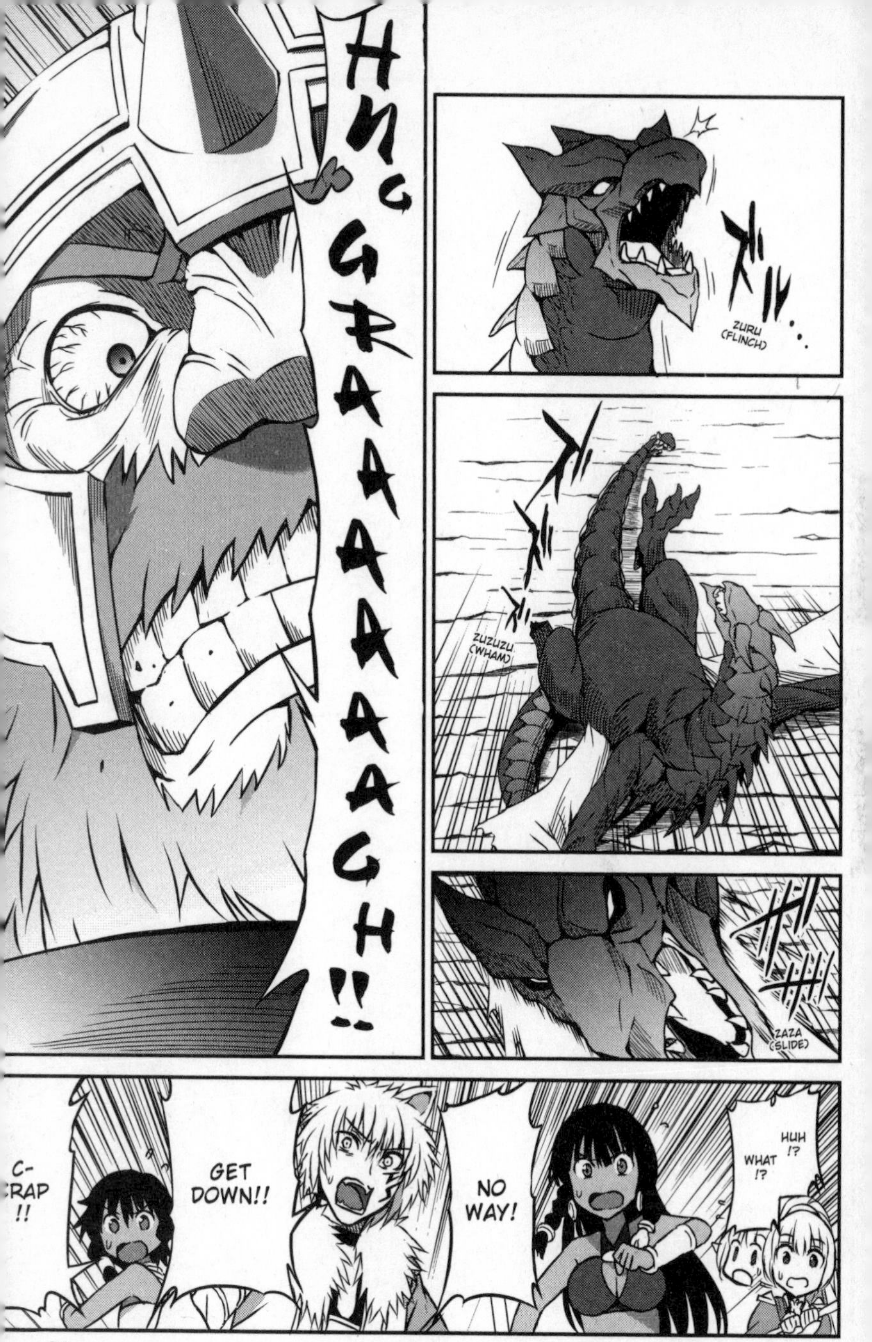
ZURU (FLINCH)
ZUZUZU (WHAM)
ZAZA (SLIDE)
HNG GRAAAAAGH!!
HUH!?
WHAT!?
NO WAY!
GET DOWN!!
C-RAP!!

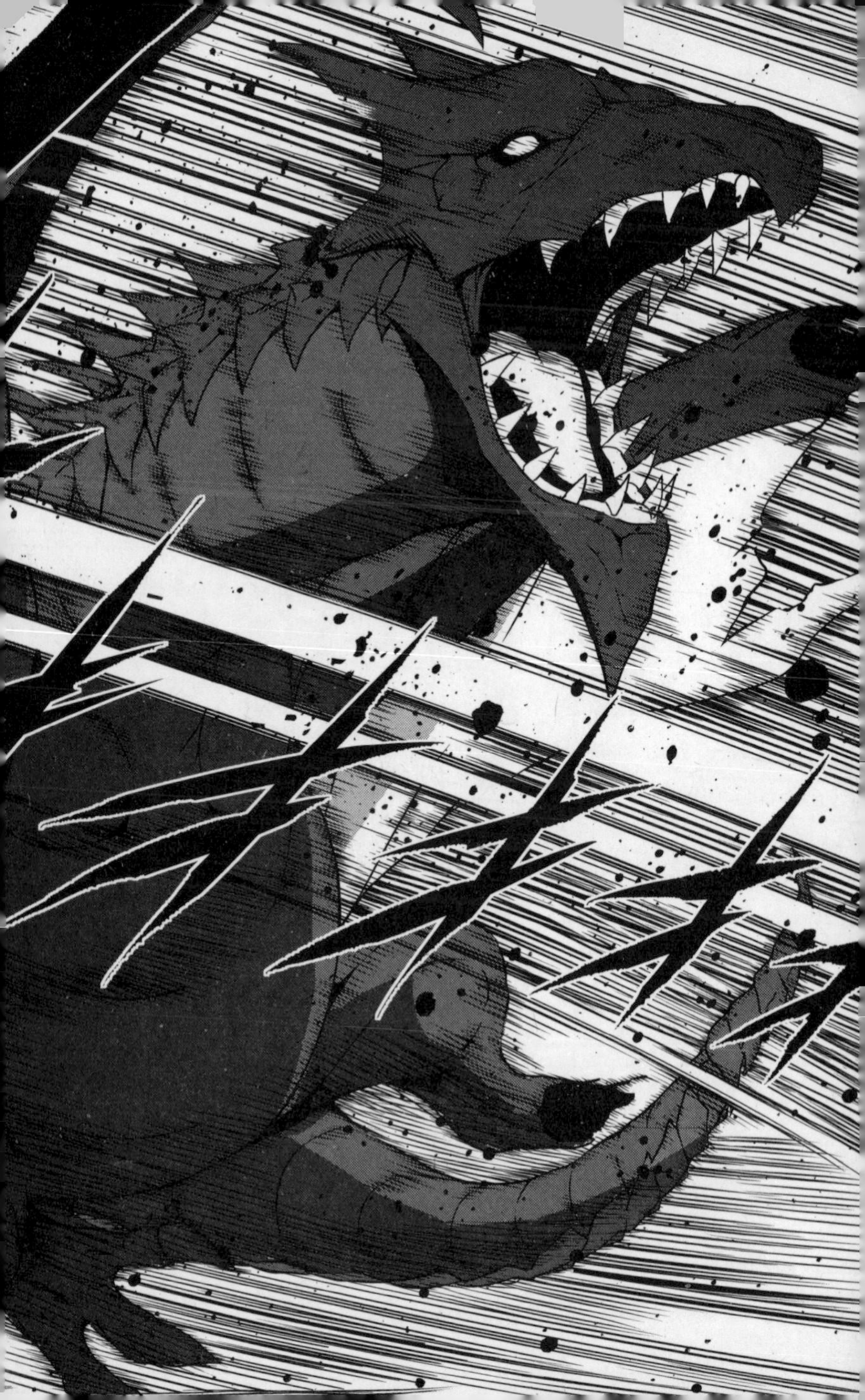

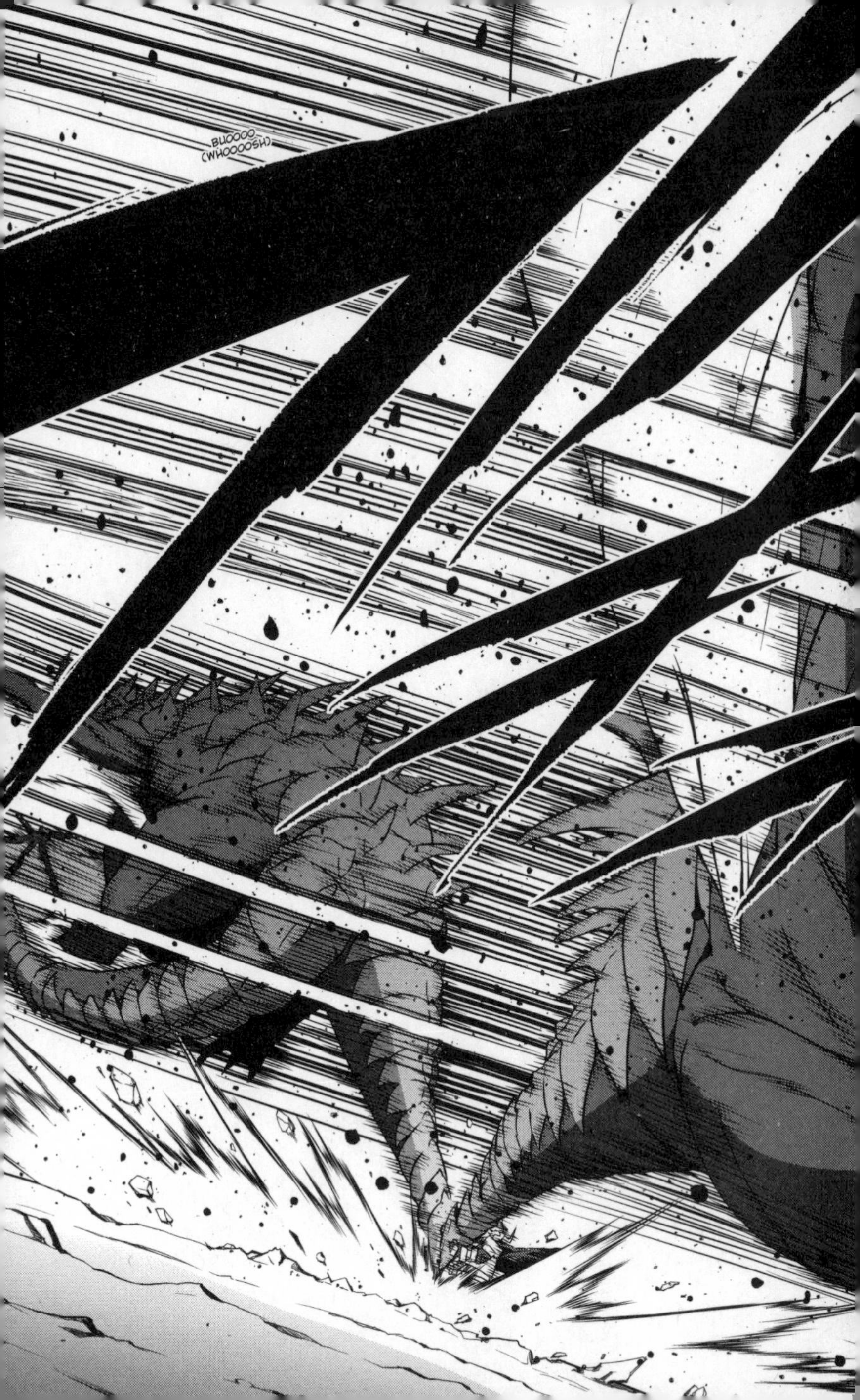
BUOOOO
(WHOOOOSH)

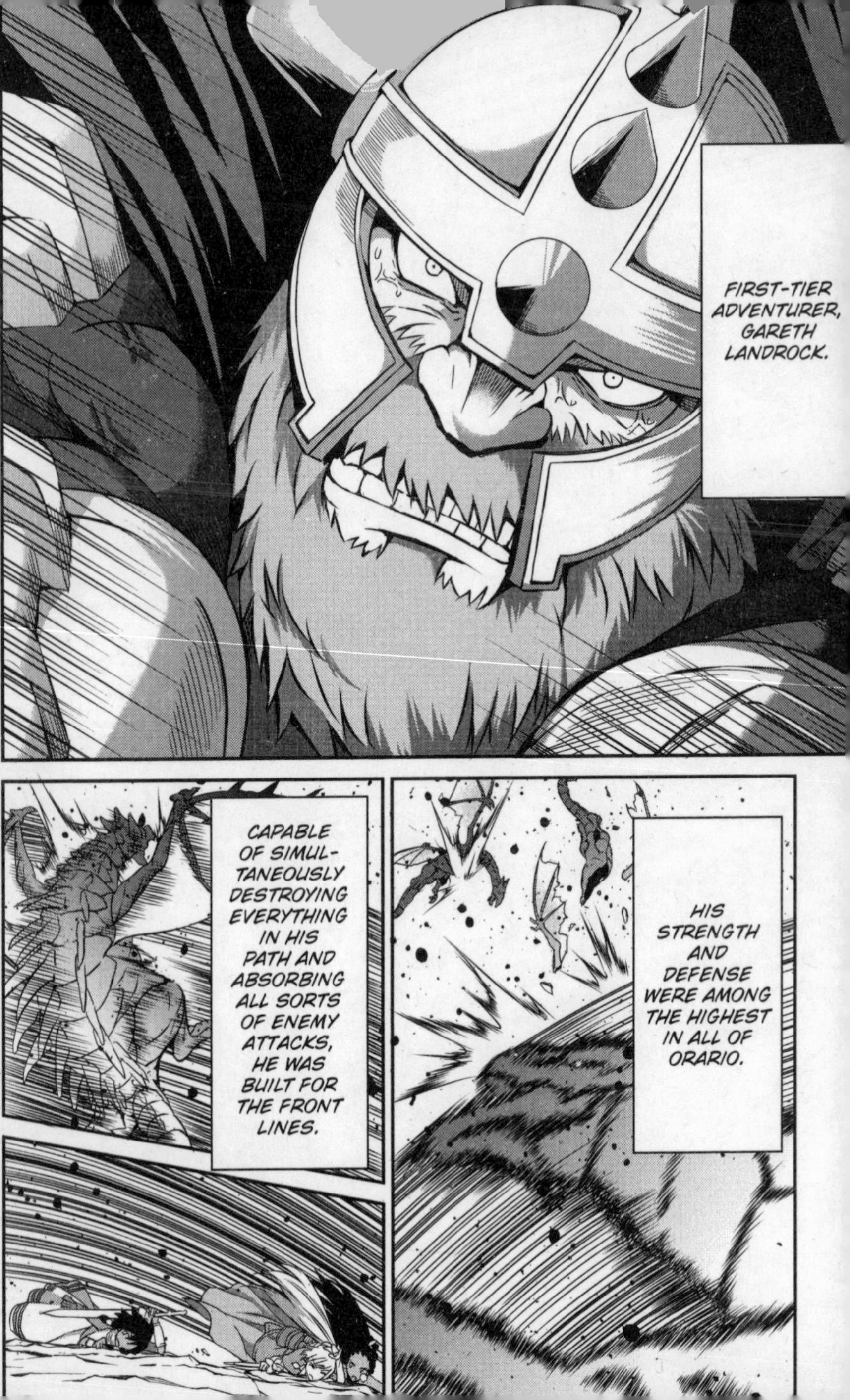
FIRST-TIER ADVENTURER, GARETH LANDROCK.
HIS STRENGTH AND DEFENSE WERE AMONG THE HIGHEST IN ALL OF ORARIO.
CAPABLE OF SIMUL-TANEOUSLY DESTROYING EVERYTHING IN HIS PATH AND ABSORBING ALL SORTS OF ENEMY ATTACKS, HE WAS BUILT FOR THE FRONT LINES.

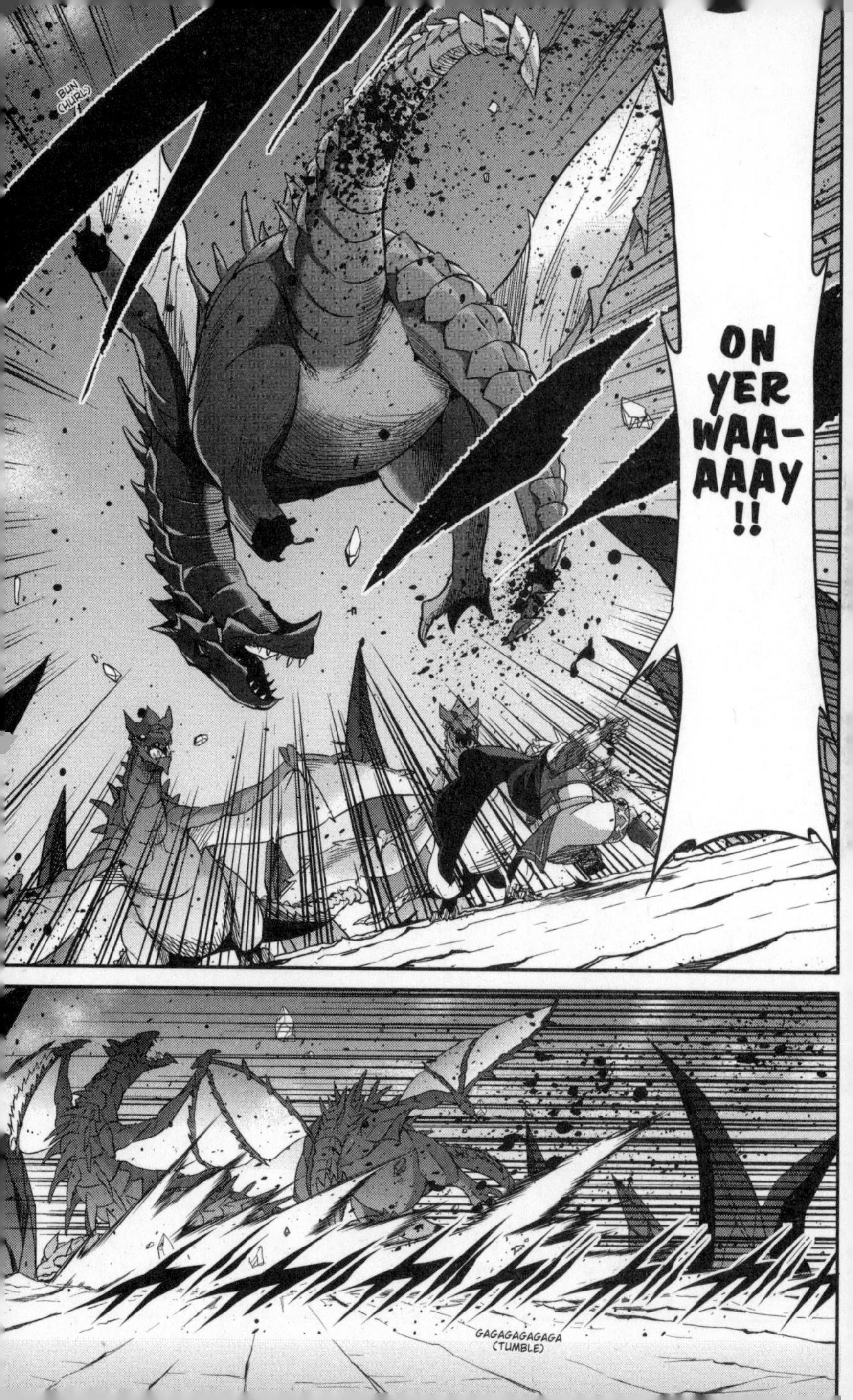
ON YER WAA-AAAY!!
BUN CHURLS
GAGAGAGAGAGA (TUMBLE)

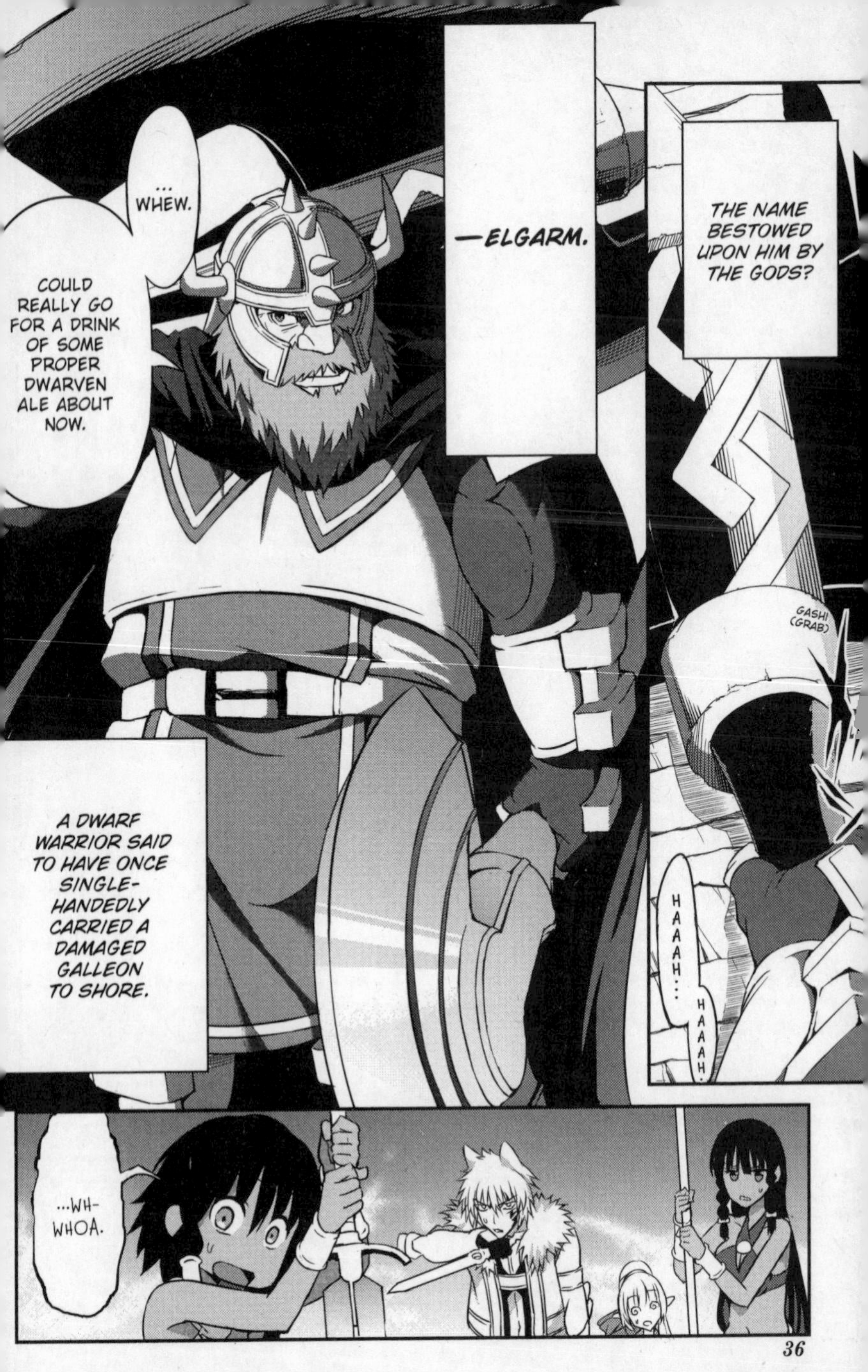

THE NAME BESTOWED UPON HIM BY THE GODS?
GASHI (GRAB)
HAAAAH... HAAAAH.
—ELGARM.
...WHEW.
COULD REALLY GO FOR A DRINK OF SOME PROPER DWARVEN ALE ABOUT NOW.
A DWARF WARRIOR SAID TO HAVE ONCE SINGLE-HANDEDLY CARRIED A DAMAGED GALLEON TO SHORE.
...WH-WHOA.

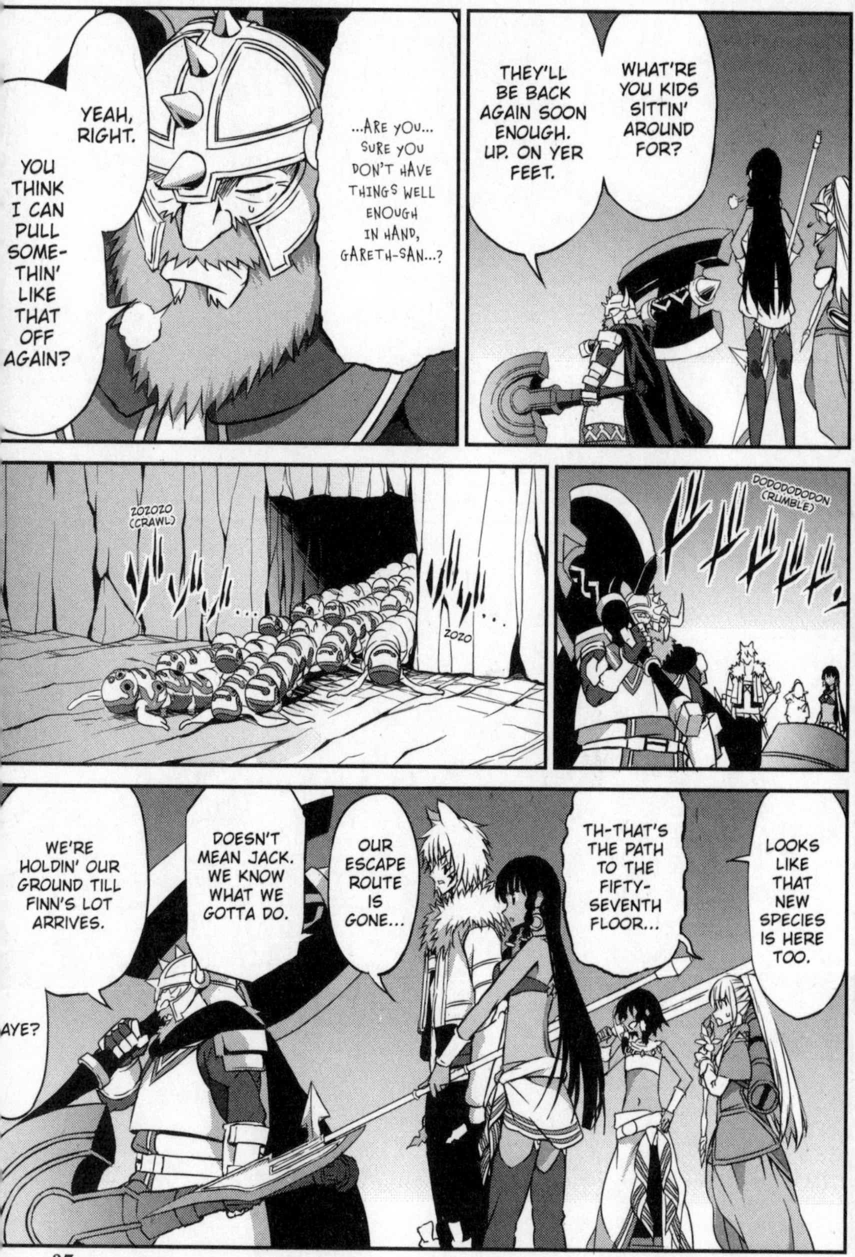
WHAT'RE YOU KIDS SITTIN' AROUND FOR?
THEY'LL BE BACK AGAIN SOON ENOUGH. UP. ON YER FEET.
...ARE YOU... SURE YOU DON'T HAVE THINGS WELL ENOUGH IN HAND, GARETH-SAN...?
YEAH, RIGHT.
YOU THINK I CAN PULL SOME-THIN' LIKE THAT OFF AGAIN?
DODODODODON (RUMBLE)
ZOZOZO (CRAWL)
ZOZO
LOOKS LIKE THAT NEW SPECIES IS HERE TOO.
TH-THAT'S THE PATH TO THE FIFTY-SEVENTH FLOOR...
OUR ESCAPE ROUTE IS GONE...
DOESN'T MEAN JACK. WE KNOW WHAT WE GOTTA DO.
WE'RE HOLDIN' OUR GROUND TILL FINN'S LOT ARRIVES.
AYE?

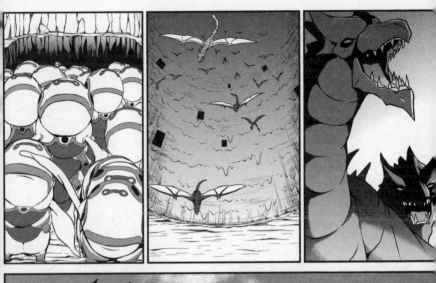

'ERE
WE
GO!!!

IS IT WRONG TO TRY TO PICK UP GIRLS IN A DUNGEON? ON THE SIDE

Sword Oratoria

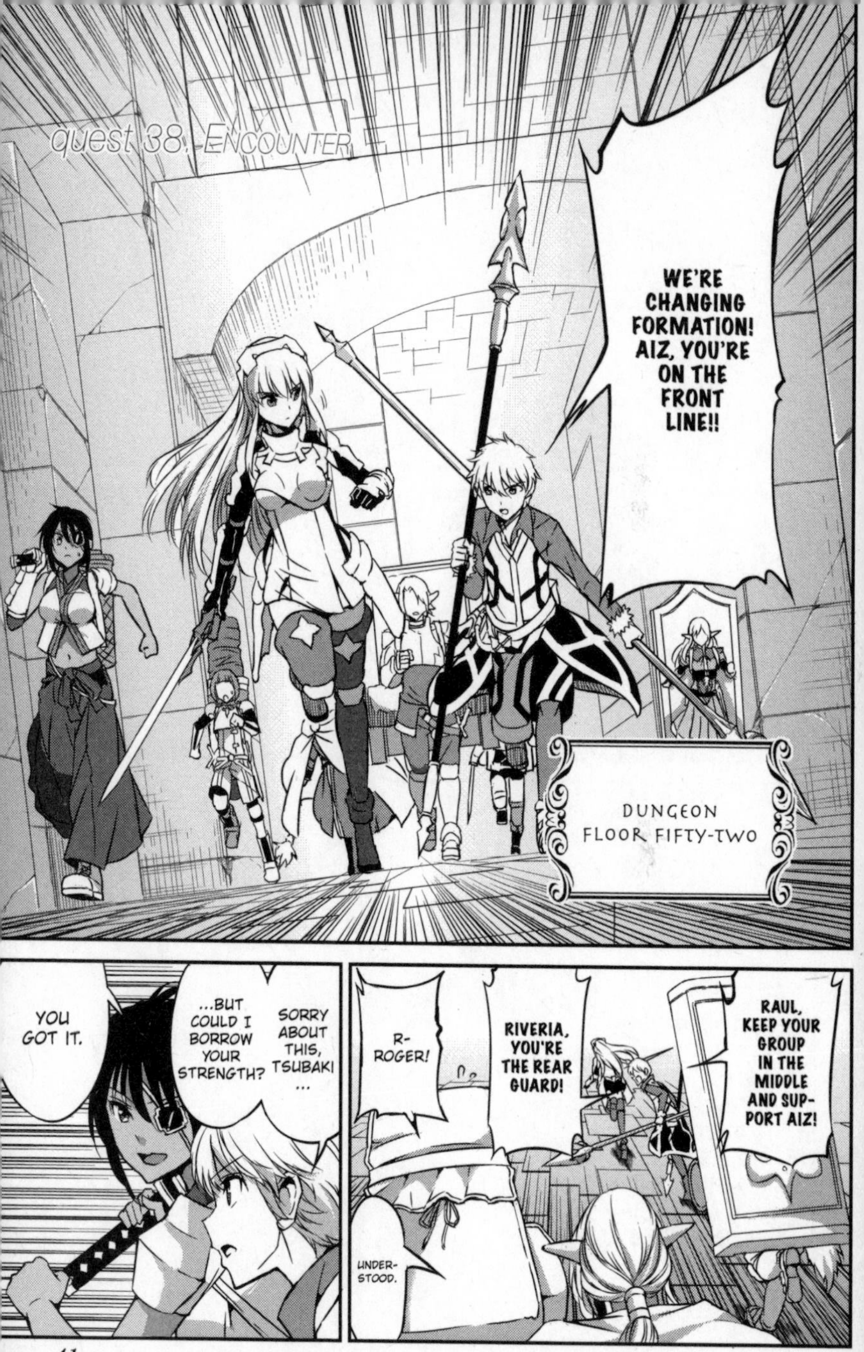
quest 38: Encounter
WE'RE CHANGING FORMATION! AIZ, YOU'RE ON THE FRONT LINE!!
DUNGEON FLOOR FIFTY-TWO
RAUL, KEEP YOUR GROUP IN THE MIDDLE AND SUP-PORT AIZ!
RIVERIA, YOU'RE THE REAR GUARD!
R-ROGER!
UNDER-STOOD.
SORRY ABOUT THIS, TSUBAKI...
...BUT COULD I BORROW YOUR STRENGTH?
YOU GOT IT.

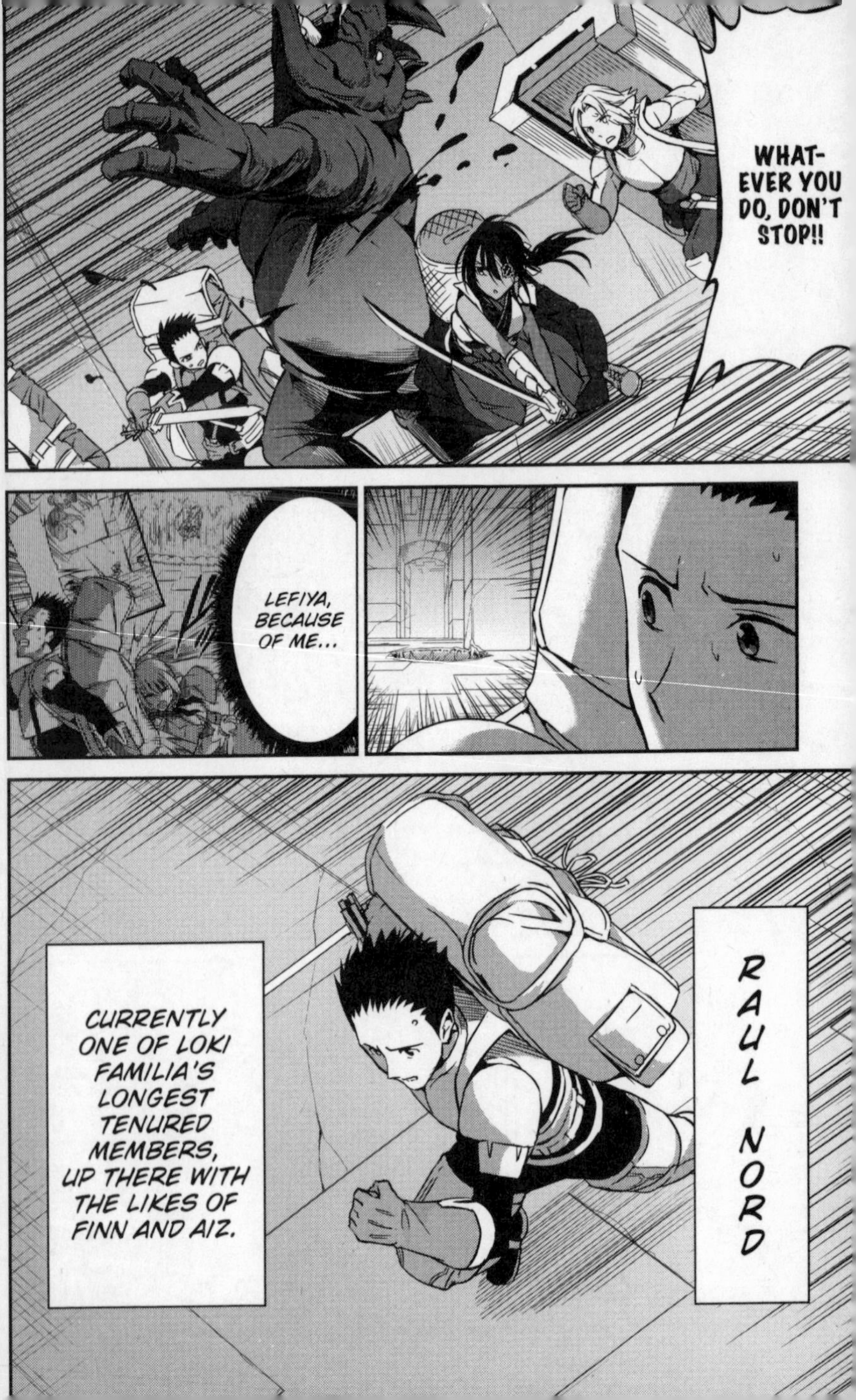
WHAT-EVER YOU DO, DON'T STOP!!
LEFIYA, BECAUSE OF ME...
RAUL NORD
CURRENTLY ONE OF LOKI FAMILIA'S LONGEST TENURED MEMBERS, UP THERE WITH THE LIKES OF FINN AND AIZ.

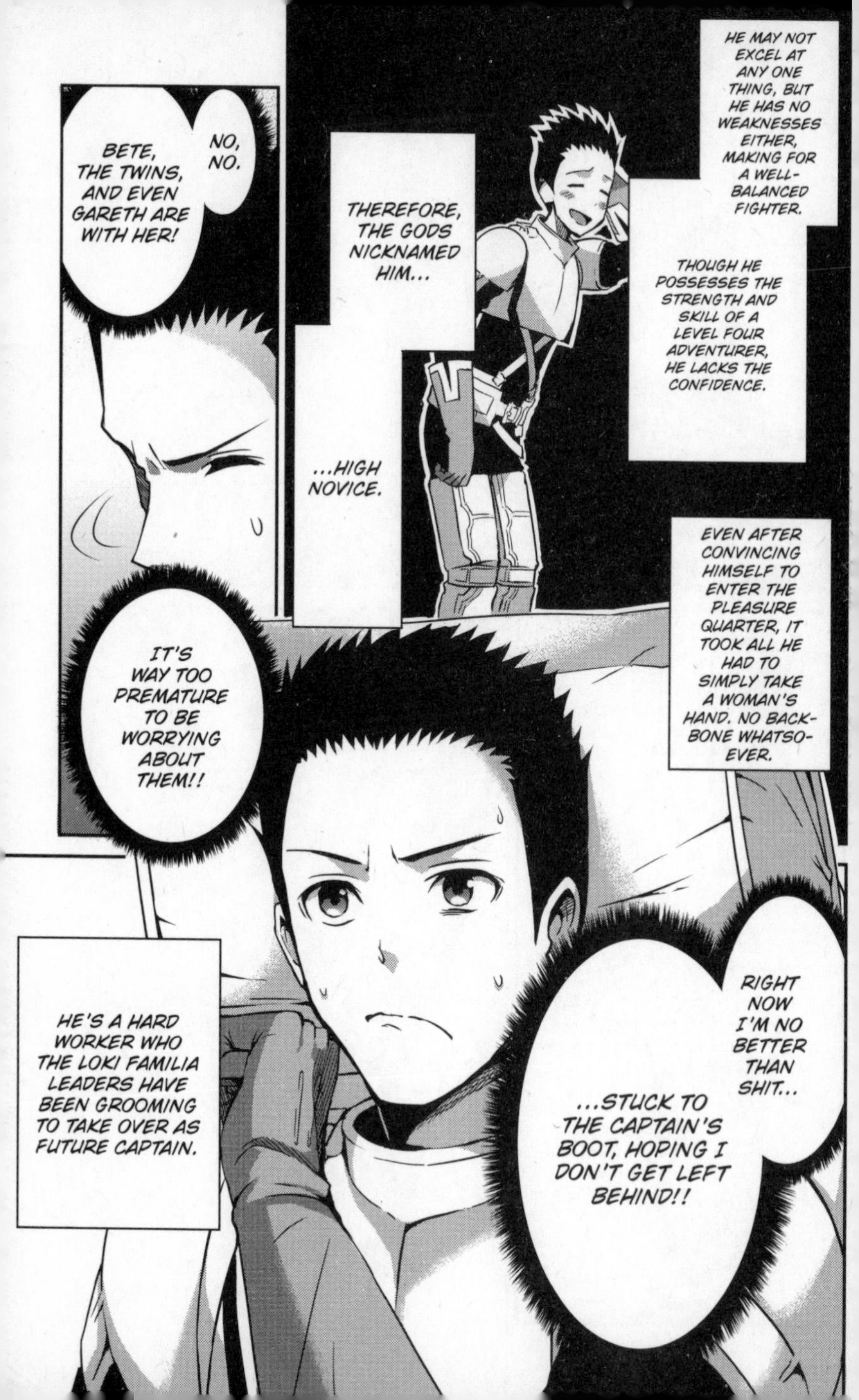
HE MAY NOT EXCEL AT ANY ONE THING, BUT HE HAS NO WEAKNESSES EITHER, MAKING FOR A WELL-BALANCED FIGHTER.
THOUGH HE POSSESSES THE STRENGTH AND SKILL OF A LEVEL FOUR ADVENTURER, HE LACKS THE CONFIDENCE.
THEREFORE, THE GODS NICKNAMED HIM...
...HIGH NOVICE.
NO, NO.
BETE, THE TWINS, AND EVEN GARETH ARE WITH HER!
IT'S WAY TOO PREMATURE TO BE WORRYING ABOUT THEM!!
EVEN AFTER CONVINCING HIMSELF TO ENTER THE PLEASURE QUARTER, IT TOOK ALL HE HAD TO SIMPLY TAKE A WOMAN'S HAND. NO BACK-BONE WHATSO-EVER.
RIGHT NOW I'M NO BETTER THAN SHIT...
...STUCK TO THE CAPTAIN'S BOOT, HOPING I DON'T GET LEFT BEHIND!!
HE'S A HARD WORKER WHO THE LOKI FAMILIA LEADERS HAVE BEEN GROOMING TO TAKE OVER AS FUTURE CAPTAIN.

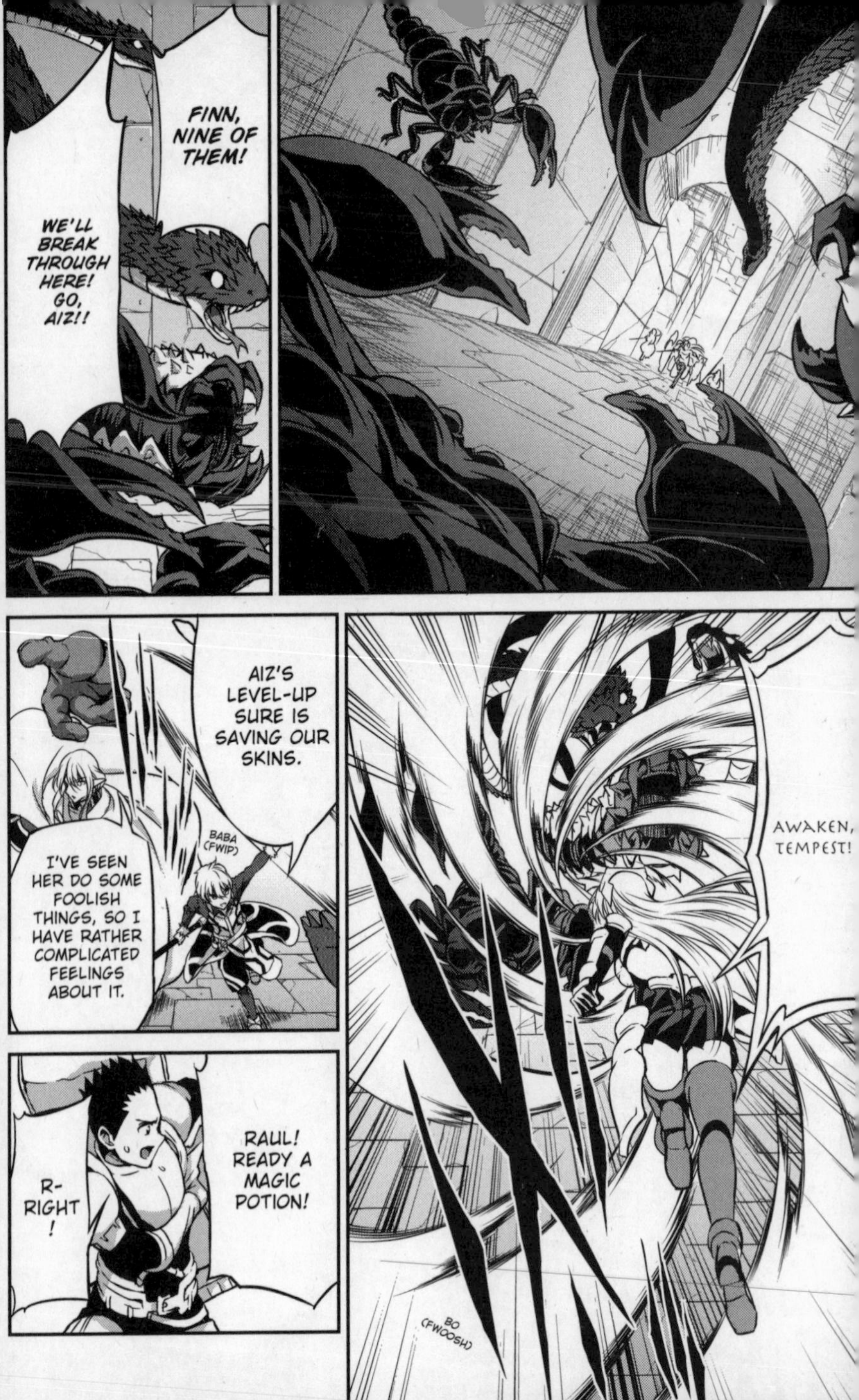
FINN, NINE OF THEM!
WE'LL BREAK THROUGH HERE! GO, AIZ!!
AWAKEN, TEMPEST!
BO (FWOOSH)
AIZ'S LEVEL-UP SURE IS SAVING OUR SKINS.
BABA (FWIP)
I'VE SEEN HER DO SOME FOOLISH THINGS, SO I HAVE RATHER COMPLICATED FEELINGS ABOUT IT.
RAUL! READY A MAGIC POTION!
R-RIGHT!

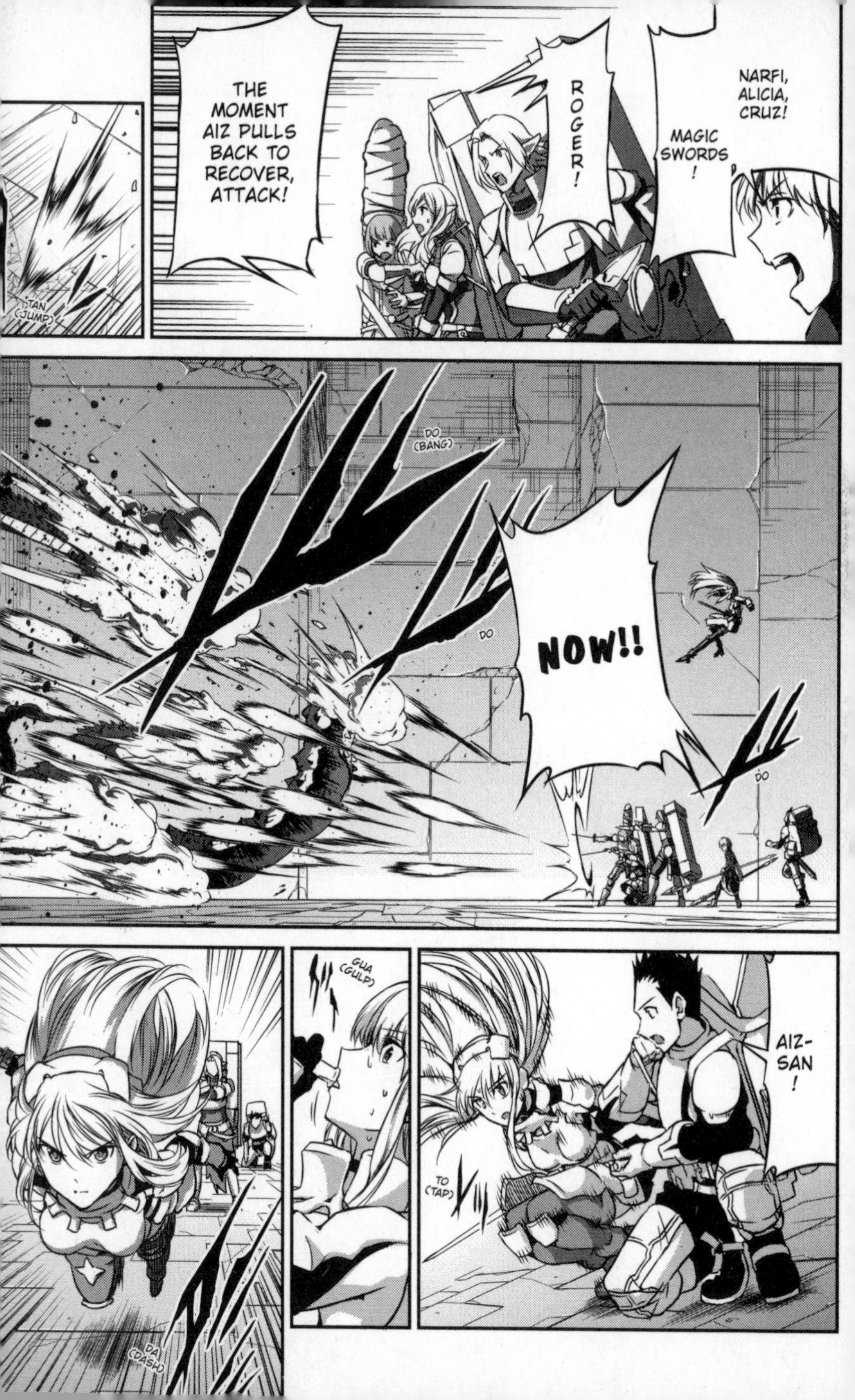
NARFI, ALICIA, CRUZ!
MAGIC SWORDS!
ROGER!
THE MOMENT AIZ PULLS BACK TO RECOVER, ATTACK!
TAN (JUMP)
NOW!!
DO (BANG)
DO
DO
AIZ-SAN!
TO (TAP)
GUA (GULP)
DA (DASH)

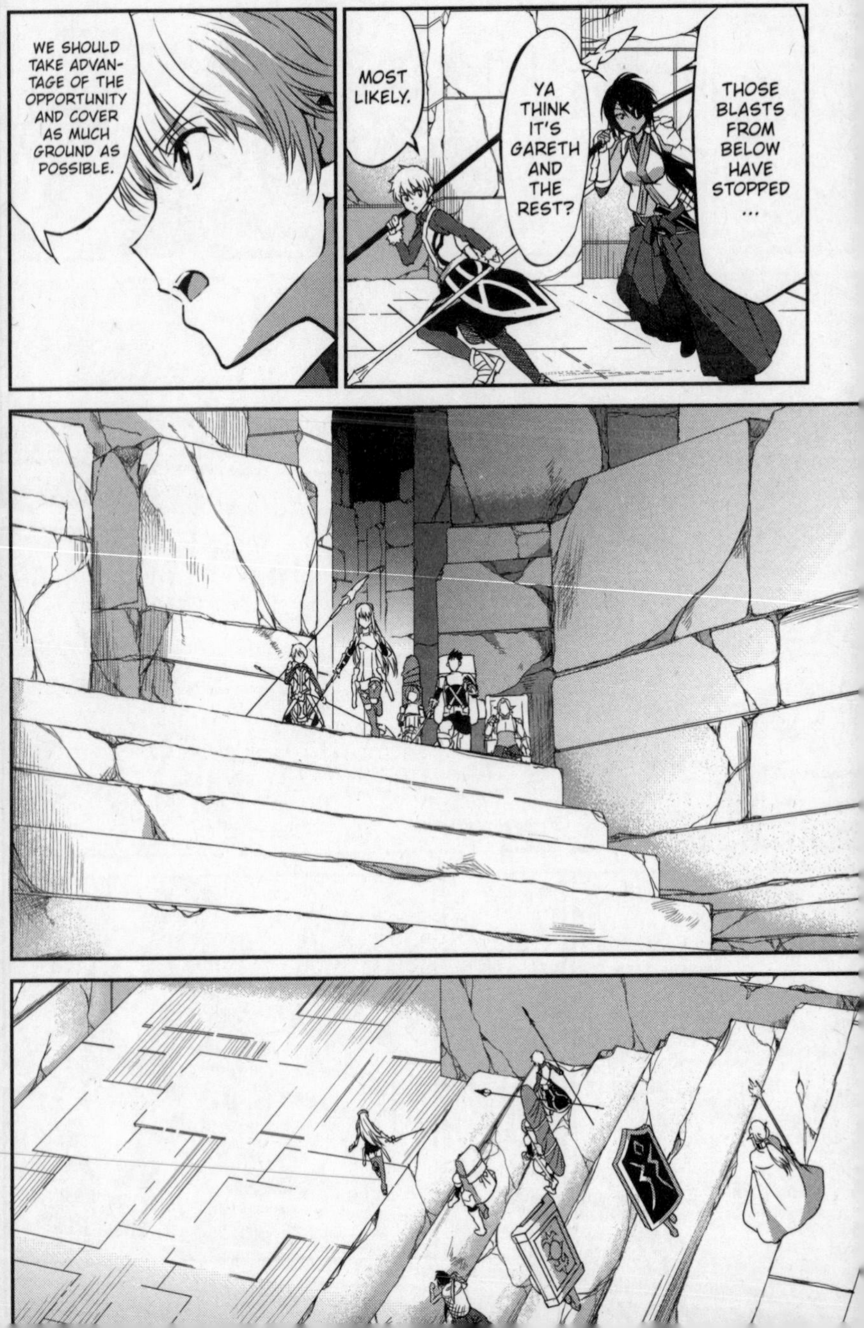
THOSE BLASTS FROM BELOW HAVE STOPPED ...
YA THINK IT'S GARETH AND THE REST?
MOST LIKELY.
WE SHOULD TAKE ADVANTAGE OF THE OPPORTUNITY AND COVER AS MUCH GROUND AS POSSIBLE.

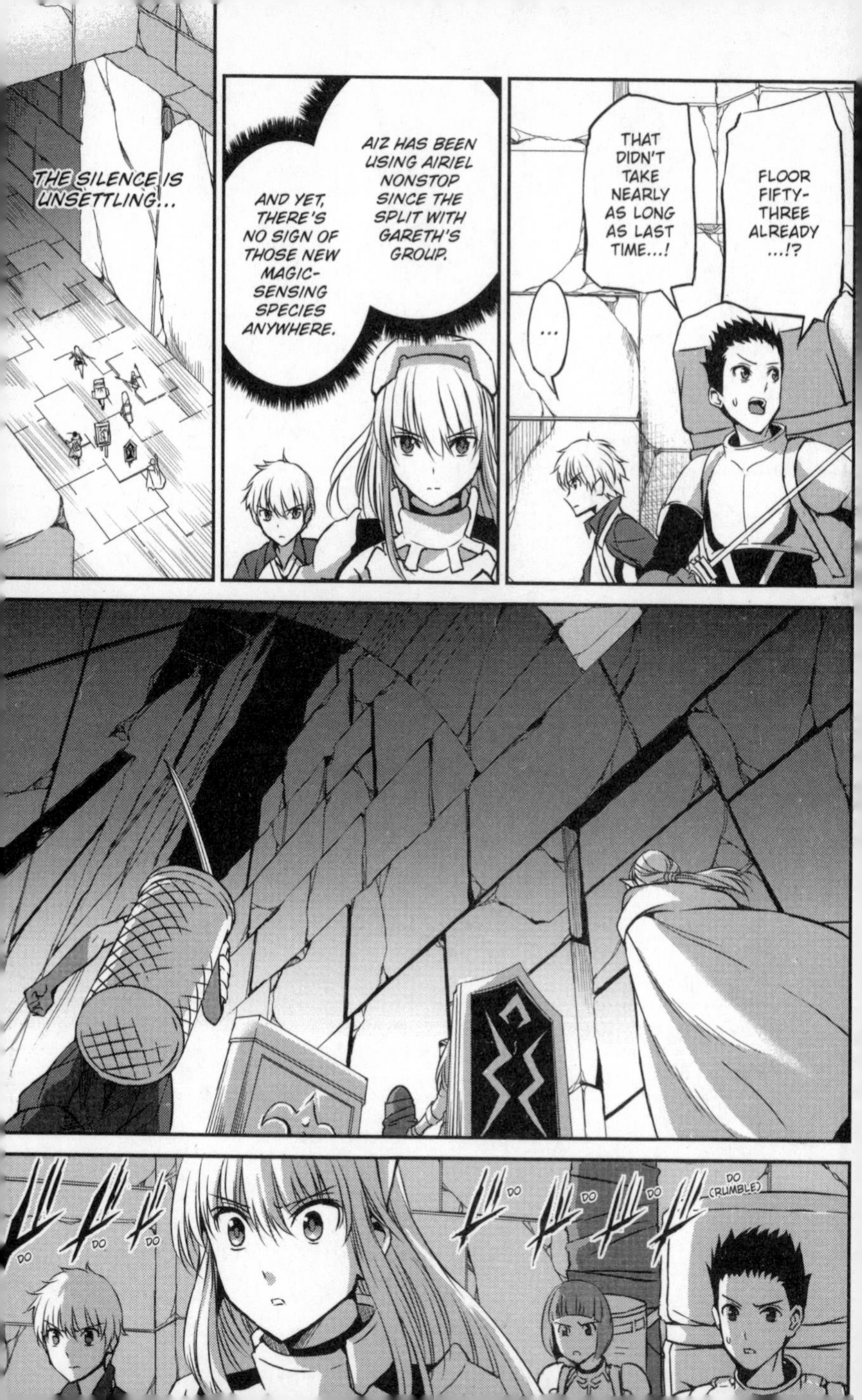
FLOOR FIFTY-THREE ALREADY ...!?
THAT DIDN'T TAKE NEARLY AS LONG AS LAST TIME...!
...
AIZ HAS BEEN USING AIRIEL NONSTOP SINCE THE SPLIT WITH GARETH'S GROUP.
AND YET, THERE'S NO SIGN OF THOSE NEW MAGIC-SENSING SPECIES ANYWHERE.
THE SILENCE IS UNSETTLING...
DO (RUMBLE)
DO
DO
DO
DO
DO
DO

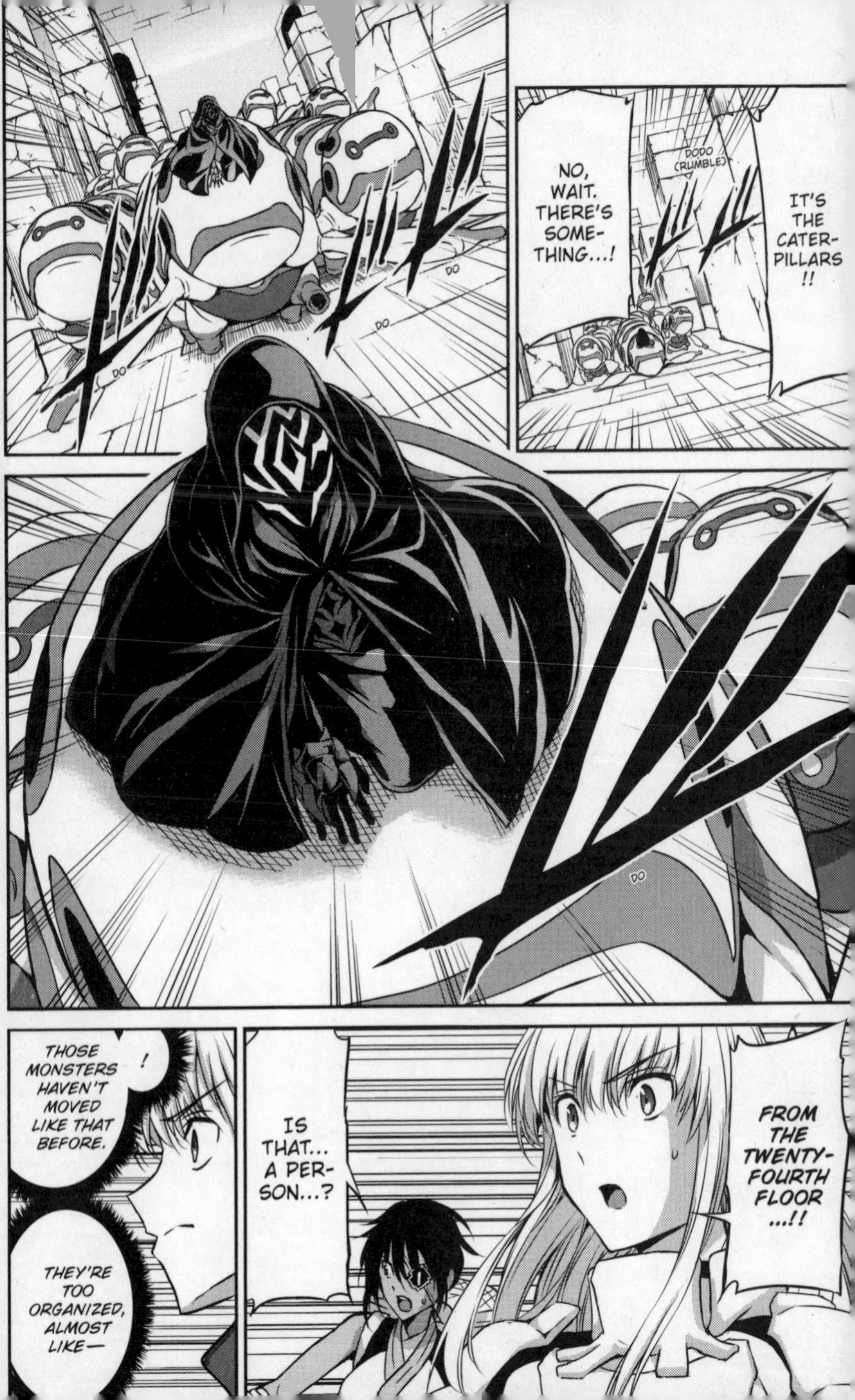
DODO (RUMBLE)
NO, WAIT. THERE'S SOME-THING...!
IT'S THE CATER-PILLARS!!
DO
DO
DO
DO
FROM THE TWENTY-FOURTH FLOOR...!!
IS THAT... A PER-SON...?
!
THOSE MONSTERS HAVEN'T MOVED LIKE THAT BEFORE.
THEY'RE TOO ORGANIZED, ALMOST LIKE—

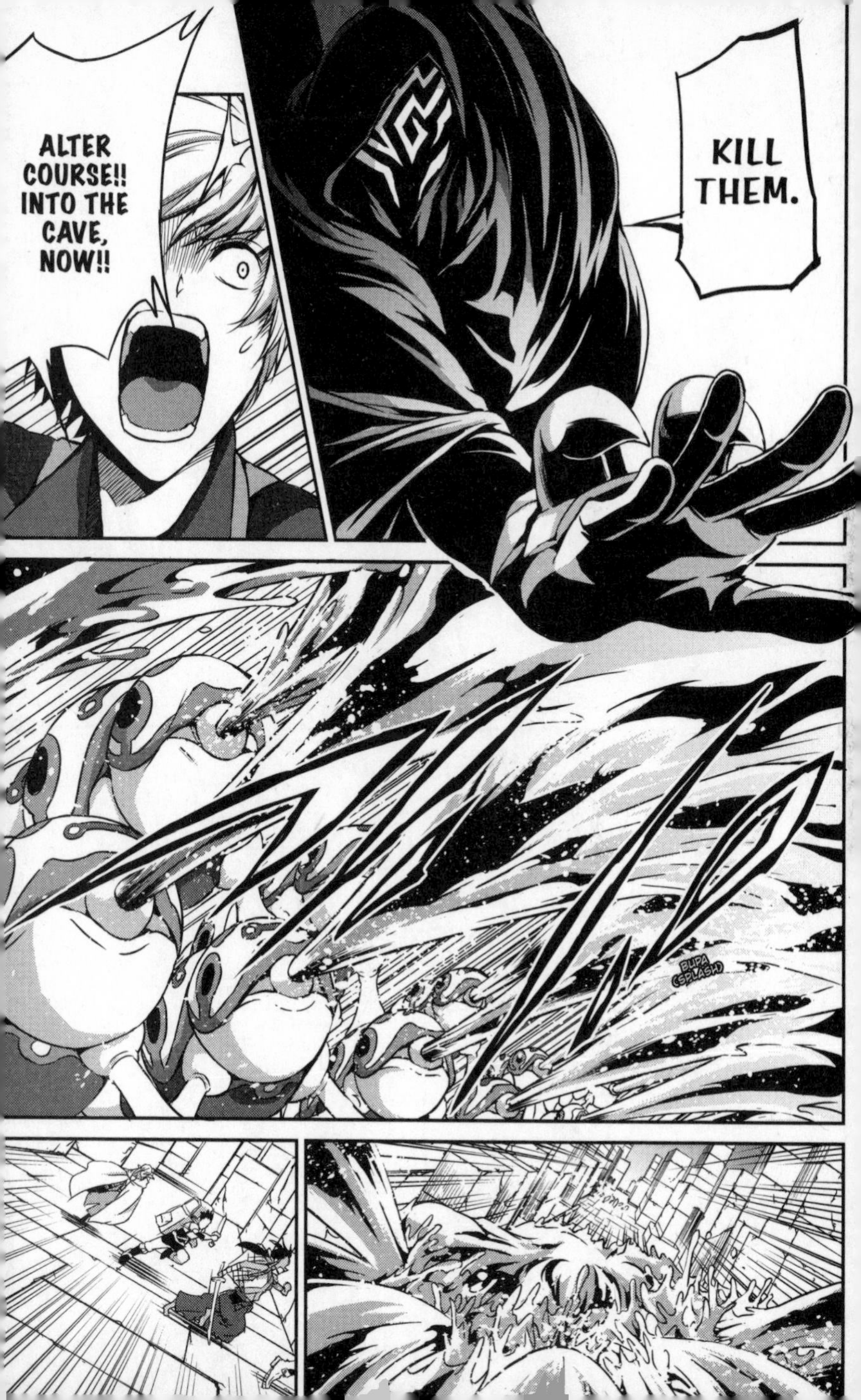
KILL THEM.
ALTER COURSE!! INTO THE CAVE, NOW!!
BUPA (SPLASH)

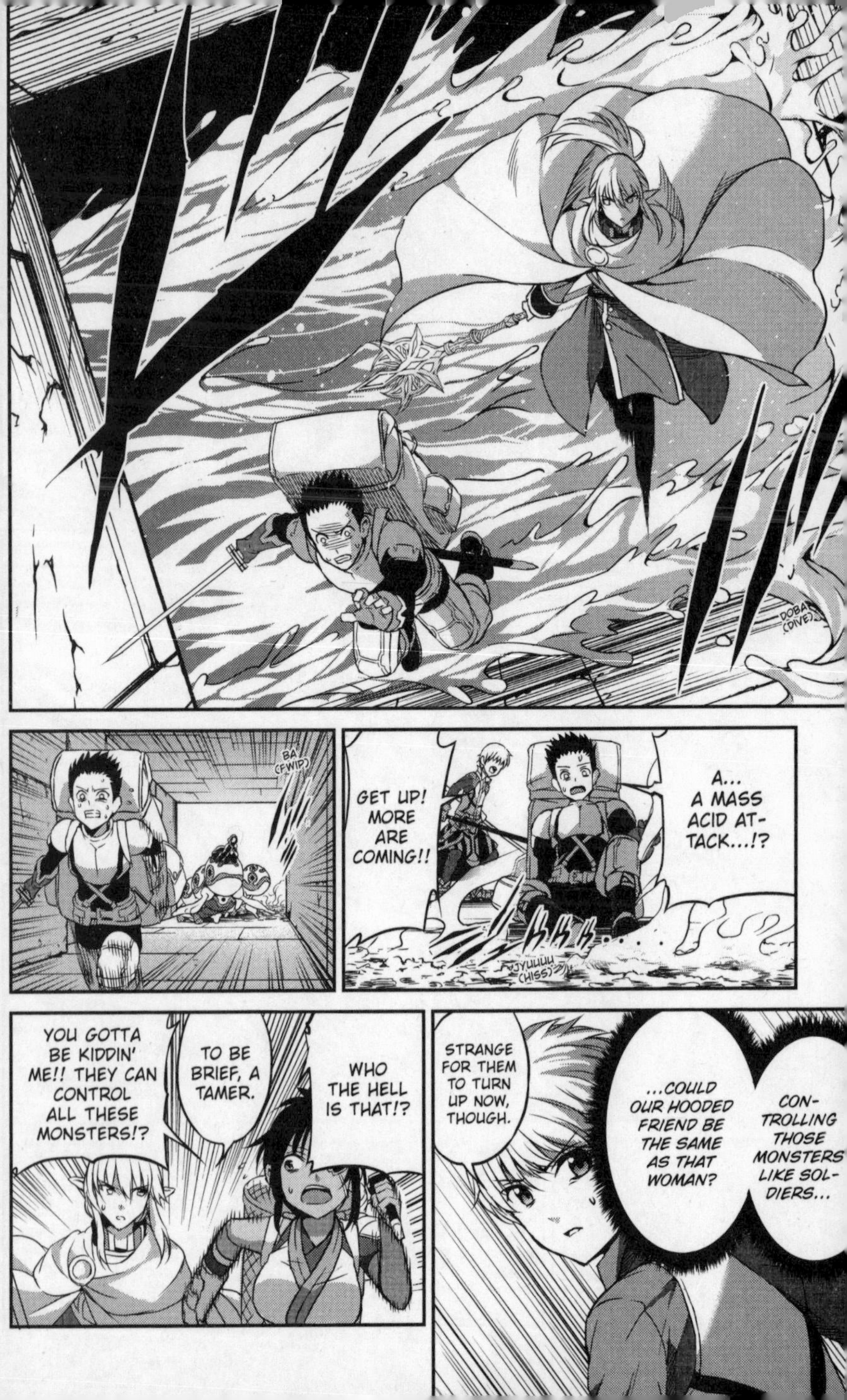
DOBA (DIVE)
A... A MASS ACID AT-TACK...!?
GET UP! MORE ARE COMING!!
JYUUUU (HISS)
BA (FWIP)
CON-TROLLING THOSE MONSTERS LIKE SOL-DIERS...
...COULD OUR HOODED FRIEND BE THE SAME AS THAT WOMAN?
STRANGE FOR THEM TO TURN UP NOW, THOUGH.
WHO THE HELL IS THAT!?
TO BE BRIEF, A TAMER.
YOU GOTTA BE KIDDIN' ME!! THEY CAN CONTROL ALL THESE MONSTERS!?

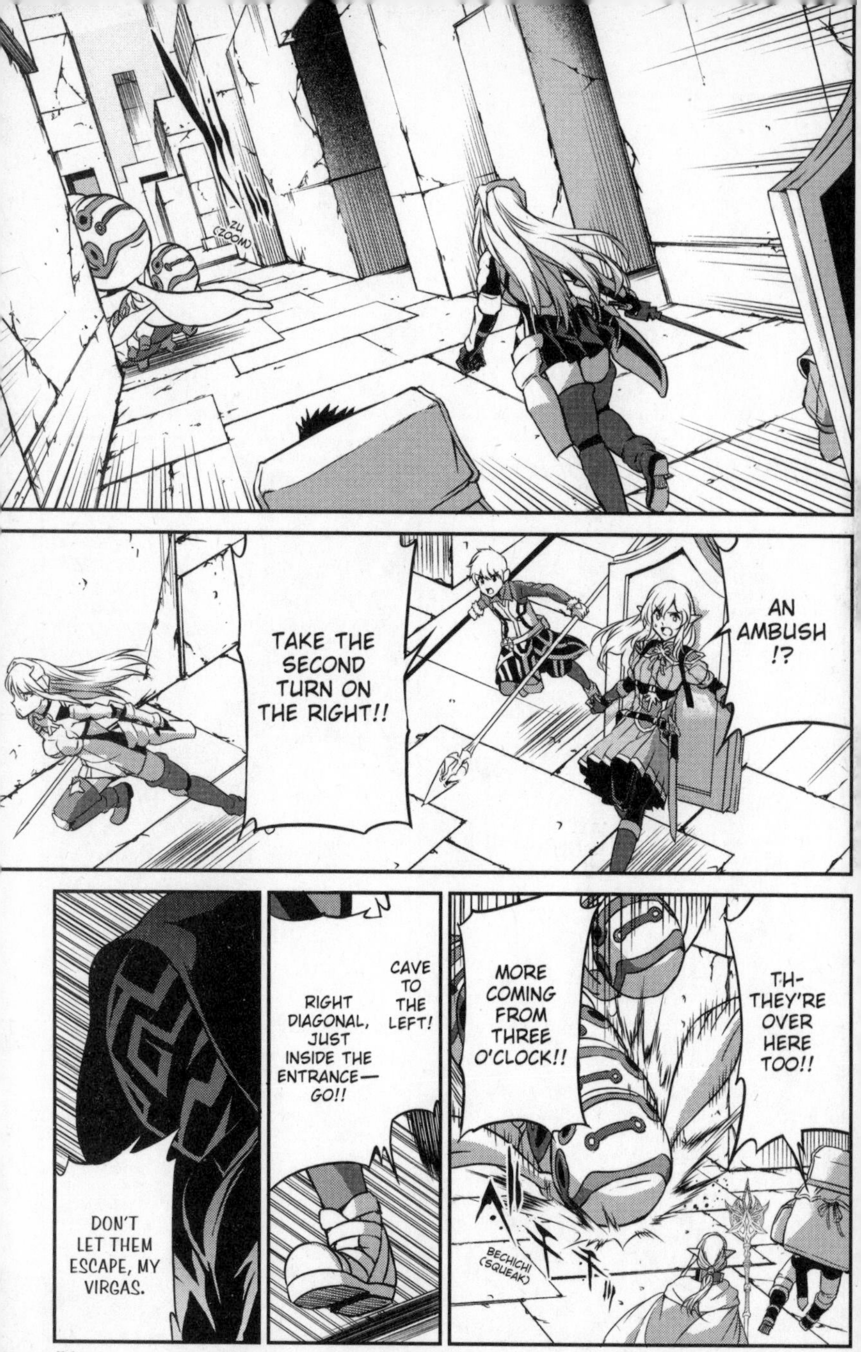
ZU (ZOOM)
AN AMBUSH!?
TAKE THE SECOND TURN ON THE RIGHT!!
TH-THEY'RE OVER HERE TOO!!
MORE COMING FROM THREE O'CLOCK!!
BECHICHI (SQUEAK)
CAVE TO THE LEFT!
RIGHT DIAGONAL, JUST INSIDE THE ENTRANCE—GO!!
DON'T LET THEM ESCAPE, MY VIRGAS.

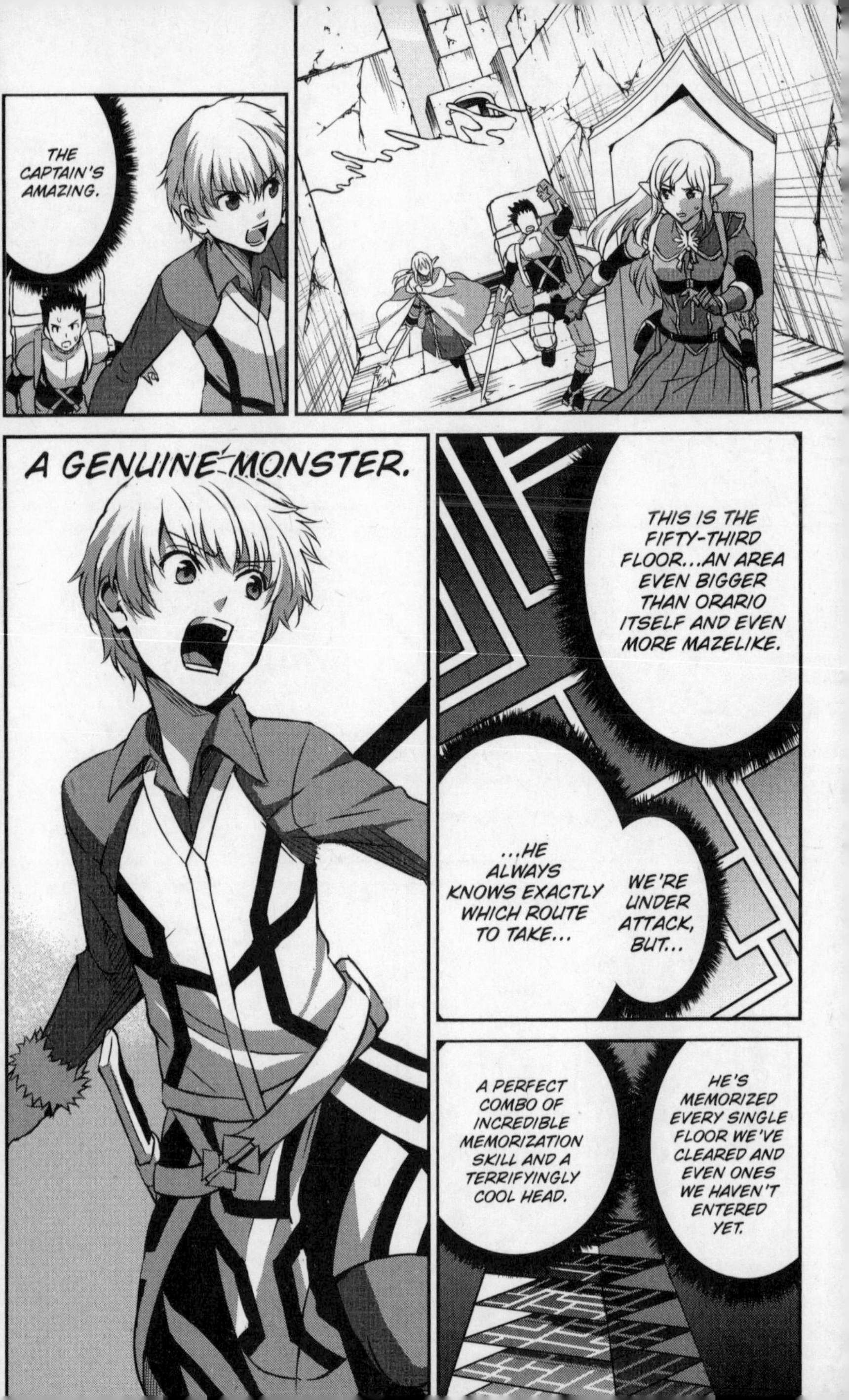
THE CAPTAIN'S AMAZING.
THIS IS THE FIFTY-THIRD FLOOR...AN AREA EVEN BIGGER THAN ORARIO ITSELF AND EVEN MORE MAZELIKE.
WE'RE UNDER ATTACK, BUT...
...HE ALWAYS KNOWS EXACTLY WHICH ROUTE TO TAKE...
HE'S MEMORIZED EVERY SINGLE FLOOR WE'VE CLEARED AND EVEN ONES WE HAVEN'T ENTERED YET.
A PERFECT COMBO OF INCREDIBLE MEMORIZATION SKILL AND A TERRIFYINGLY COOL HEAD.
A GENUINE MONSTER.

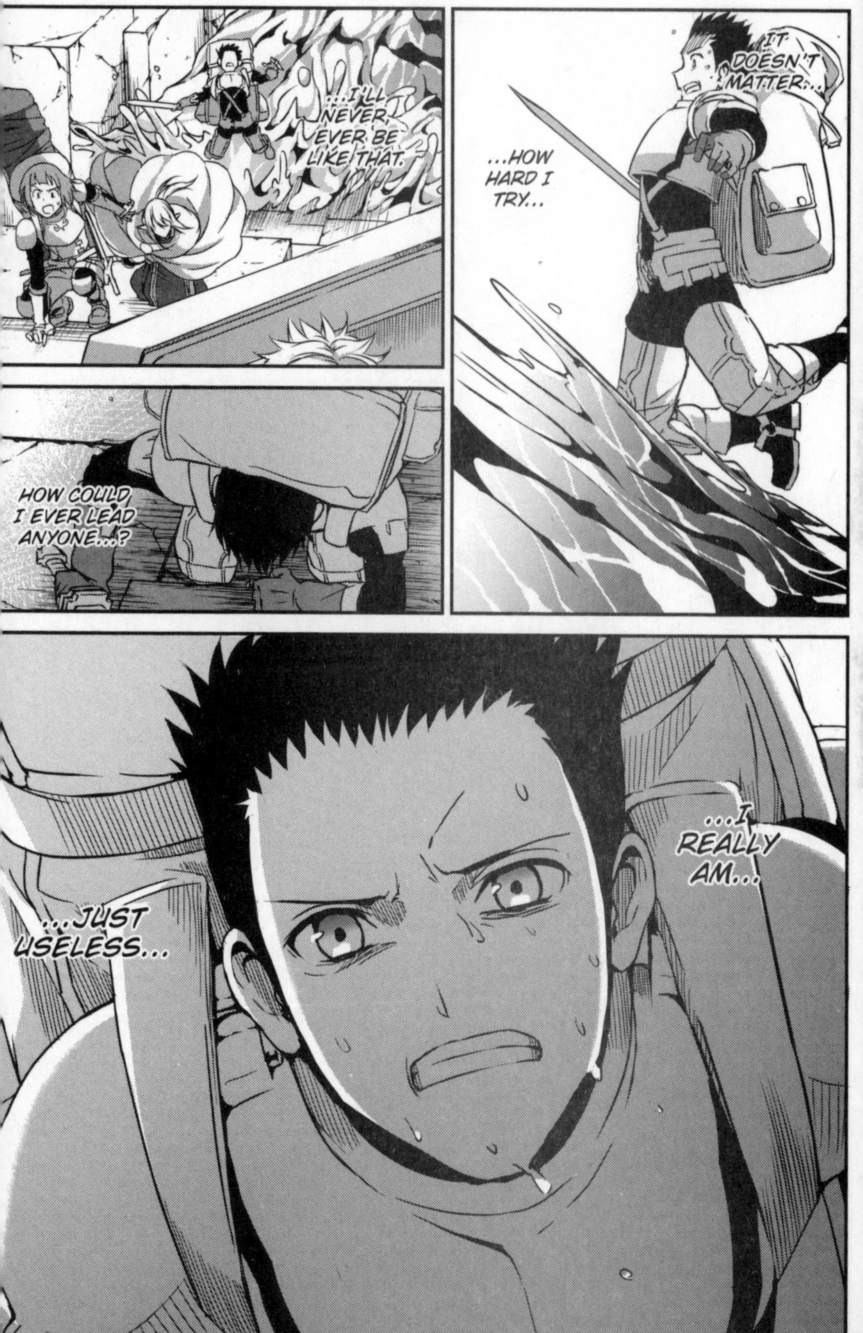
IT DOESN'T MATTER...
...HOW HARD I TRY...
...I'LL NEVER, EVER BE LIKE THAT.
HOW COULD I EVER LEAD ANYONE...?
...I REALLY AM...
...JUST USELESS...

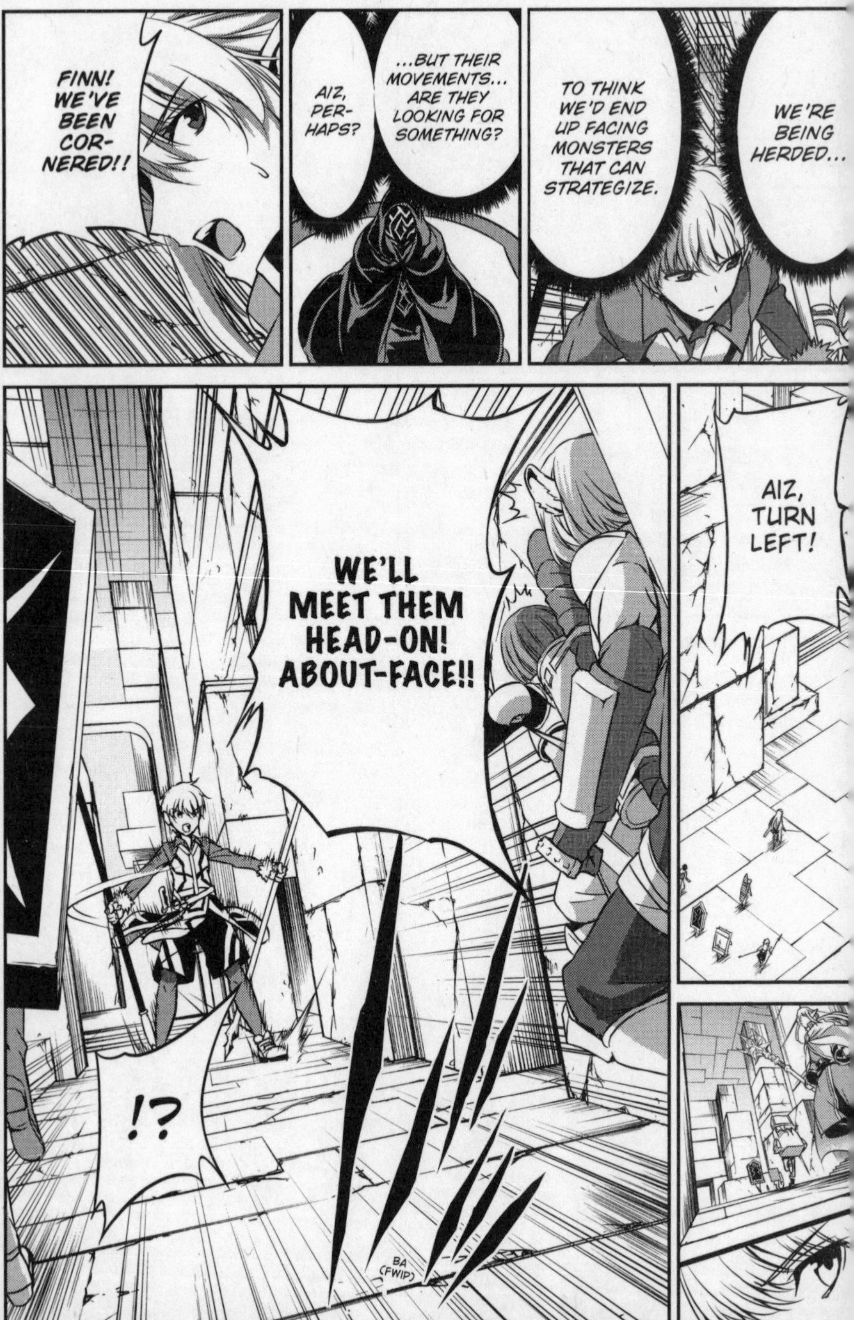
WE'RE BEING HERDED...
TO THINK WE'D END UP FACING MONSTERS THAT CAN STRATEGIZE.
...BUT THEIR MOVEMENTS... ARE THEY LOOKING FOR SOMETHING?
AIZ, PER-HAPS?
FINN! WE'VE BEEN COR-NERED!!
AIZ, TURN LEFT!
WE'LL MEET THEM HEAD-ON! ABOUT-FACE!!
!?
BA (FWIP)

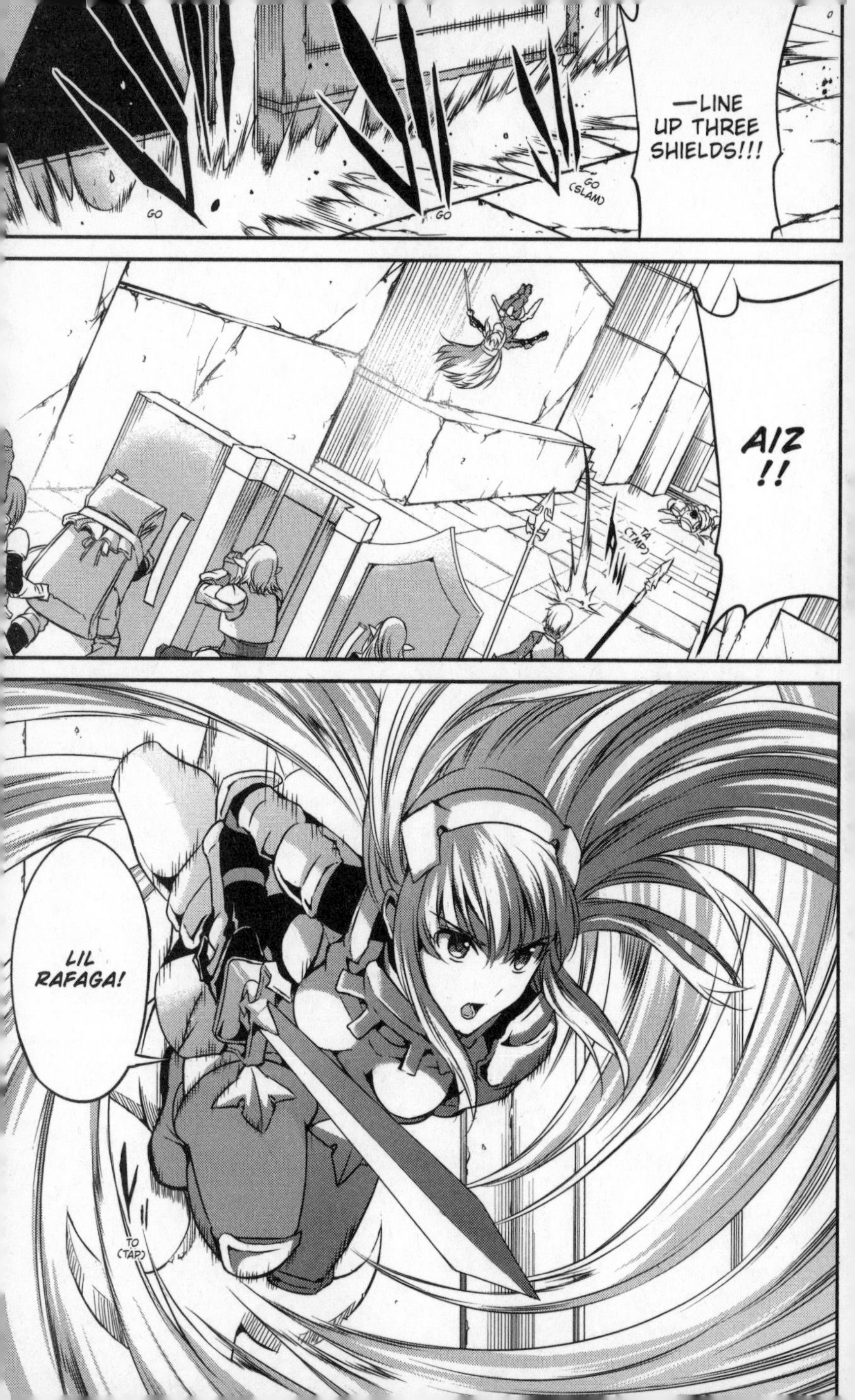
—LINE UP THREE SHIELDS!!!
GO (SLAM)
GO
GO
AIZ !!
TA (TMP)
LIL RAFAGA!
TO (TAP)

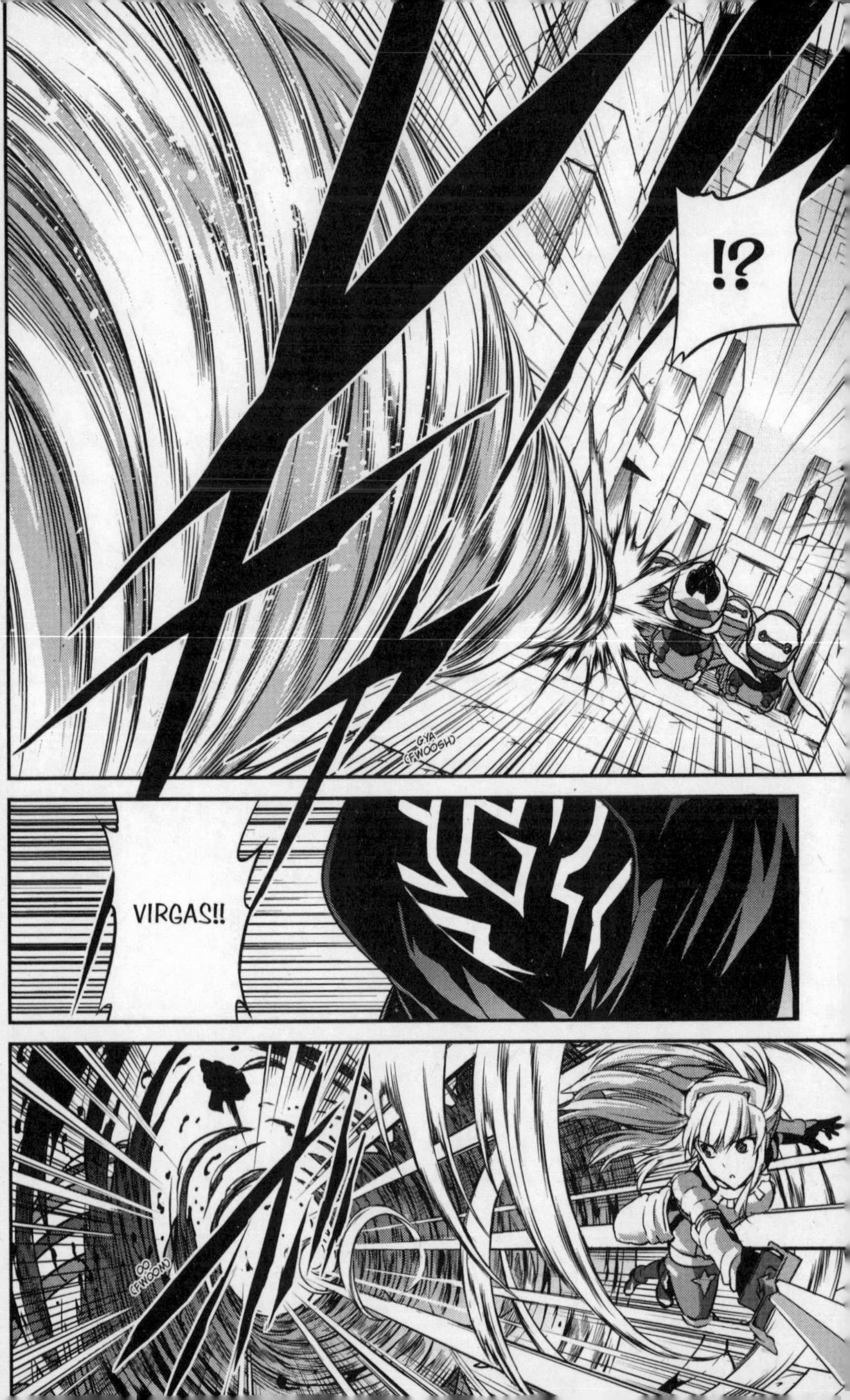
!?
GYA
(FWOOSH)
VIRGAS!!
OO
(FWOOM)

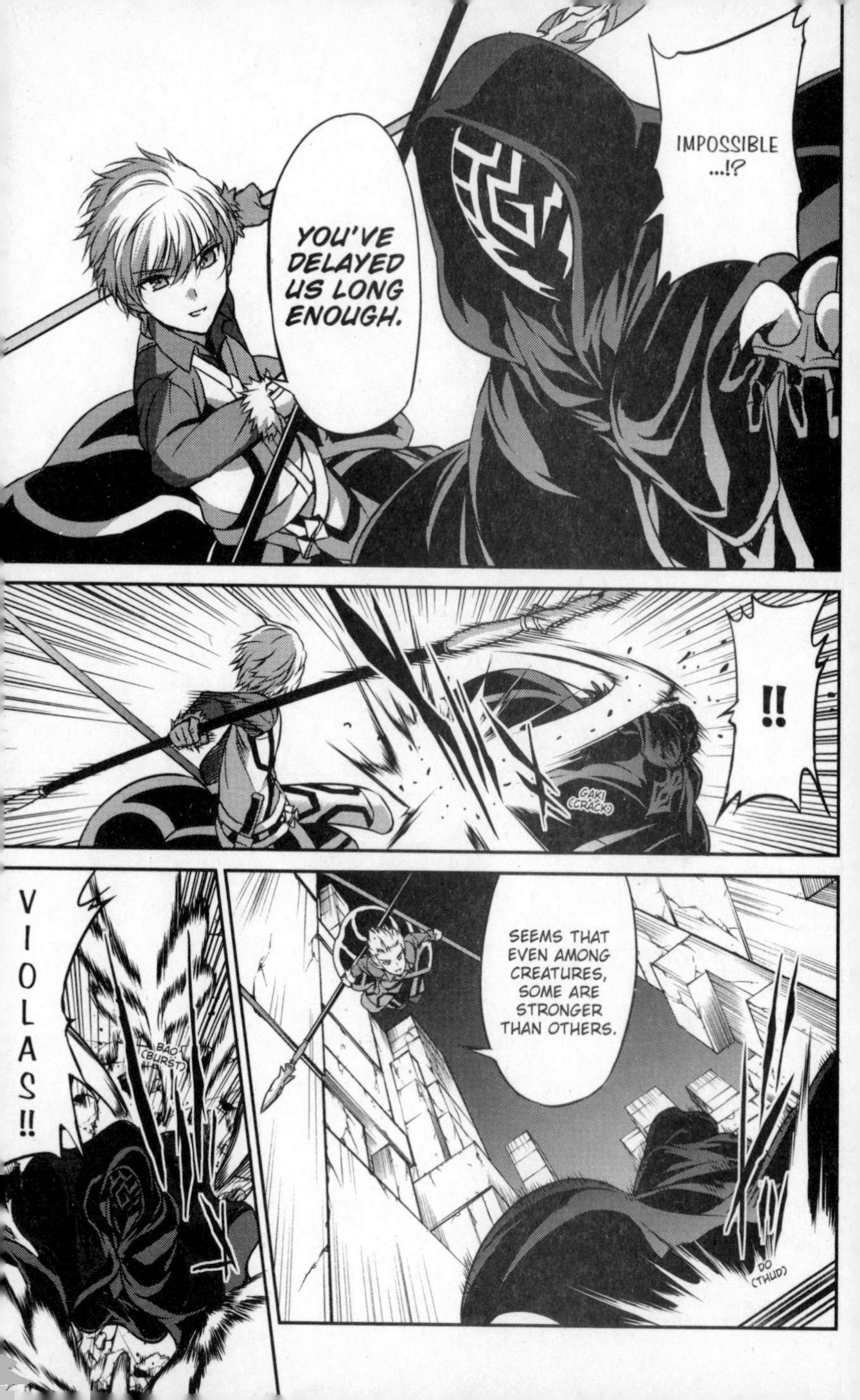
IMPOSSIBLE ...!?
YOU'VE DELAYED US LONG ENOUGH.
!!
GAKI (CRACK)
SEEMS THAT EVEN AMONG CREATURES, SOME ARE STRONGER THAN OTHERS.
DO (THUD)
VIOLAS!!
BAO (BURST)

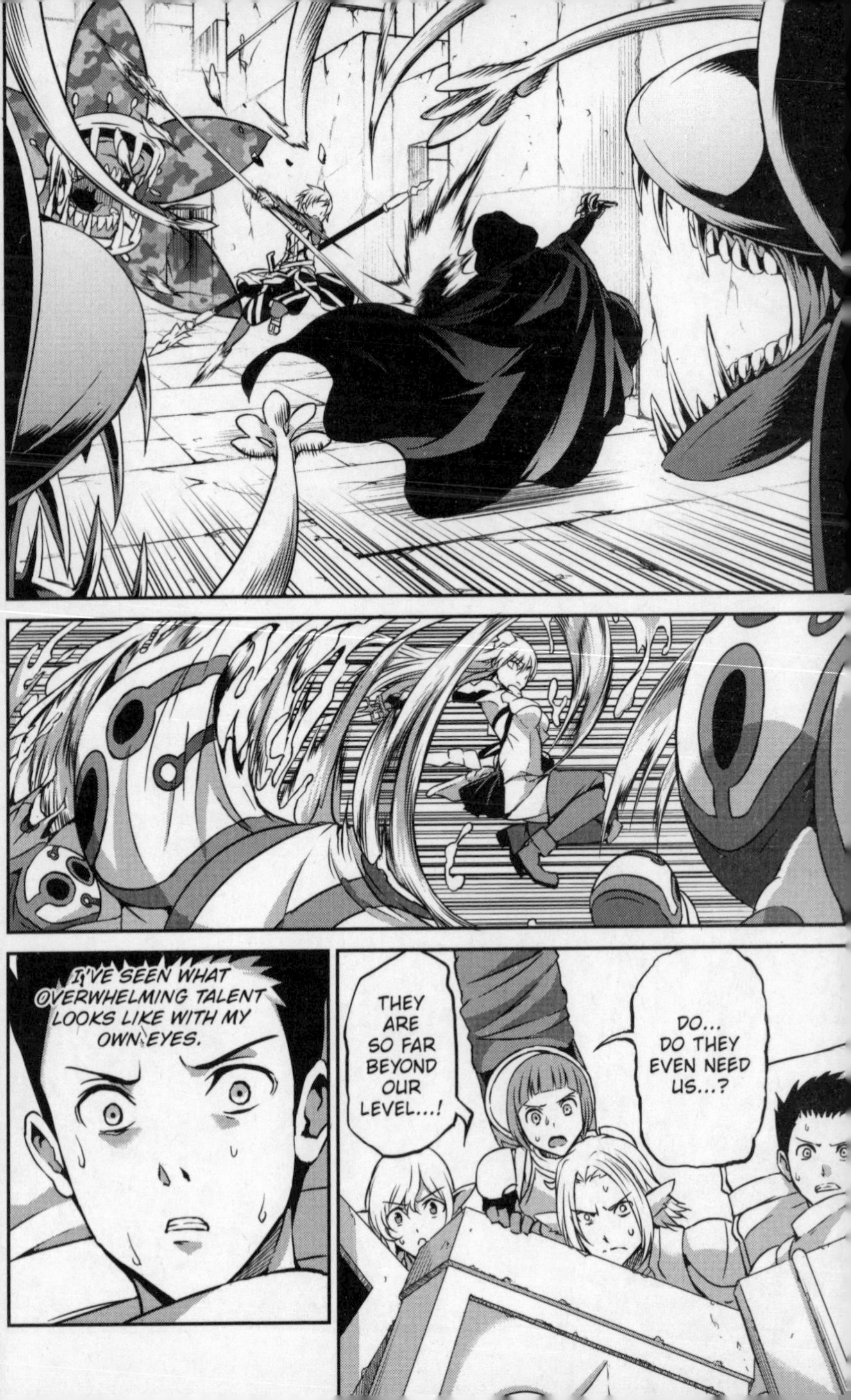
DO... DO THEY EVEN NEED US...?
THEY ARE SO FAR BEYOND OUR LEVEL...!
I'VE SEEN WHAT OVERWHELMING TALENT LOOKS LIKE WITH MY OWN EYES.

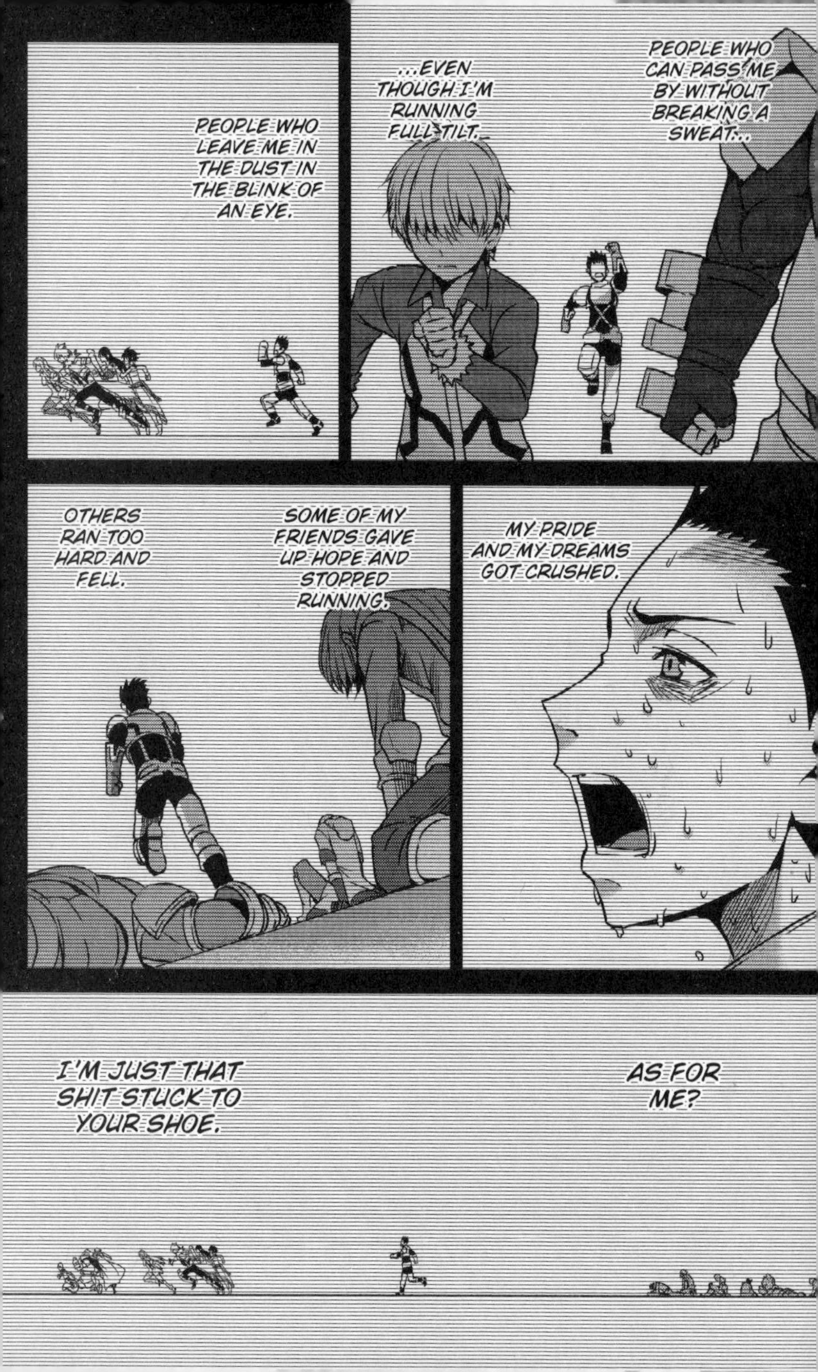
PEOPLE WHO CAN PASS ME BY WITHOUT BREAKING A SWEAT...
...EVEN THOUGH I'M RUNNING FULL TILT.
PEOPLE WHO LEAVE ME IN THE DUST IN THE BLINK OF AN EYE.
MY PRIDE AND MY DREAMS GOT CRUSHED.
SOME OF MY FRIENDS GAVE UP HOPE AND STOPPED RUNNING.
OTHERS RAN TOO HARD AND FELL.
AS FOR ME?
I'M JUST THAT SHIT STUCK TO YOUR SHOE.

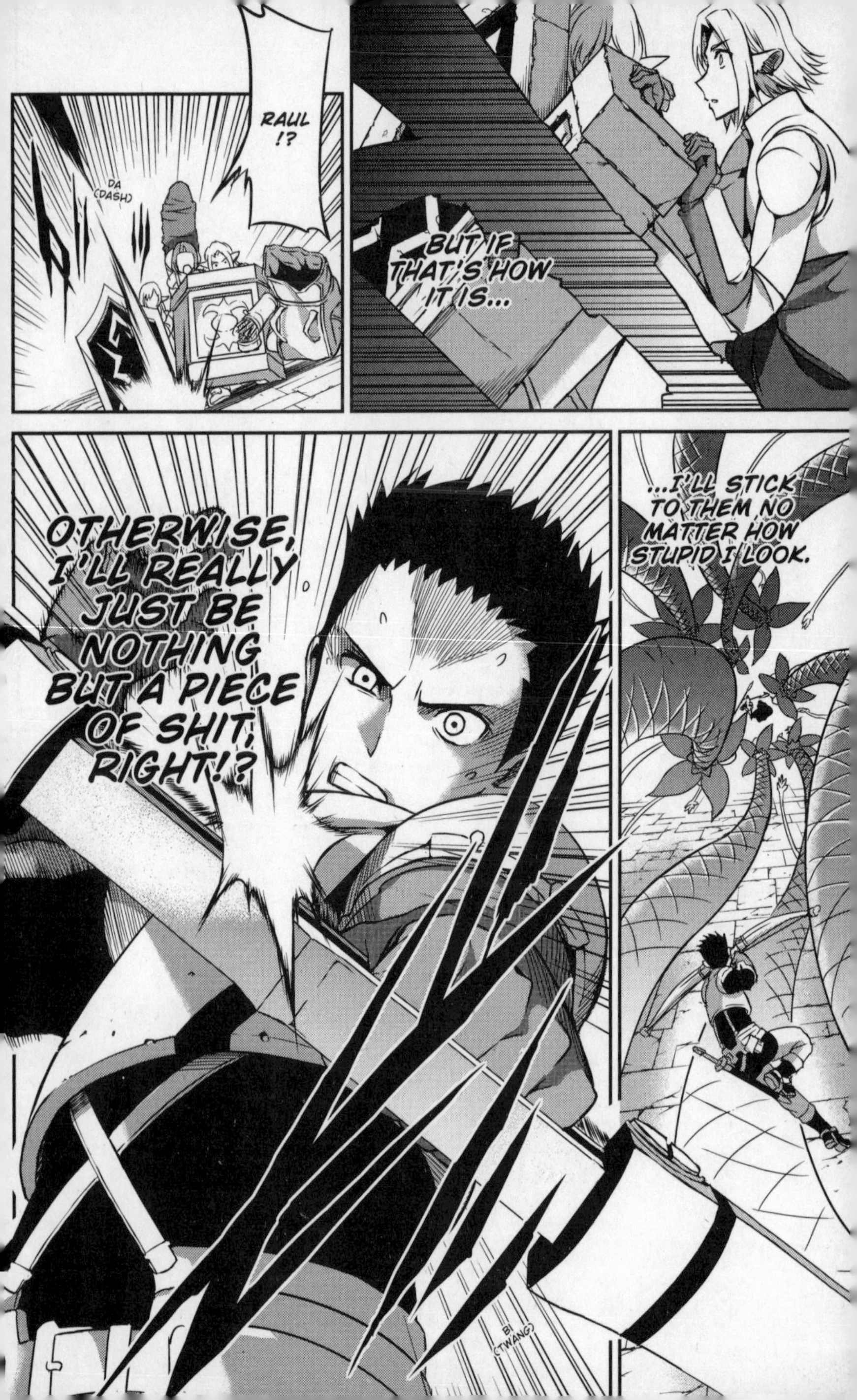
BUT IF THAT'S HOW IT IS...
RAUL !?
DA (DASH)
...I'LL STICK TO THEM NO MATTER HOW STUPID I LOOK.
OTHERWISE, I'LL REALLY JUST BE NOTHING BUT A PIECE OF SHIT, RIGHT!?
BI (TWANG)

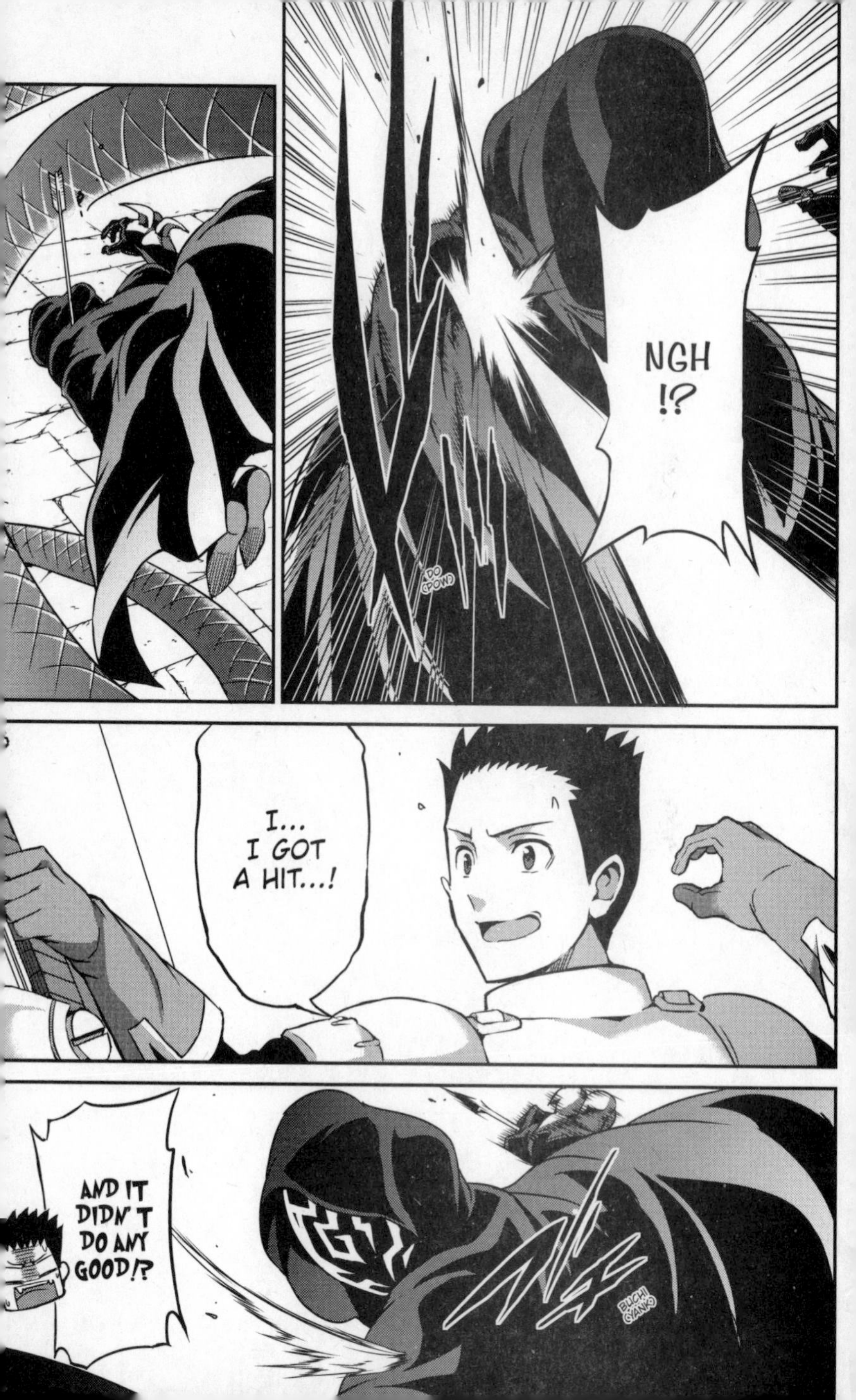
NGH !?
DO (POW)
I... I GOT A HIT...!
BUCHI (YANK)
AND IT DIDN'T DO ANY GOOD!?

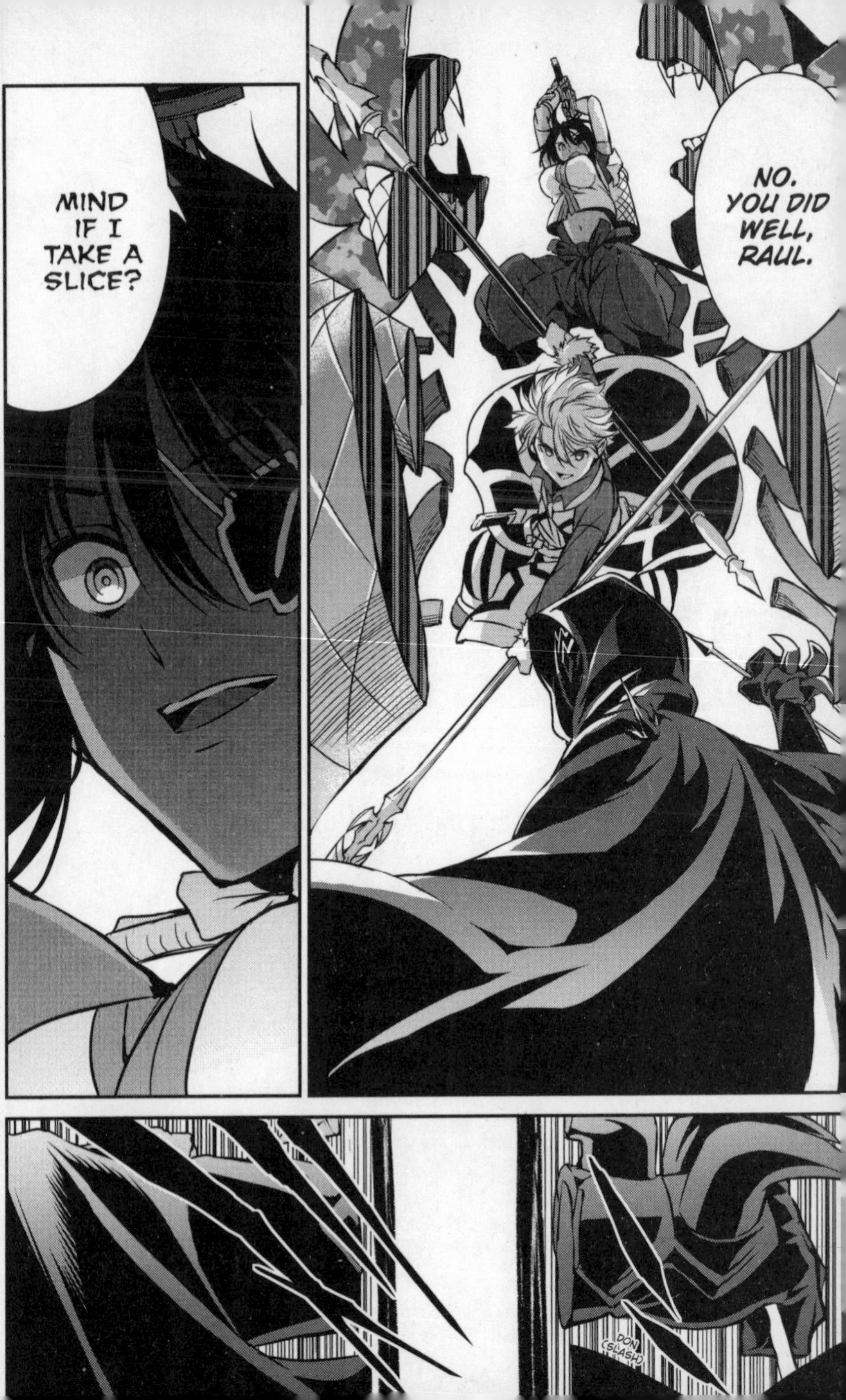
NO. YOU DID WELL, RAUL.
MIND IF I TAKE A SLICE?
DON (SLASH)

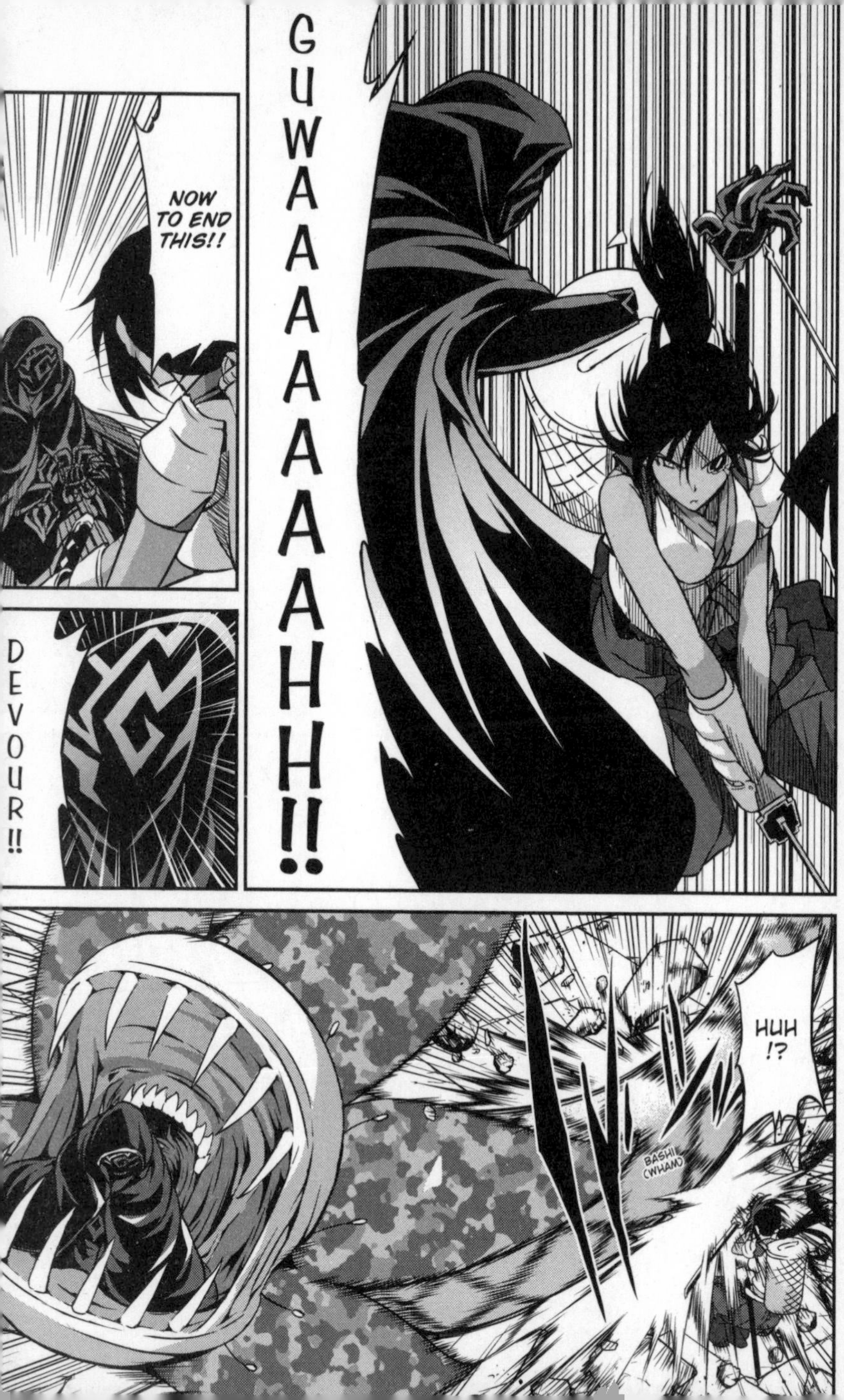
GUWAAAAAAAHH!!
NOW TO END THIS!!
DEVOUR!!
HUH!?
BASHI (WHAM)

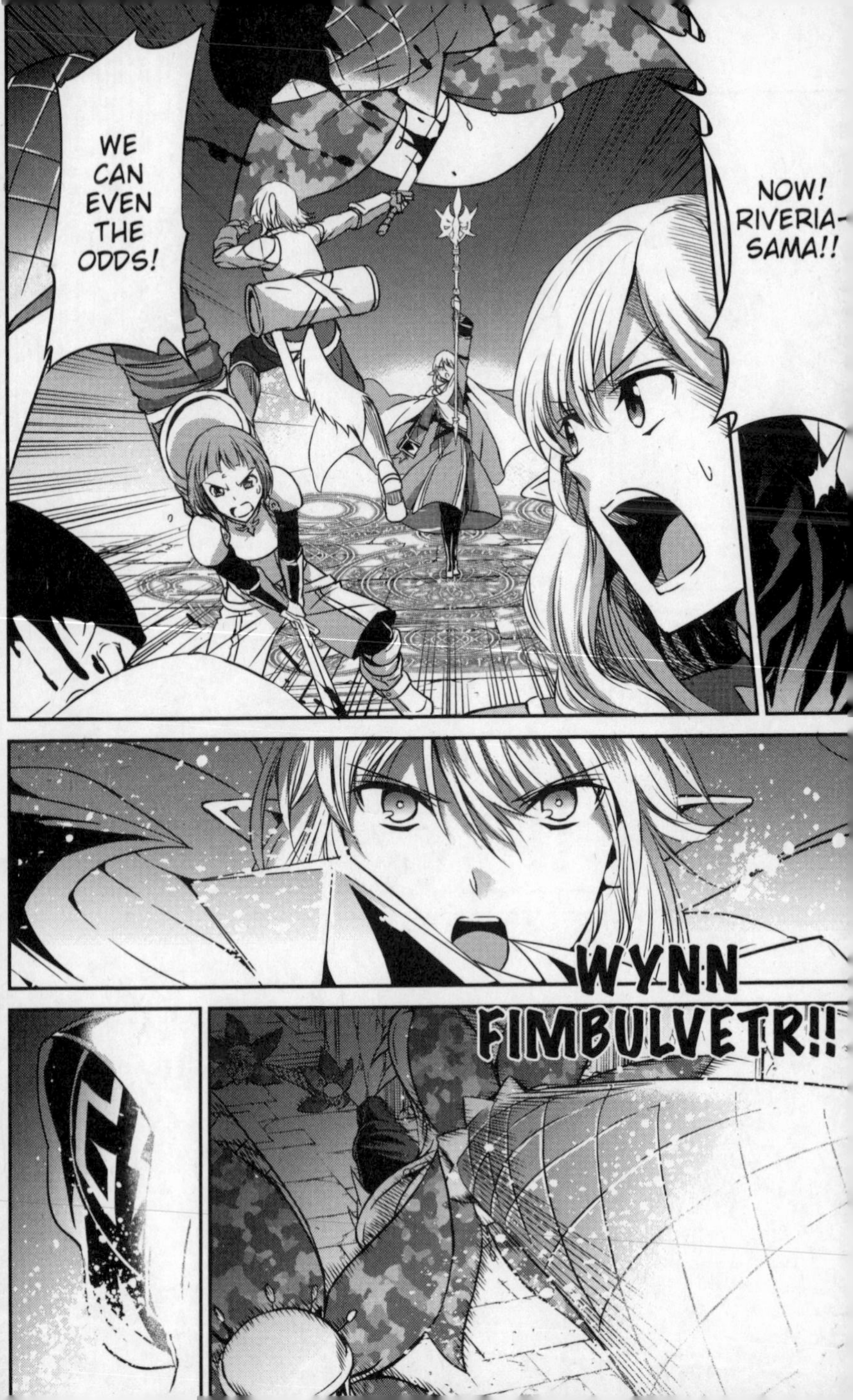
NOW! RIVERIA-SAMA!!
WE CAN EVEN THE ODDS!
WYNN FIMBULVETR!!

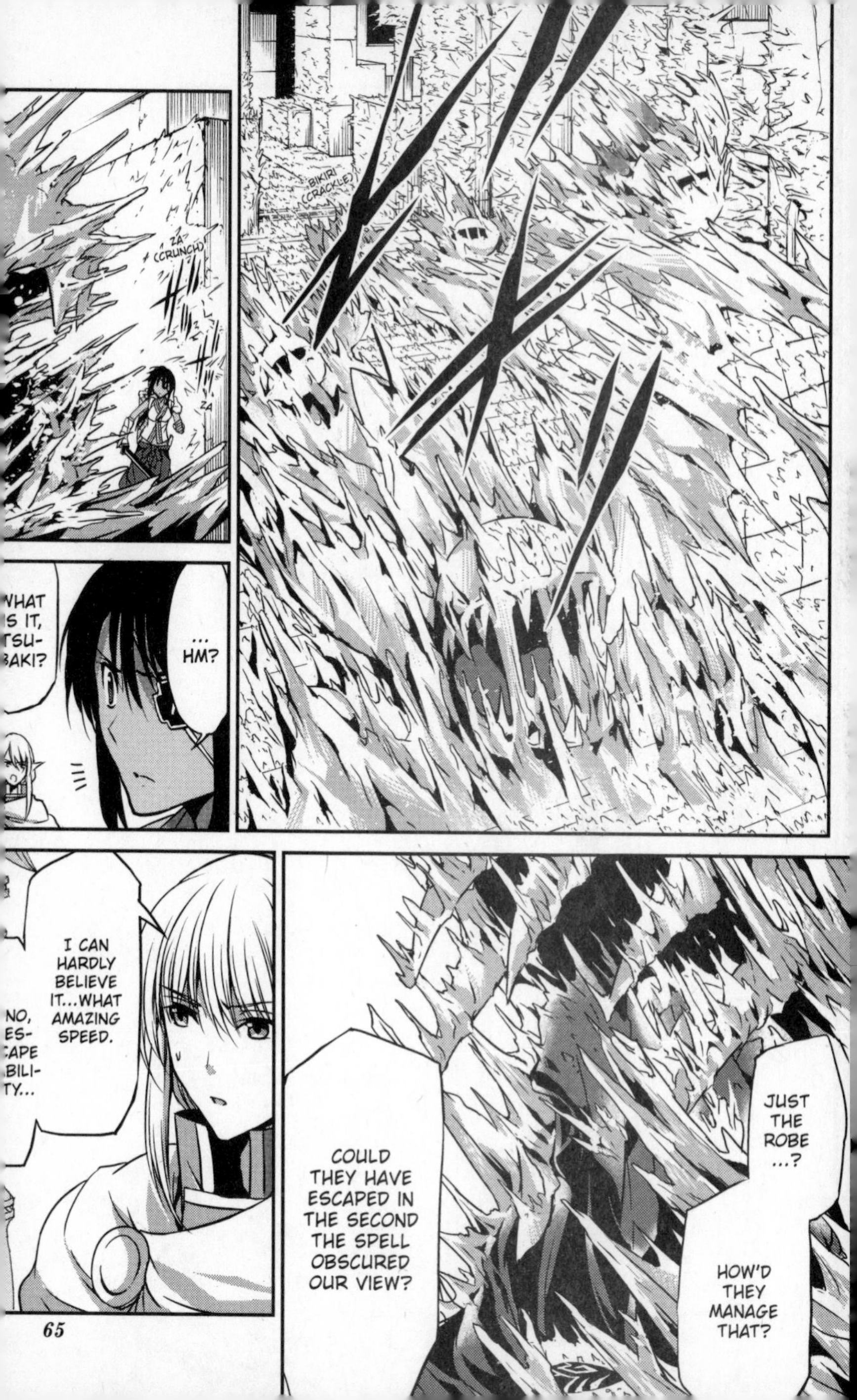
BIKIRI (CRACKLE)
ZA (CRUNCH)
ZA
...HM?
WHAT S IT, TSU- BAKI?
JUST THE ROBE...?
HOW'D THEY MANAGE THAT?
COULD THEY HAVE ESCAPED IN THE SECOND THE SPELL OBSCURED OUR VIEW?
I CAN HARDLY BELIEVE IT...WHAT AMAZING SPEED.
NO, ES- CAPE BILI- TY...

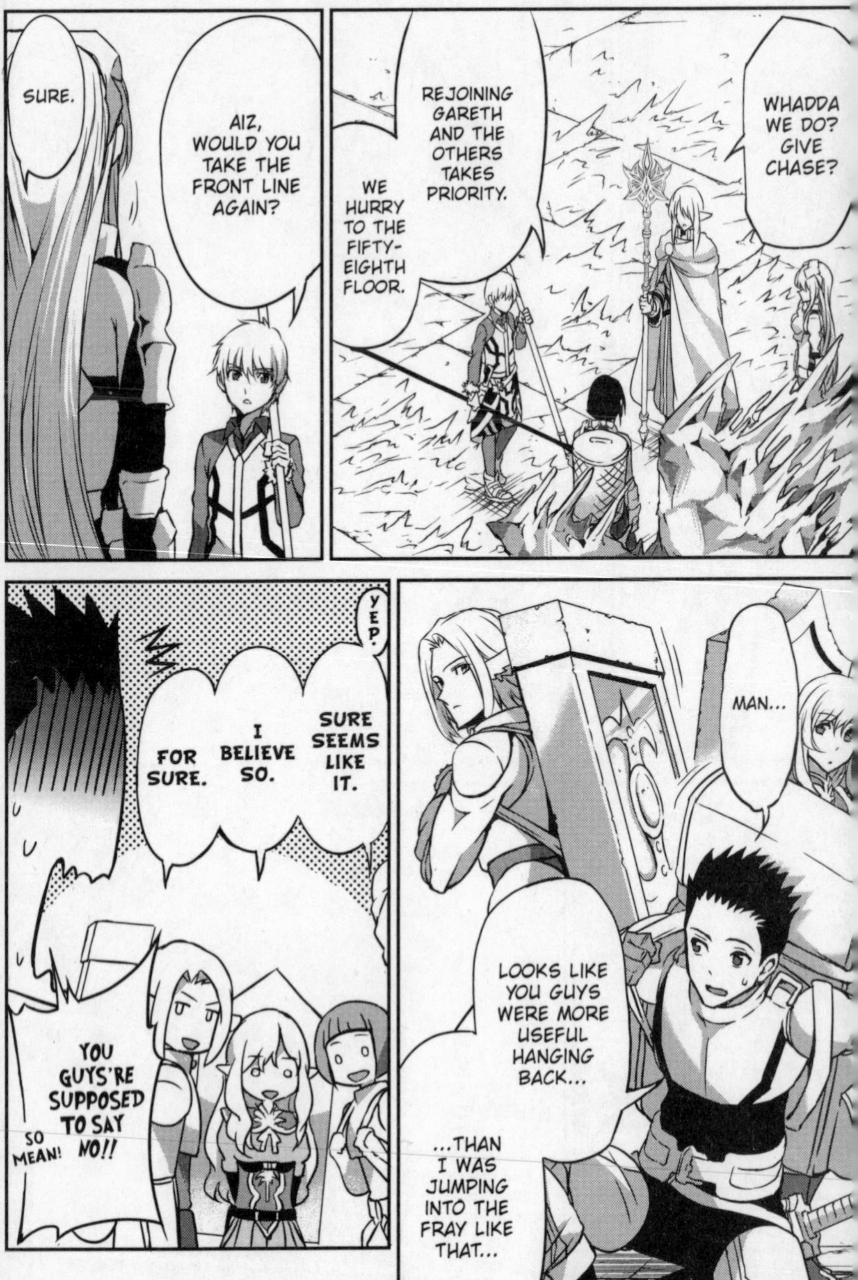
WHADDA WE DO? GIVE CHASE?
REJOINING GARETH AND THE OTHERS TAKES PRIORITY.
WE HURRY TO THE FIFTY-EIGHTH FLOOR.
AIZ, WOULD YOU TAKE THE FRONT LINE AGAIN?
SURE.
MAN...
LOOKS LIKE YOU GUYS WERE MORE USEFUL HANGING BACK...
...THAN I WAS JUMPING INTO THE FRAY LIKE THAT...
YEP.
SURE SEEMS LIKE IT.
I BELIEVE SO.
FOR SURE.
YOU GUYS'RE SUPPOSED TO SAY NO!!
SO MEAN!

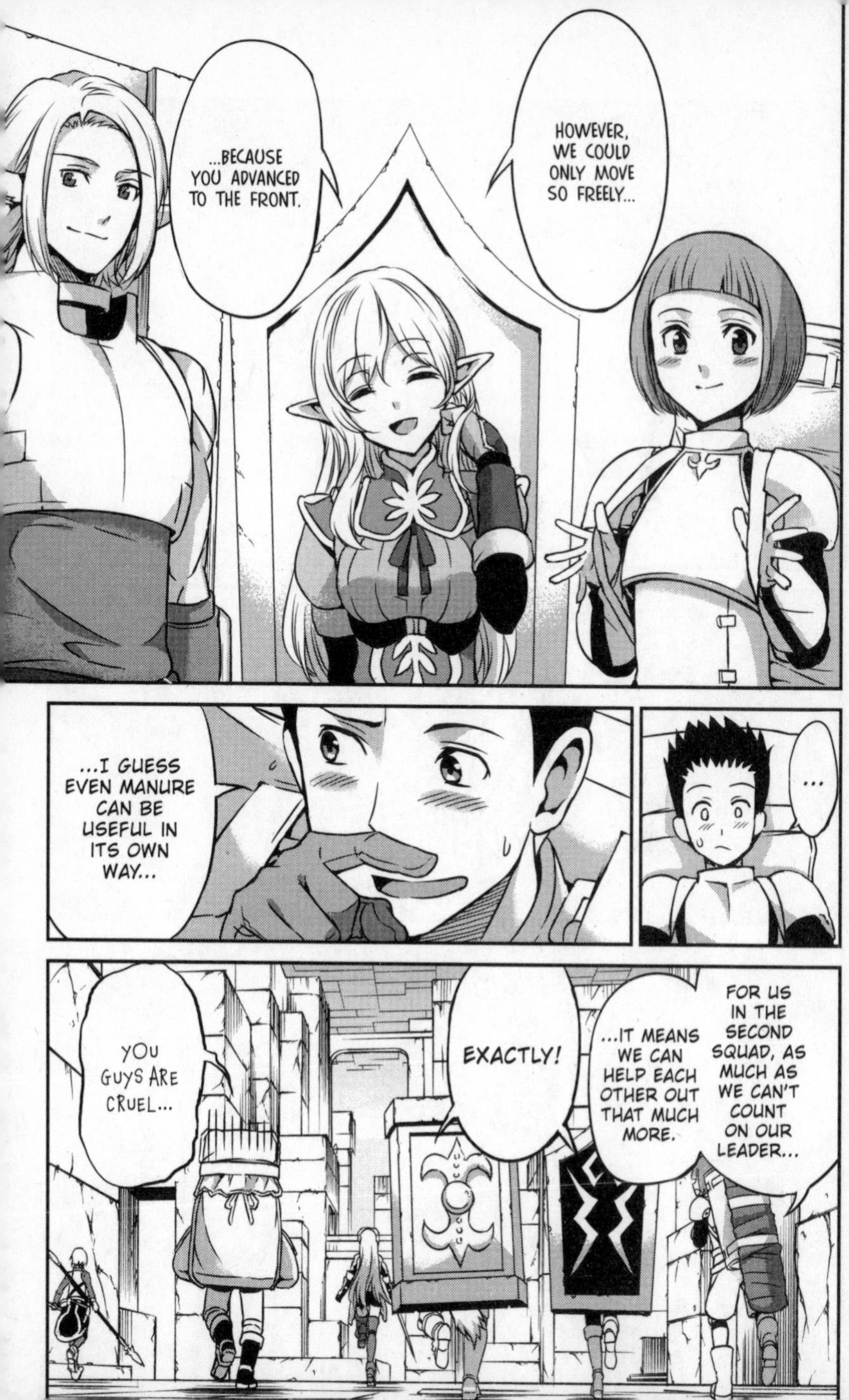
HOWEVER, WE COULD ONLY MOVE SO FREELY...
...BECAUSE YOU ADVANCED TO THE FRONT.
...
...I GUESS EVEN MANURE CAN BE USEFUL IN ITS OWN WAY...
FOR US IN THE SECOND SQUAD, AS MUCH AS WE CAN'T COUNT ON OUR LEADER...
...IT MEANS WE CAN HELP EACH OTHER OUT THAT MUCH MORE.
EXACTLY!
YOU GUYS ARE CRUEL...

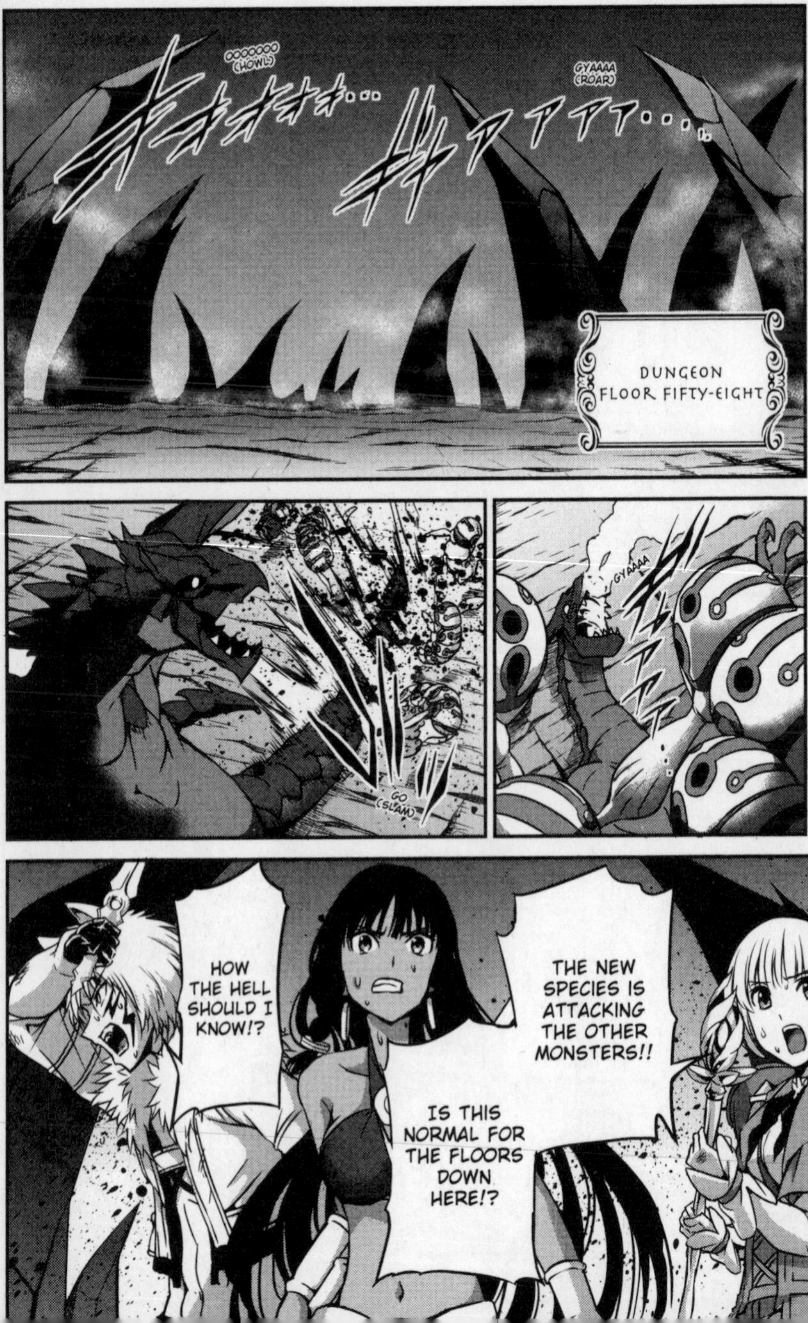
GYAAAA (ROAR)
OOOOOOO (HOWL)
DUNGEON FLOOR FIFTY-EIGHT
GYAAAA
GO (SLAM)
THE NEW SPECIES IS ATTACKING THE OTHER MONSTERS!!
IS THIS NORMAL FOR THE FLOORS DOWN HERE!?
HOW THE HELL SHOULD I KNOW!?

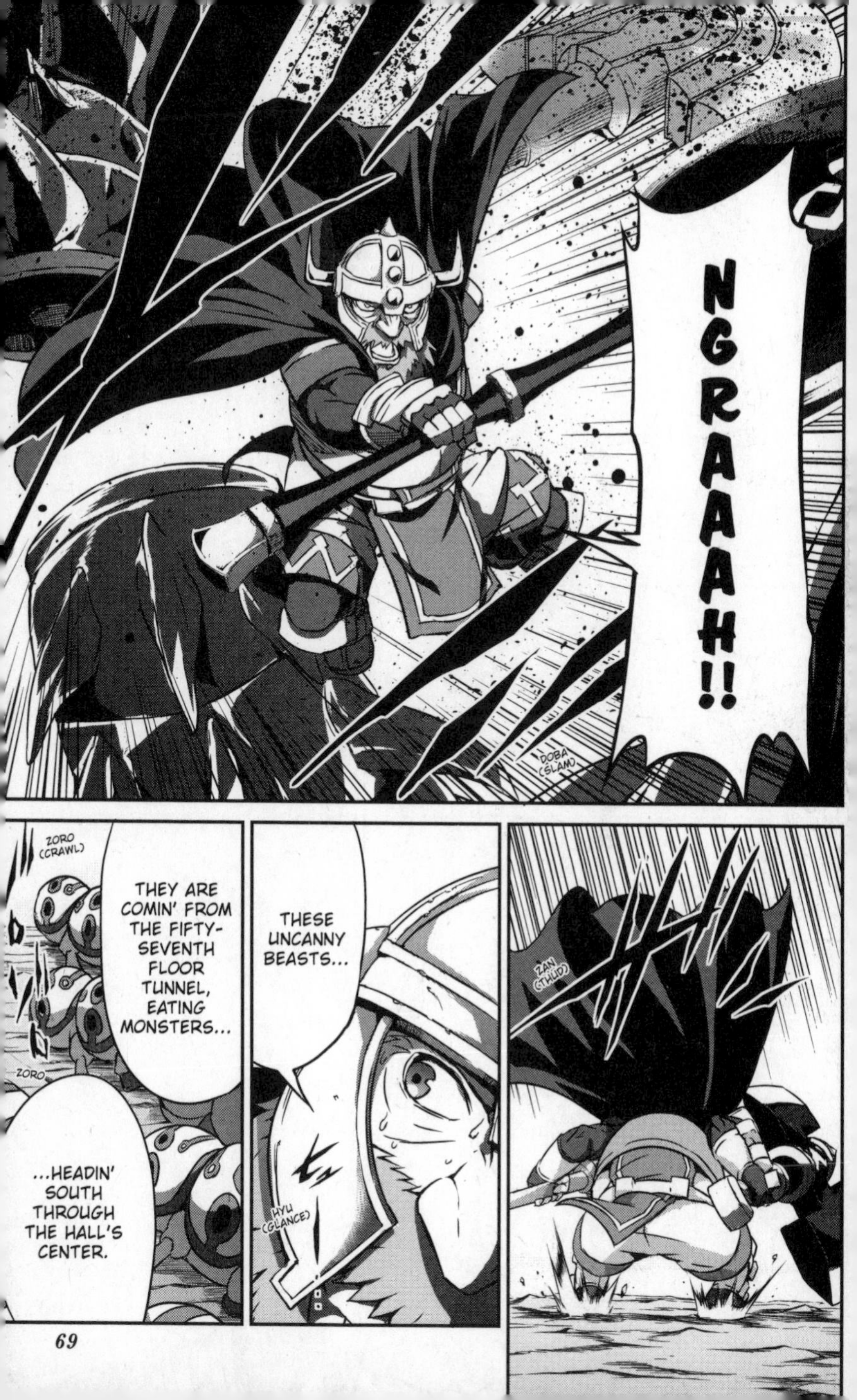

NGRAAAH!!
DOBA (SLAM)
ZAN (THUD)
THESE UNCANNY BEASTS...
HYU (GLANCE)
ZORO (CRAWL)
THEY ARE COMIN' FROM THE FIFTY-SEVENTH FLOOR TUNNEL, EATING MONSTERS...
ZORO
...HEADIN' SOUTH THROUGH THE HALL'S CENTER.

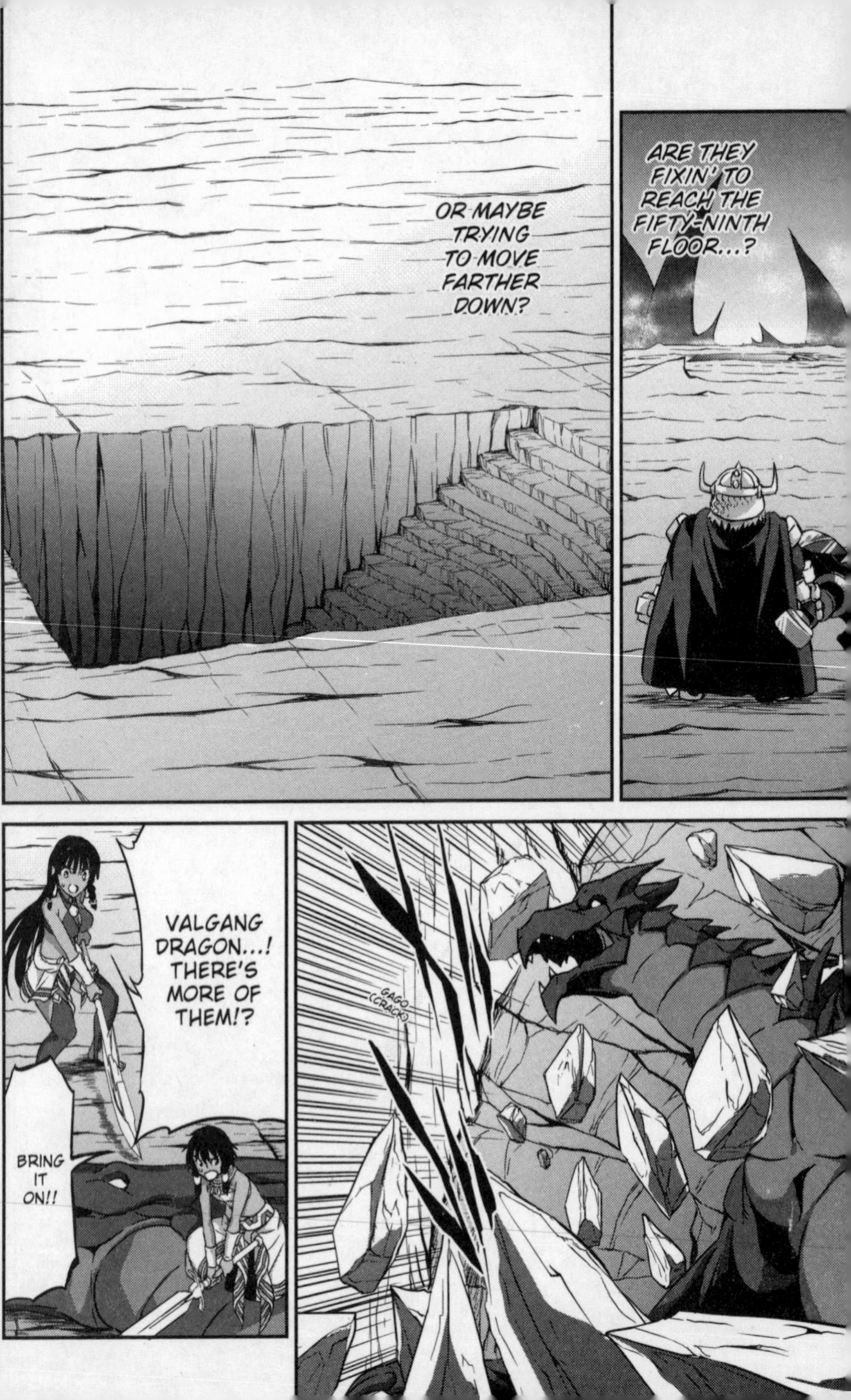
ARE THEY FIXIN' TO REACH THE FIFTY-NINTH FLOOR...?
OR MAYBE TRYING TO MOVE FARTHER DOWN?
GAGO (CRACK)
VALGANG DRAGON...! THERE'S MORE OF THEM!?
BRING IT ON!!

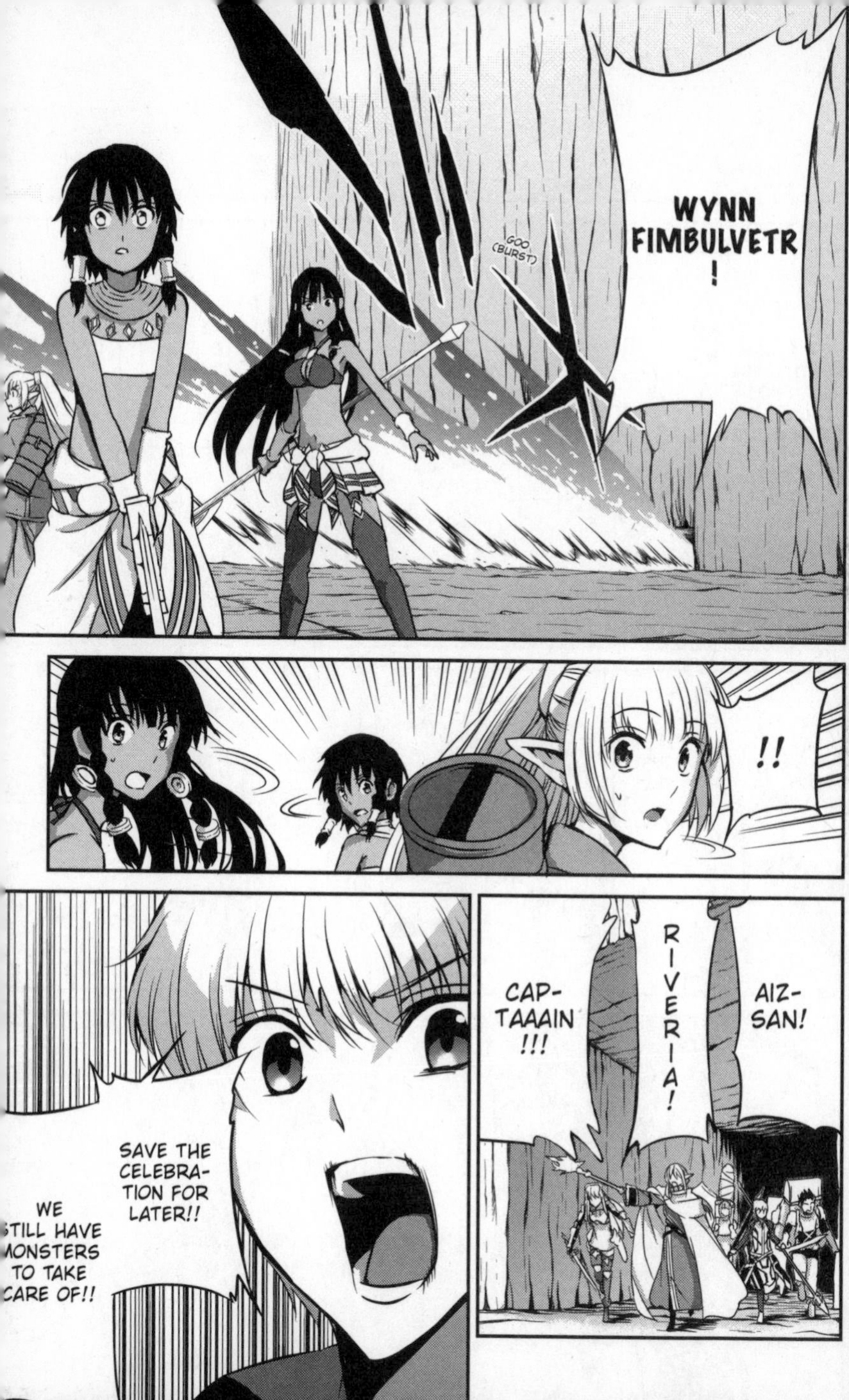
WYNN FIMBULVETR!
GOO (BURST)
!!
AIZ-SAN!
RIVERIA!
CAP-TAAAIN!!!
SAVE THE CELEBRATION FOR LATER!!
WE STILL HAVE MONSTERS TO TAKE CARE OF!!

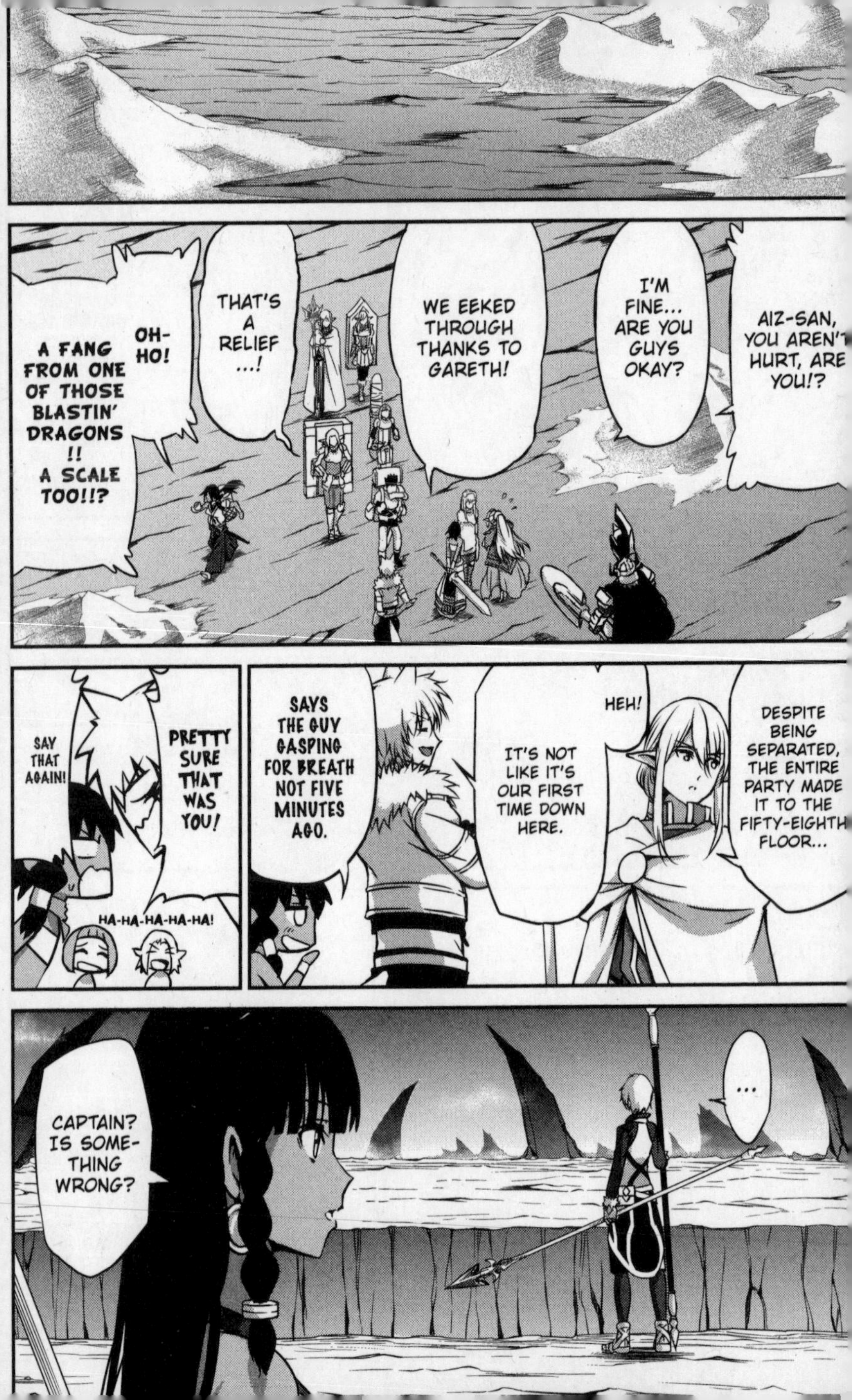
AIZ-SAN, YOU AREN'T HURT, ARE YOU!?
I'M FINE... ARE YOU GUYS OKAY?
WE EEKED THROUGH THANKS TO GARETH!
THAT'S A RELIEF ...!
OH-HO!
A FANG FROM ONE OF THOSE BLASTIN' DRAGONS!! A SCALE TOO!!?
DESPITE BEING SEPARATED, THE ENTIRE PARTY MADE IT TO THE FIFTY-EIGHTH FLOOR...
HEH!
IT'S NOT LIKE IT'S OUR FIRST TIME DOWN HERE.
SAYS THE GUY GASPING FOR BREATH NOT FIVE MINUTES AGO.
PRETTY SURE THAT WAS YOU!
SAY THAT AGAIN!
HA-HA-HA-HA-HA!
...
CAPTAIN? IS SOMETHING WRONG?

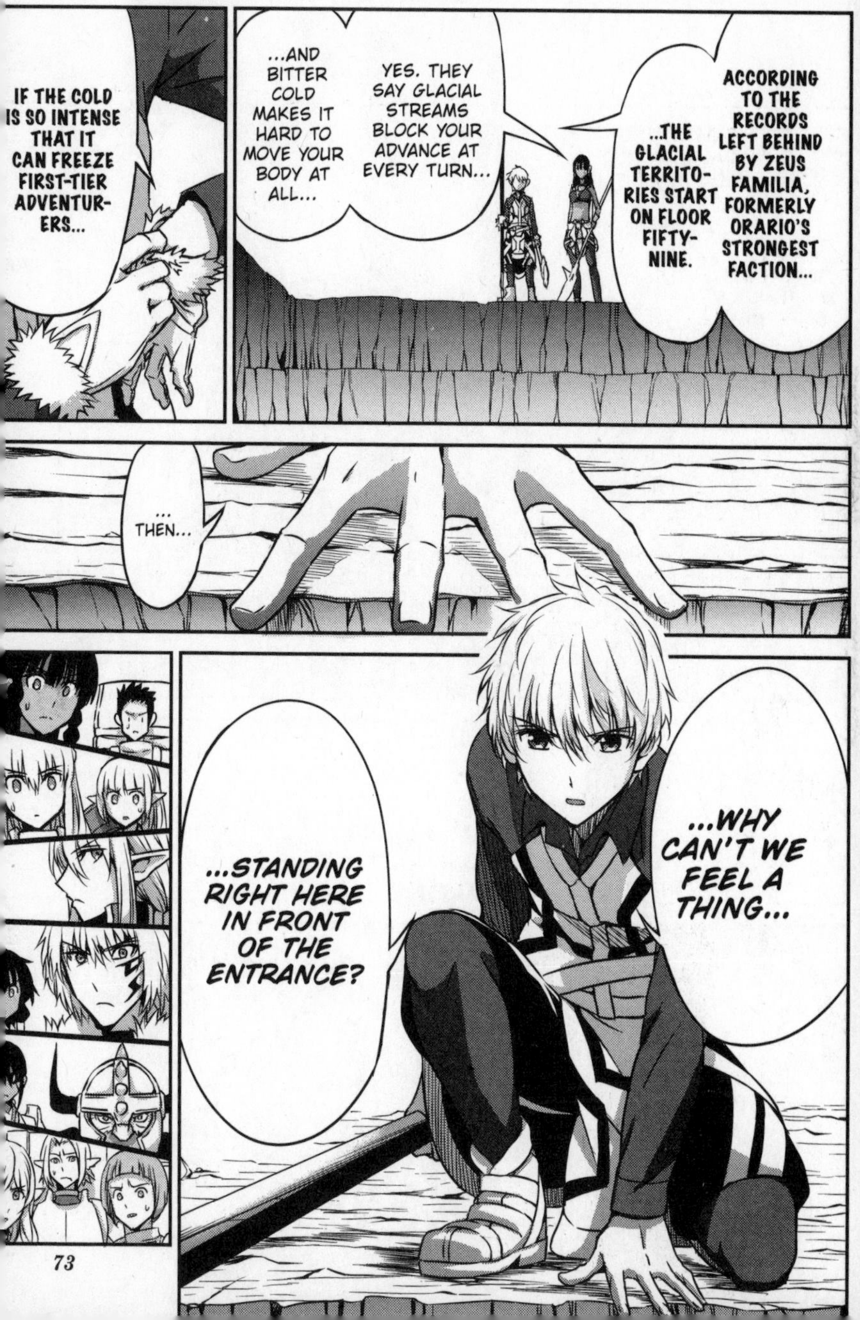
ACCORDING TO THE RECORDS LEFT BEHIND BY ZEUS FAMILIA, FORMERLY ORARIO'S STRONGEST FACTION...
...THE GLACIAL TERRITO-RIES START ON FLOOR FIFTY-NINE.
YES. THEY SAY GLACIAL STREAMS BLOCK YOUR ADVANCE AT EVERY TURN...
...AND BITTER COLD MAKES IT HARD TO MOVE YOUR BODY AT ALL...
IF THE COLD IS SO INTENSE THAT IT CAN FREEZE FIRST-TIER ADVENTURERS...
... THEN...
...WHY CAN'T WE FEEL A THING...
...STANDING RIGHT HERE IN FRONT OF THE ENTRANCE?

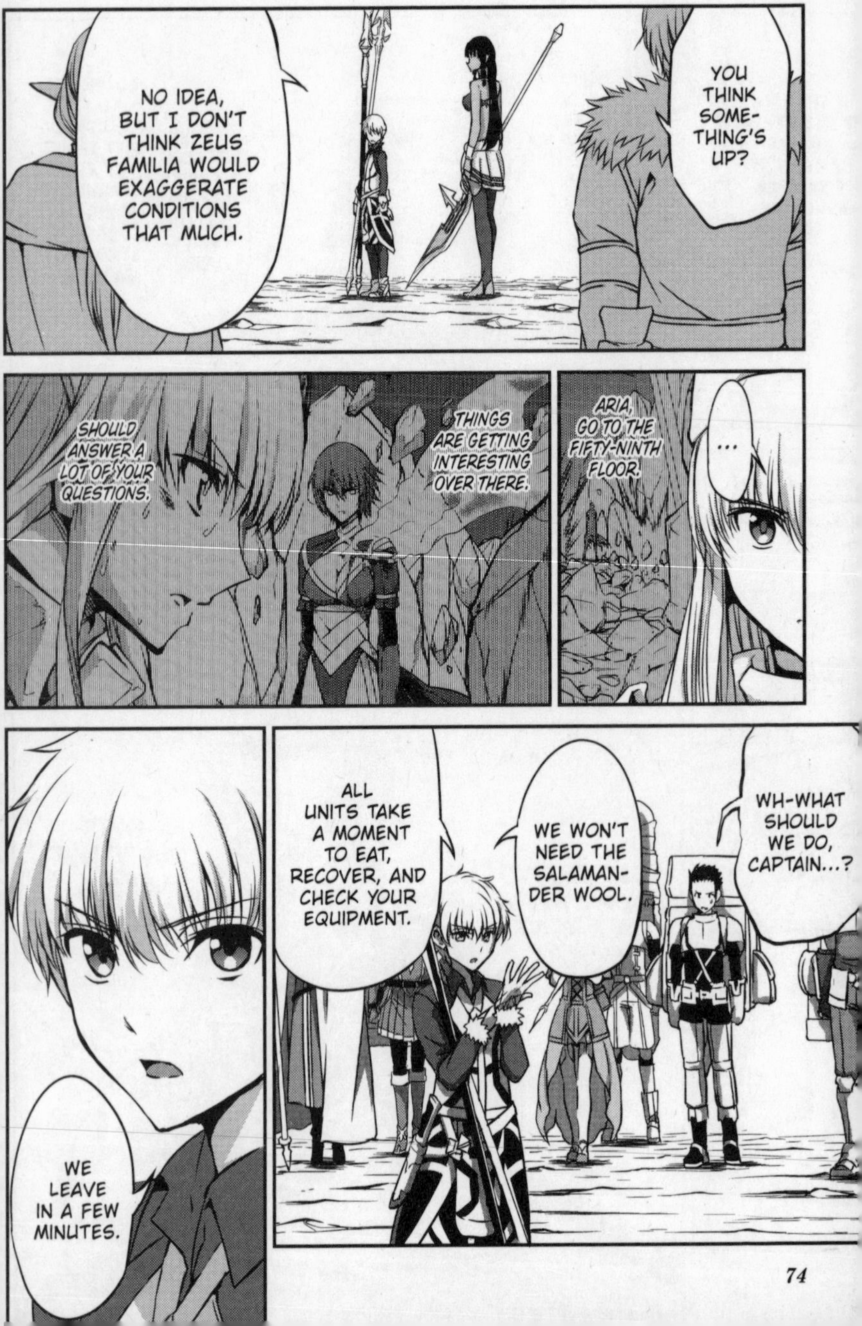
YOU THINK SOME-THING'S UP?
NO IDEA, BUT I DON'T THINK ZEUS FAMILIA WOULD EXAGGERATE CONDITIONS THAT MUCH.
...
ARIA. GO TO THE FIFTY-NINTH FLOOR.
THINGS ARE GETTING INTERESTING OVER THERE.
SHOULD ANSWER A LOT OF YOUR QUESTIONS.
WH-WHAT SHOULD WE DO, CAPTAIN...?
WE WON'T NEED THE SALAMAN-DER WOOL.
ALL UNITS TAKE A MOMENT TO EAT, RECOVER, AND CHECK YOUR EQUIPMENT.
WE LEAVE IN A FEW MINUTES.

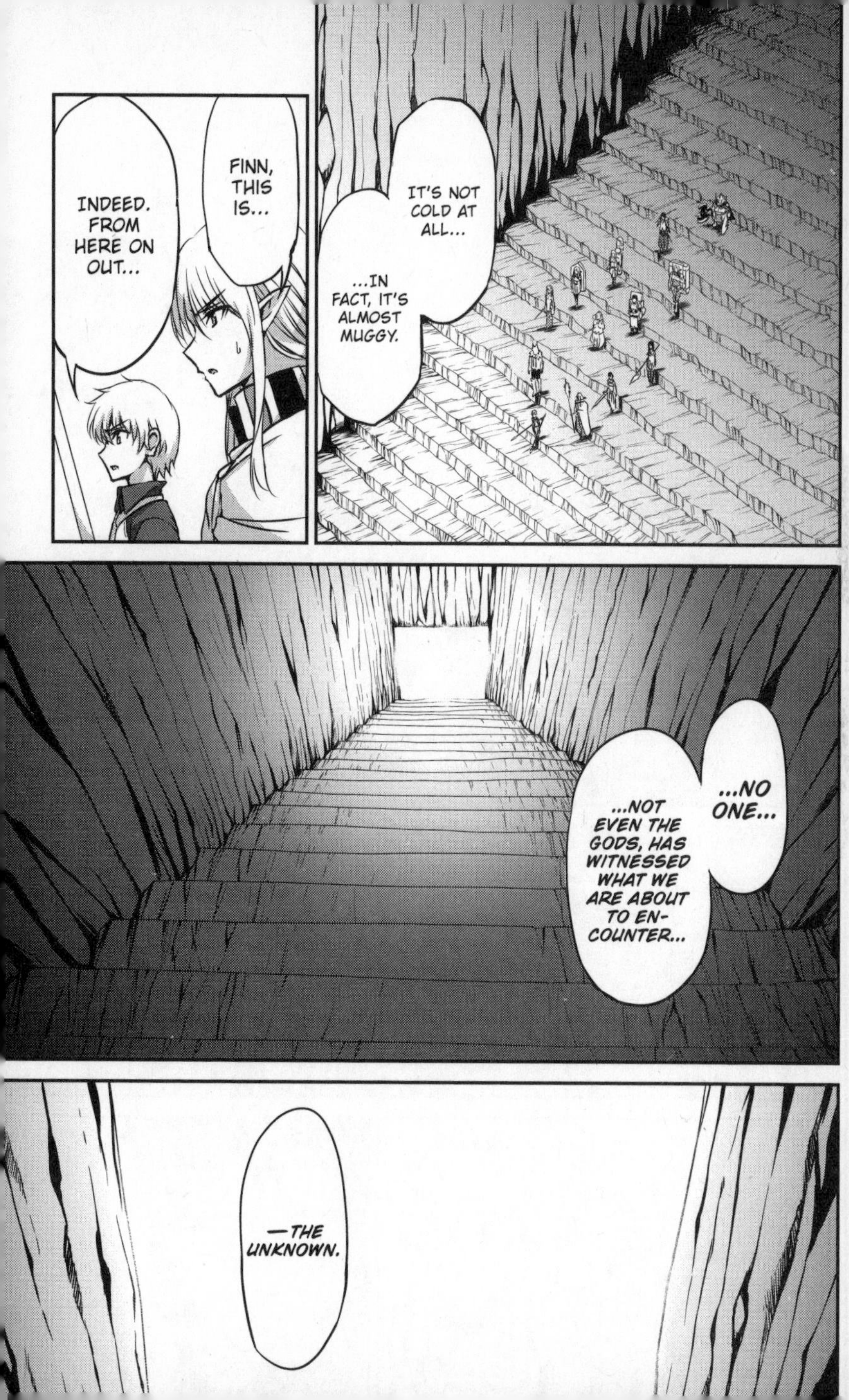
IT'S NOT COLD AT ALL...
...IN FACT, IT'S ALMOST MUGGY.
FINN, THIS IS...
INDEED. FROM HERE ON OUT...
...NO ONE...
...NOT EVEN THE GODS, HAS WITNESSED WHAT WE ARE ABOUT TO EN-COUNTER...
—THE UNKNOWN.

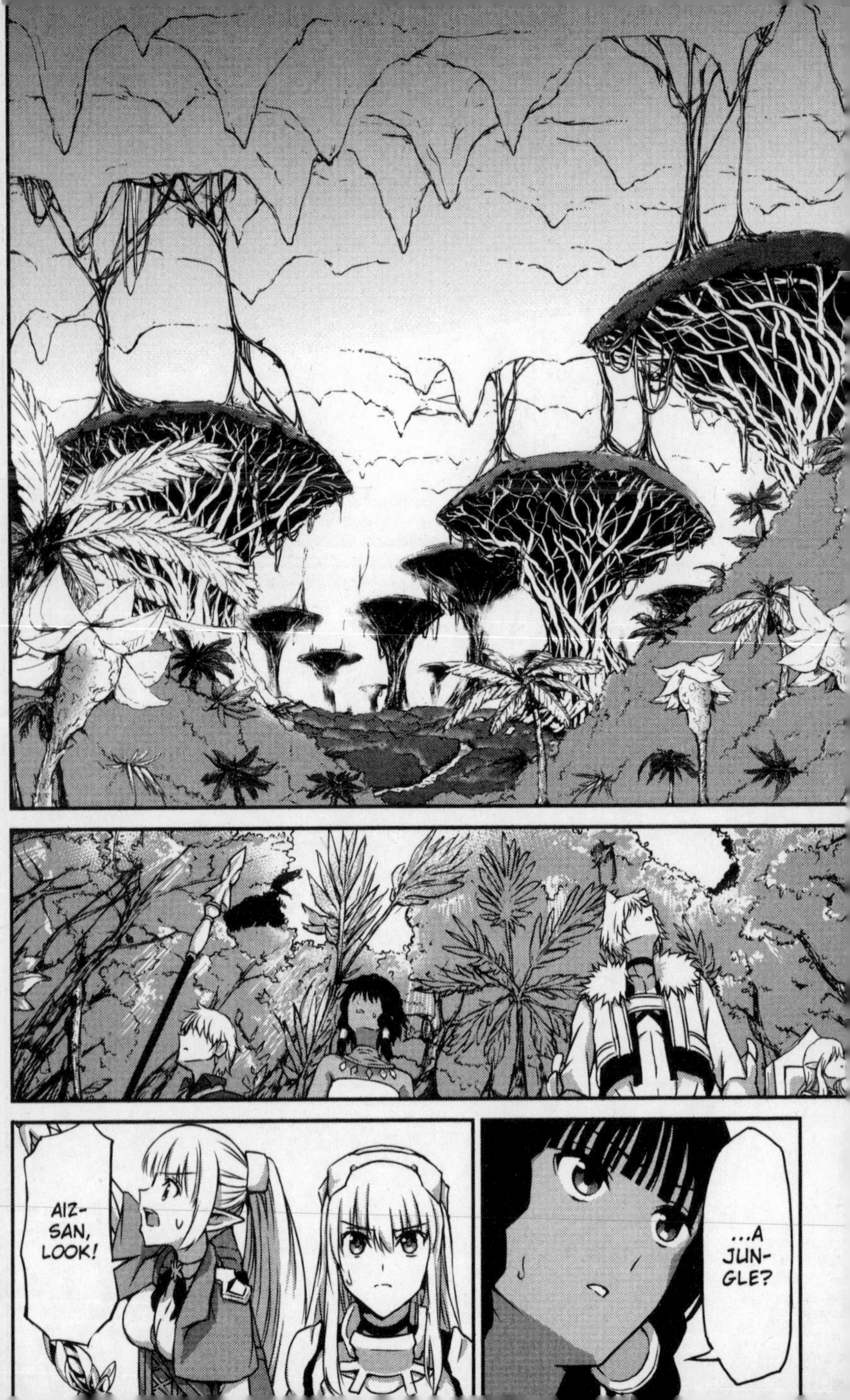
...A JUNGLE?
AIZ-SAN, LOOK!

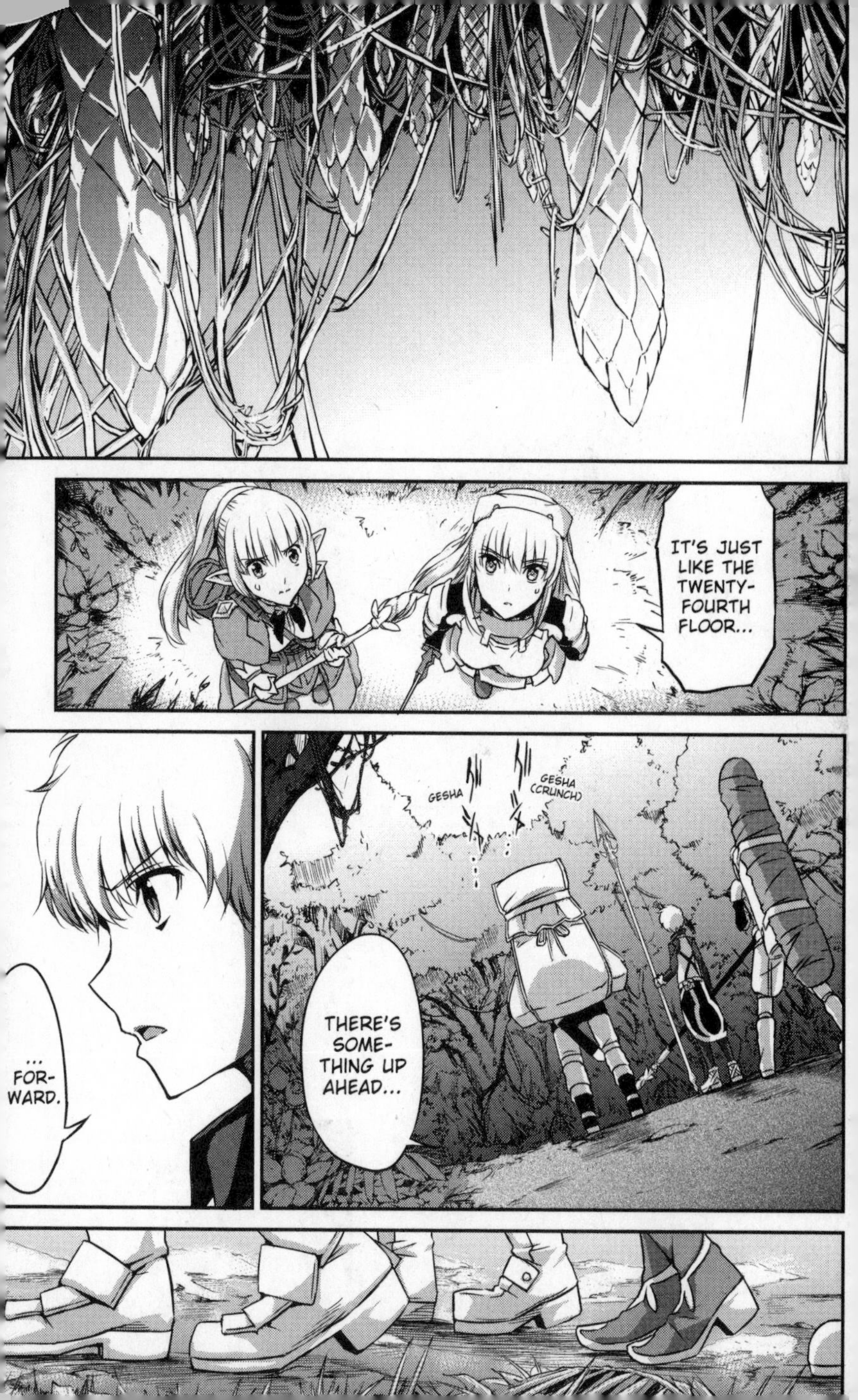
IT'S JUST LIKE THE TWENTY-FOURTH FLOOR...
GESHA (CRUNCH)
GESHA
THERE'S SOME-THING UP AHEAD...
... FOR-WARD.

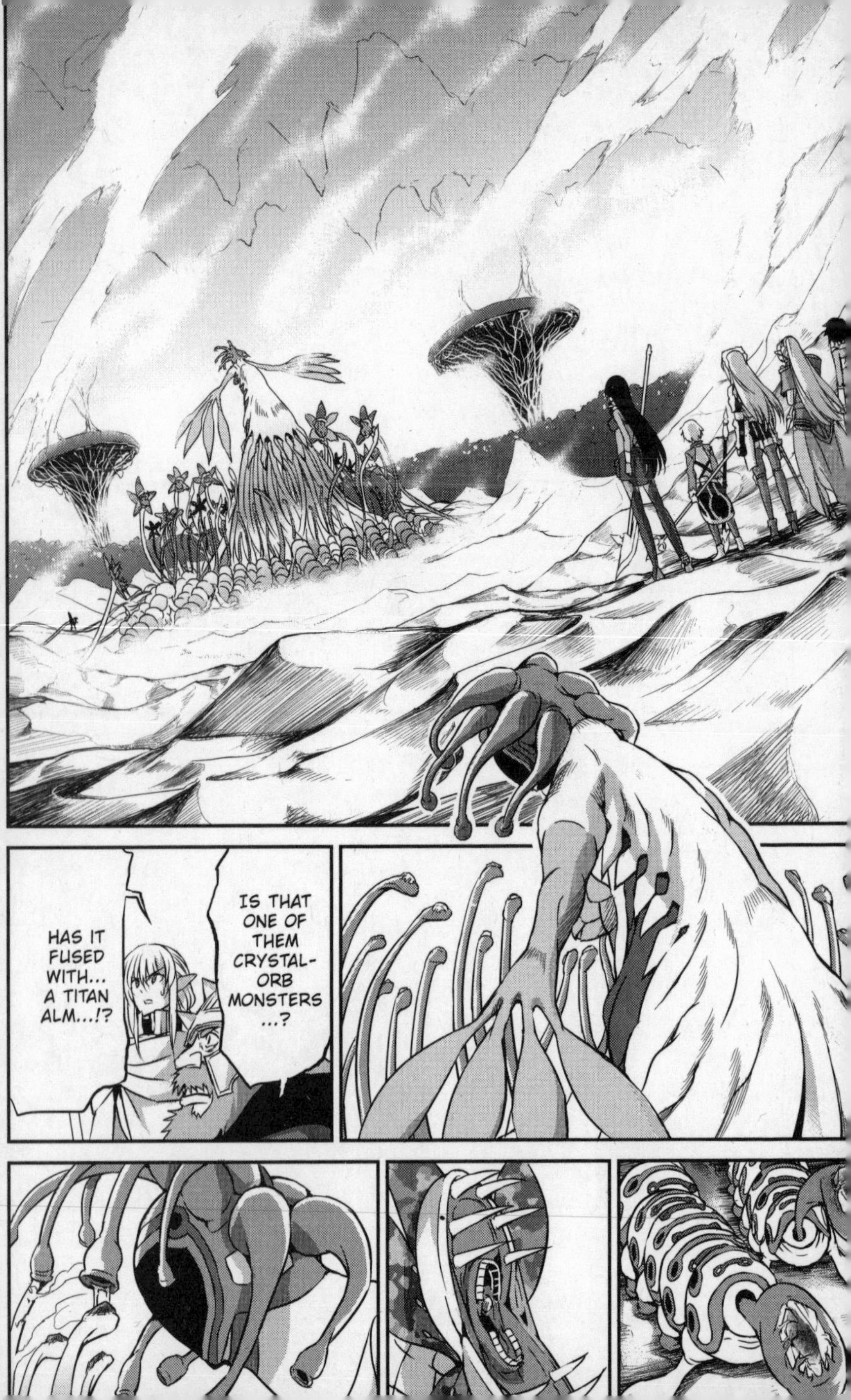
IS THAT ONE OF THEM CRYSTAL-ORB MONSTERS...?
HAS IT FUSED WITH... A TITAN ALM...!?

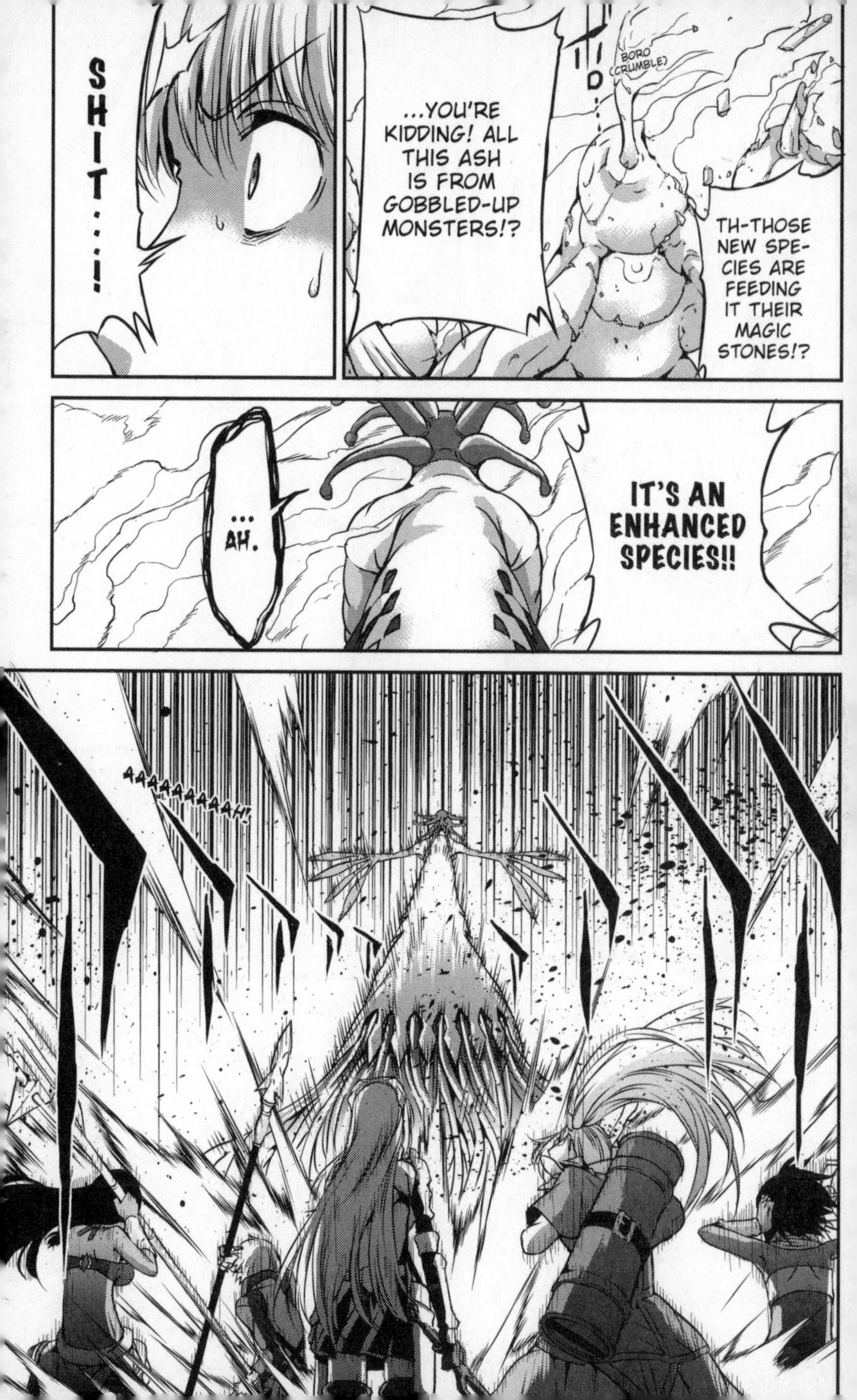
BORO (CRUMBLE)
D...
TH-THOSE NEW SPECIES ARE FEEDING IT THEIR MAGIC STONES!?
...YOU'RE KIDDING! ALL THIS ASH IS FROM GOBBLED-UP MONSTERS!?
SHIT...!
IT'S AN ENHANCED SPECIES!!
...AH.
AAAAAAAAAAAH!

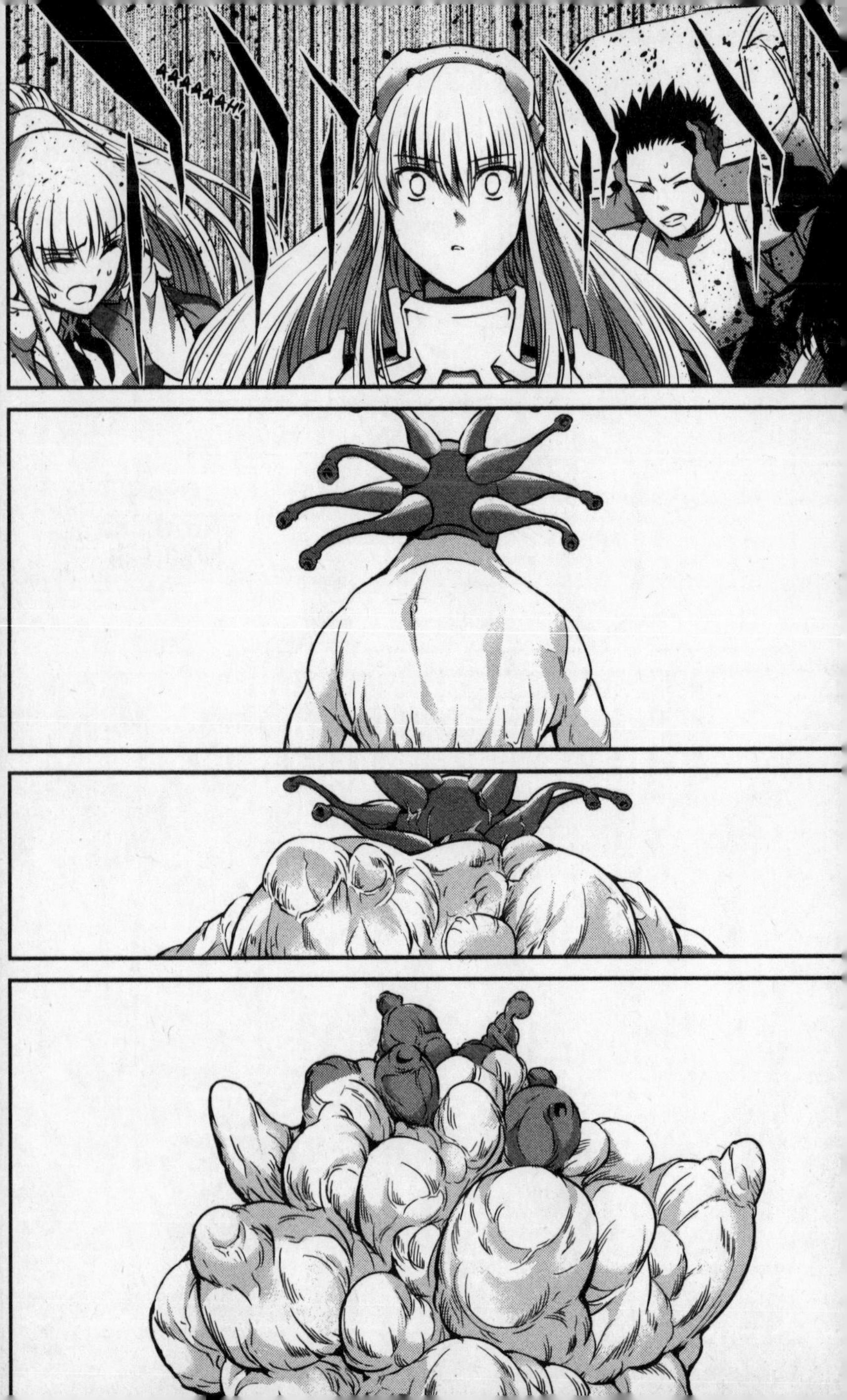
AAAAAAH!!

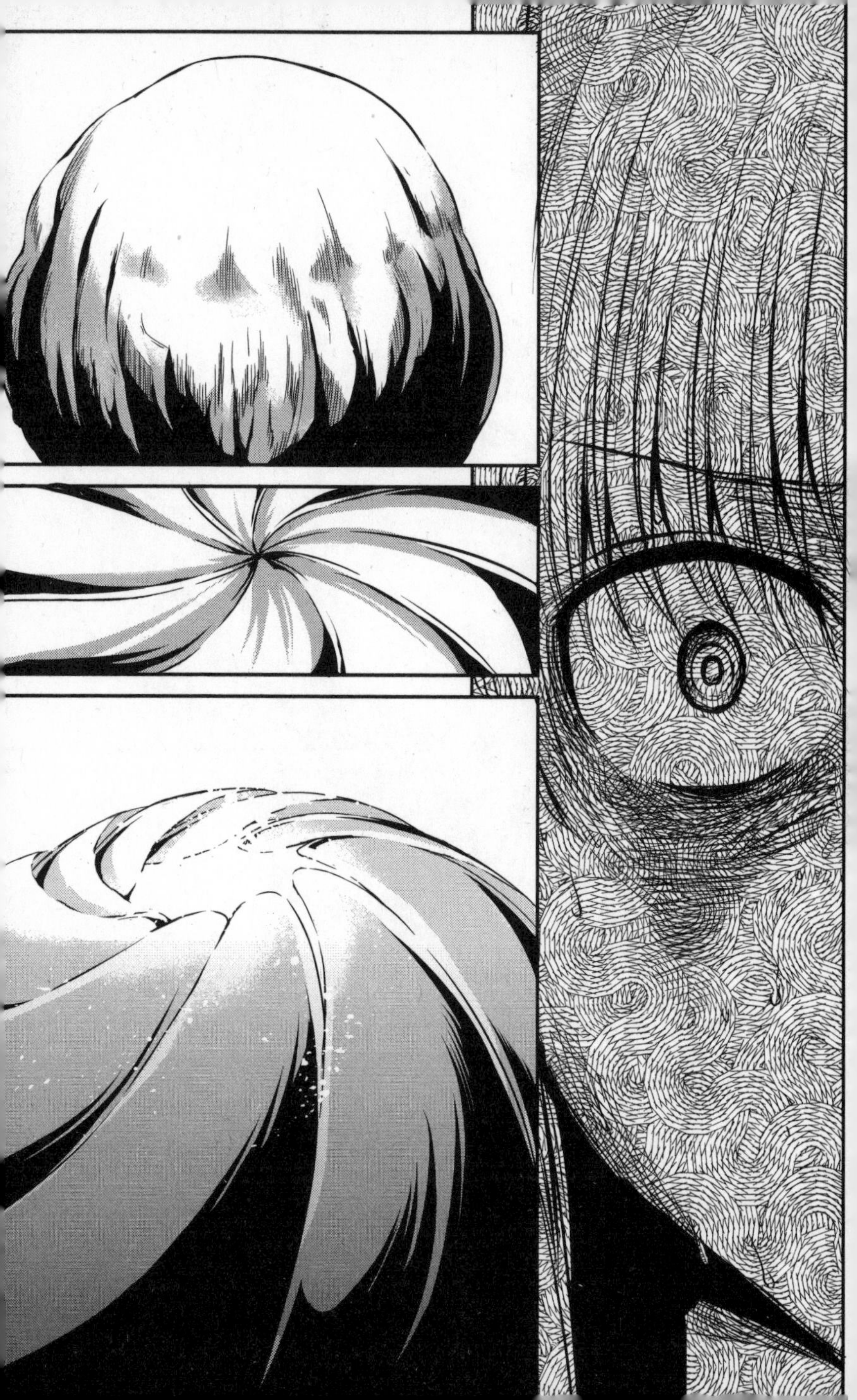

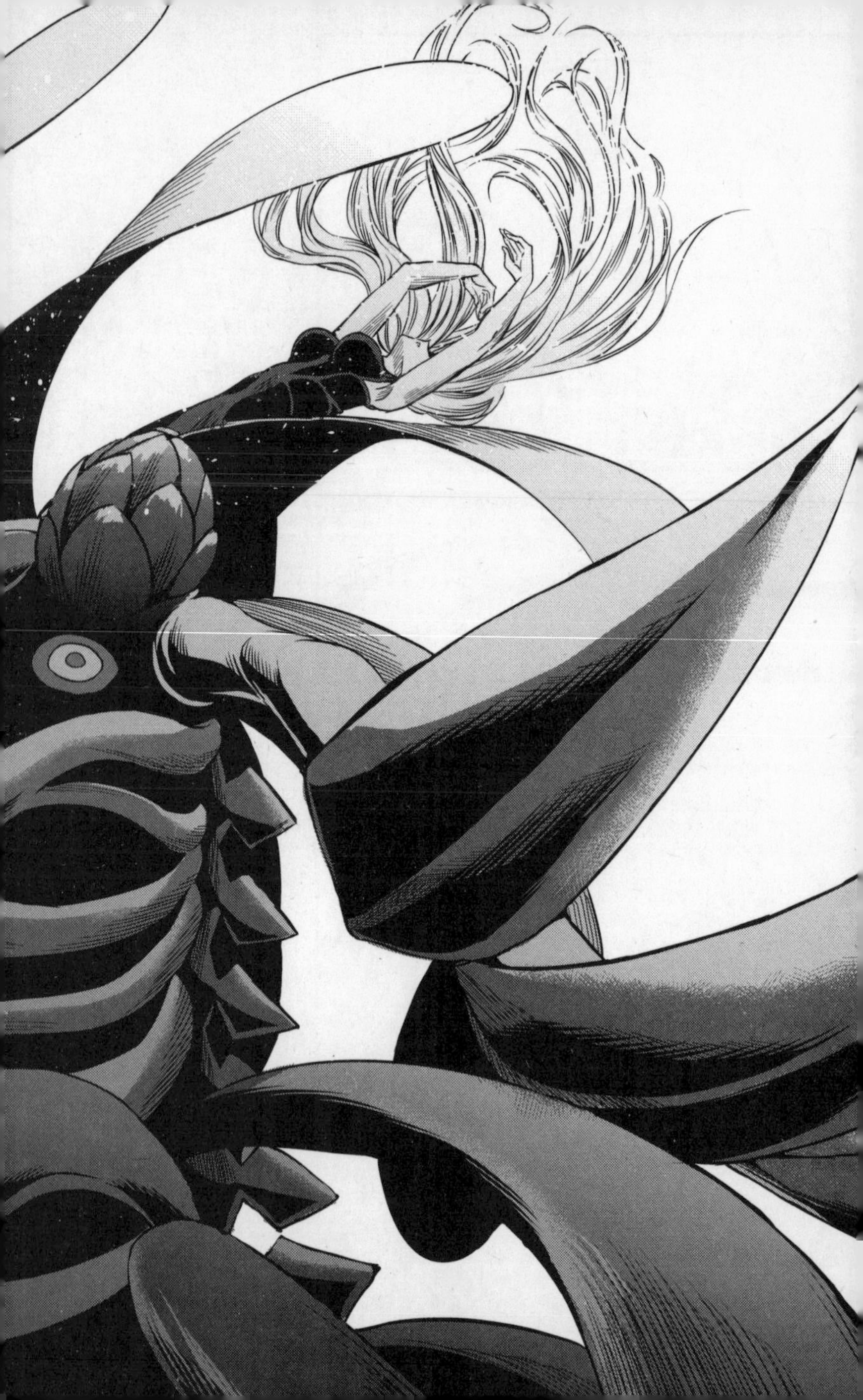

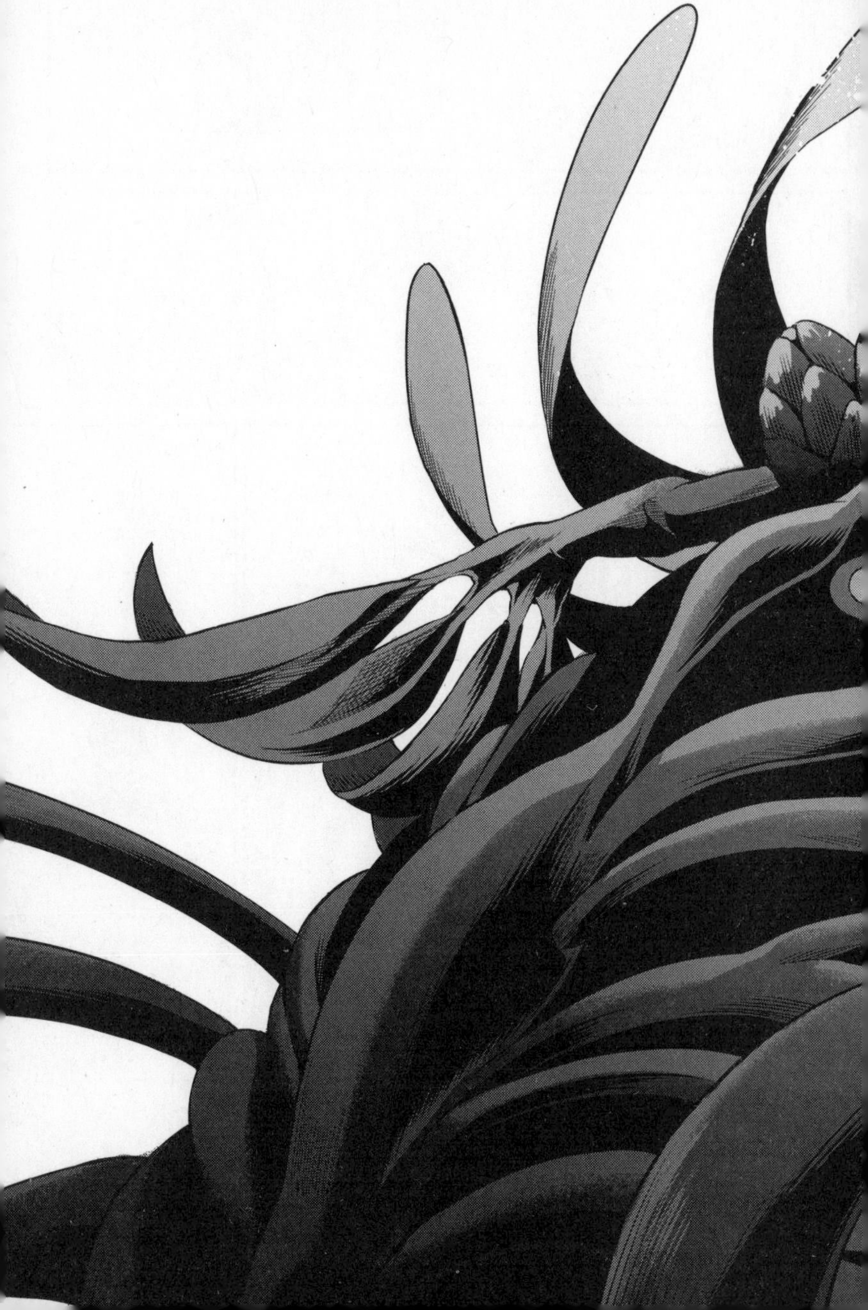

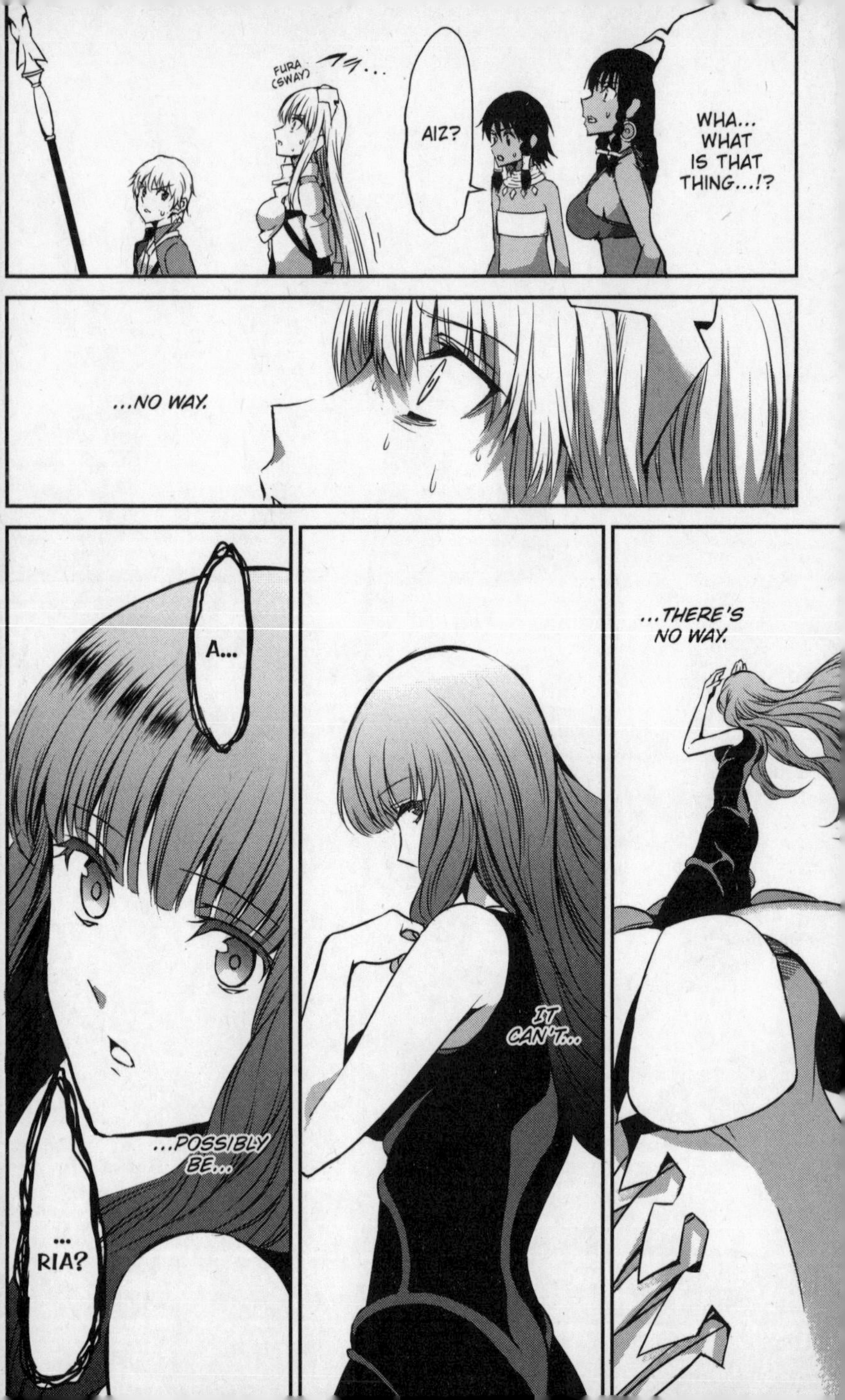
WHA... WHAT IS THAT THING...!?
AIZ?
FURA (SWAY)
...NO WAY.
...THERE'S NO WAY.
IT CAN'T...
A...
...POSSIBLY BE...
...RIA?

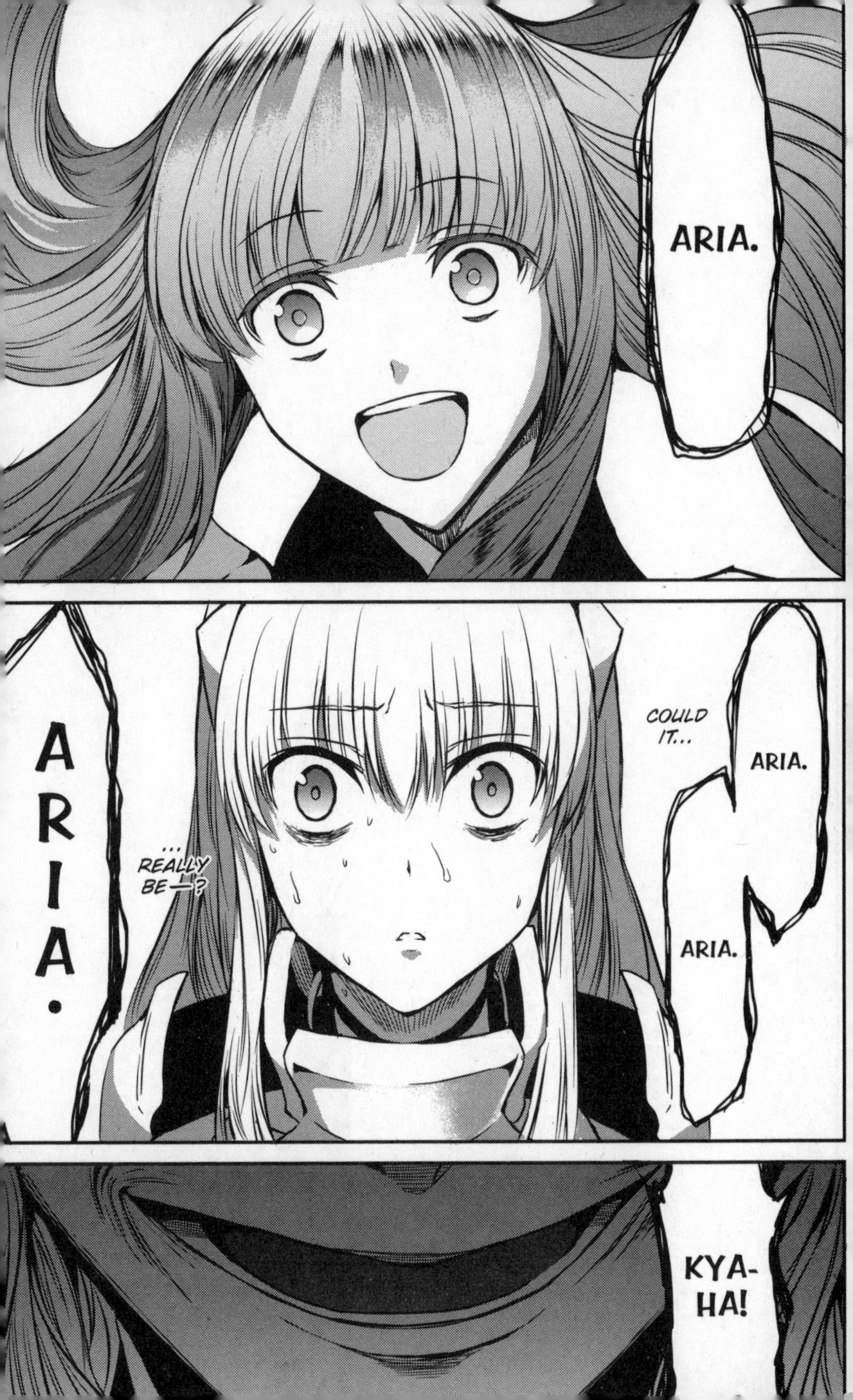
ARIA.
ARIA.
ARIA.
COULD IT...
...REALLY BE—?
ARIA.
KYA-HA!

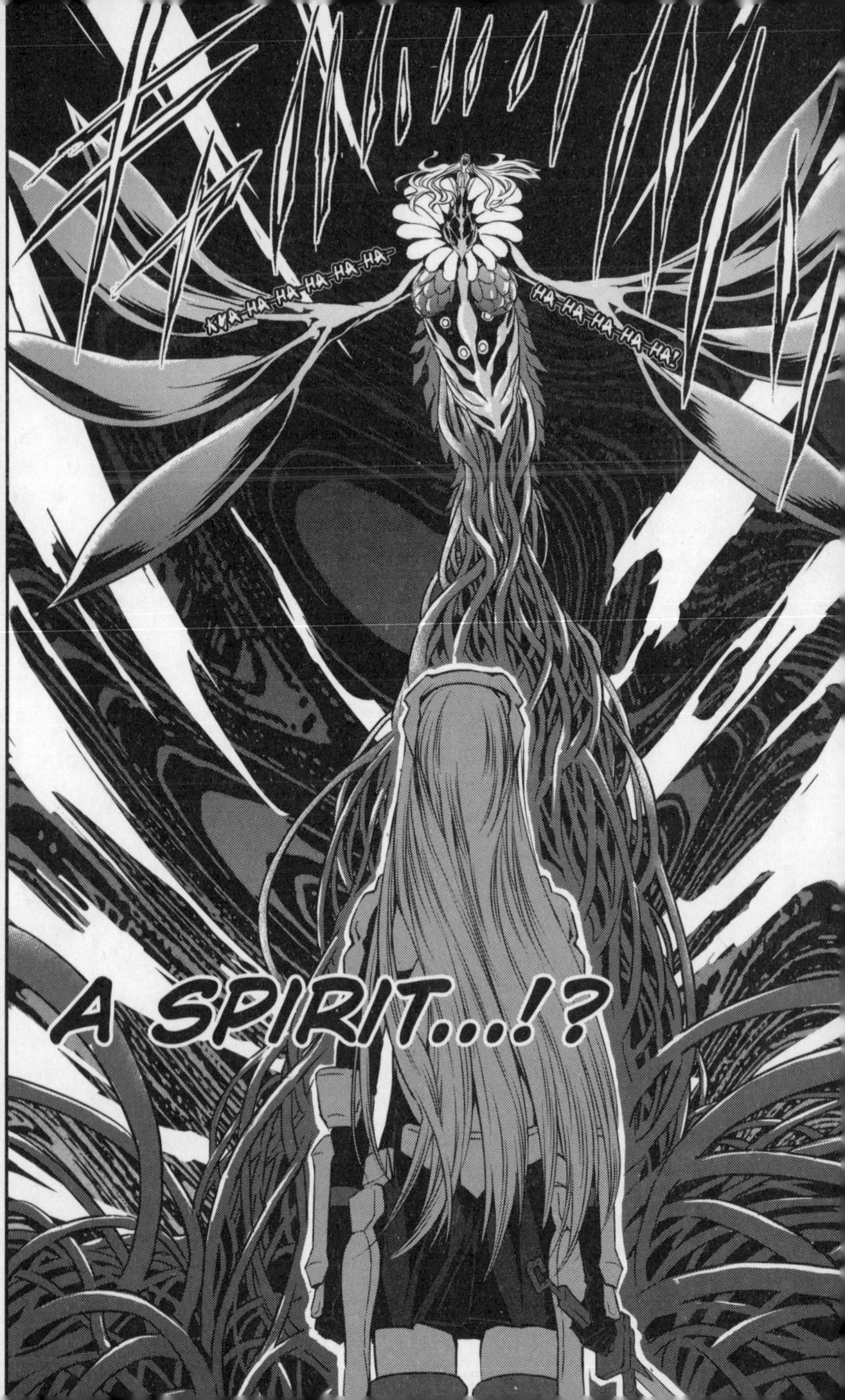
KYA-HA-HA-HA-HA-HA-
HA-HA-HA-HA-HA-HA!
A SPIRIT...!?

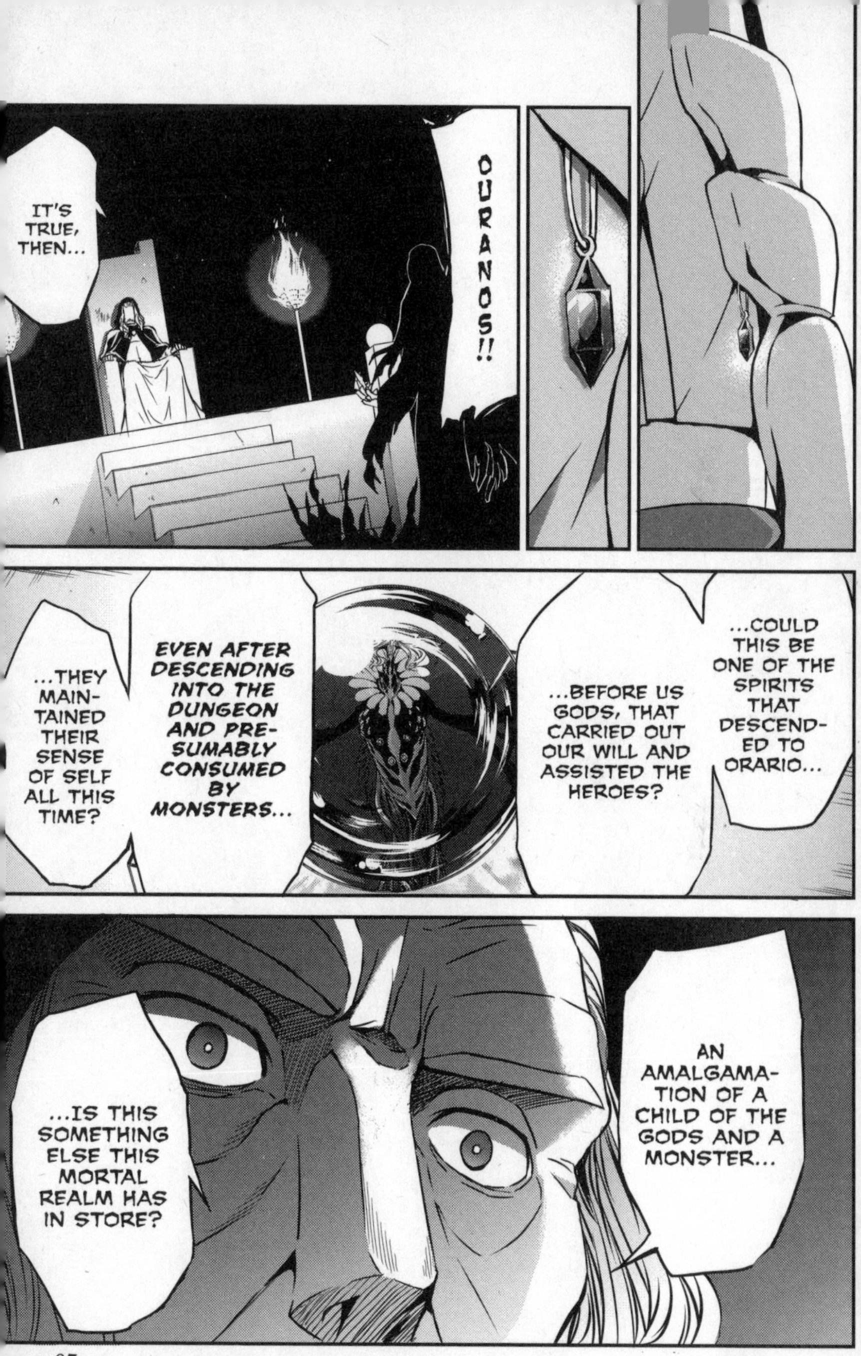
OURANOS!!
IT'S TRUE, THEN...
...COULD THIS BE ONE OF THE SPIRITS THAT DESCEND-ED TO ORARIO...
...BEFORE US GODS, THAT CARRIED OUT OUR WILL AND ASSISTED THE HEROES?
EVEN AFTER DESCENDING INTO THE DUNGEON AND PRE-SUMABLY CONSUMED BY MONSTERS...
...THEY MAIN-TAINED THEIR SENSE OF SELF ALL THIS TIME?
AN AMALGAMA-TION OF A CHILD OF THE GODS AND A MONSTER...
...IS THIS SOMETHING ELSE THIS MORTAL REALM HAS IN STORE?

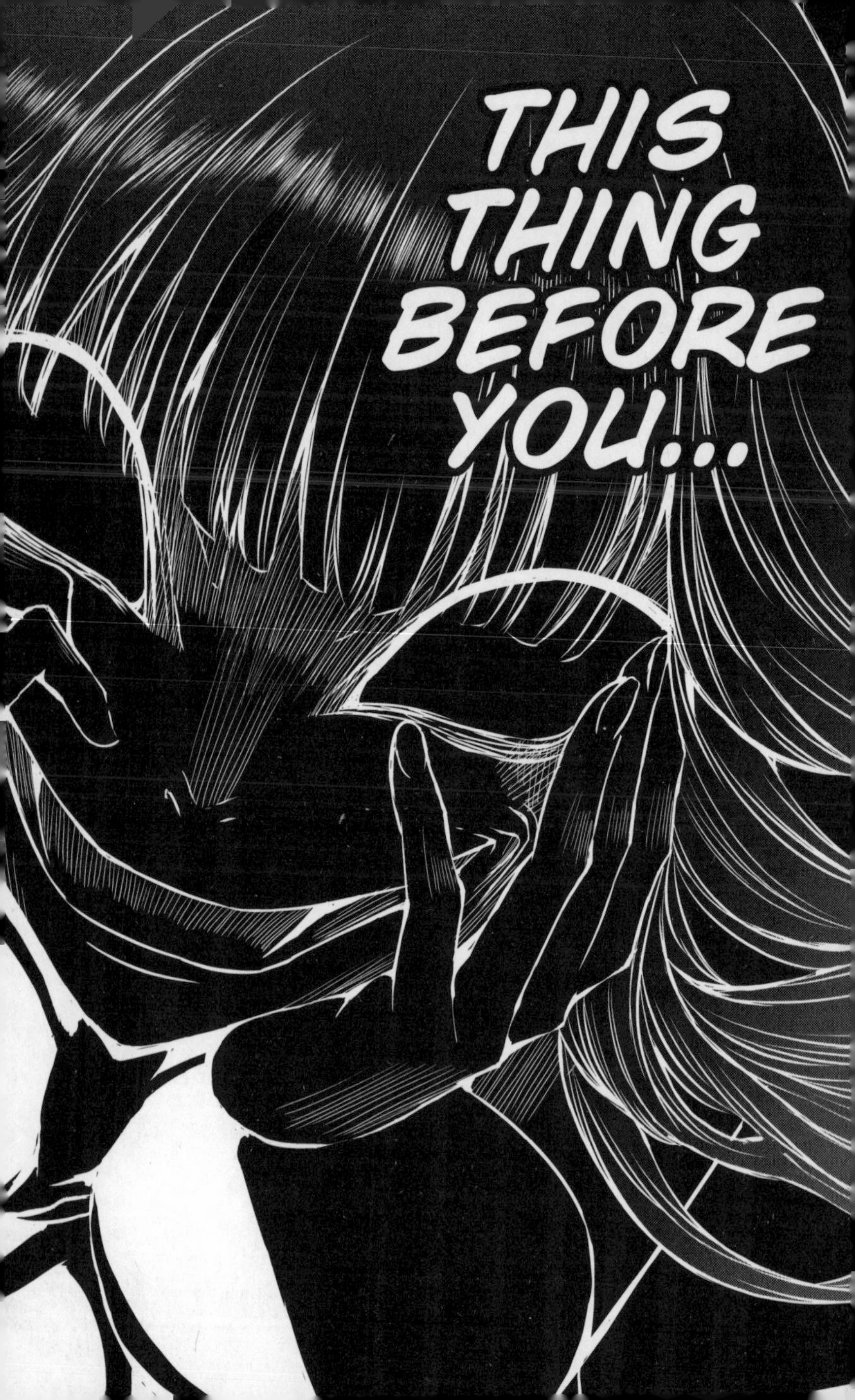
THIS THING BEFORE YOU...

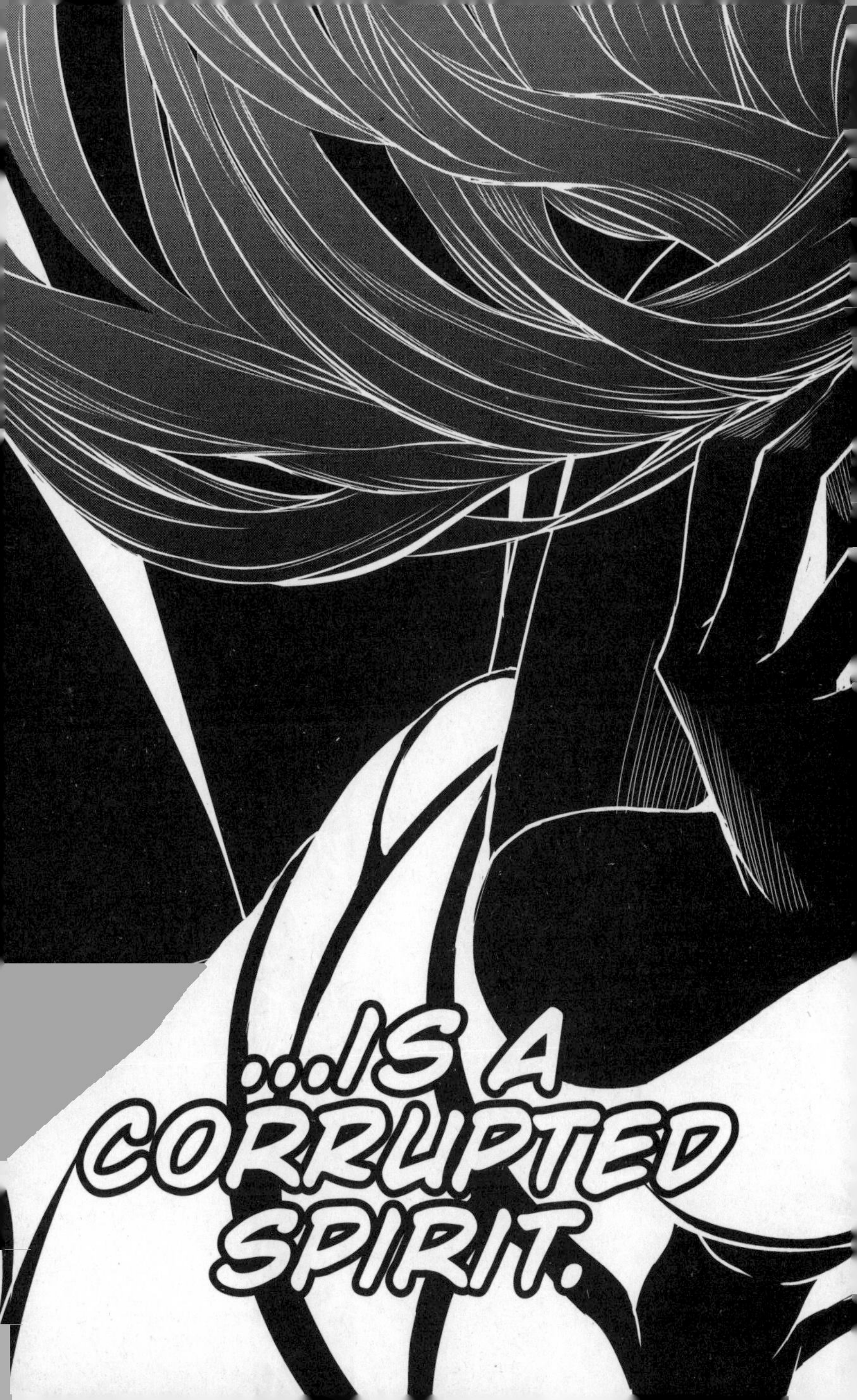
...IS A CORRUPTED SPIRIT.

Is it Wrong to Try to Pick Up Girls in a Dungeon? On the Side

Sword Oratoria

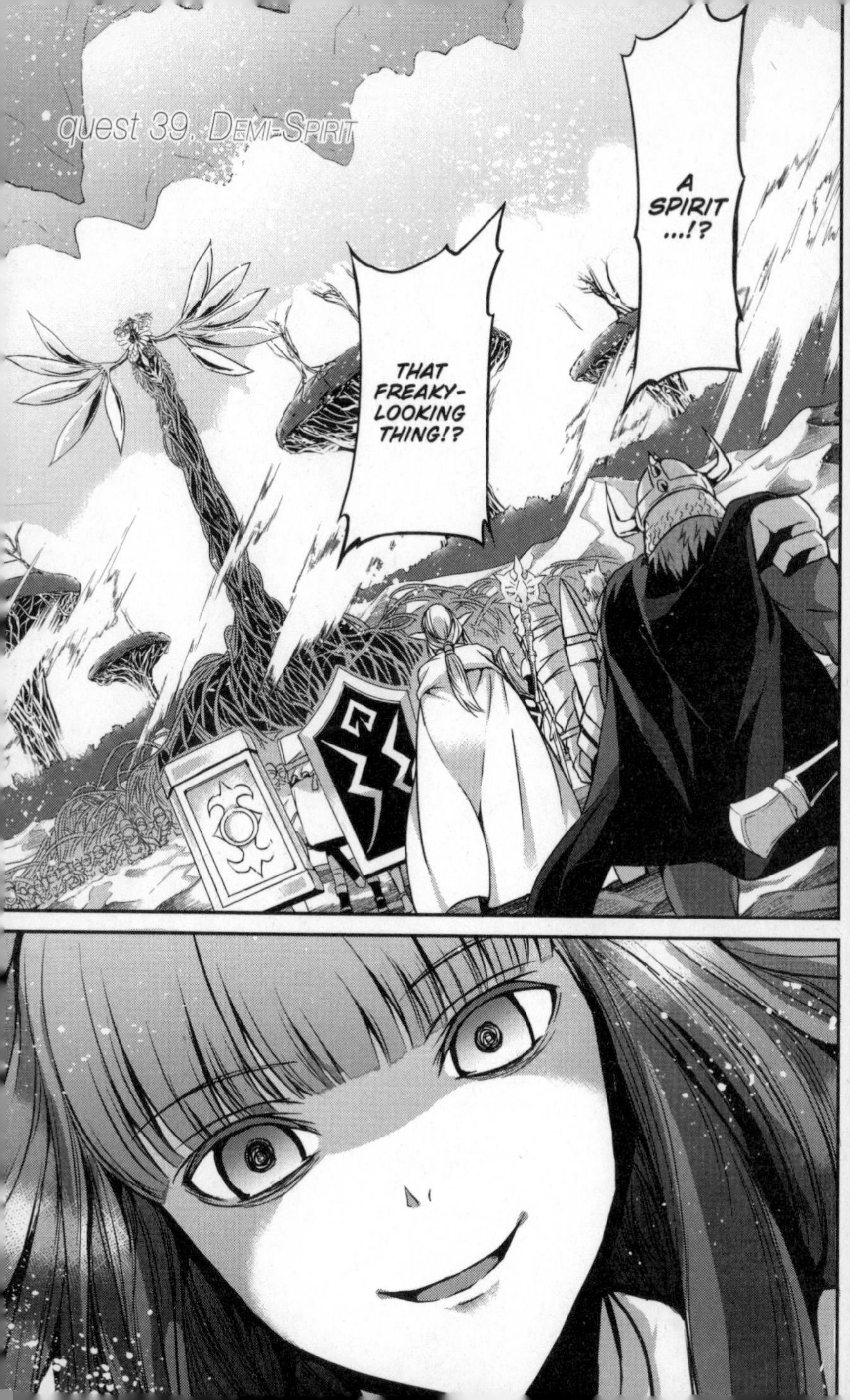
quest 39. Demi-Spirit
A SPIRIT ...!?
THAT FREAKY-LOOKING THING!?

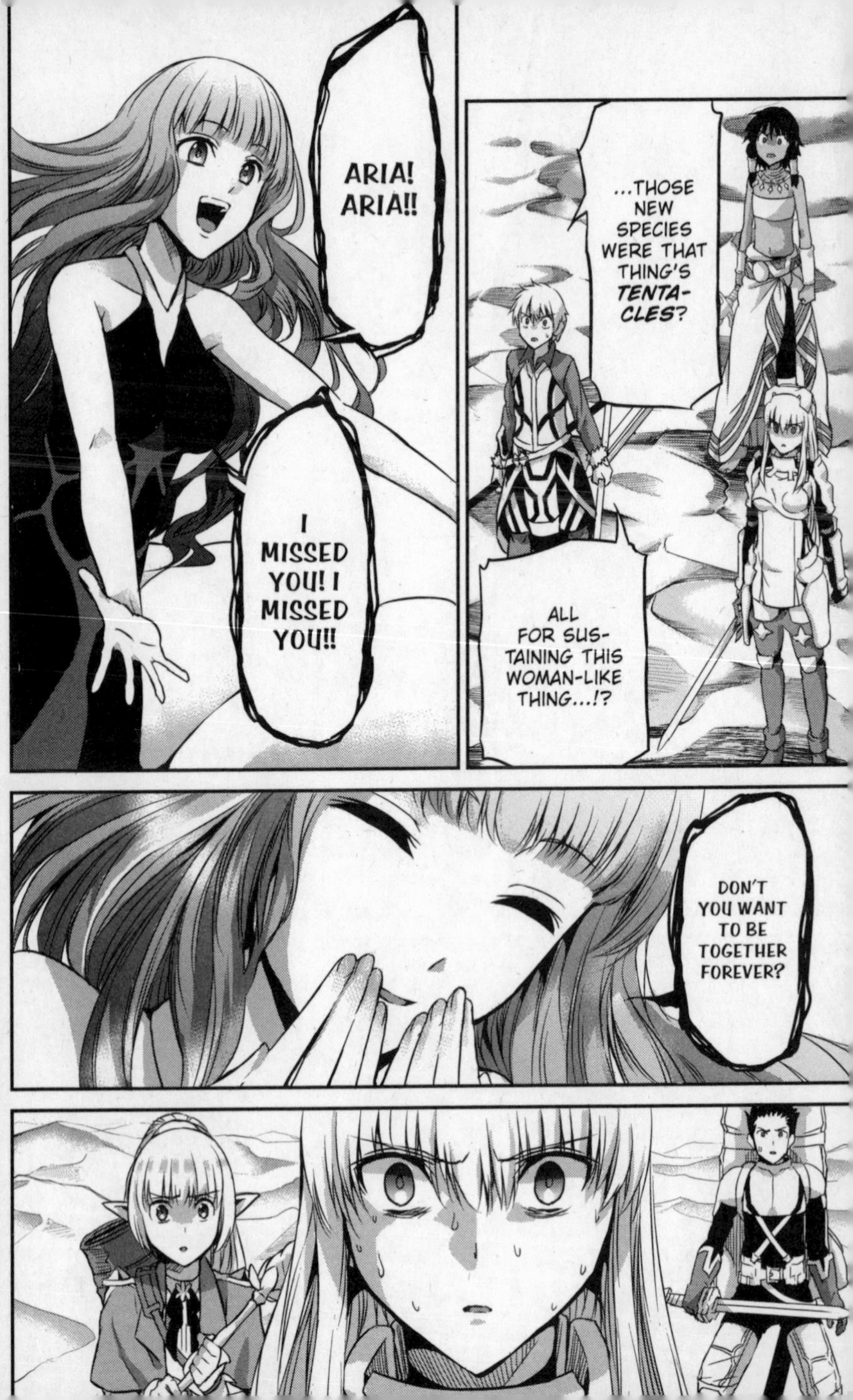
...THOSE NEW SPECIES WERE THAT THING'S *TENTACLES*?
ALL FOR SUSTAINING THIS WOMAN-LIKE THING...!?
ARIA! ARIA!!
I MISSED YOU! I MISSED YOU!!
DON'T YOU WANT TO BE TOGETHER FOREVER?

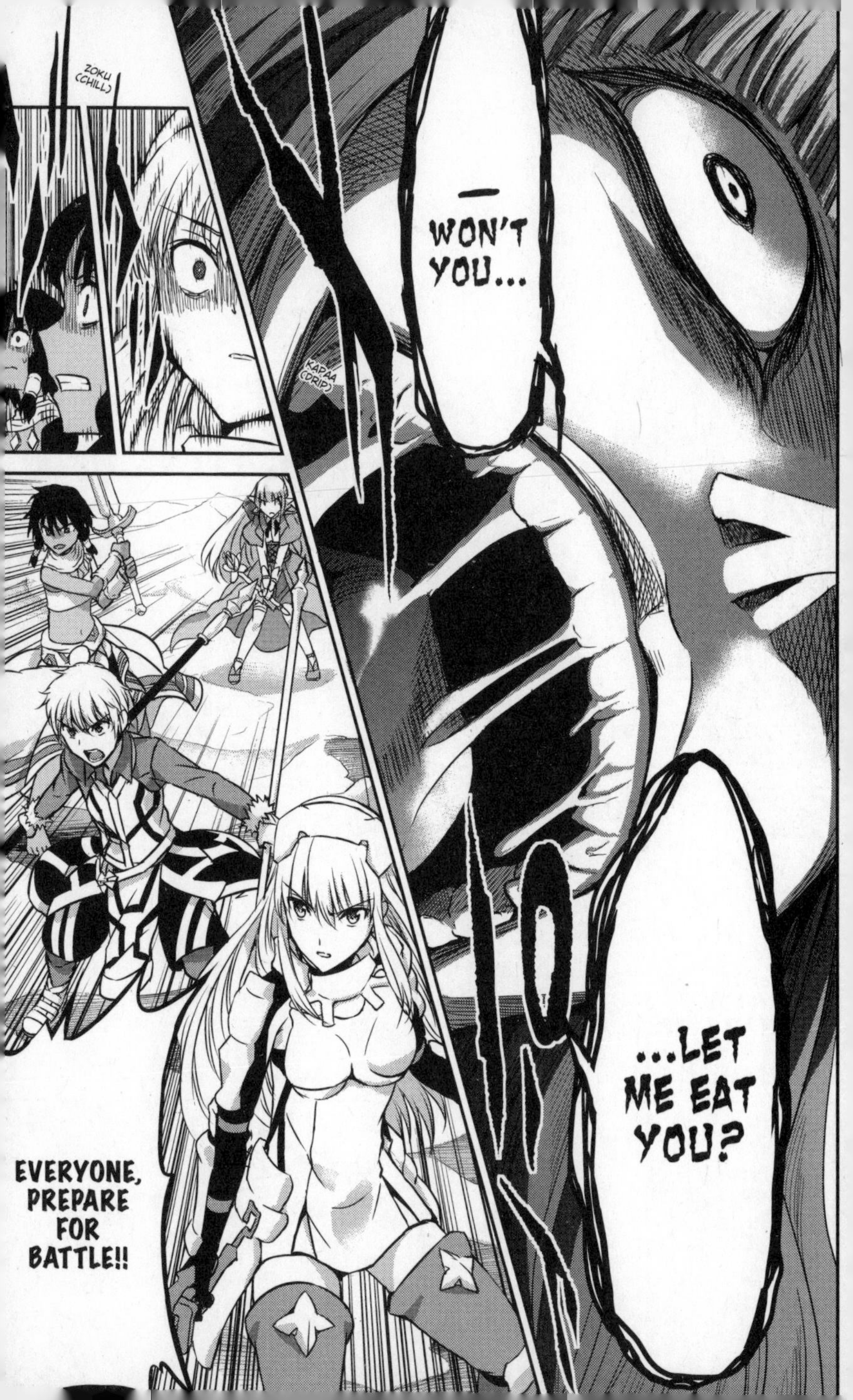
— WON'T YOU...
KAPAA (DRIP)
...LET ME EAT YOU?
ZOKU (CHILL)
EVERYONE, PREPARE FOR BATTLE!!

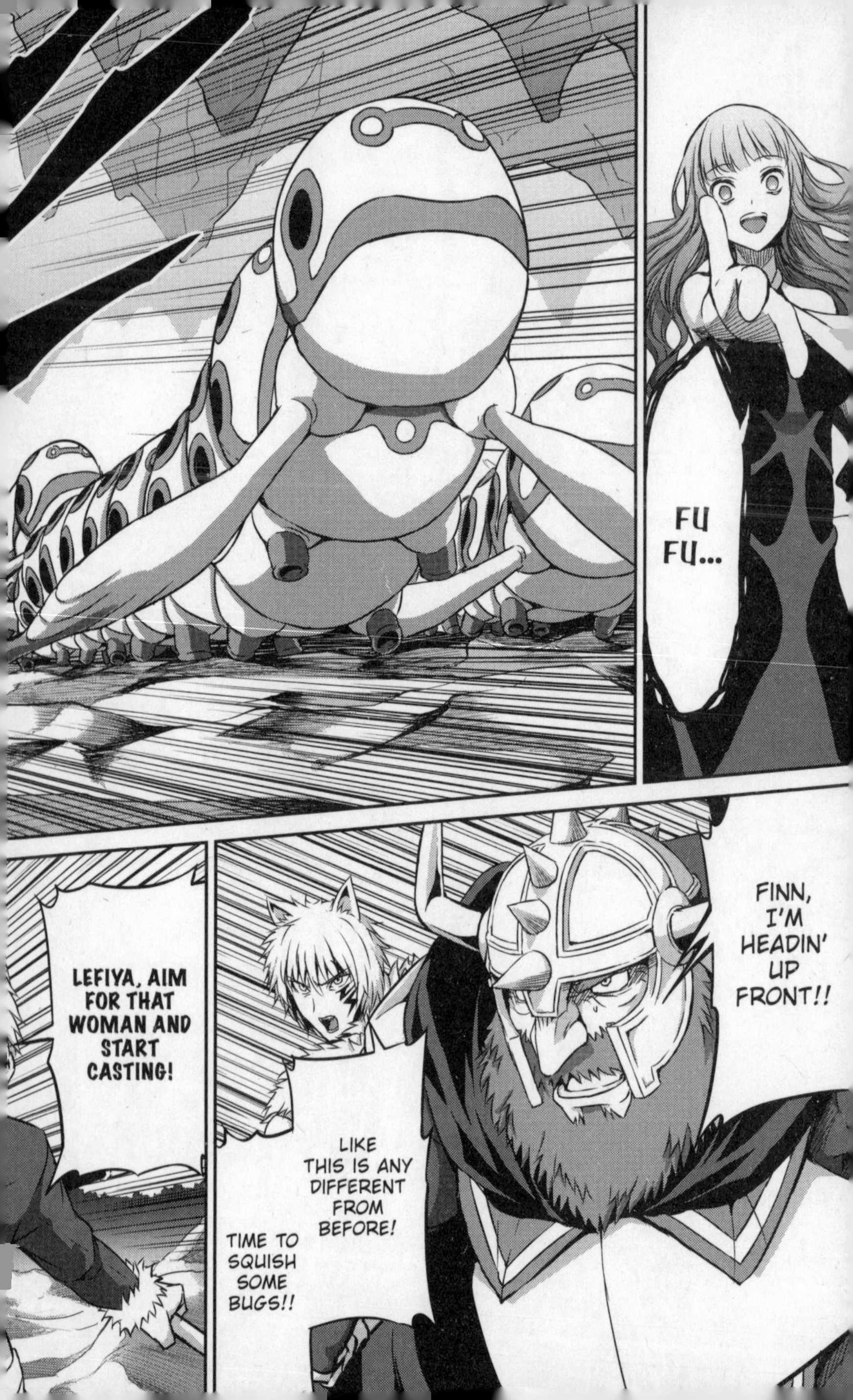
FU FU...
FINN, I'M HEADIN' UP FRONT!!
LIKE THIS IS ANY DIFFERENT FROM BEFORE!
TIME TO SQUISH SOME BUGS!!
LEFIYA, AIM FOR THAT WOMAN AND START CASTING!

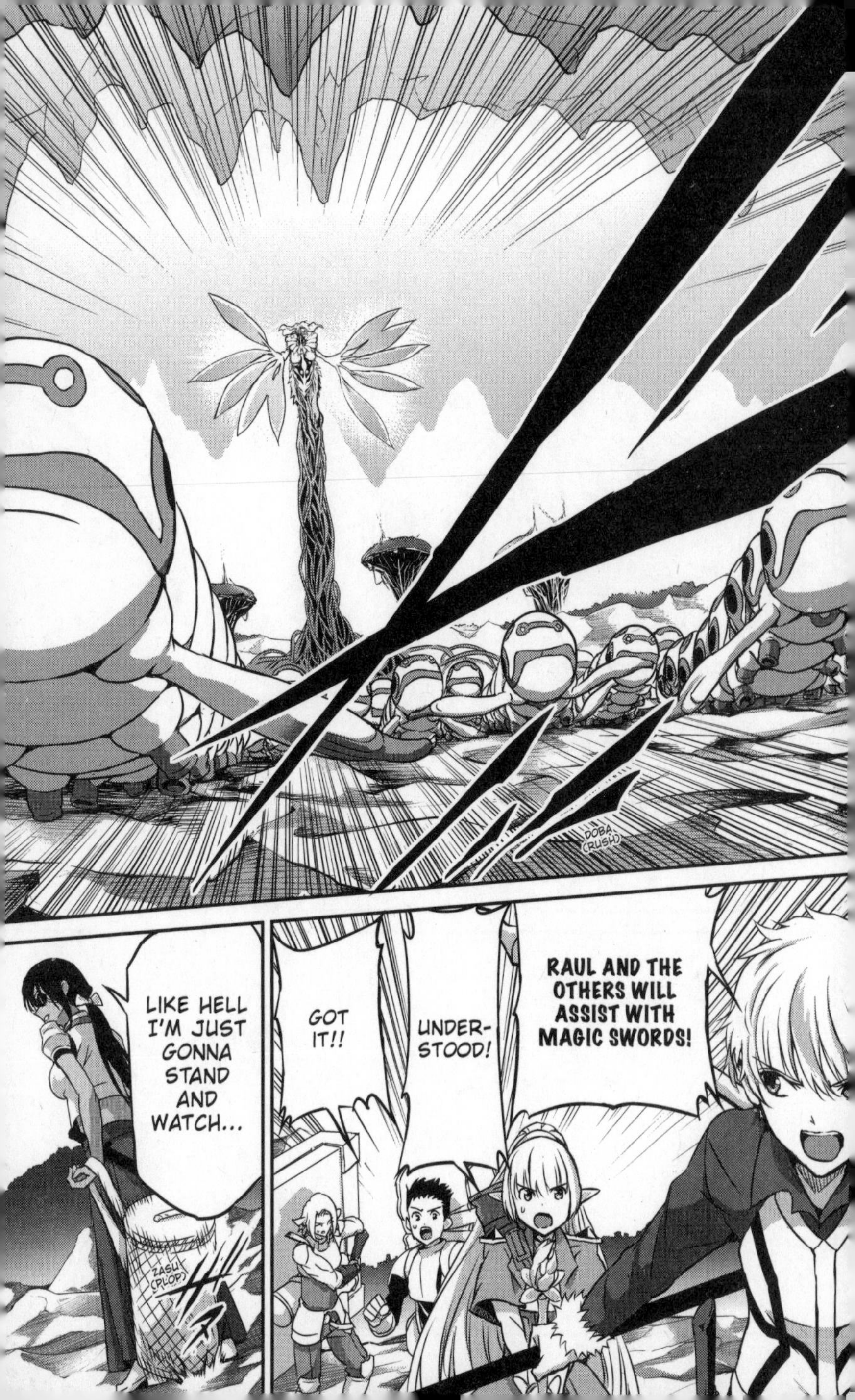
DOBA (RUSH)
RAUL AND THE OTHERS WILL ASSIST WITH MAGIC SWORDS!
UNDER-STOOD!
GOT IT!!
LIKE HELL I'M JUST GONNA STAND AND WATCH...
ZASU (PLOP)

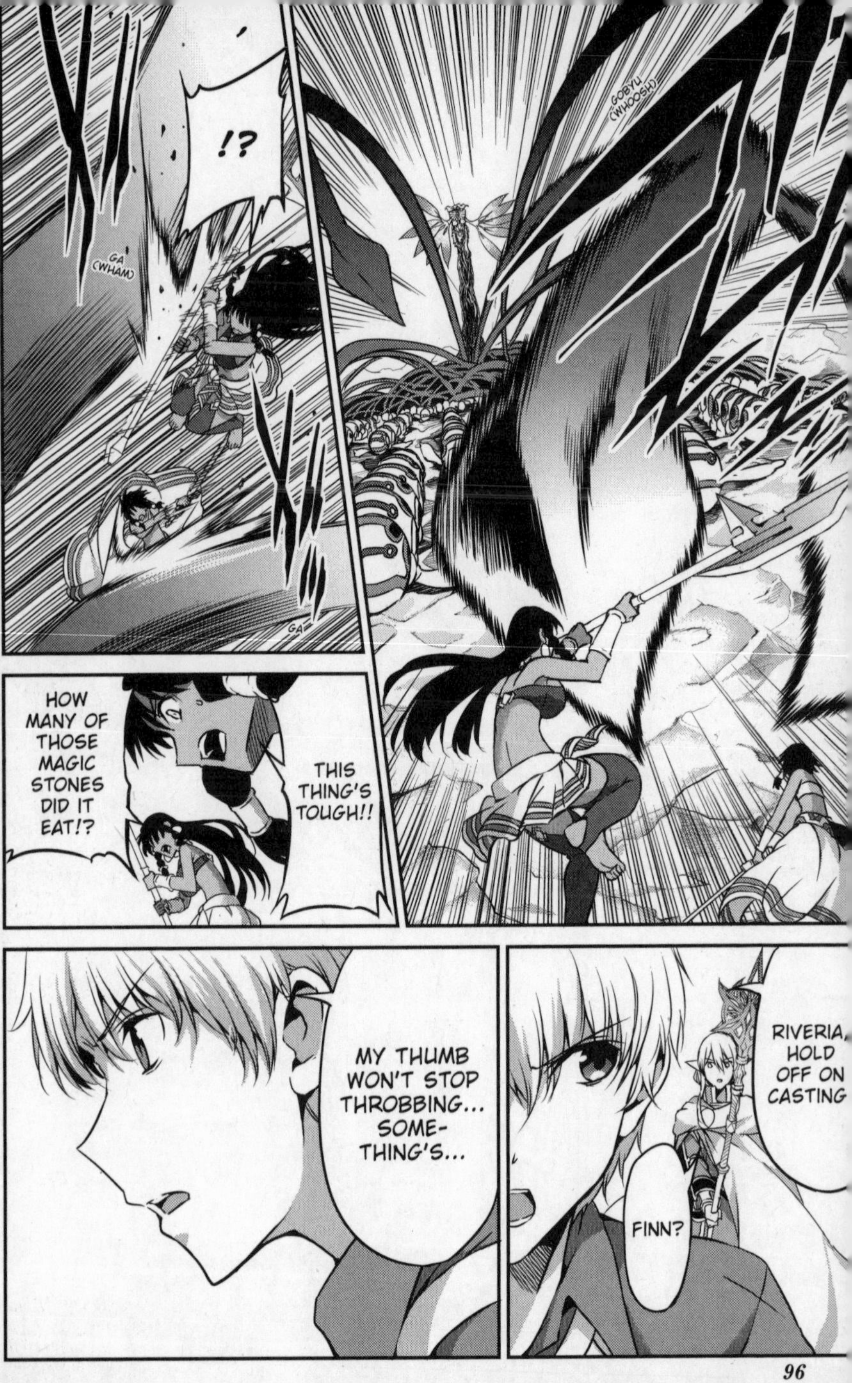
GOBYU (WHOOSH)
!?
GA (WHAM)
GA
THIS THING'S TOUGH!!
HOW MANY OF THOSE MAGIC STONES DID IT EAT!?
RIVERIA, HOLD OFF ON CASTING
FINN?
MY THUMB WON'T STOP THROBBING... SOMETHING'S...

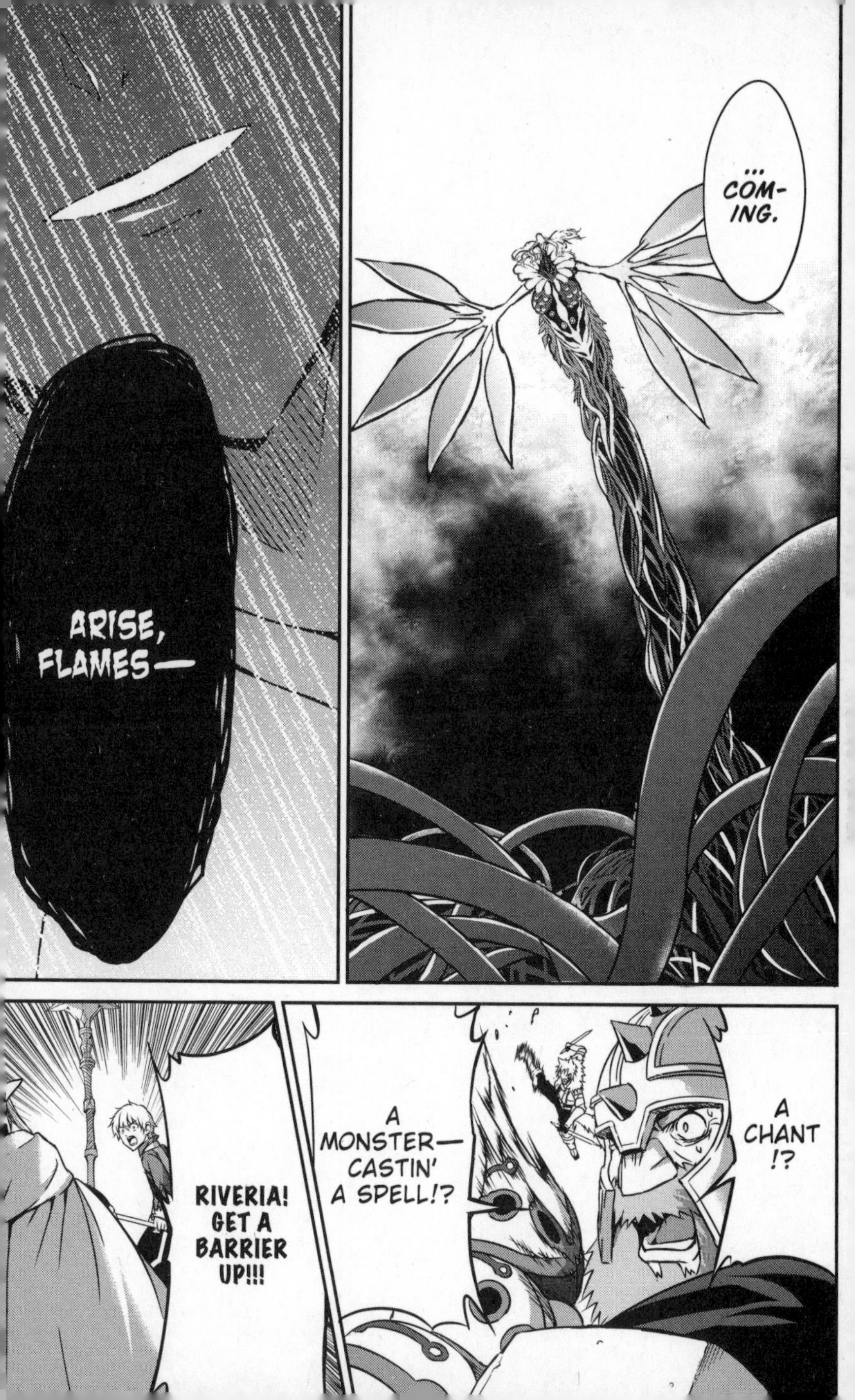
...COMING.
ARISE, FLAMES—
A CHANT!?
A MONSTER—CASTIN' A SPELL!?
RIVERIA! GET A BARRIER UP!!!

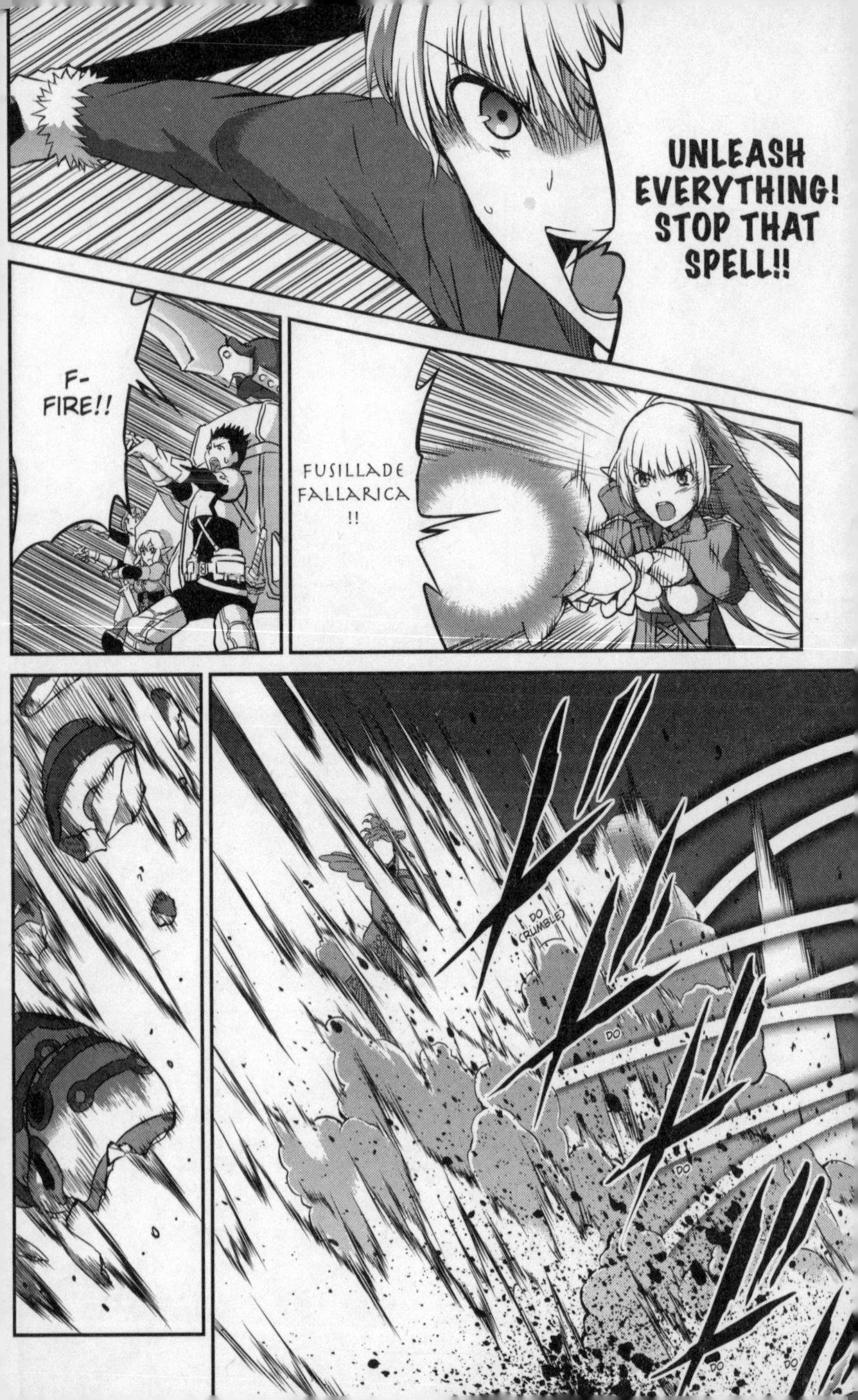
UNLEASH EVERYTHING! STOP THAT SPELL!!
FUSILLADE FALLARICA !!
F- FIRE!!
DO (CRUMBLE)
DO
DO
DO
DO

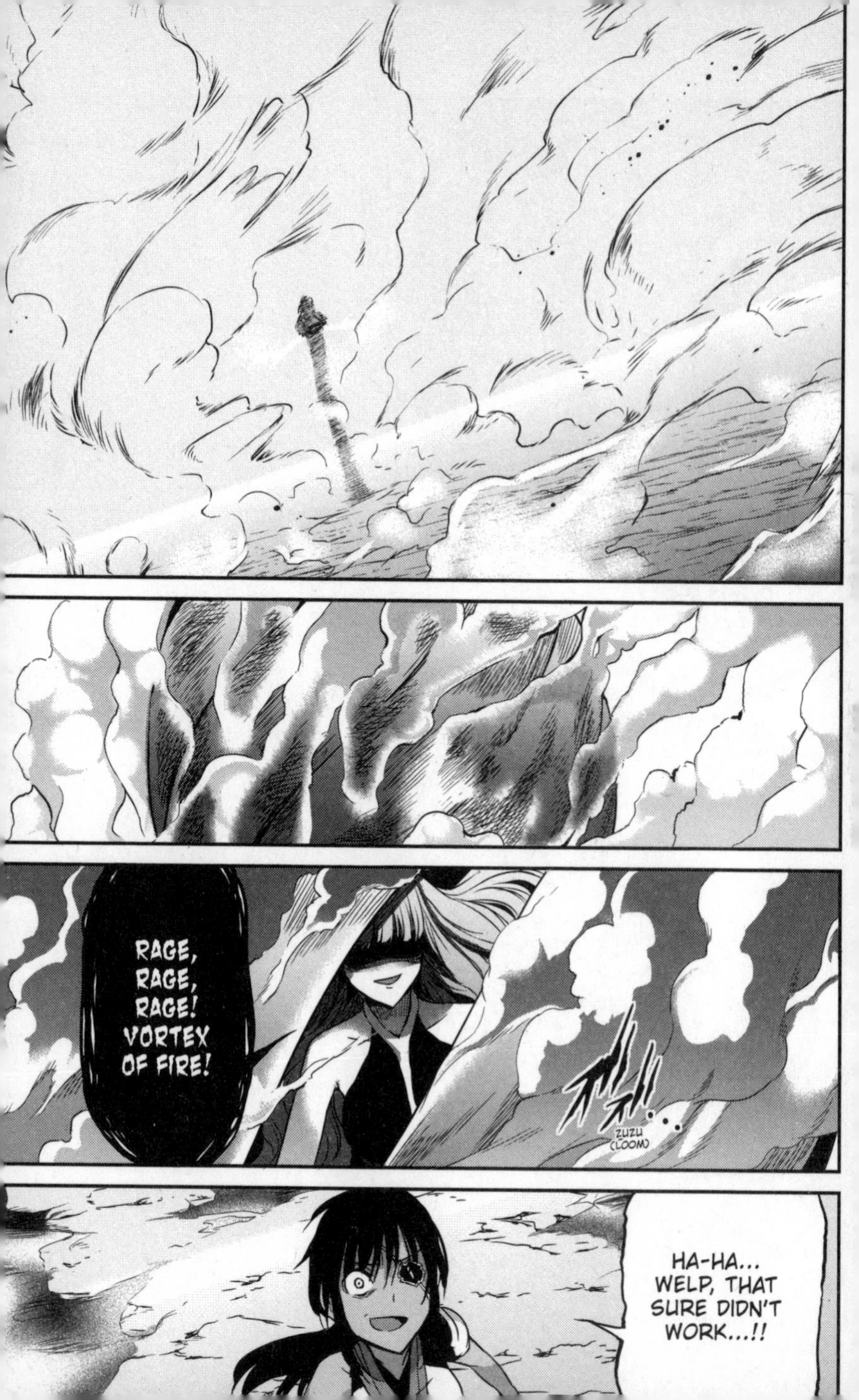
RAGE, RAGE, RAGE! VORTEX OF FIRE!
ZUZU (LOOM)
HA-HA... WELP, THAT SURE DIDN'T WORK...!!

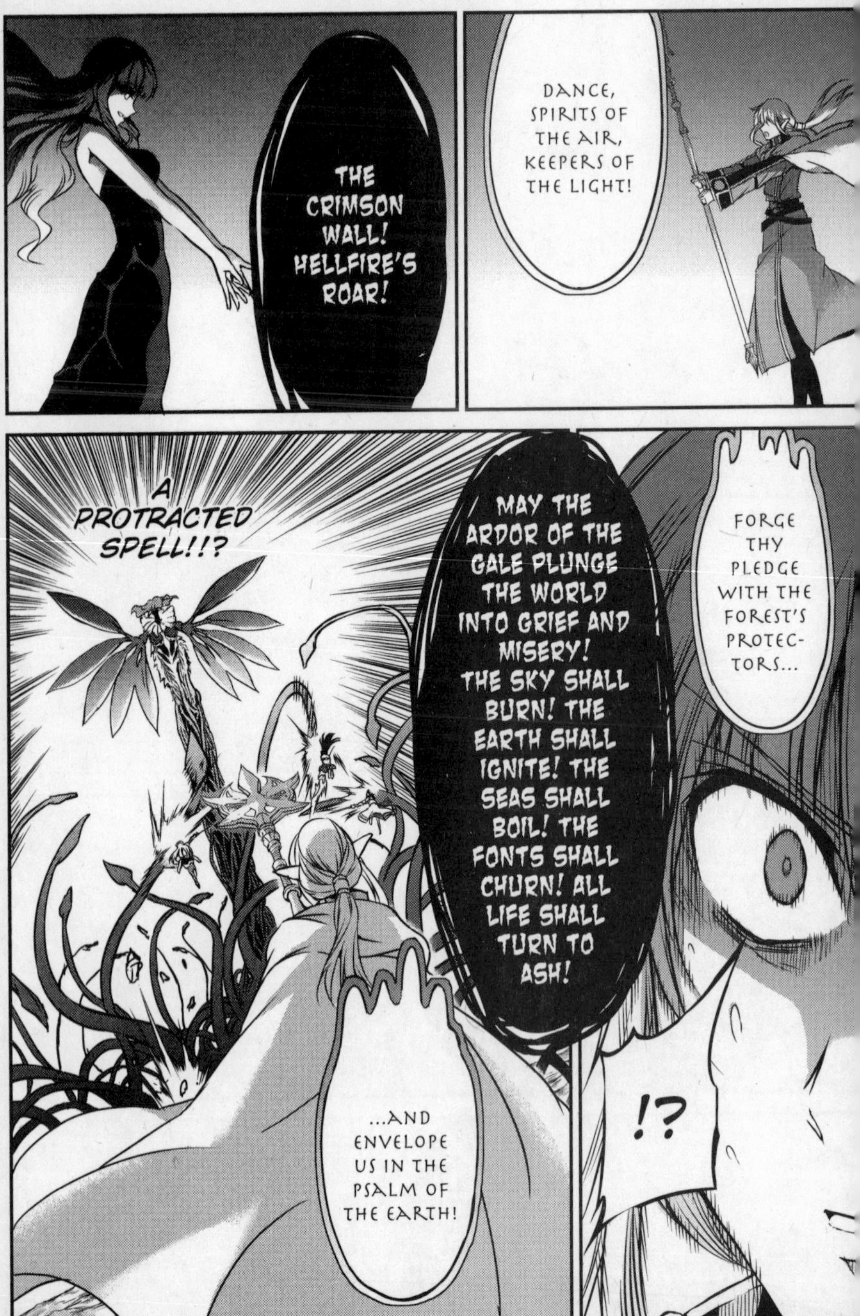
DANCE, SPIRITS OF THE AIR, KEEPERS OF THE LIGHT!
THE CRIMSON WALL! HELLFIRE'S ROAR!
FORGE THY PLEDGE WITH THE FOREST'S PROTEC-TORS...
MAY THE ARDOR OF THE GALE PLUNGE THE WORLD INTO GRIEF AND MISERY! THE SKY SHALL BURN! THE EARTH SHALL IGNITE! THE SEAS SHALL BOIL! THE FONTS SHALL CHURN! ALL LIFE SHALL TURN TO ASH!
A PROTRACTED SPELL!!?
!?
...AND ENVELOPE US IN THE PSALM OF THE EARTH!

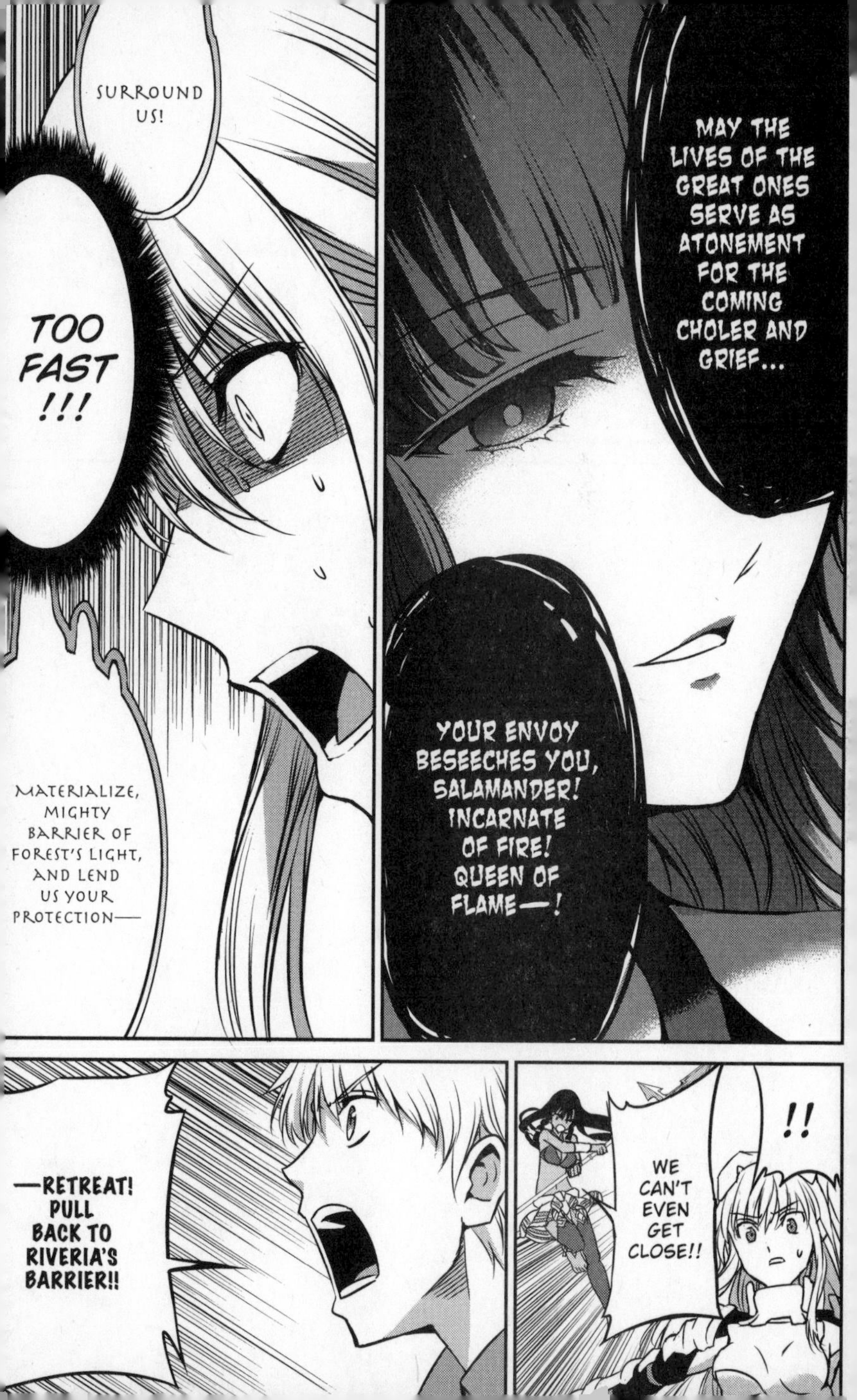
MAY THE LIVES OF THE GREAT ONES SERVE AS ATONEMENT FOR THE COMING CHOLER AND GRIEF...
YOUR ENVOY BESEECHES YOU, SALAMANDER! INCARNATE OF FIRE! QUEEN OF FLAME—!
SURROUND US!
TOO FAST!!!
MATERIALIZE, MIGHTY BARRIER OF FOREST'S LIGHT, AND LEND US YOUR PROTECTION—
!!
WE CAN'T EVEN GET CLOSE!!
—RETREAT! PULL BACK TO RIVERIA'S BARRIER!!

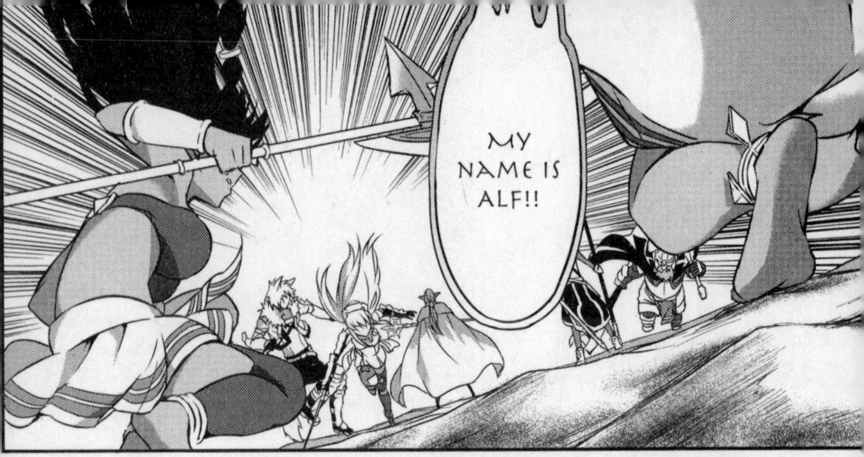
MY NAME IS ALF!!
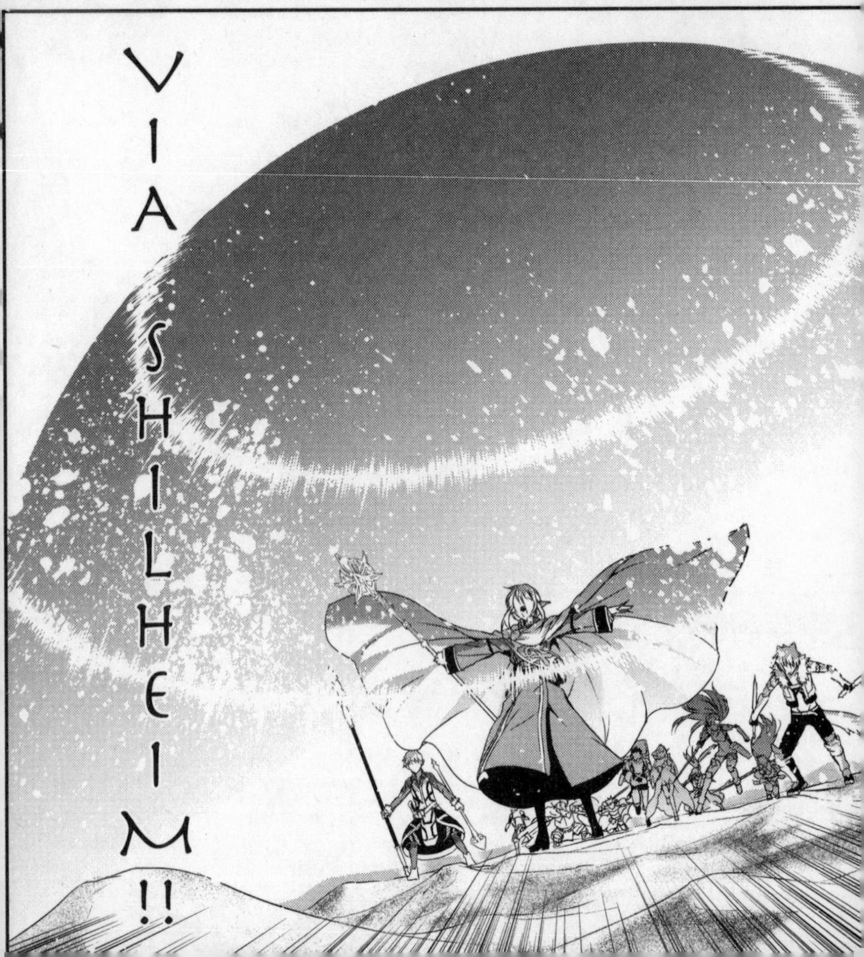
VIA SHILHEIM!!

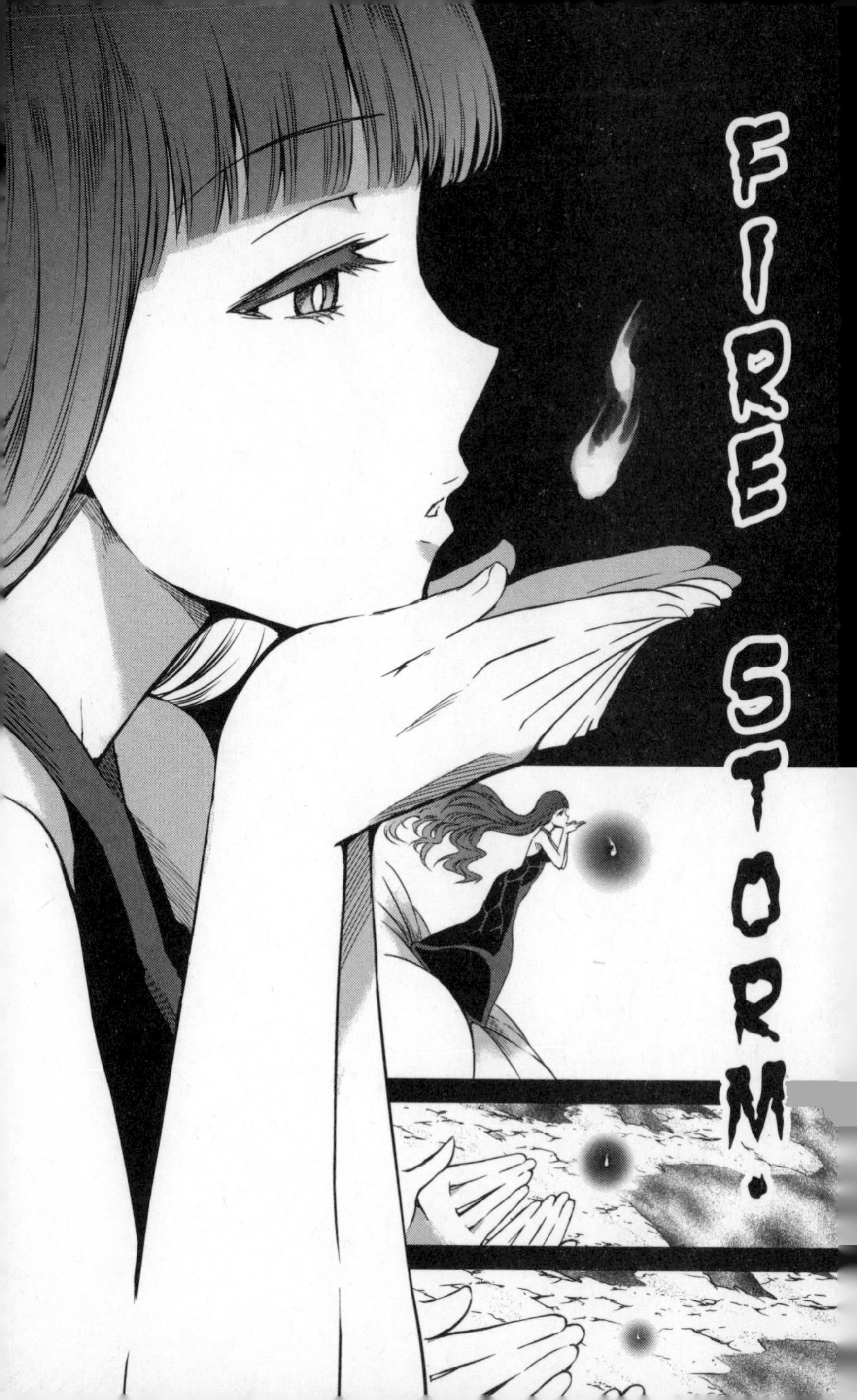
FIRE STORM.

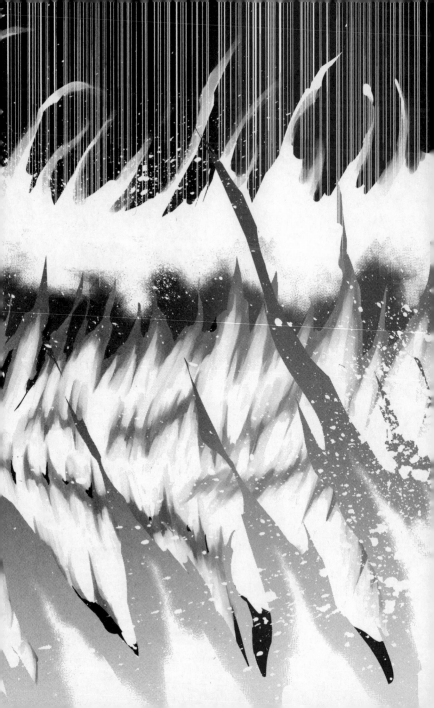

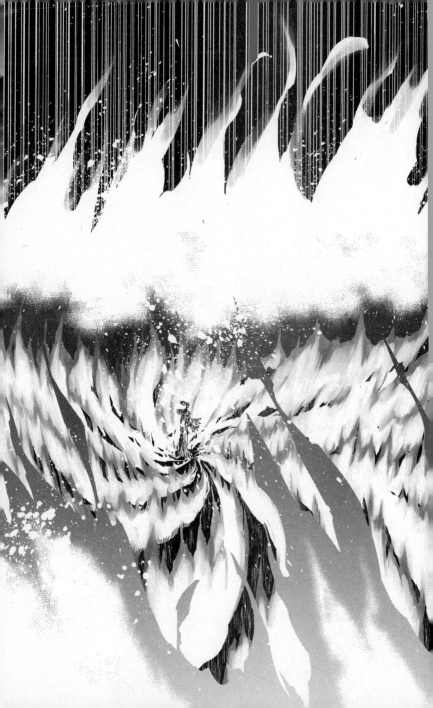

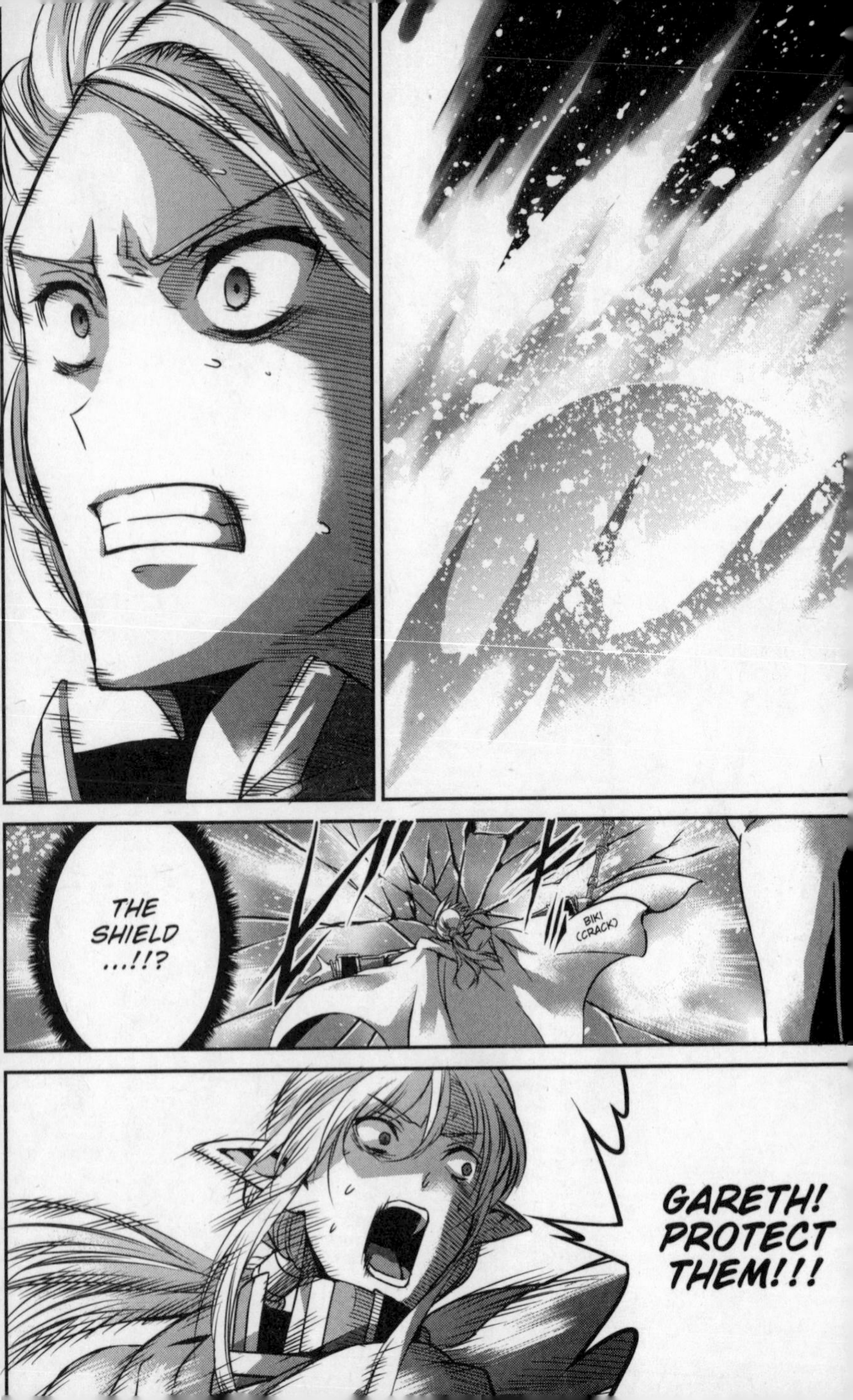
BIKI (CRACK)
THE SHIELD ...!!?
GARETH! PROTECT THEM!!!

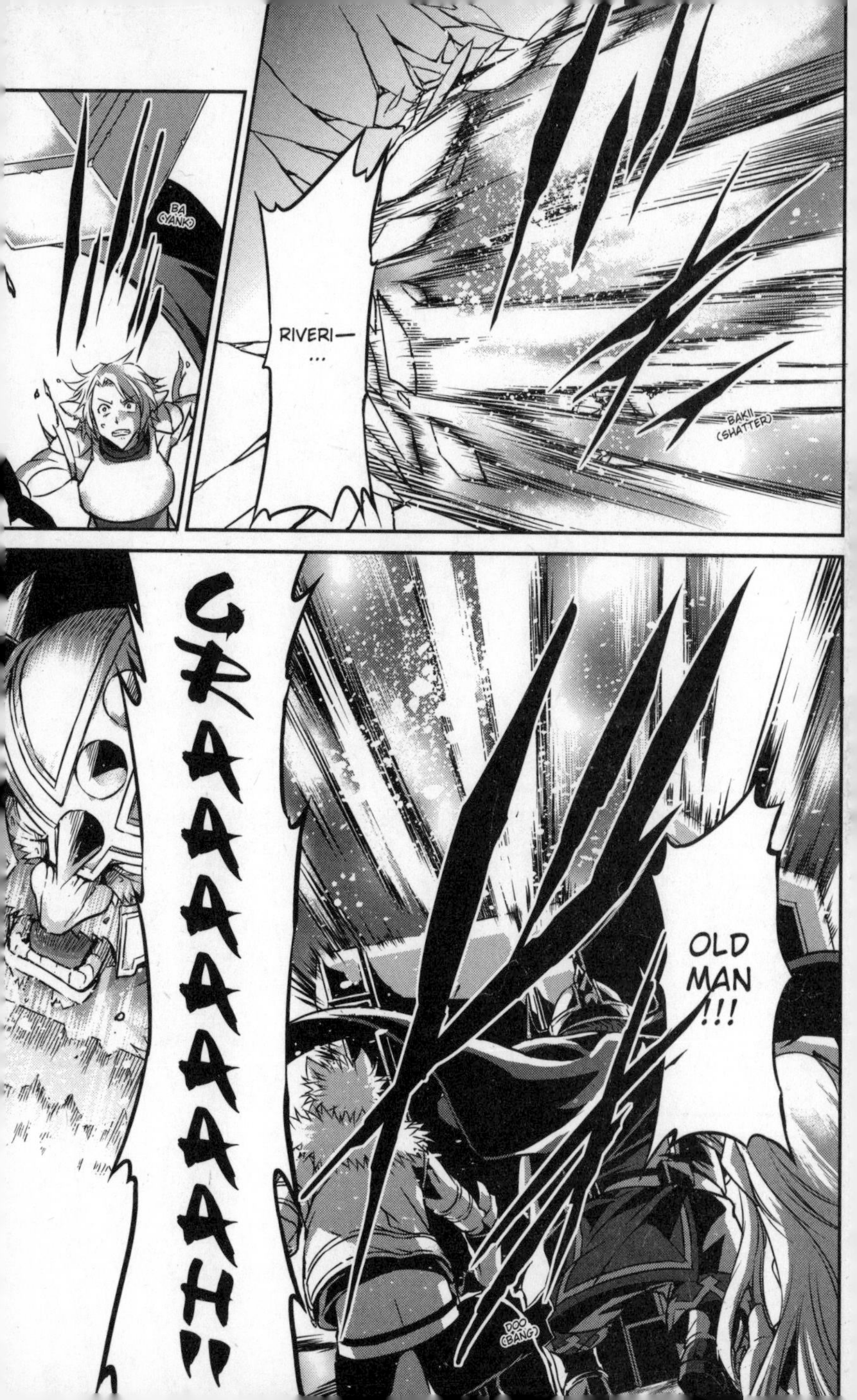
RIVERI—
...
BAKI! (SHATTER)
BA (GANK)
OLD MAN!!!
DOO (BANG)
GRAAAAAAAH!!

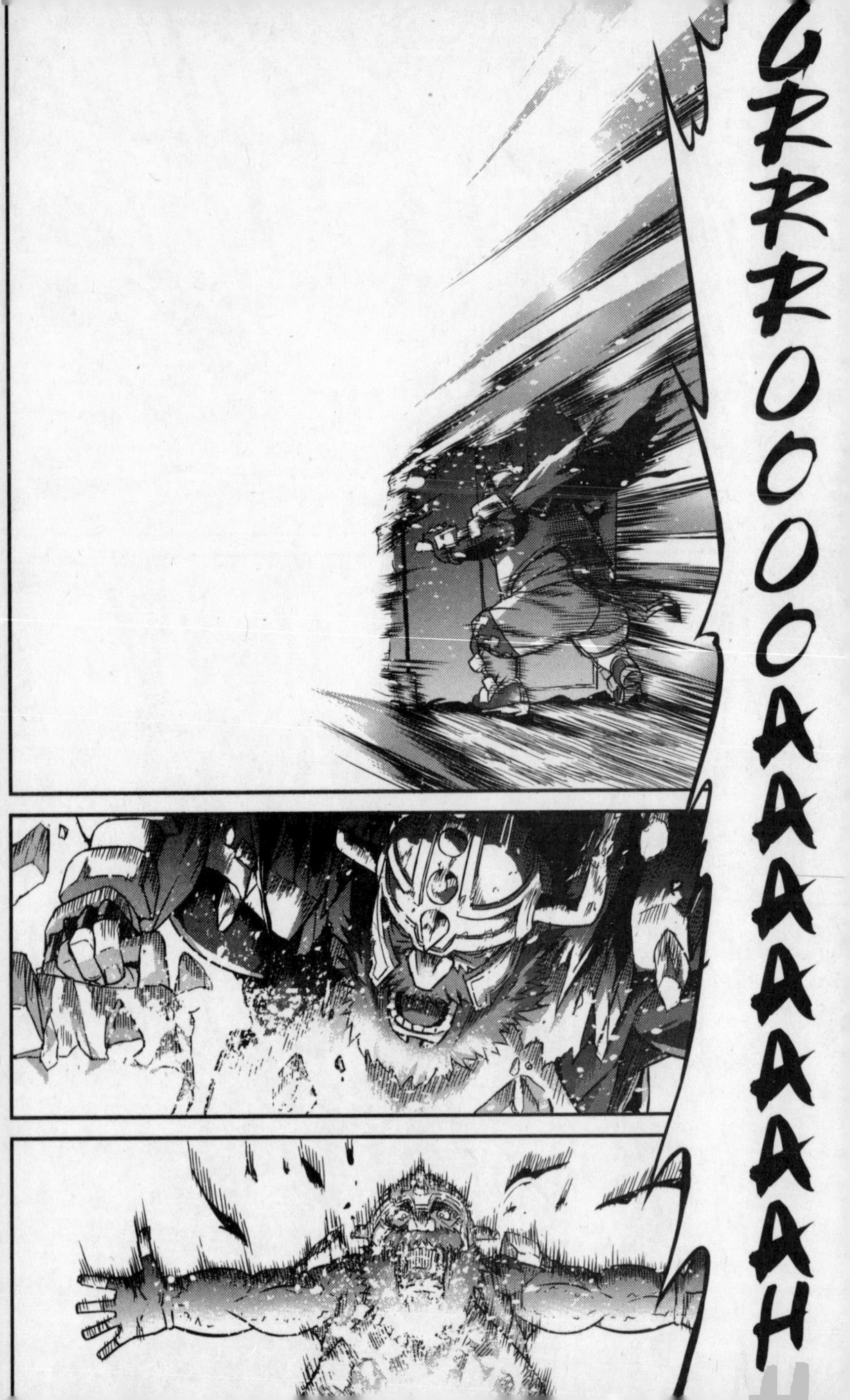
GRRROOOOAAAAAAAH

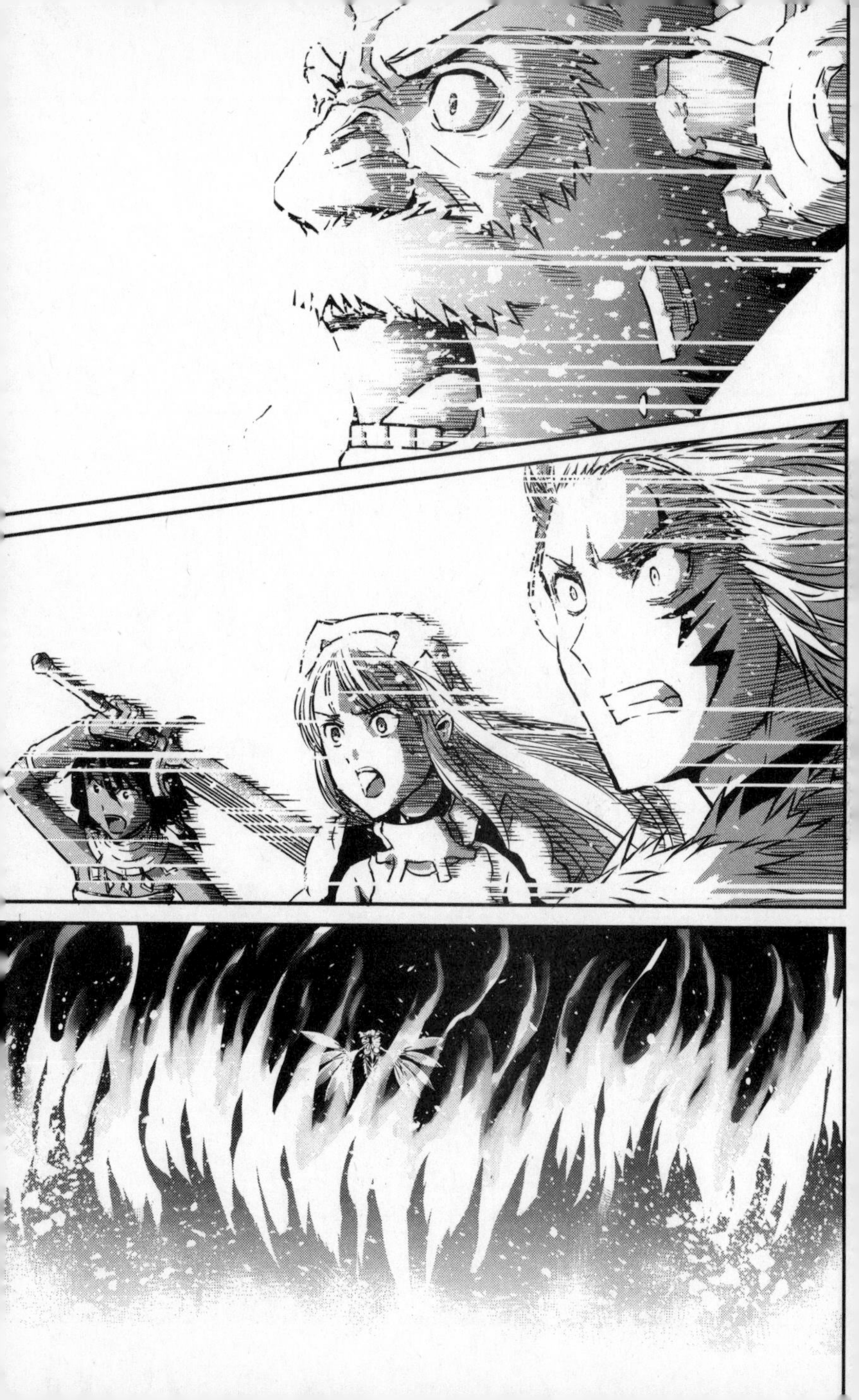

 GEH...!
...HAH!

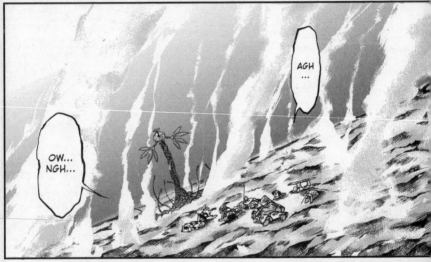

AGH
...

OW...
NGH...

 ERASING
THE WHOLE
LANDSCAPE,
JUST LIKE
THAT...!?

TH...
THE
FOR-
EST...

 RIVERIA...
GARETH
...

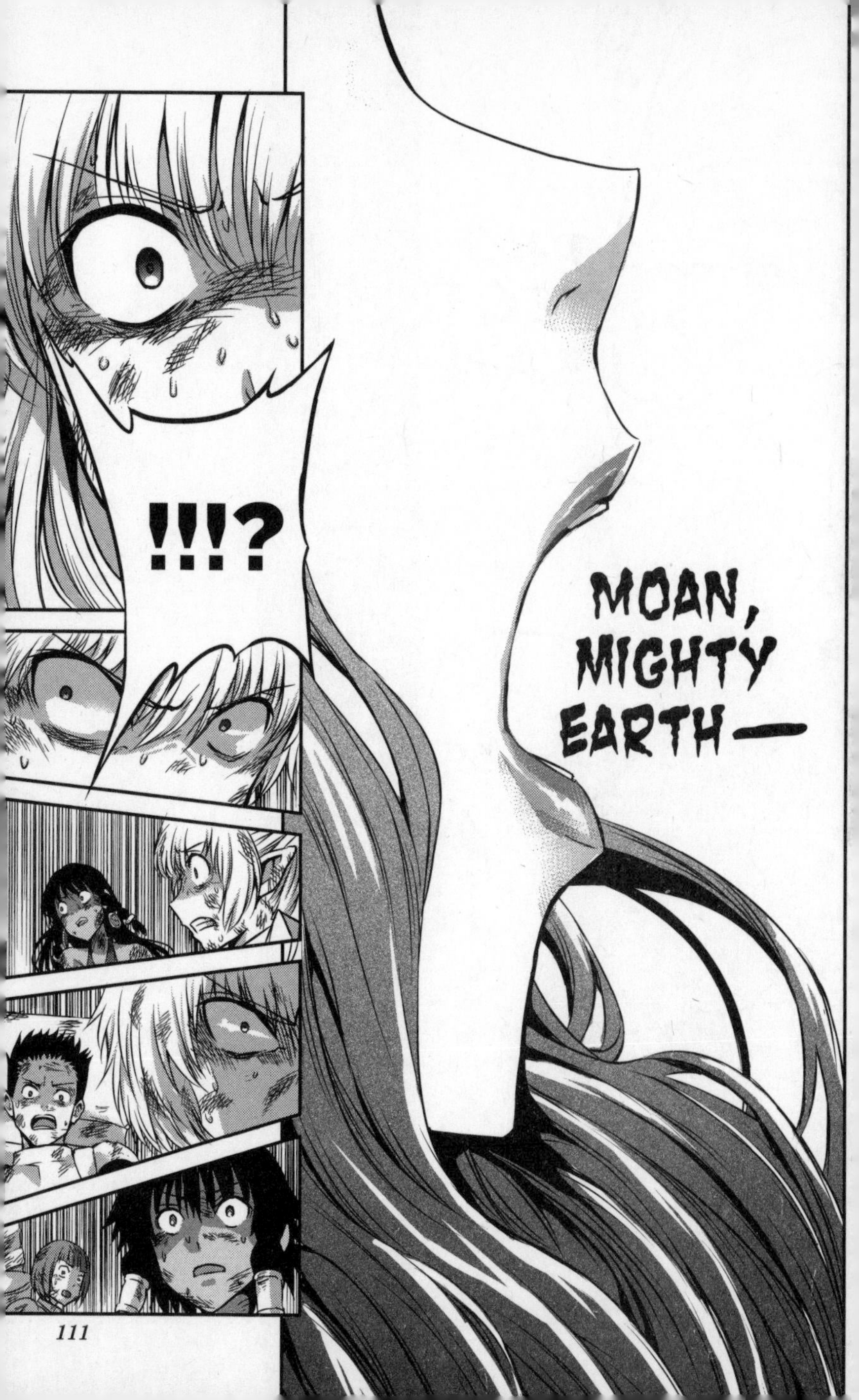
MOAN, MIGHTY EARTH—
!!!?

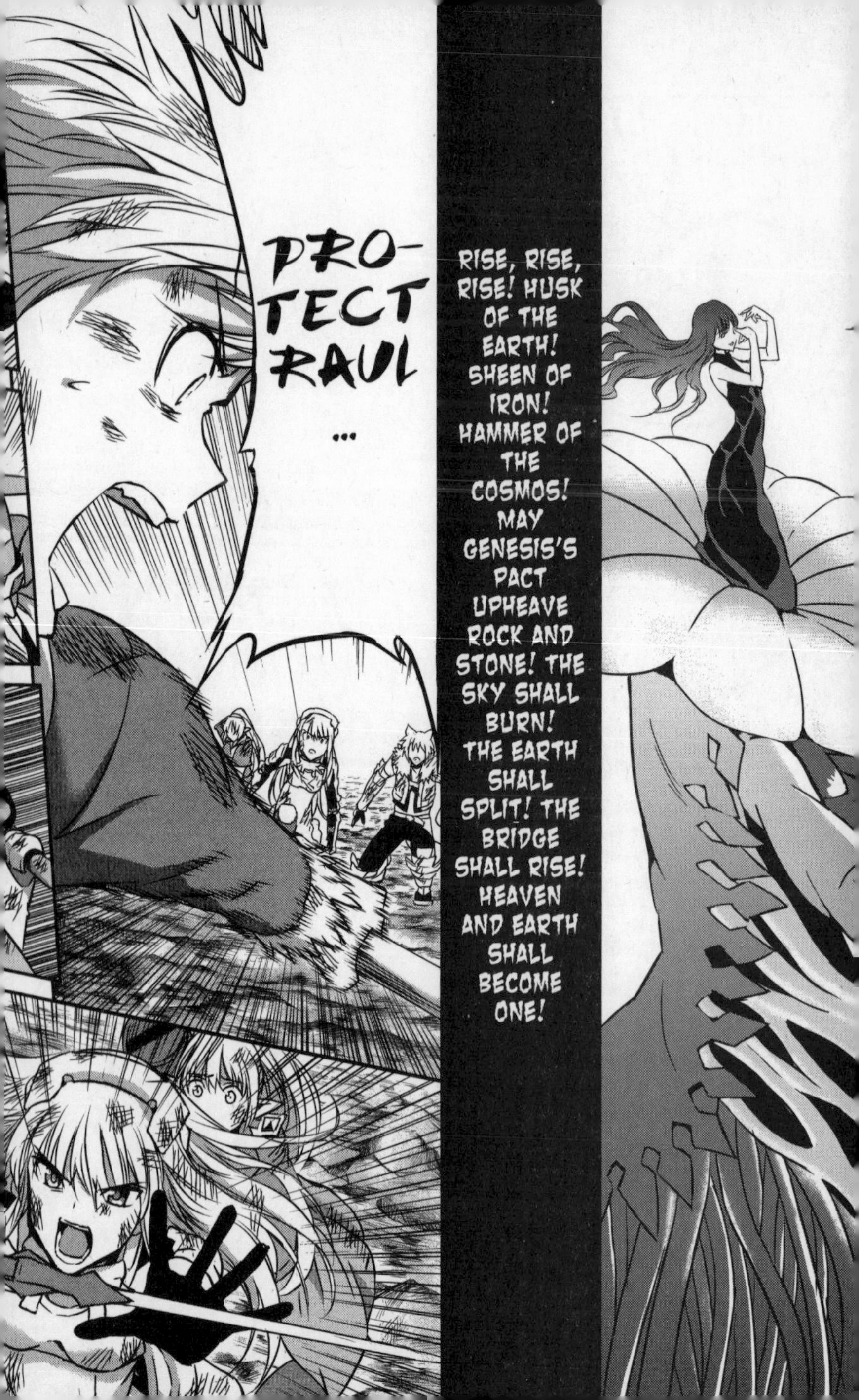
RISE, RISE, RISE! HUSK OF THE EARTH! SHEEN OF IRON! HAMMER OF THE COSMOS! MAY GENESIS'S PACT UPHEAVE ROCK AND STONE! THE SKY SHALL BURN! THE EARTH SHALL SPLIT! THE BRIDGE SHALL RISE! HEAVEN AND EARTH SHALL BECOME ONE!
PRO-TECT RAUL
...

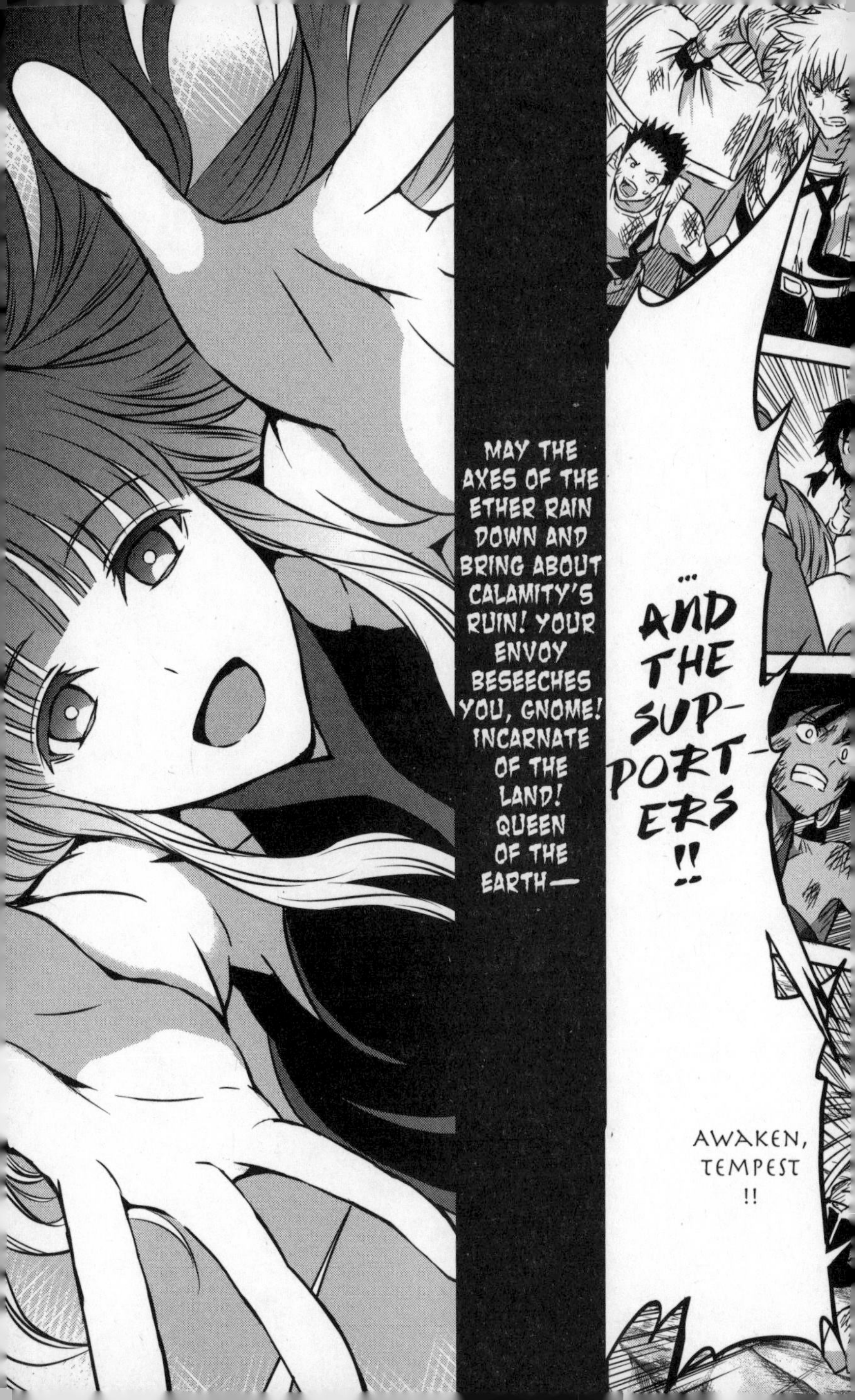
...AND THE SUPPORTERS!!
AWAKEN, TEMPEST!!
MAY THE AXES OF THE ETHER RAIN DOWN AND BRING ABOUT CALAMITY'S RUIN! YOUR ENVOY BESEECHES YOU, GNOME! INCARNATE OF THE LAND! QUEEN OF THE EARTH—

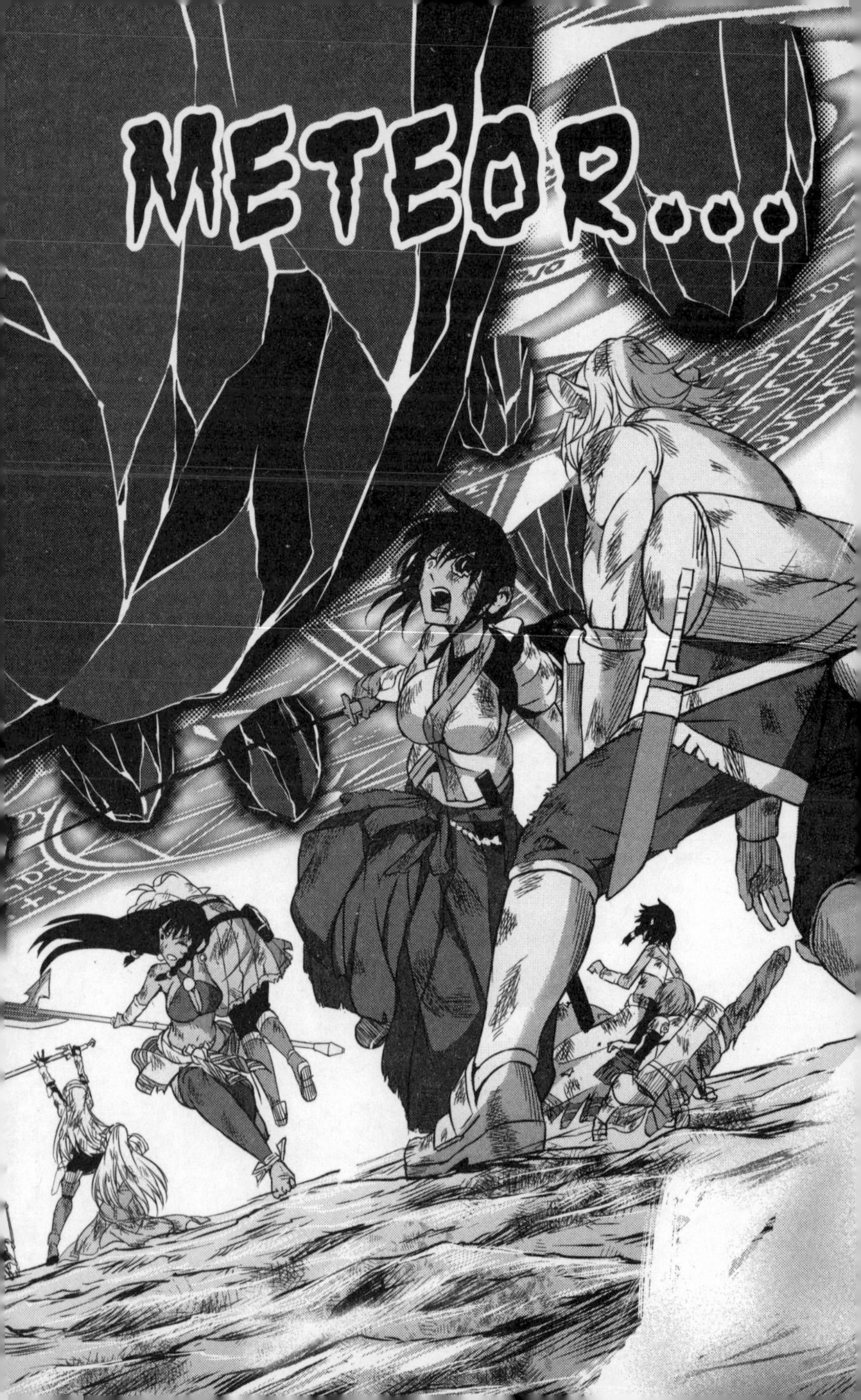
METEOR...!

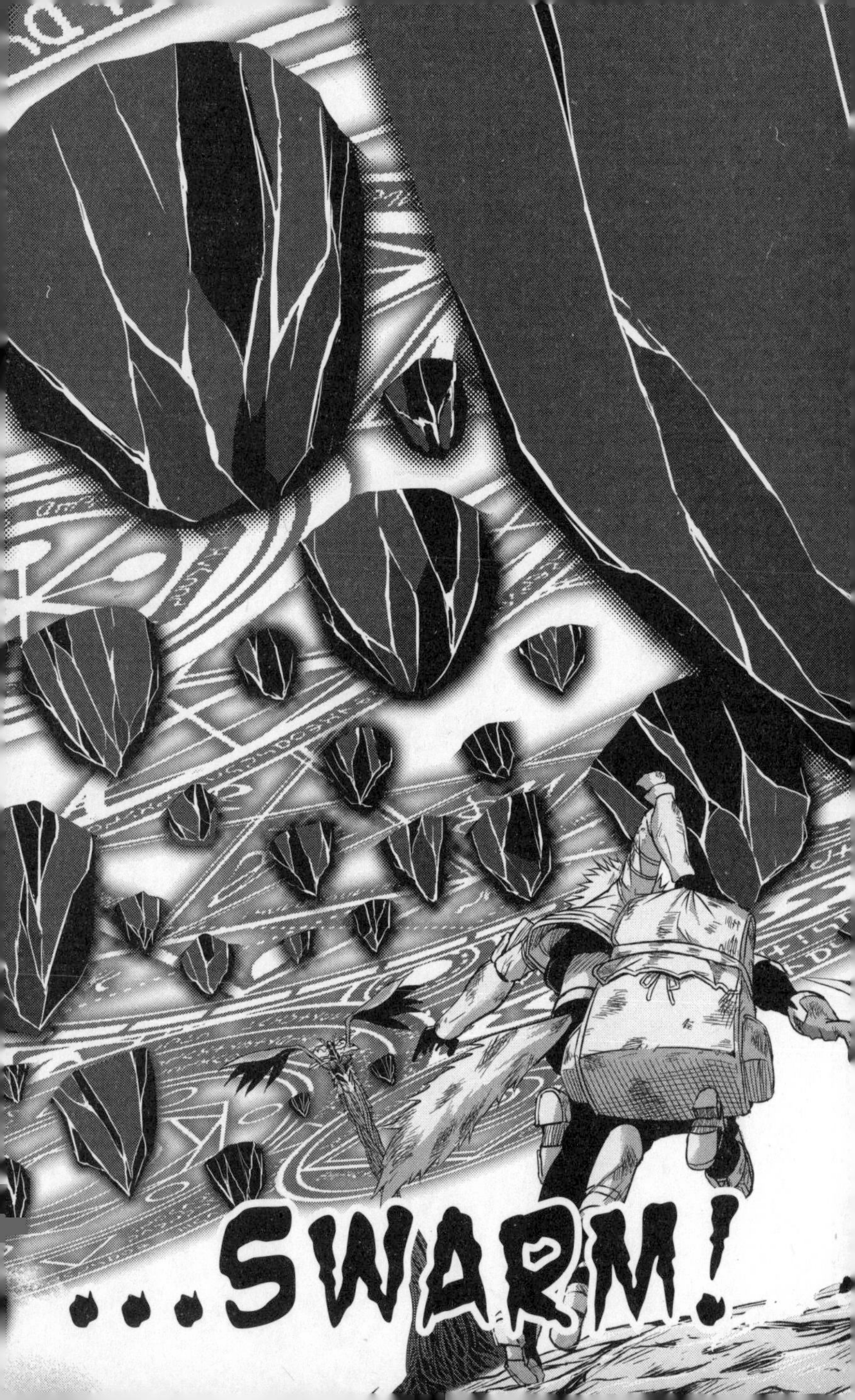
...SWARM!

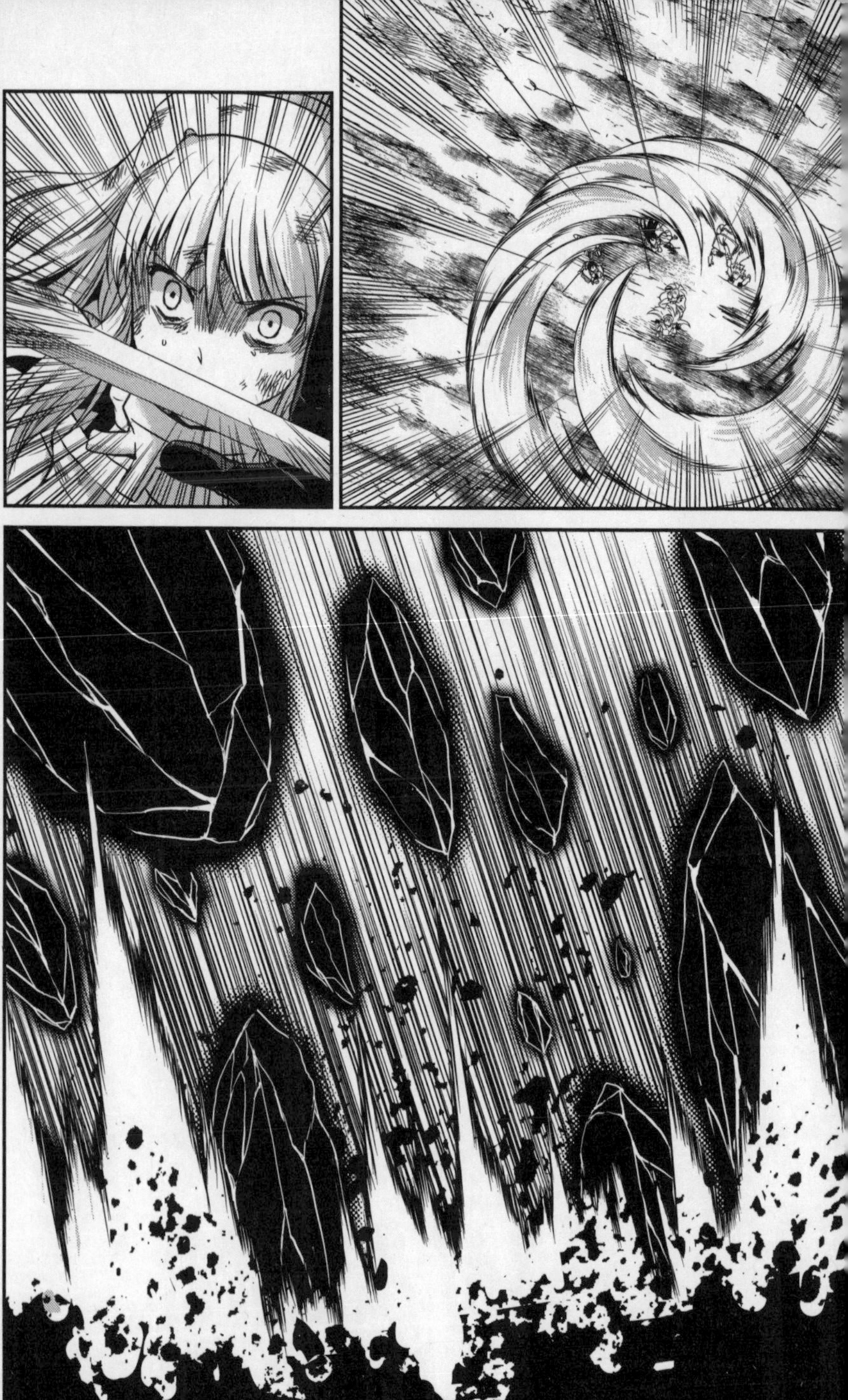

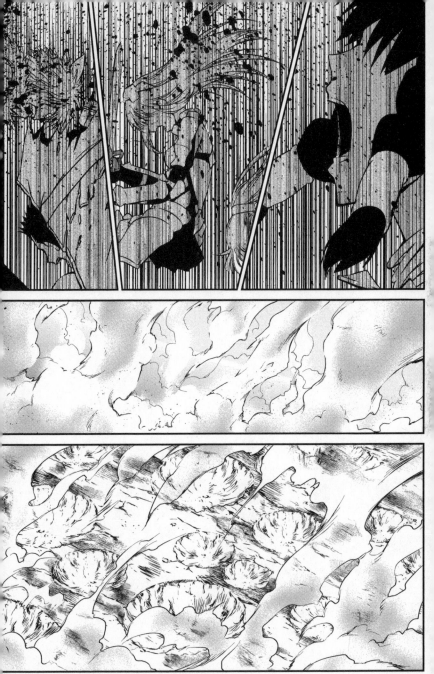

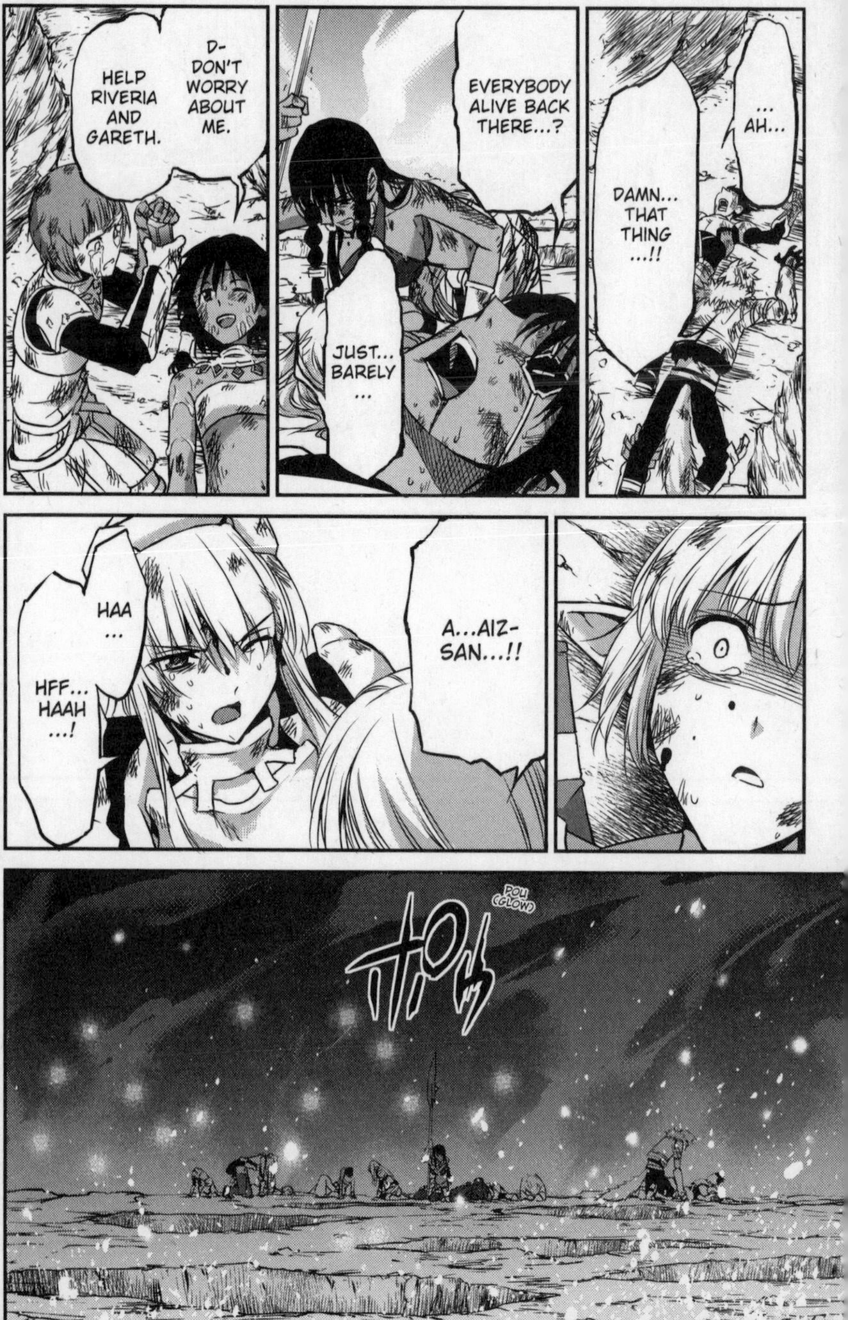
... AH...
DAMN... THAT THING ...!!
EVERYBODY ALIVE BACK THERE...?
JUST... BARELY ...
D- DON'T WORRY ABOUT ME.
HELP RIVERIA AND GARETH.
A...AIZ-SAN...!!
HAA ...
HFF... HAAH ...!
POU (GLOW)

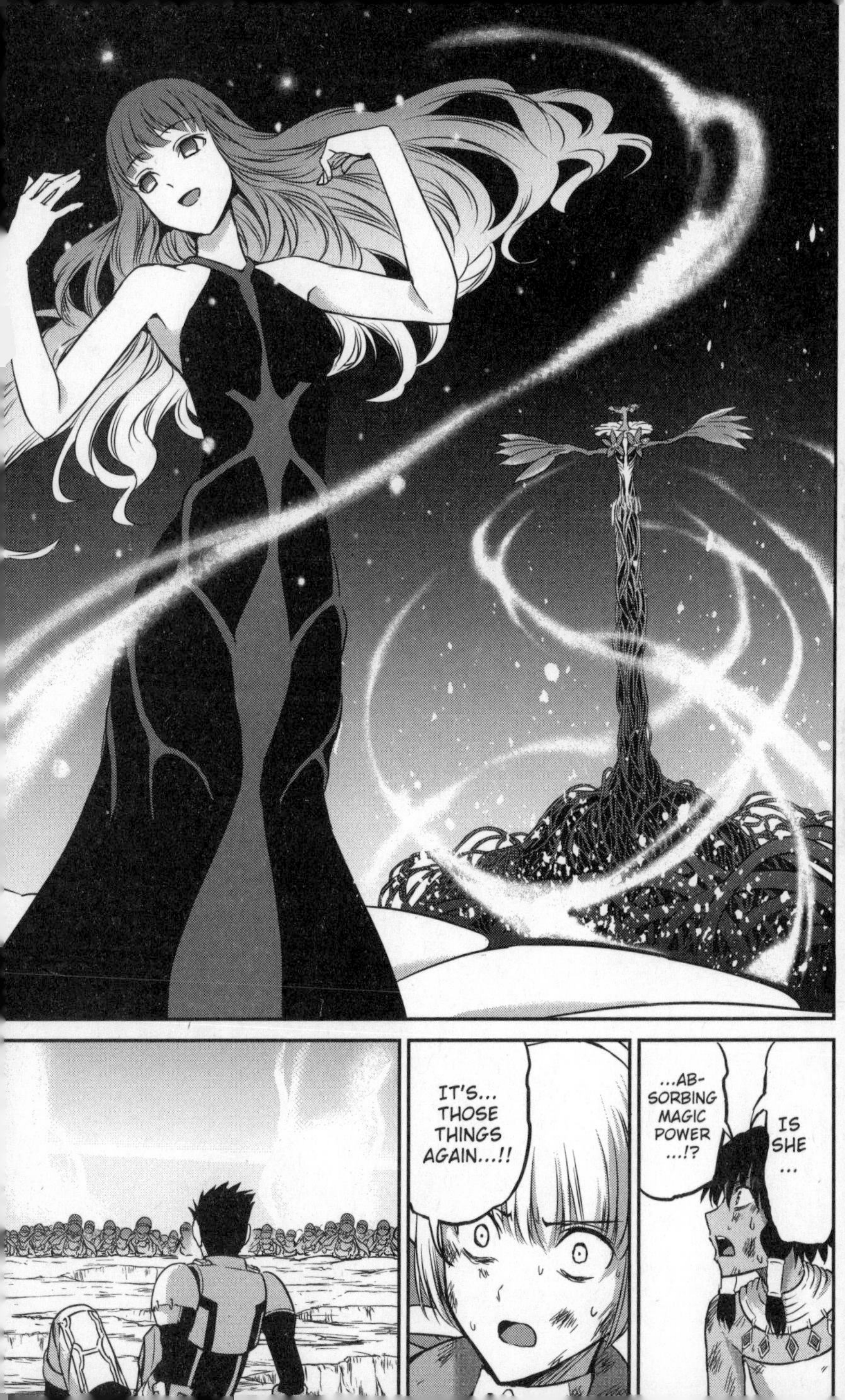
IS SHE ...
...AB-SORBING MAGIC POWER ...!?
IT'S... THOSE THINGS AGAIN...!!

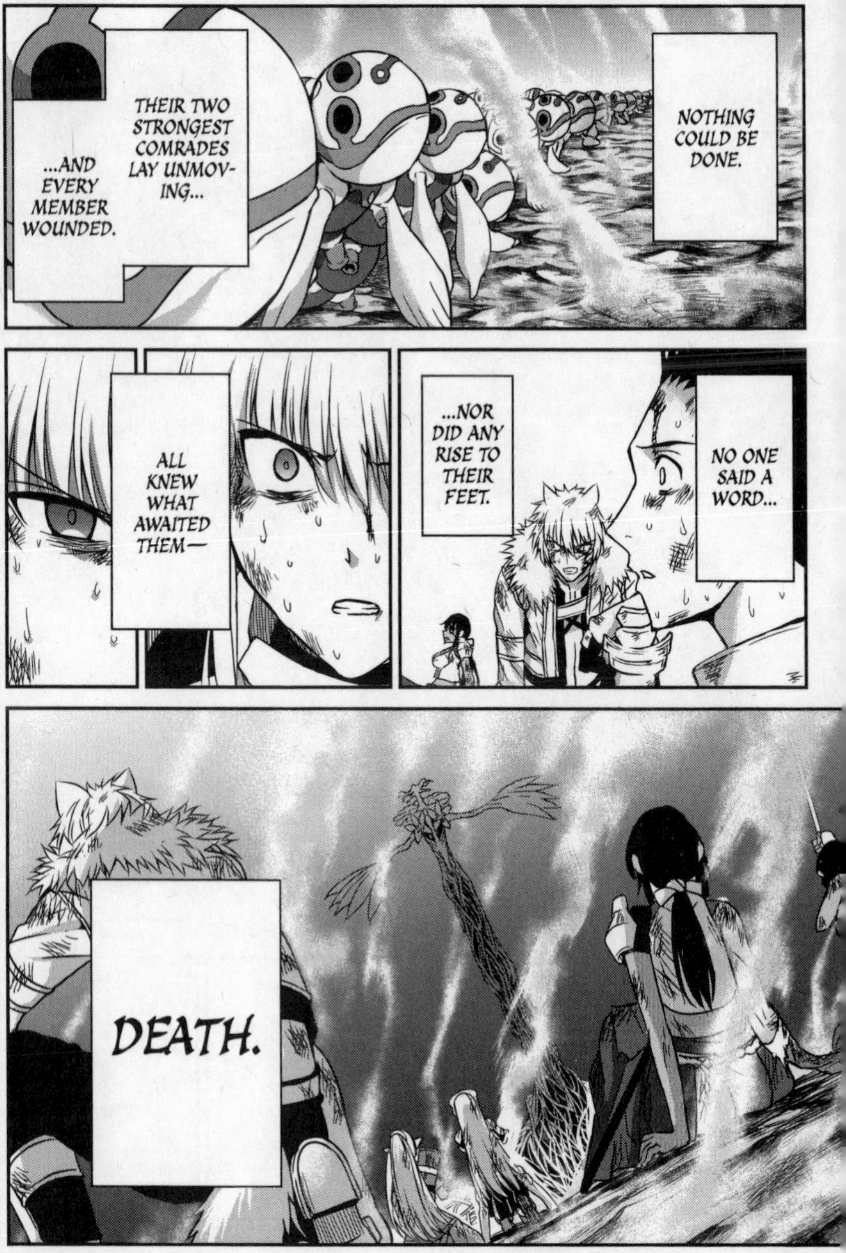
NOTHING COULD BE DONE.
THEIR TWO STRONGEST COMRADES LAY UNMOVING...
...AND EVERY MEMBER WOUNDED.
NO ONE SAID A WORD...
...NOR DID ANY RISE TO THEIR FEET.
ALL KNEW WHAT AWAITED THEM—
DEATH.

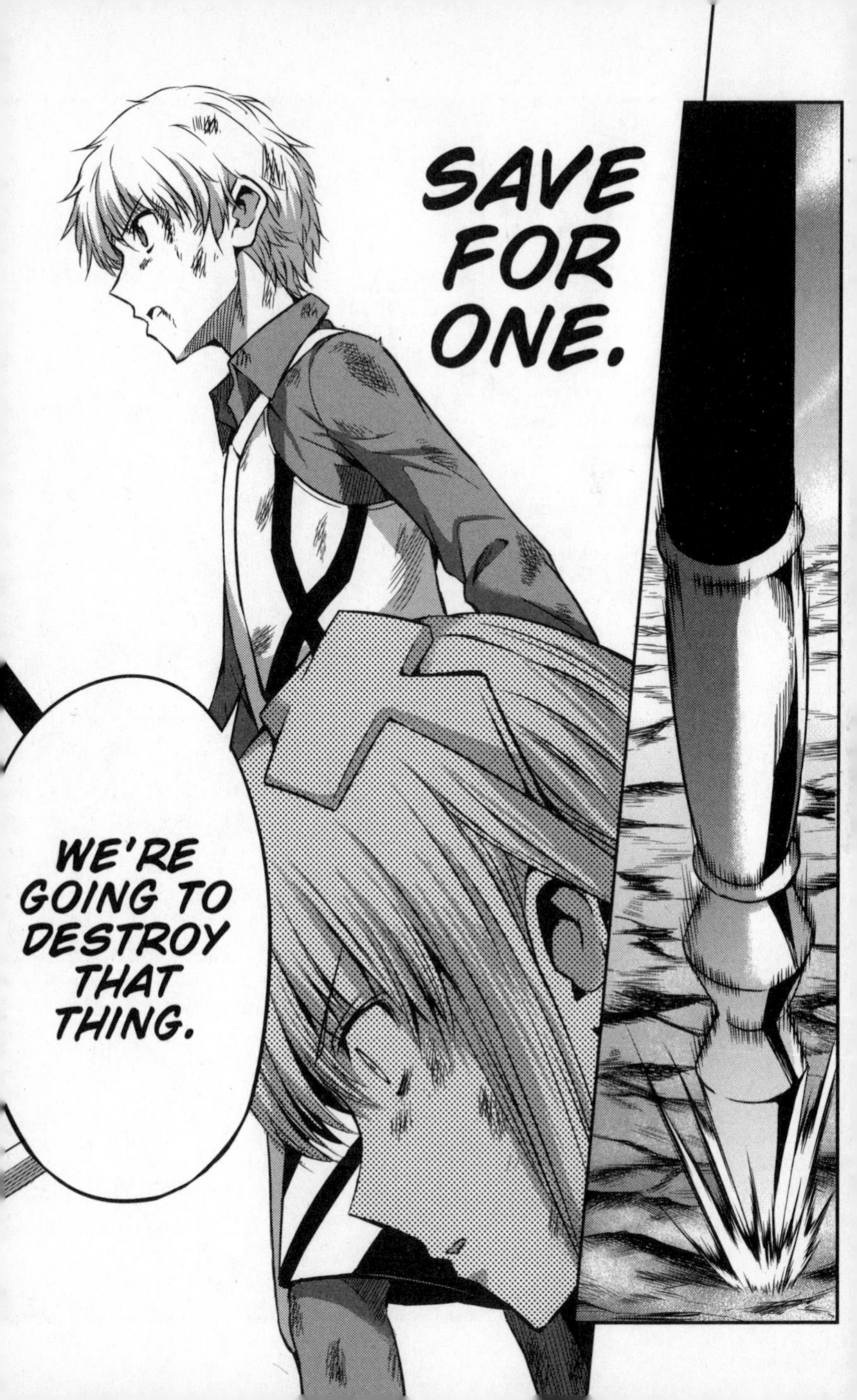
SAVE FOR ONE.
WE'RE GOING TO DESTROY THAT THING.

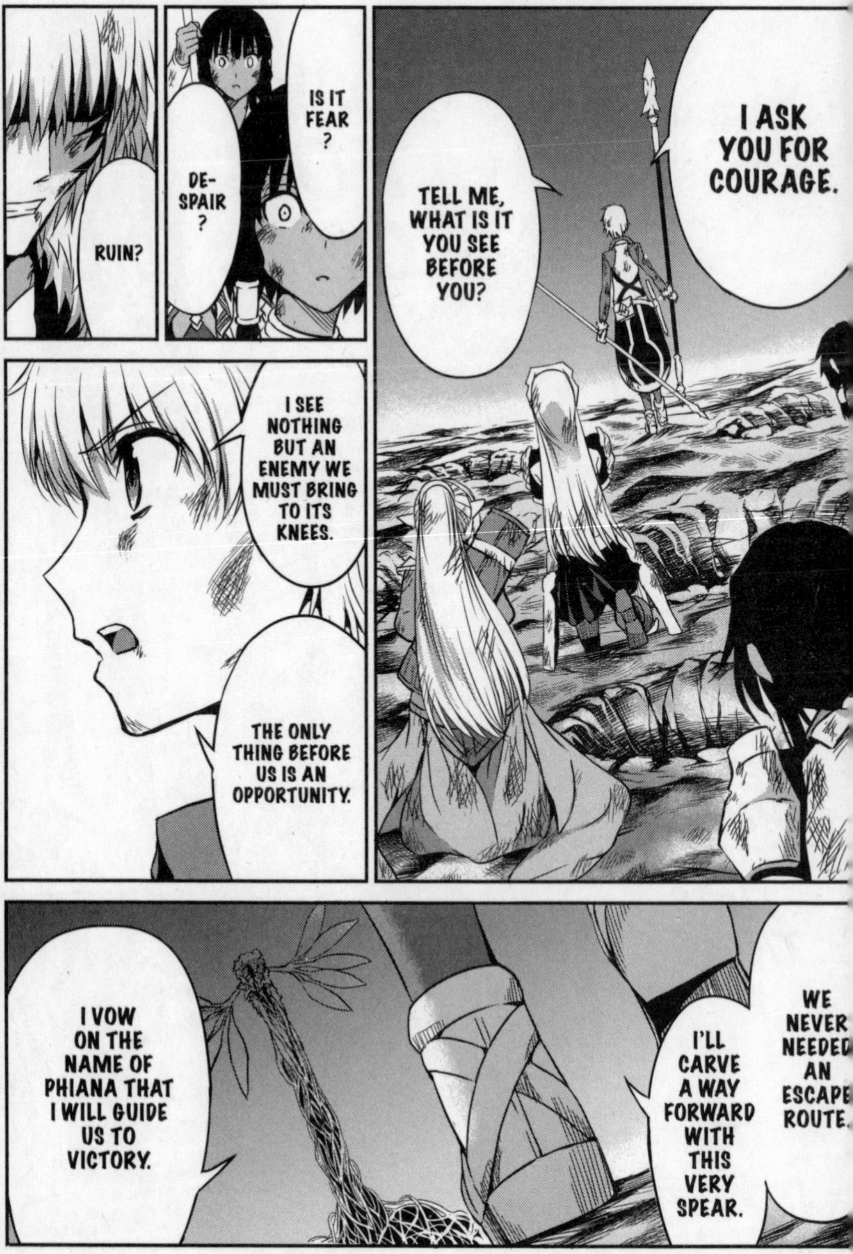
I ASK YOU FOR COURAGE.
TELL ME, WHAT IS IT YOU SEE BEFORE YOU?
IS IT FEAR?
DE-SPAIR?
RUIN?
I SEE NOTHING BUT AN ENEMY WE MUST BRING TO ITS KNEES.
THE ONLY THING BEFORE US IS AN OPPORTUNITY.
WE NEVER NEEDED AN ESCAPE ROUTE.
I'LL CARVE A WAY FORWARD WITH THIS VERY SPEAR.
I VOW ON THE NAME OF PHIANA THAT I WILL GUIDE US TO VICTORY.

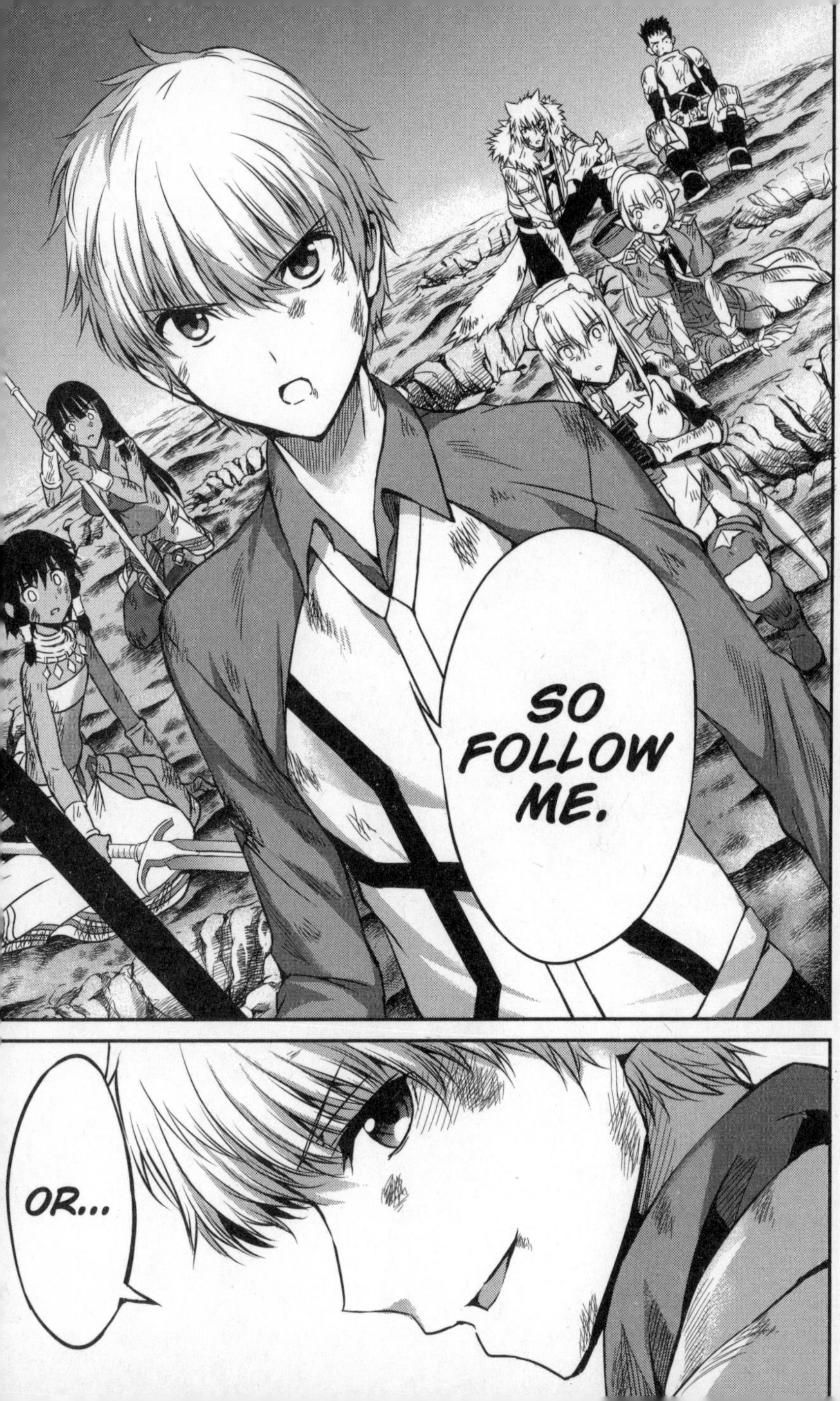
SO FOLLOW ME.
OR...

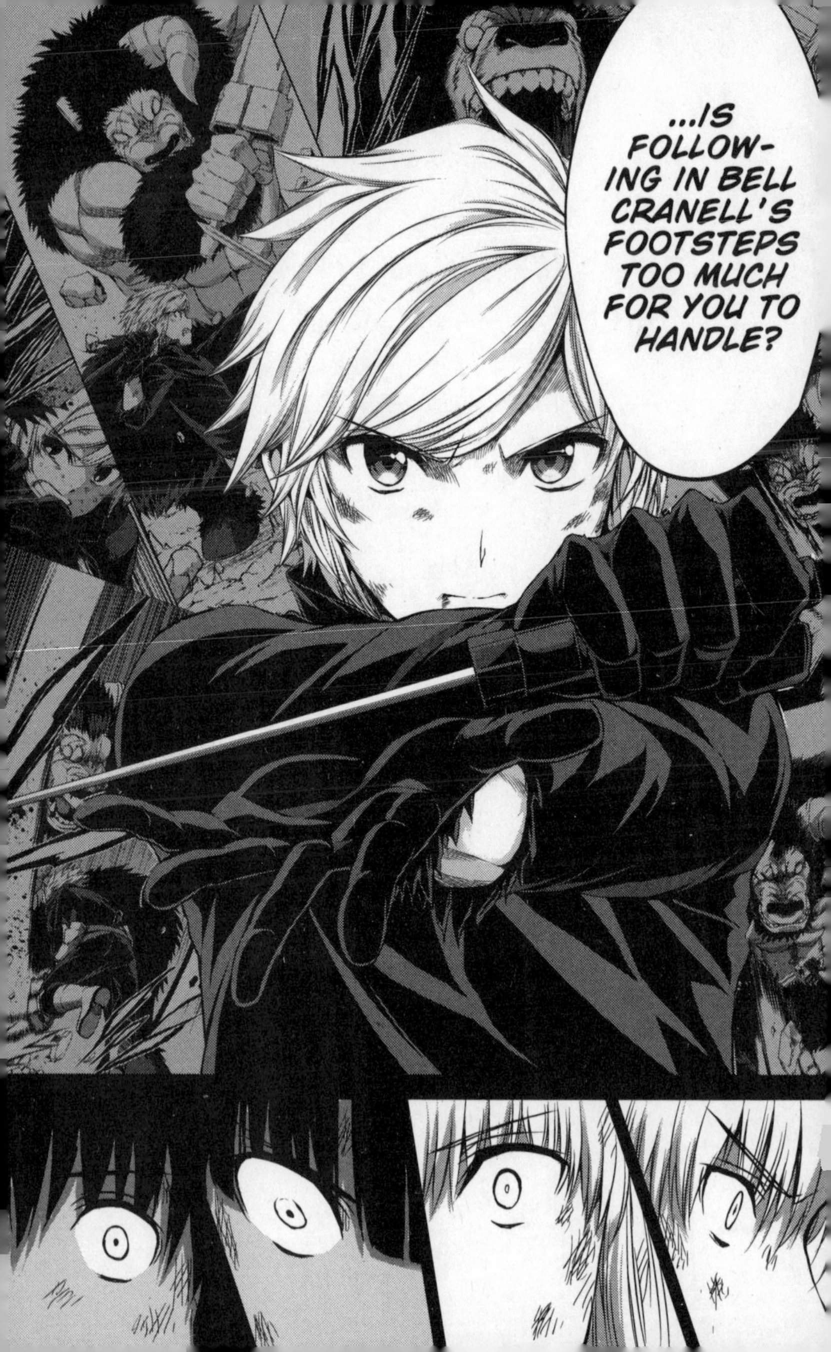
...IS FOLLOWING IN BELL CRANELL'S FOOTSTEPS TOO MUCH FOR YOU TO HANDLE?

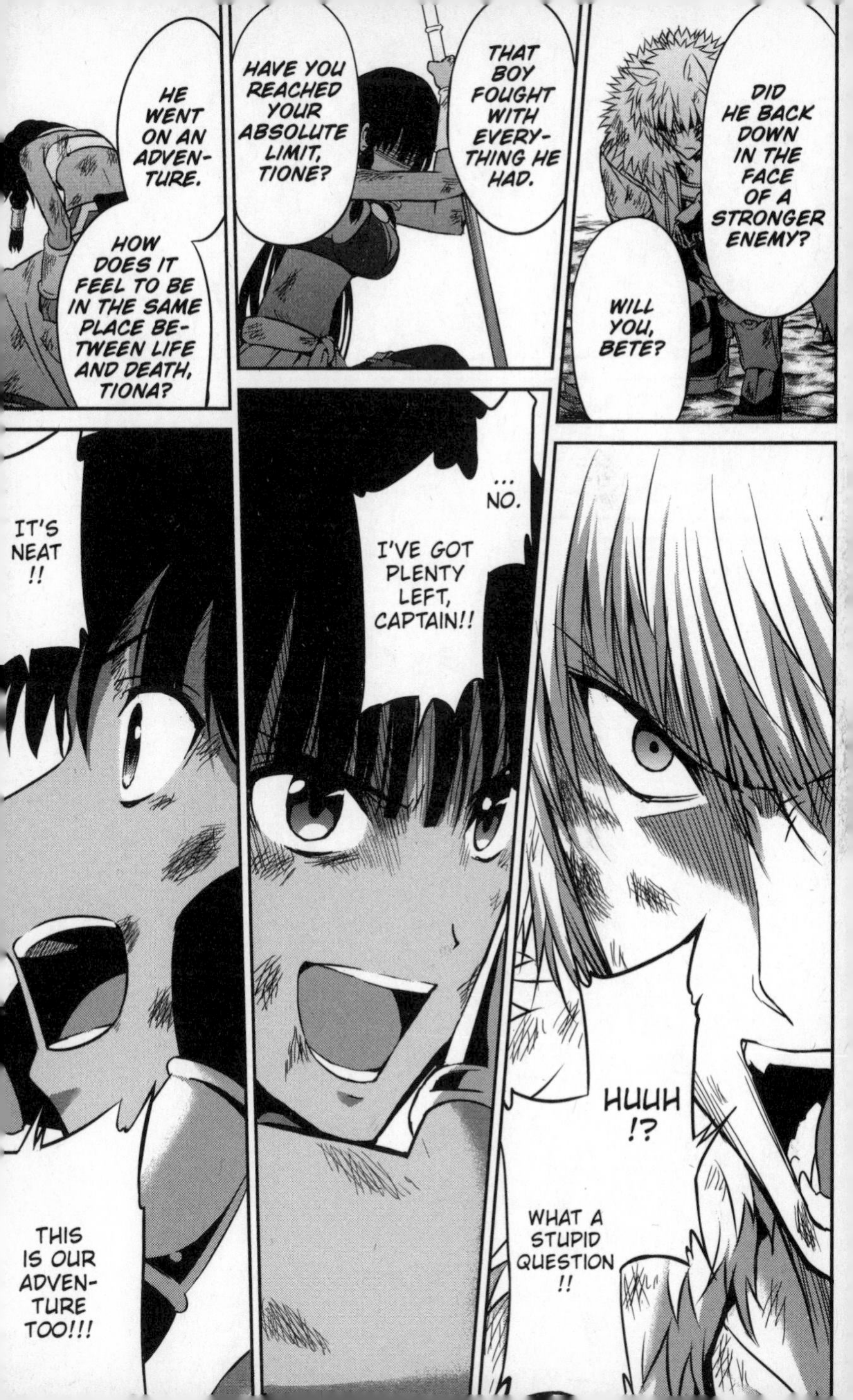
DID HE BACK DOWN IN THE FACE OF A STRONGER ENEMY?
WILL YOU, BETE?
THAT BOY FOUGHT WITH EVERY-THING HE HAD.
HAVE YOU REACHED YOUR ABSOLUTE LIMIT, TIONE?
HE WENT ON AN ADVEN-TURE.
HOW DOES IT FEEL TO BE IN THE SAME PLACE BE-TWEEN LIFE AND DEATH, TIONA?
HUUH!?
WHAT A STUPID QUESTION!!
...NO.
I'VE GOT PLENTY LEFT, CAPTAIN!!
IT'S NEAT!!
THIS IS OUR ADVEN-TURE TOO!!!

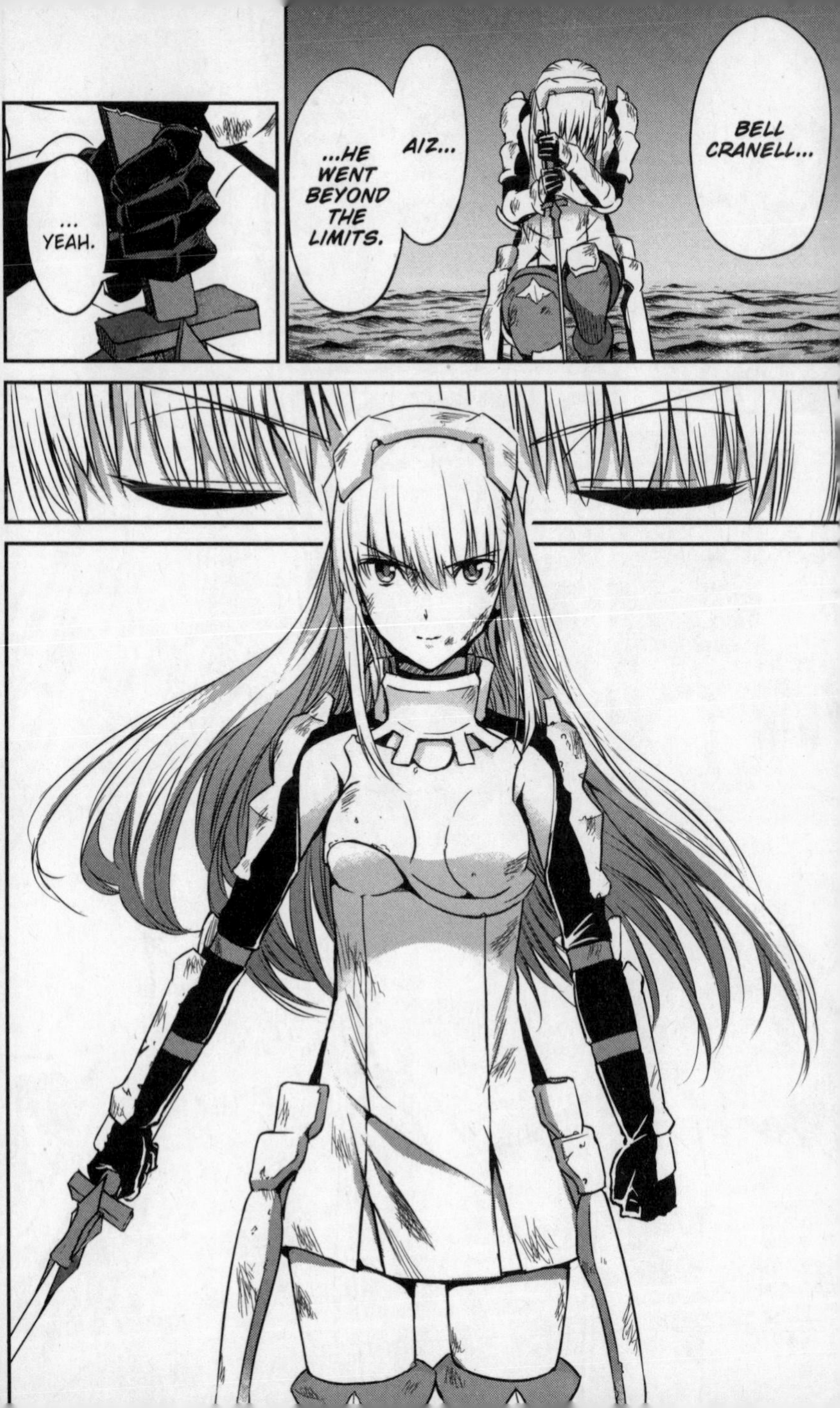
BELL CRANELL...
AIZ...
...HE WENT BEYOND THE LIMITS.
... YEAH.

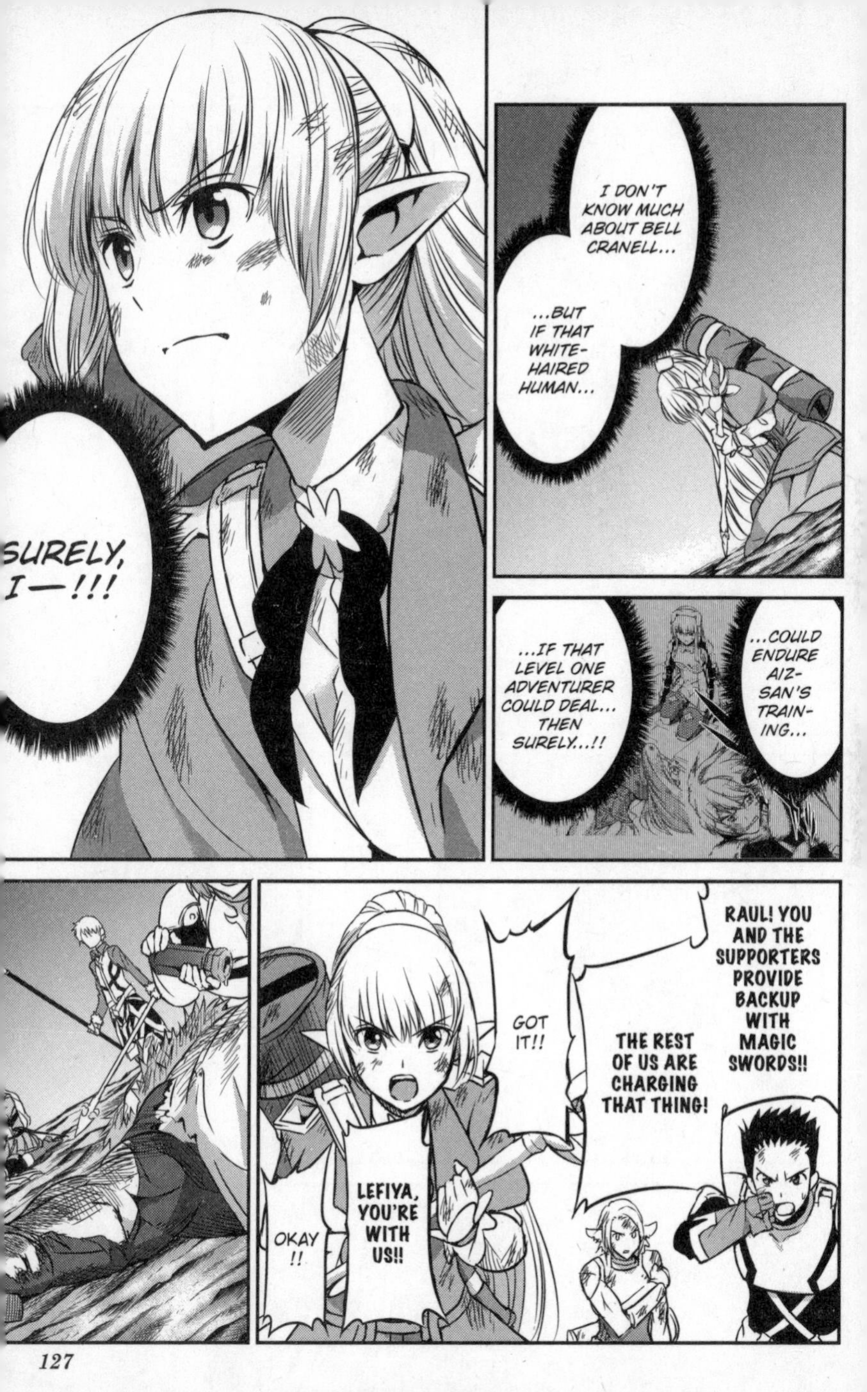
I DON'T KNOW MUCH ABOUT BELL CRANELL...
...BUT IF THAT WHITE-HAIRED HUMAN...
...COULD ENDURE AIZ-SAN'S TRAIN-ING...
...IF THAT LEVEL ONE ADVENTURER COULD DEAL... THEN SURELY...!!
SURELY, I—!!!
RAUL! YOU AND THE SUPPORTERS PROVIDE BACKUP WITH MAGIC SWORDS!!
THE REST OF US ARE CHARGING THAT THING!
GOT IT!!
LEFIYA, YOU'RE WITH US!!
OKAY!!

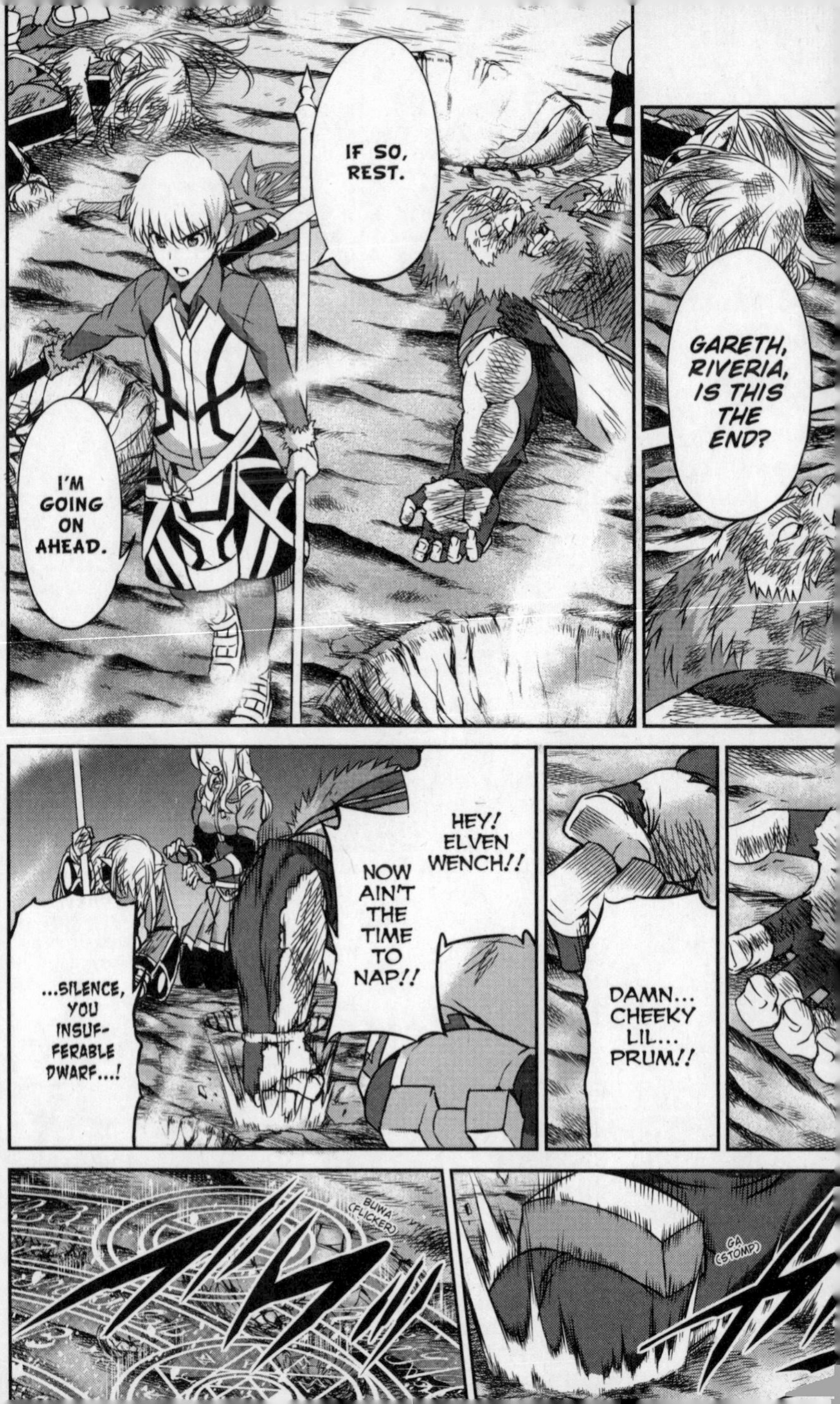
GARETH, RIVERIA, IS THIS THE END?
IF SO, REST.
I'M GOING ON AHEAD.
DAMN... CHEEKY LIL... PRUM!!
HEY! ELVEN WENCH!!
NOW AIN'T THE TIME TO NAP!!
...SILENCE, YOU INSUF-FERABLE DWARF...!
GA (STOMP)
BUWA (FLICKER)

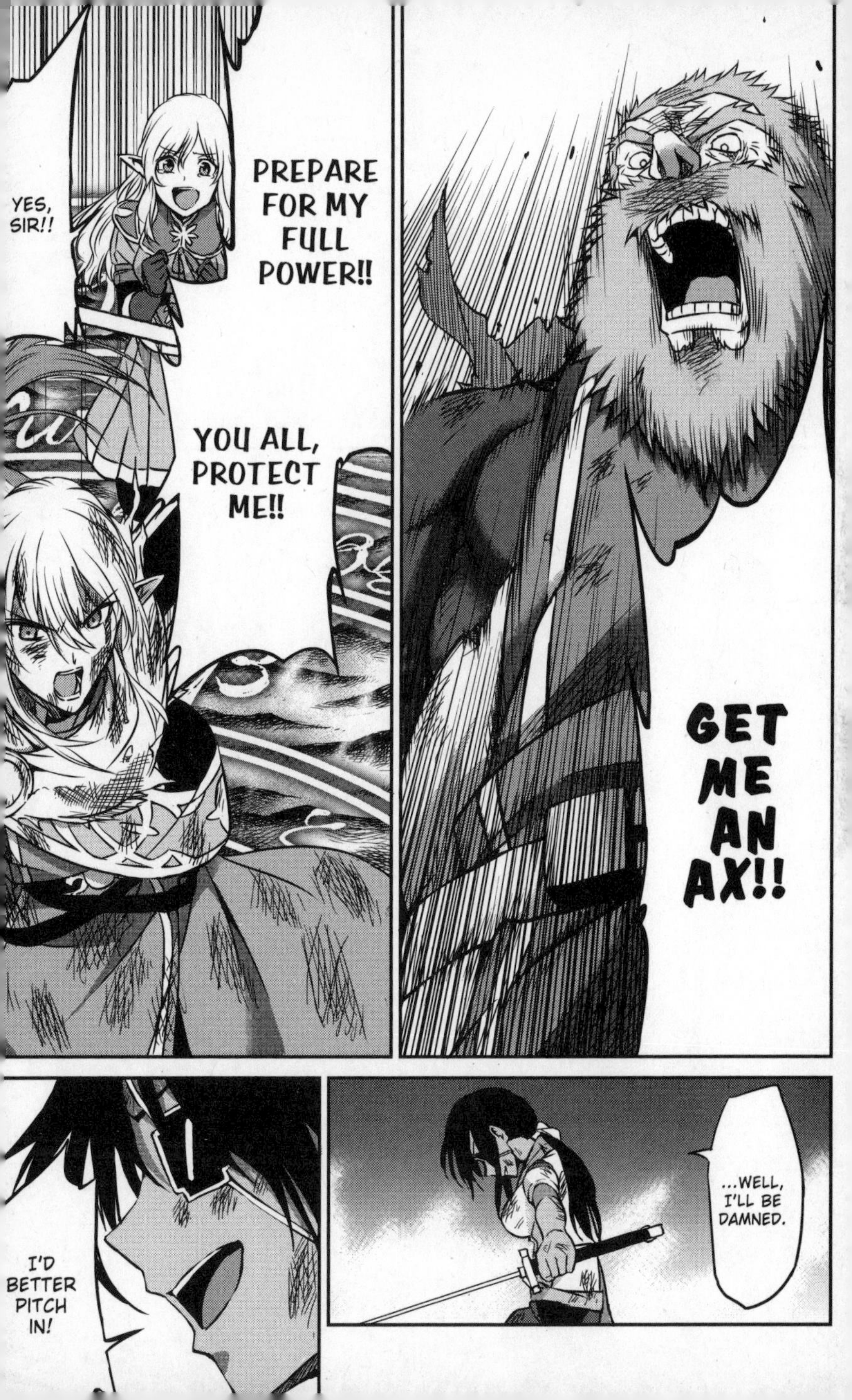
GET ME AN AX!!
PREPARE FOR MY FULL POWER!!
YES, SIR!!
YOU ALL, PROTECT ME!!
...WELL, I'LL BE DAMNED.
I'D BETTER PITCH IN!

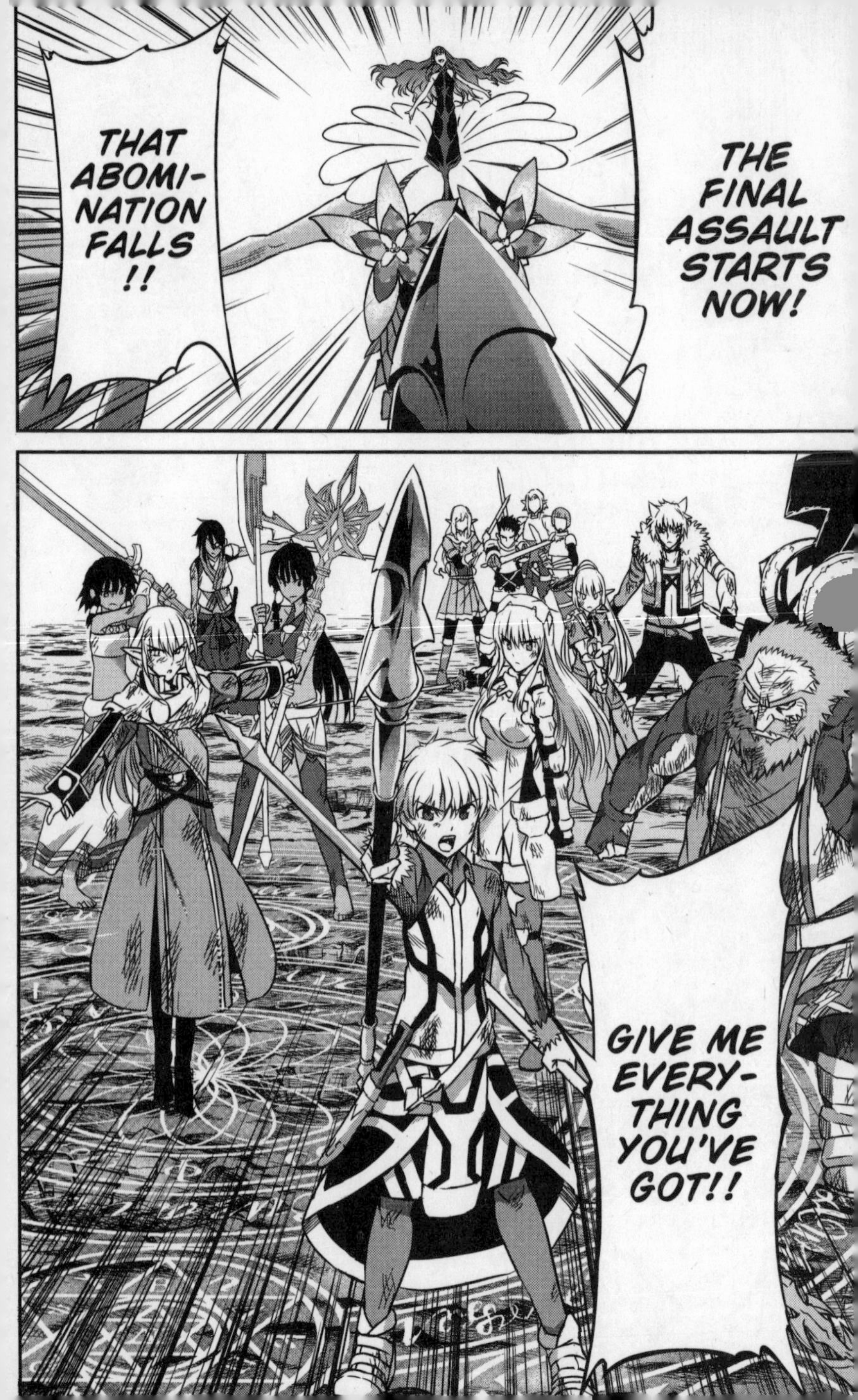
THE FINAL ASSAULT STARTS NOW!
THAT ABOMI-NATION FALLS !!
GIVE ME EVERY-THING YOU'VE GOT!!

Is it **WRONG** to try to **PICK-UP** GIRLS IN A **DUNGEON**? ON THE SIDE

Sword Oratoria

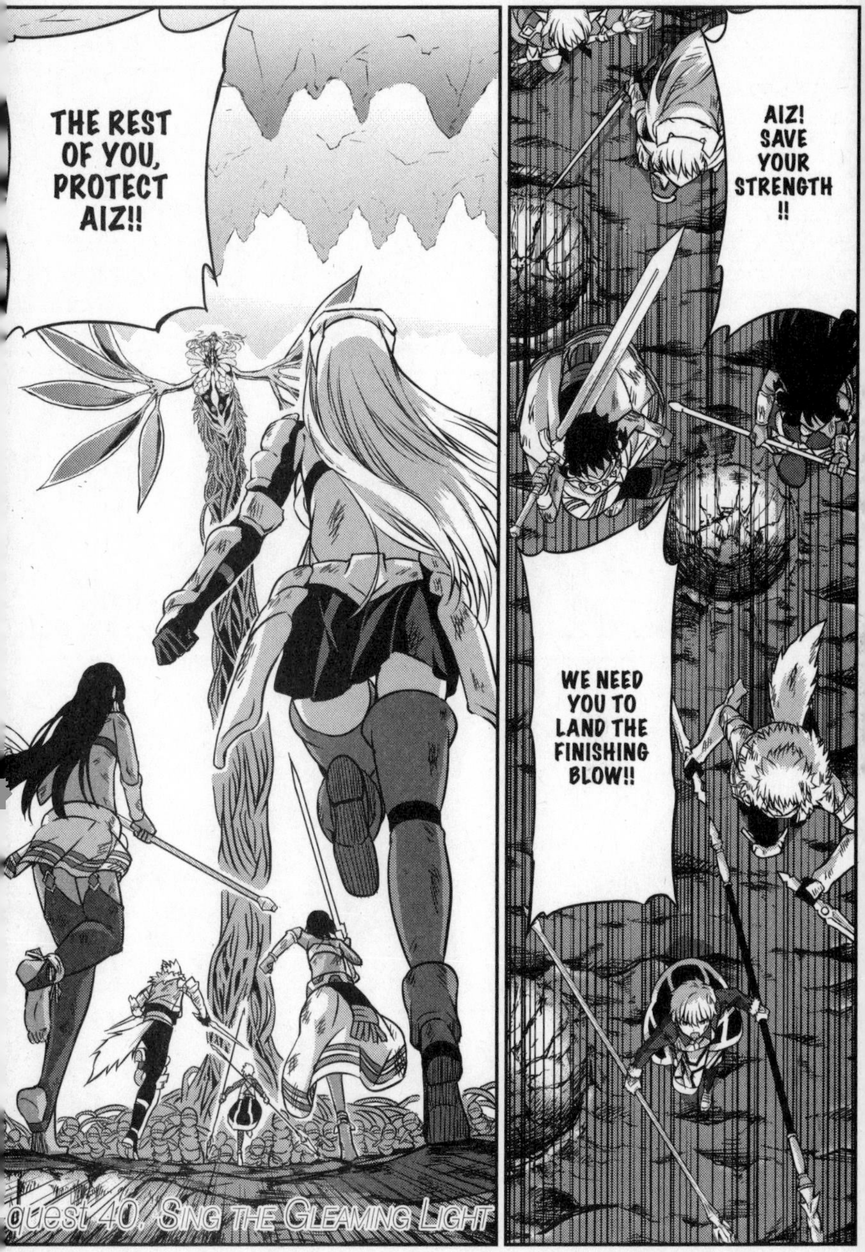
AIZ! SAVE YOUR STRENGTH!!
WE NEED YOU TO LAND THE FINISHING BLOW!!
THE REST OF YOU, PROTECT AIZ!!
quest 40: Sing the Gleaming Light

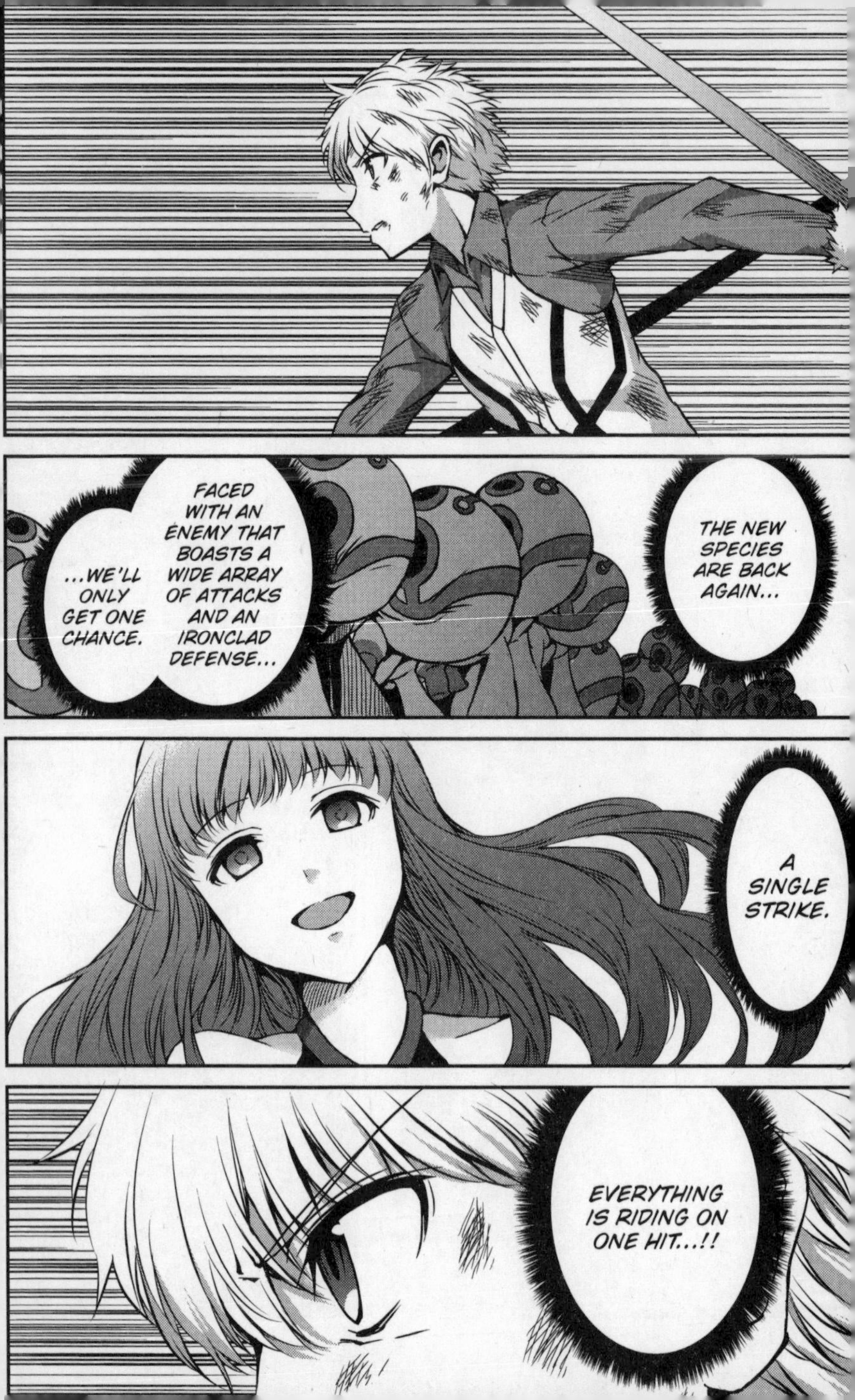
THE NEW SPECIES ARE BACK AGAIN...
FACED WITH AN ENEMY THAT BOASTS A WIDE ARRAY OF ATTACKS AND AN IRONCLAD DEFENSE...
...WE'LL ONLY GET ONE CHANCE.
A SINGLE STRIKE.
EVERYTHING IS RIDING ON ONE HIT...!!

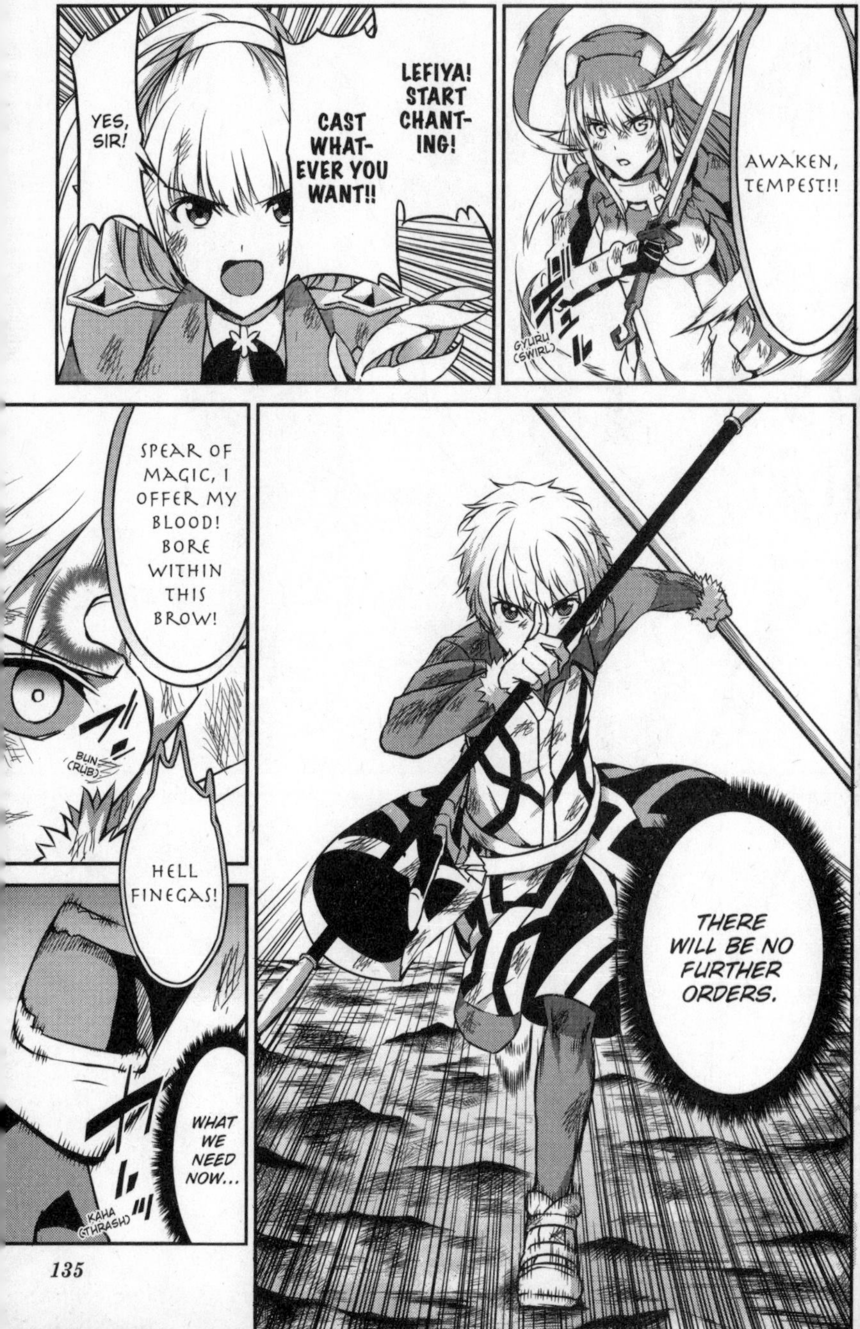
AWAKEN, TEMPEST!!
GYURU (SWIRL)
LEFIYA! START CHANT-ING!
CAST WHAT-EVER YOU WANT!!
YES, SIR!
THERE WILL BE NO FURTHER ORDERS.
SPEAR OF MAGIC, I OFFER MY BLOOD! BORE WITHIN THIS BROW!
BUN (RUB)
HELL FINEGAS!
WHAT WE NEED NOW...
KAHA (THRASH)

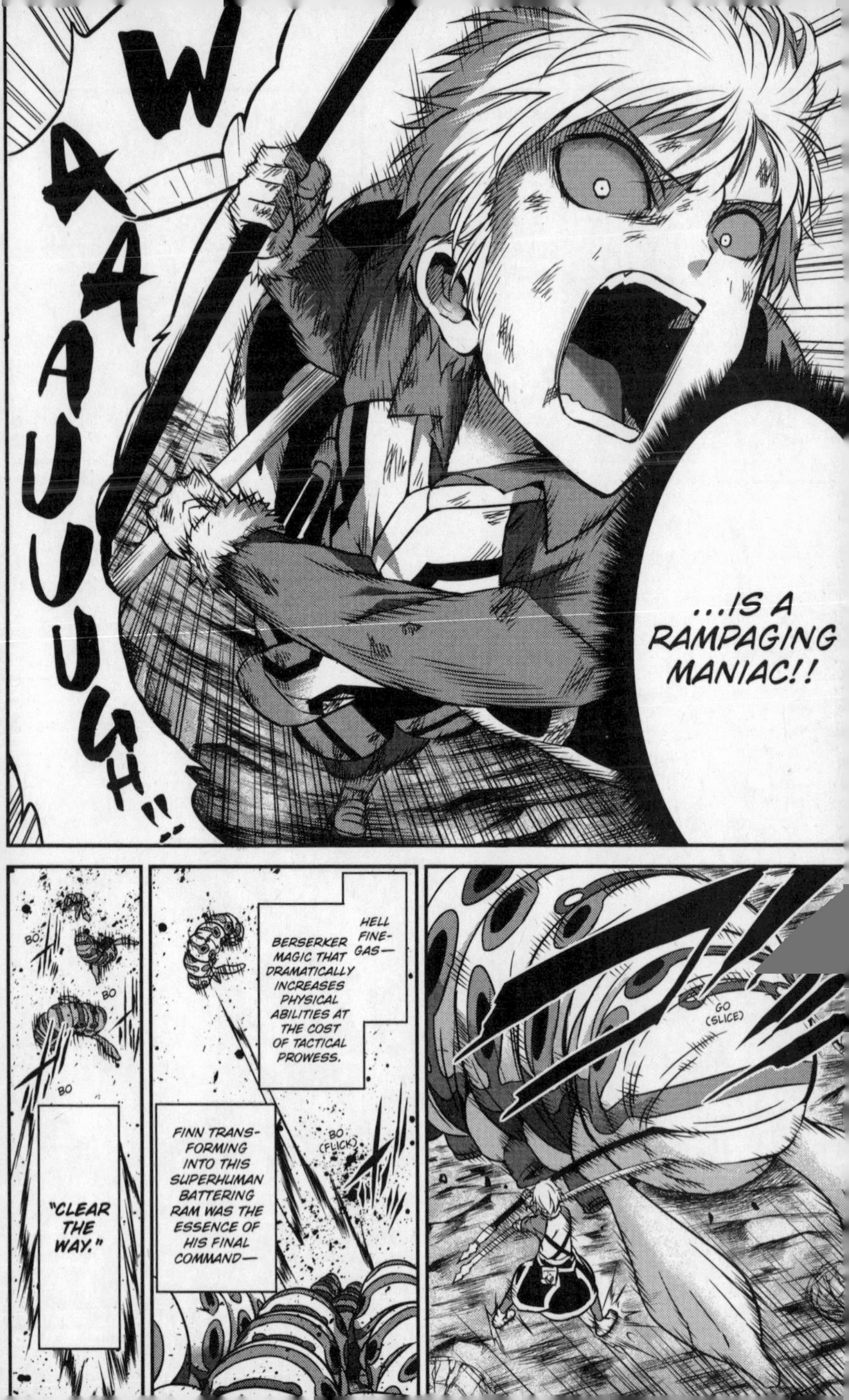
...IS A RAMPAGING MANIAC!!
WAAAUUUGH!!
GO (SLICE)
HELL FINE-GAS—
BERSERKER MAGIC THAT DRAMATICALLY INCREASES PHYSICAL ABILITIES AT THE COST OF TACTICAL PROWESS.
BO (FLICK)
FINN TRANS-FORMING INTO THIS SUPERHUMAN BATTERING RAM WAS THE ESSENCE OF HIS FINAL COMMAND—
BO
BO
BO
"CLEAR THE WAY."

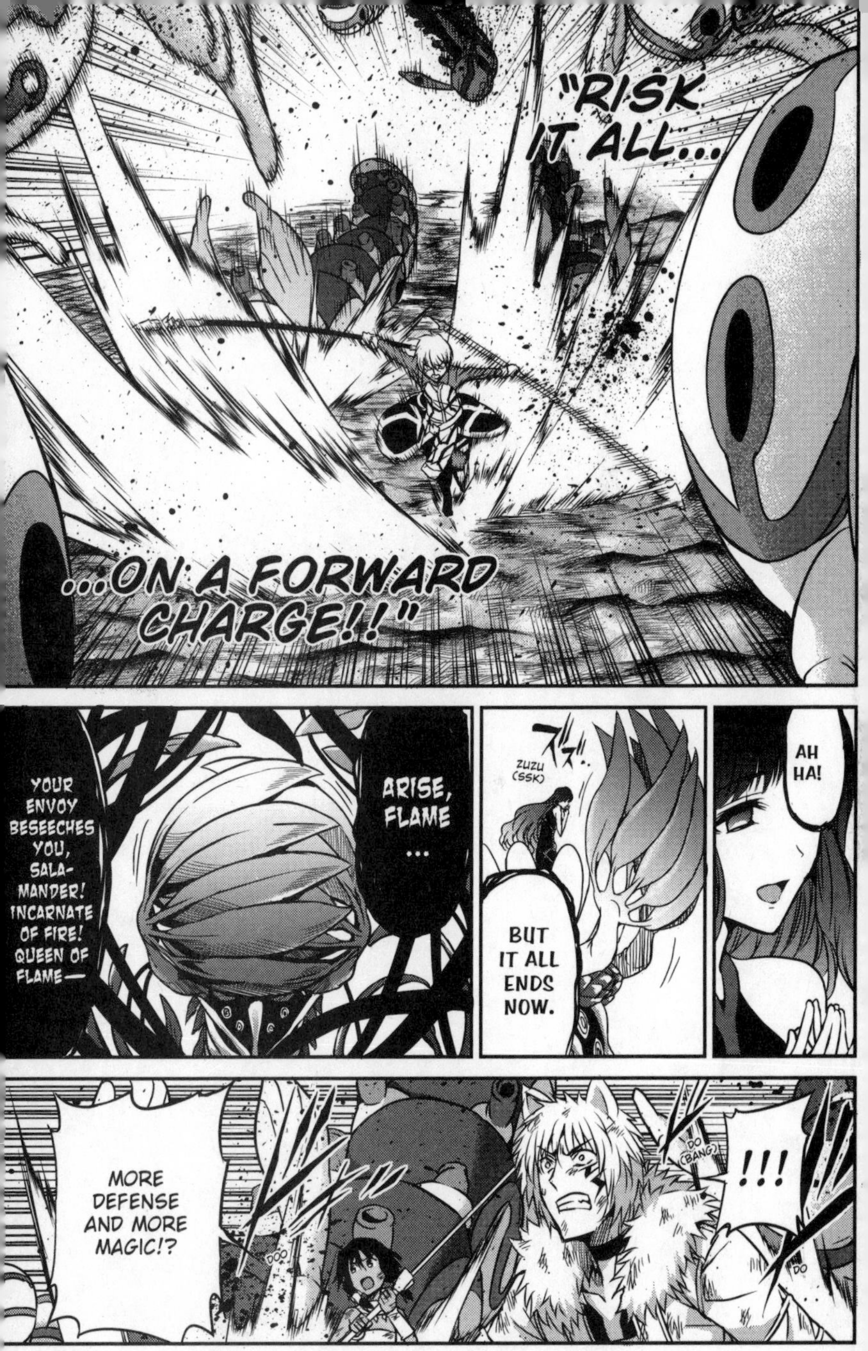
"RISK IT ALL...
...ON A FORWARD CHARGE!!"
AH HA!
ZUZU (SSK)
BUT IT ALL ENDS NOW.
ARISE, FLAME ...
YOUR ENVOY BESEECHES YOU, SALAMANDER! INCARNATE OF FIRE! QUEEN OF FLAME—
DO (BANG)
!!!
MORE DEFENSE AND MORE MAGIC!?
DOO
DO

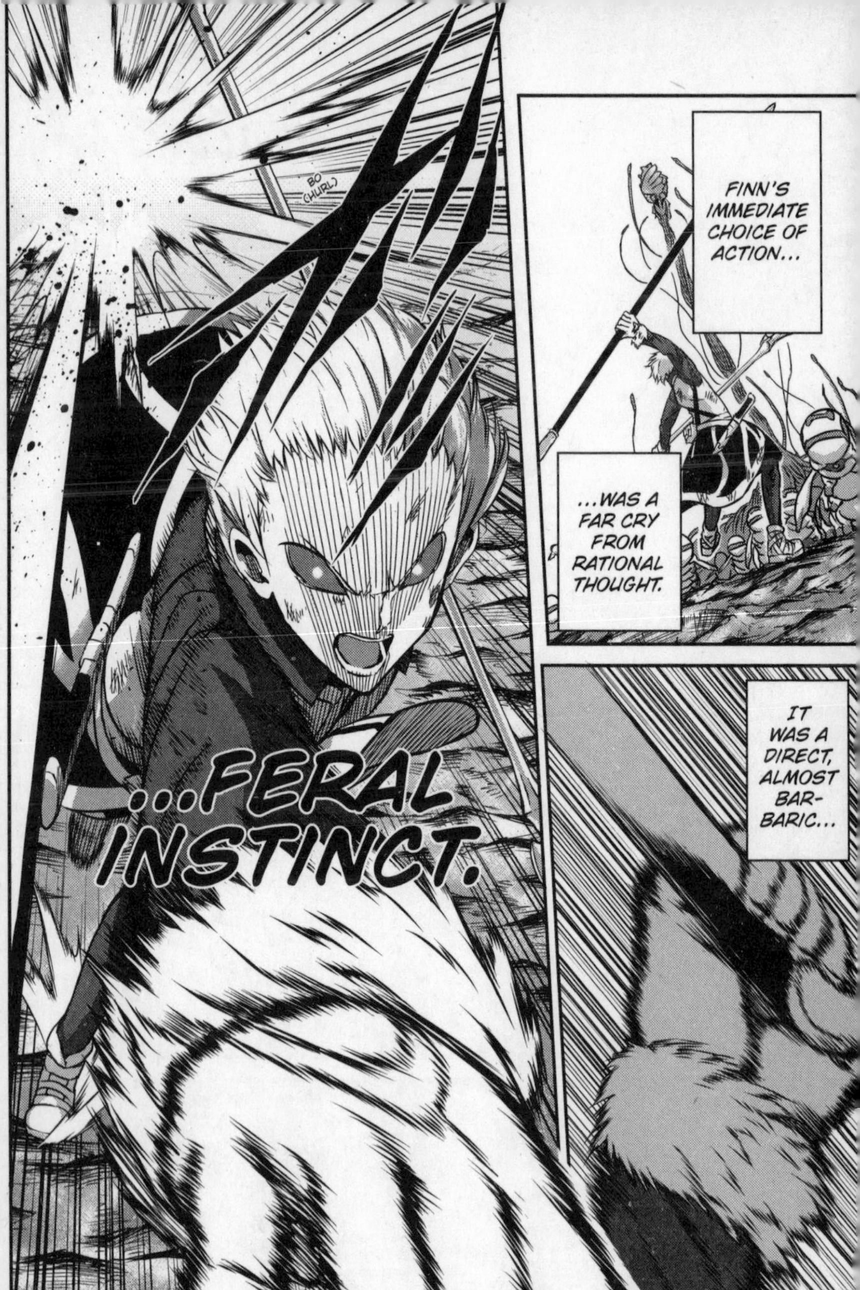

FINN'S IMMEDIATE CHOICE OF ACTION...
...WAS A FAR CRY FROM RATIONAL THOUGHT.
IT WAS A DIRECT, ALMOST BAR-BARIC...
BO (HURL)
...FERAL INSTINCT.

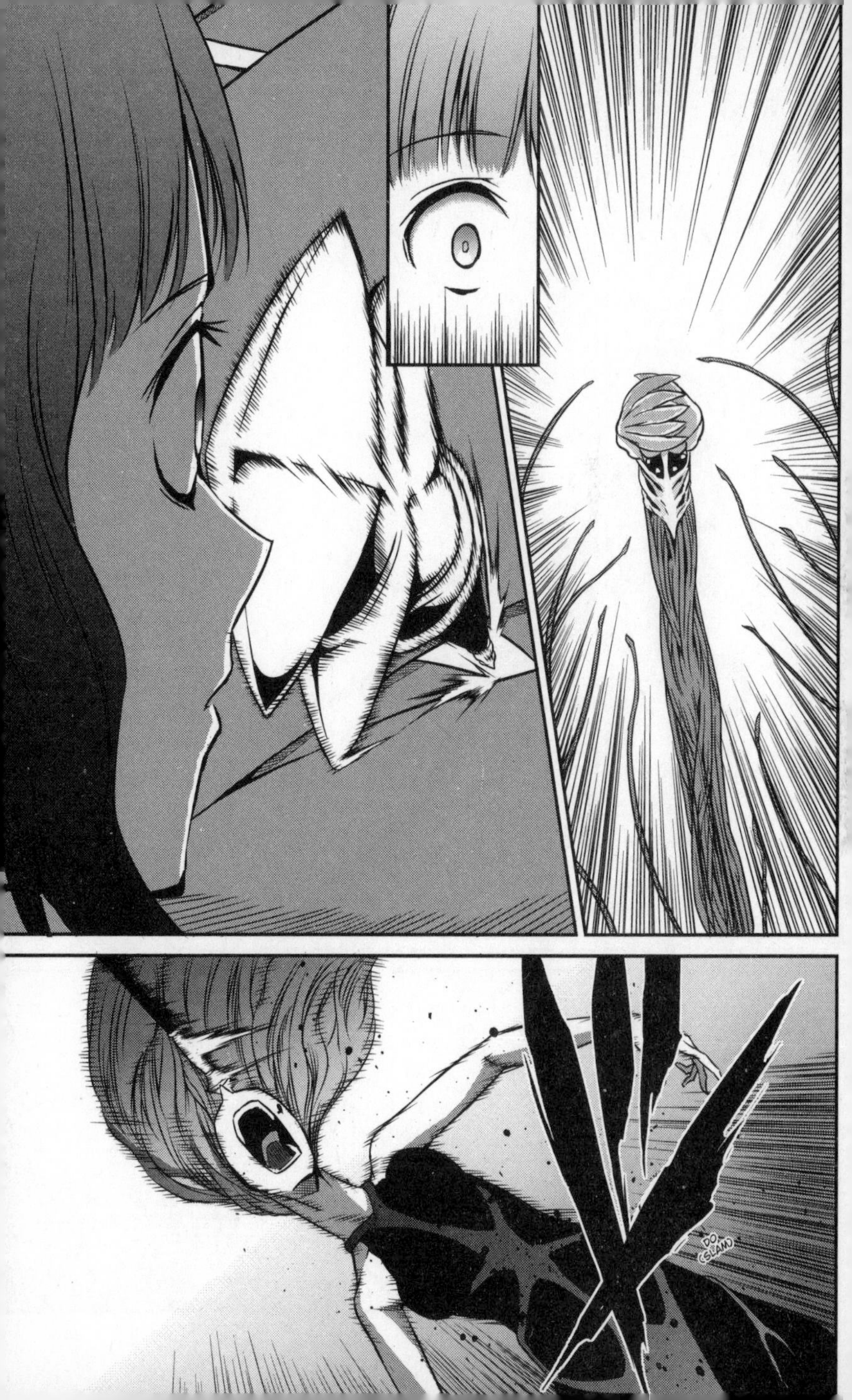
DO
(SLAM)

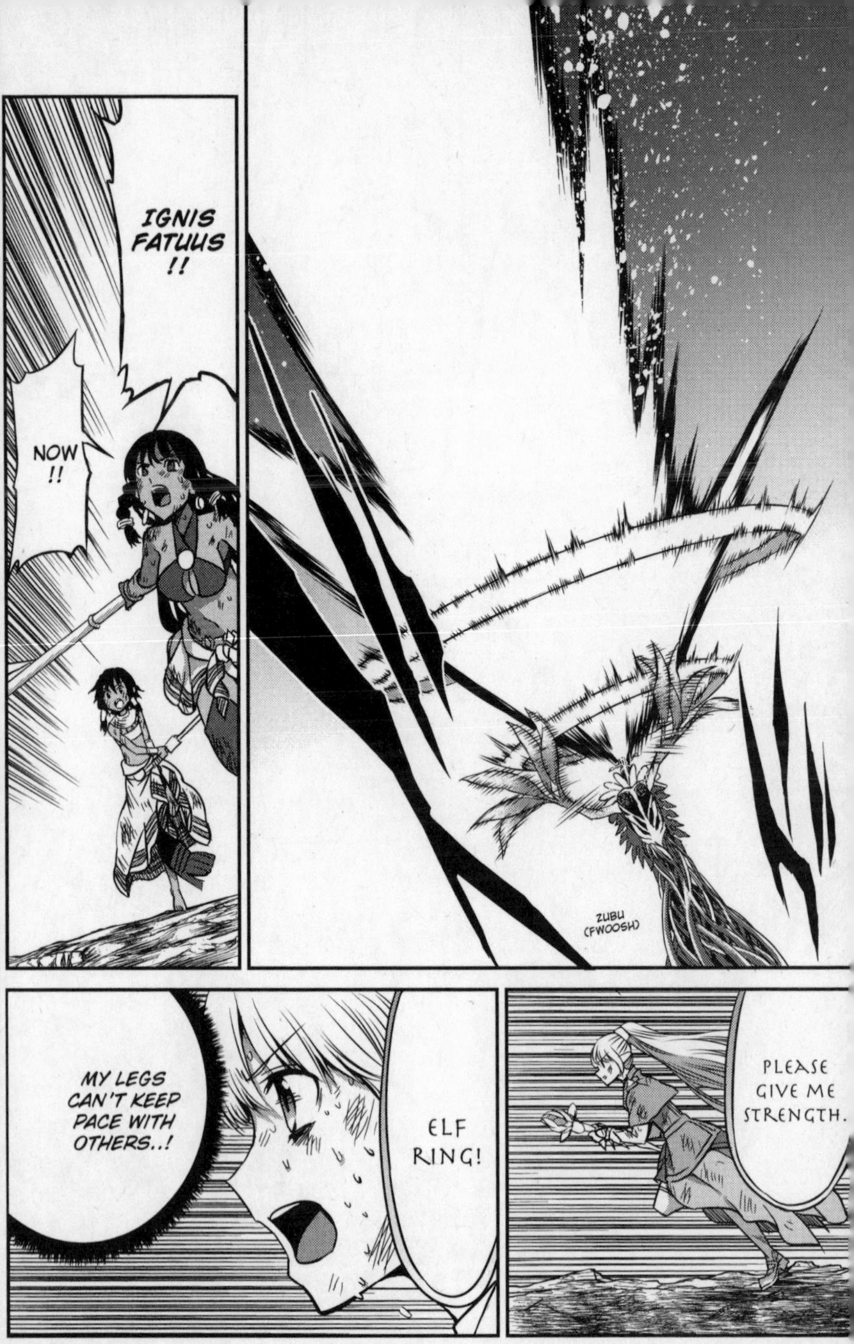
ZUBU (FWOOSH)
IGNIS FATUUS !!
NOW !!
PLEASE GIVE ME STRENGTH.
ELF RING!
MY LEGS CAN'T KEEP PACE WITH OTHERS..!

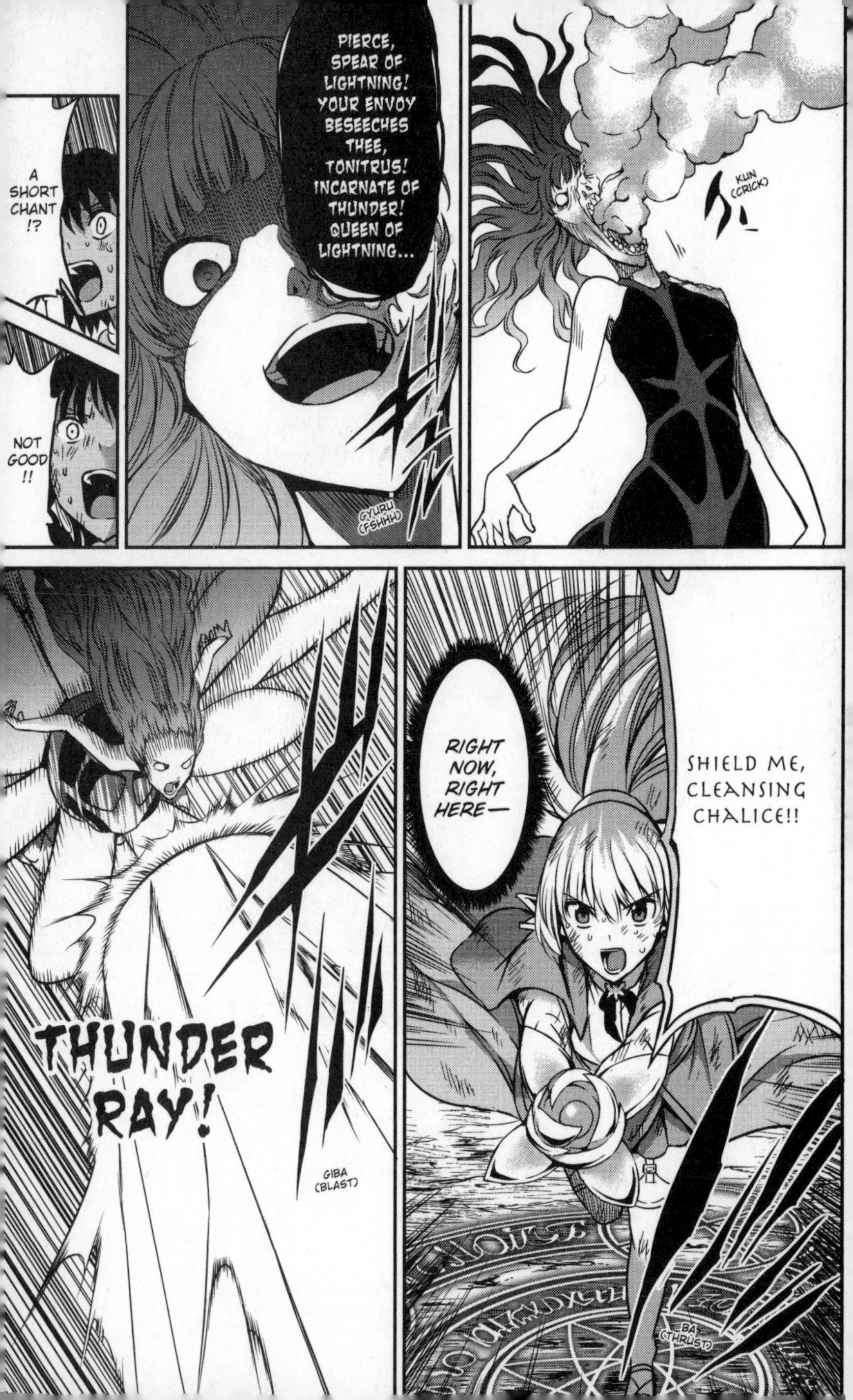
KUN (CRICK)
PIERCE, SPEAR OF LIGHTNING! YOUR ENVOY BESEECHES THEE, TONITRUS! INCARNATE OF THUNDER! QUEEN OF LIGHTNING...
GYURU (FSHHH)
A SHORT CHANT !?
NOT GOOD !!
RIGHT NOW, RIGHT HERE—
SHIELD ME, CLEANSING CHALICE!!
BA (THRUST)
THUNDER RAY!
GIBA (BLAST)

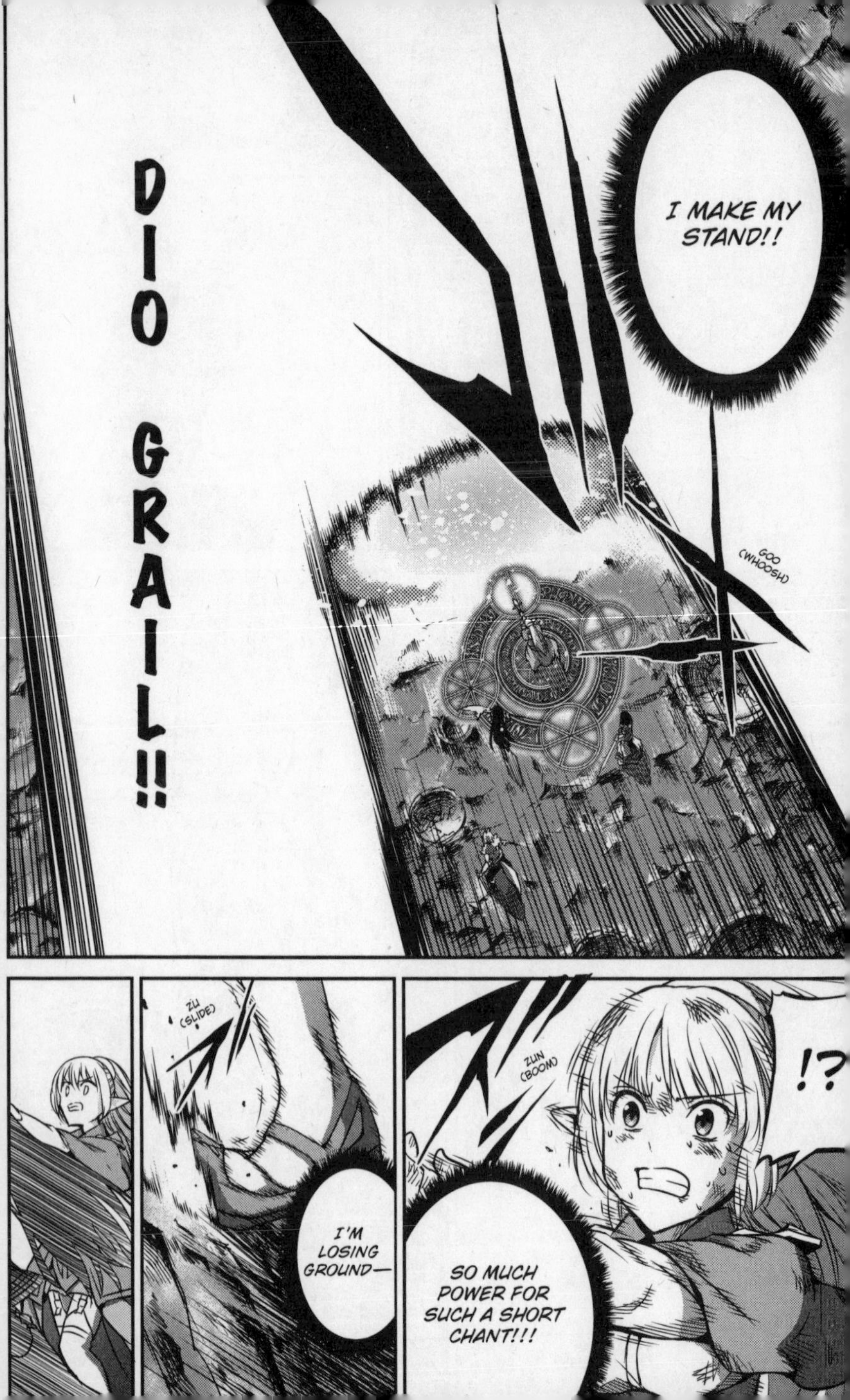
I MAKE MY STAND!!
DIO GRAIL!!
GOO (WHOOSH)
!?
ZUN (BOOM)
SO MUCH POWER FOR SUCH A SHORT CHANT!!!
I'M LOSING GROUND—
ZU (SLIDE)

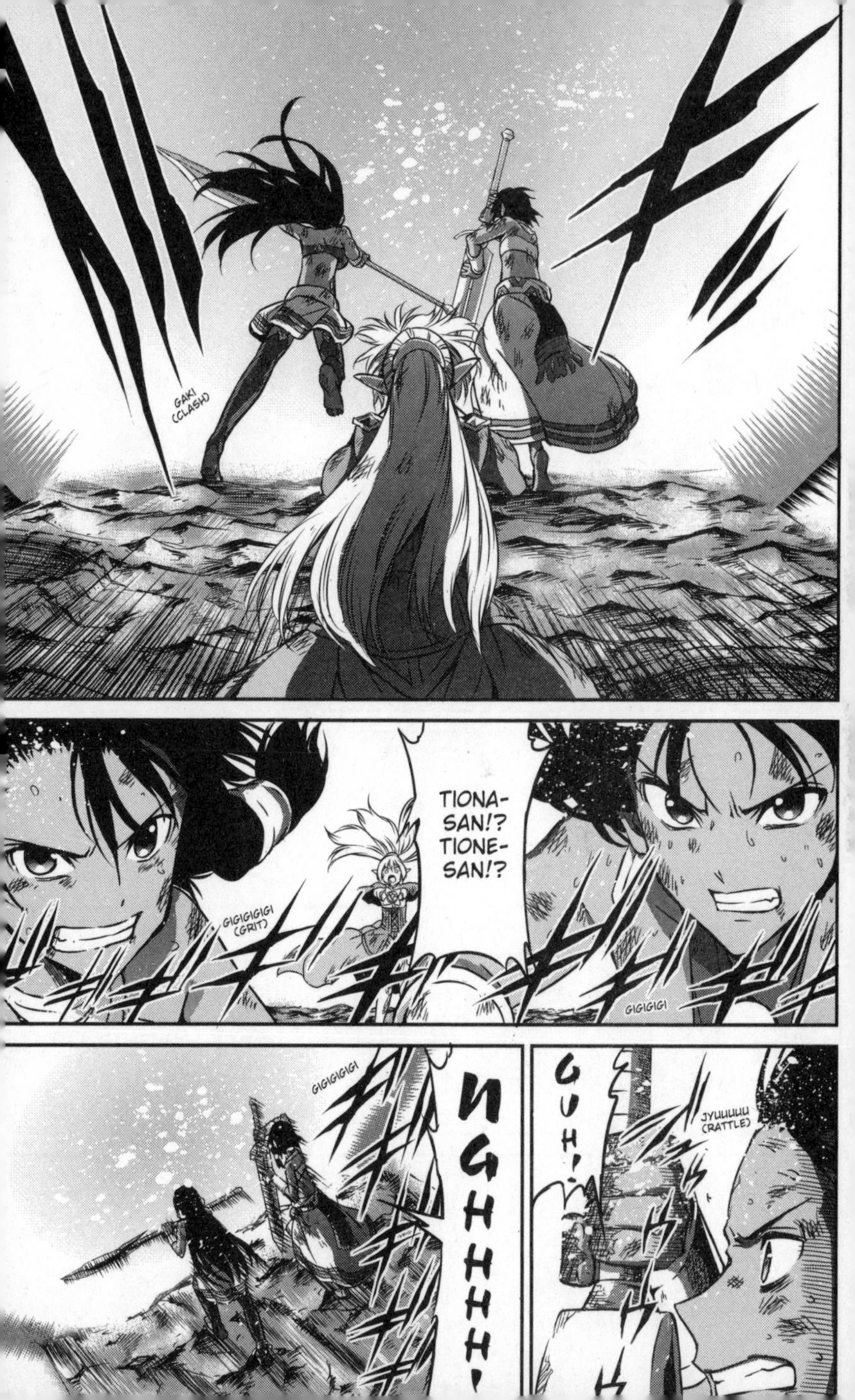
GAKI
(CLASH)
TIONA-SAN!? TIONE-SAN!?
GIGIGIGI
(GRIT)
GIGIGIGI
GUH!
JYUUUUU
(RATTLE)
GIGIGIGI
NGHHHH!

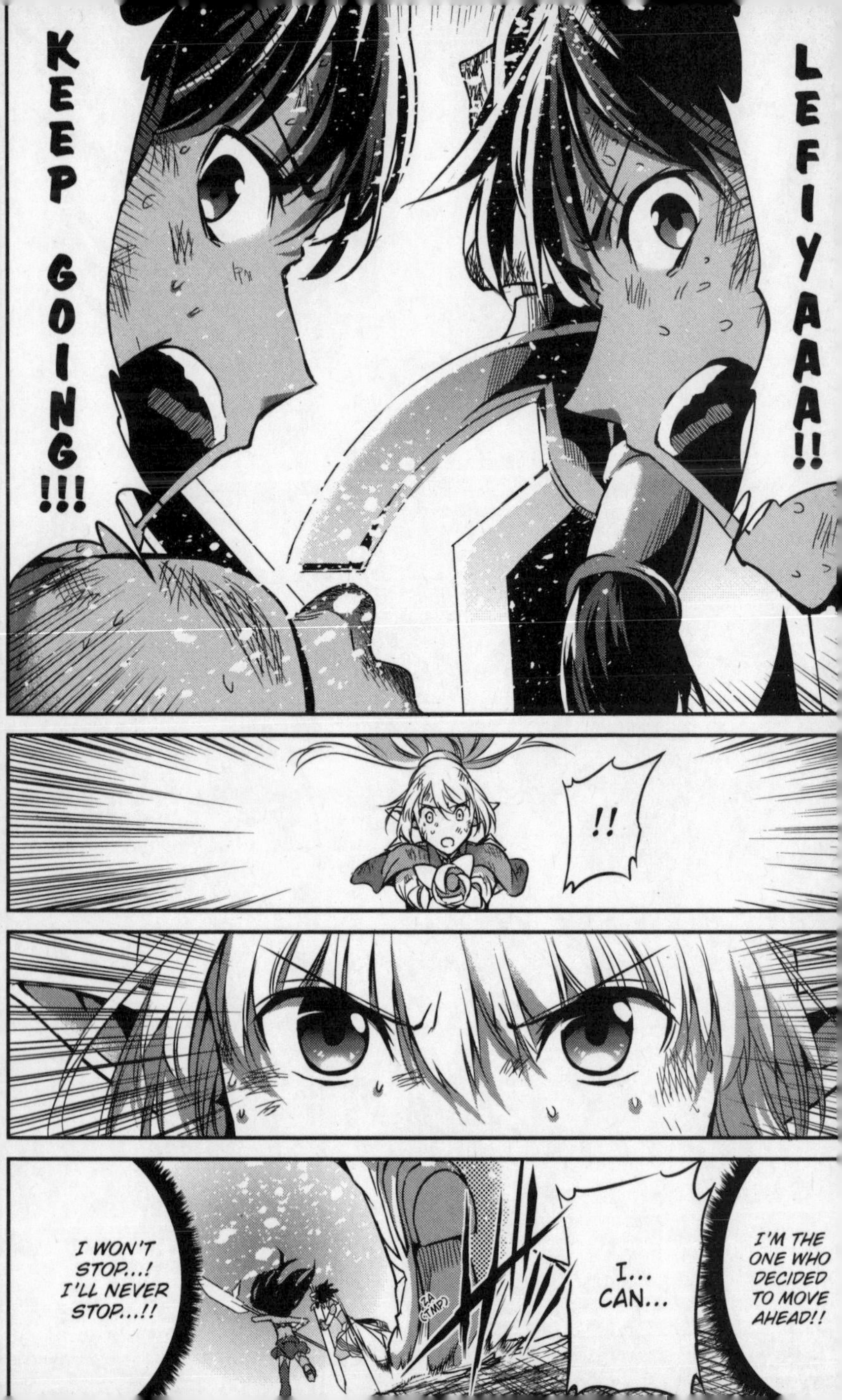
LEFIYAAA!!
KEEP GOING!!!
!!
I'M THE ONE WHO DECIDED TO MOVE AHEAD!!
I... CAN...
ZA (TMP)
I WON'T STOP...! I'LL NEVER STOP...!!

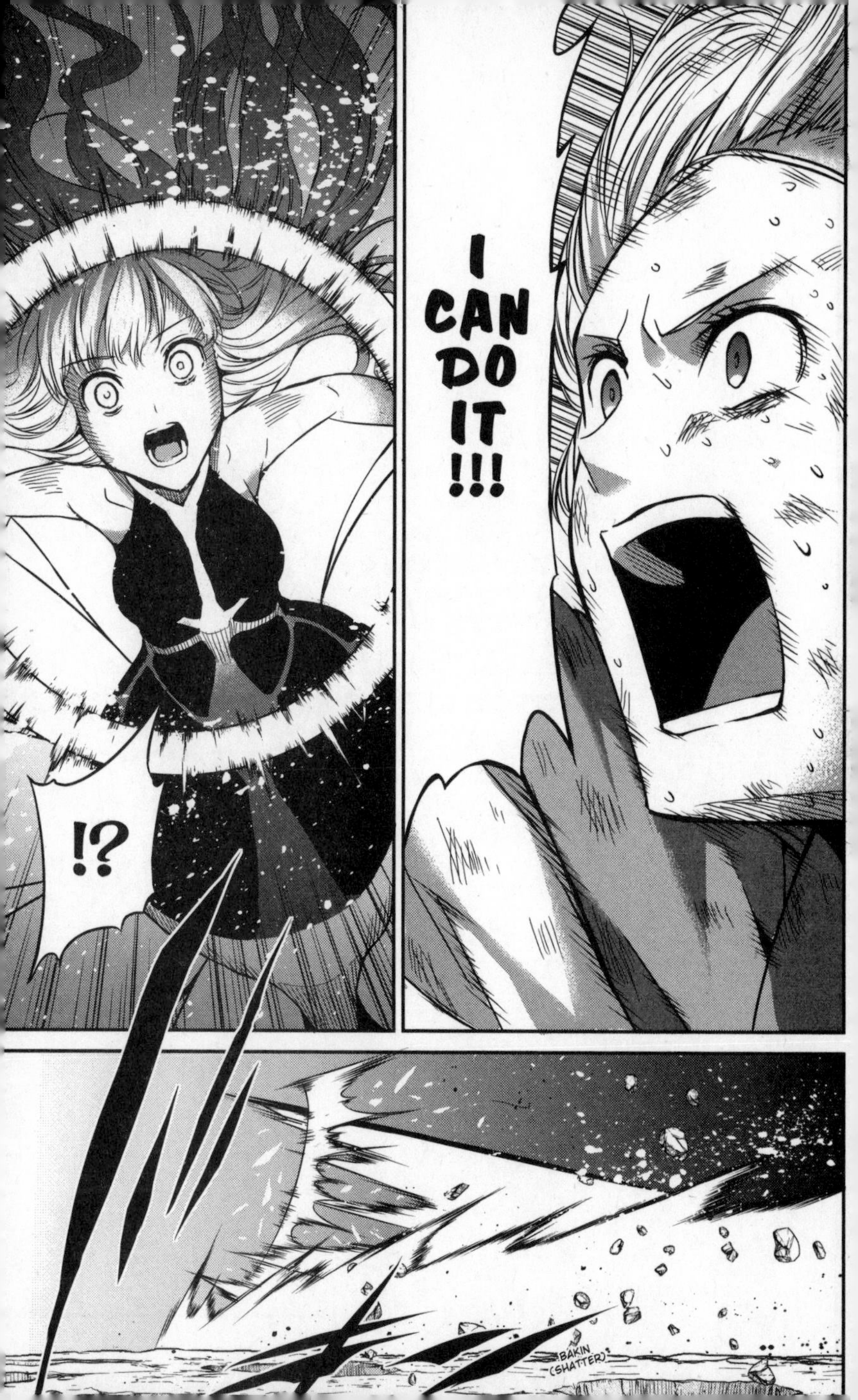
I CAN DO IT!!!
!?
BAKIN (SHATTER)

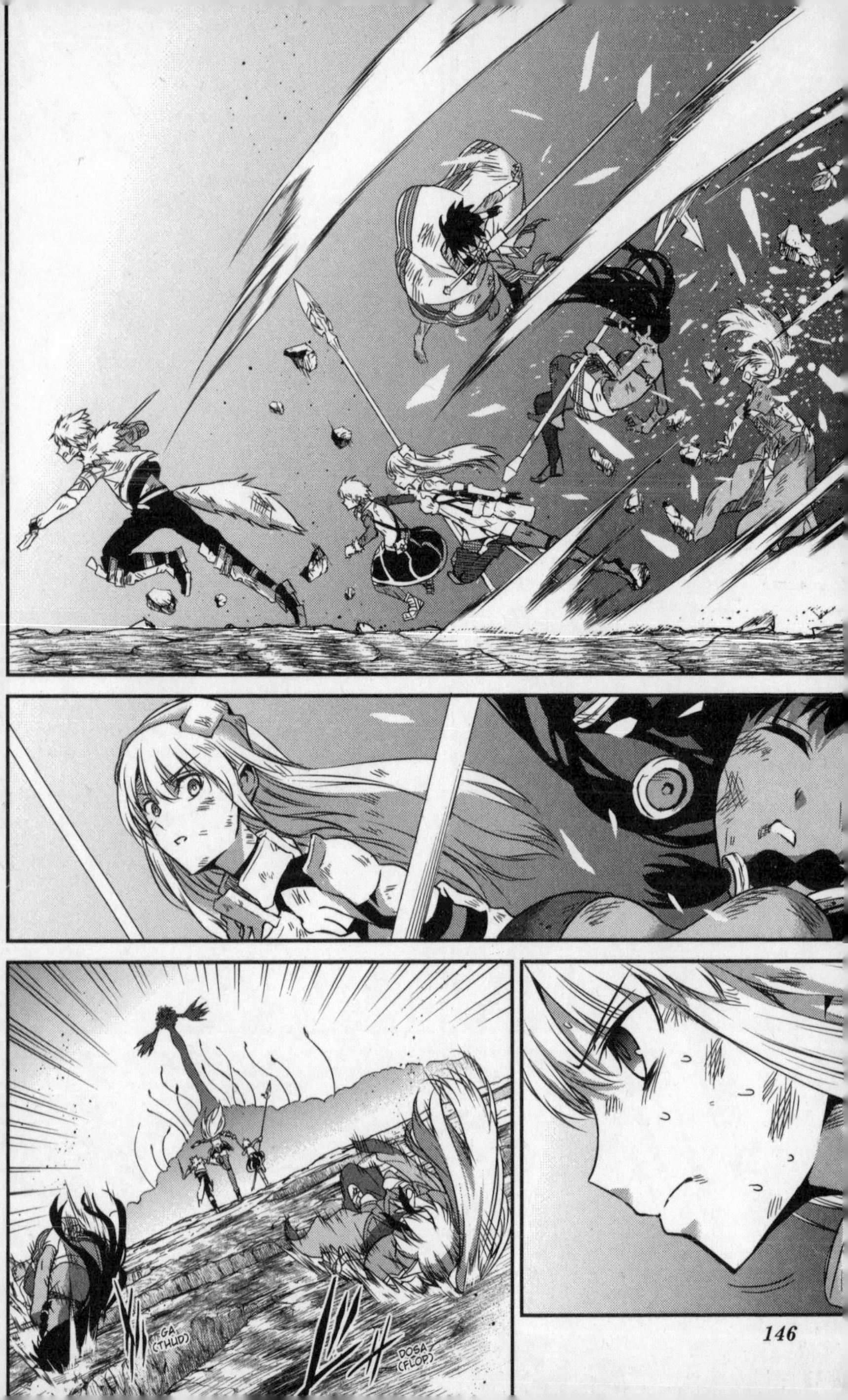
DOSA (FLOP)
GA (THUD)

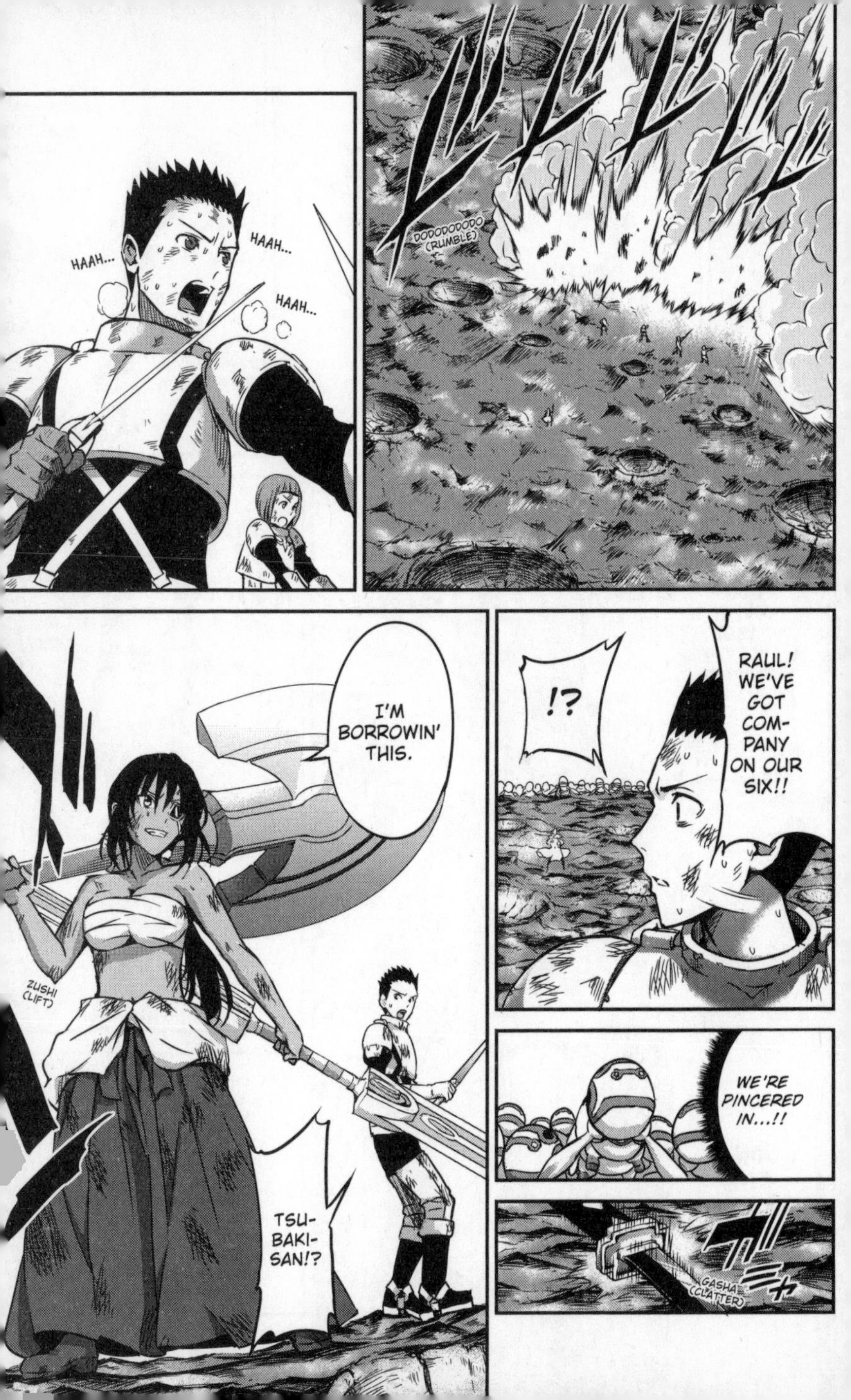
DODODODODO (RUMBLE)
HAAH...
HAAH...
HAAH...
RAUL! WE'VE GOT COM-PANY ON OUR SIX!!
!?
WE'RE PINCERED IN...!!
GASHA (CLATTER)
I'M BORROWIN' THIS.
ZUSHI (LIFT)
TSU-BAKI-SAN!?

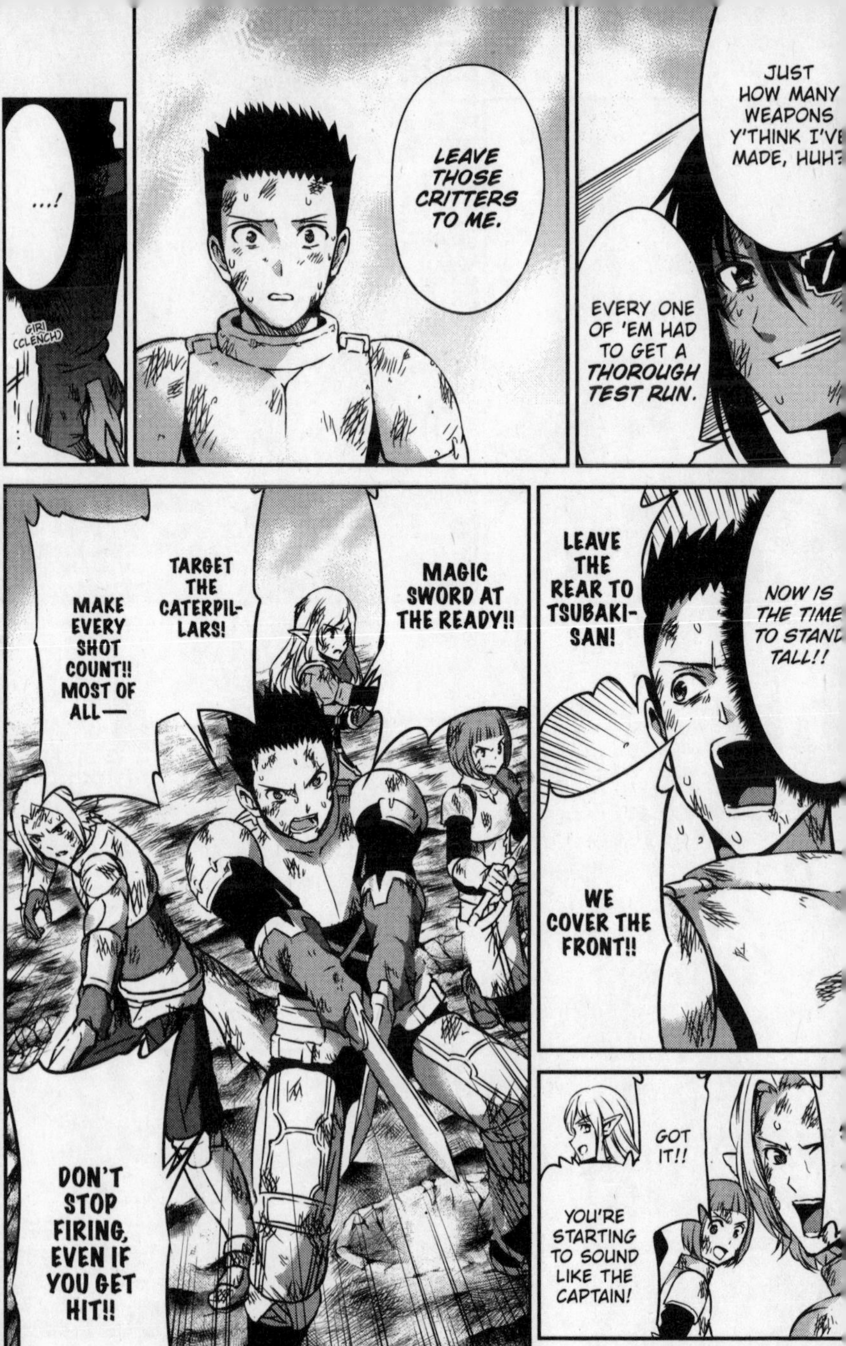
JUST HOW MANY WEAPONS Y'THINK I'VE MADE, HUH?
EVERY ONE OF 'EM HAD TO GET A *THOROUGH TEST RUN.*
LEAVE THOSE CRITTERS TO ME.
...!
GIRI (CLENCH)
NOW IS THE TIME TO STAND TALL!!
LEAVE THE REAR TO TSUBAKI-SAN!
WE COVER THE FRONT!!
GOT IT!!
YOU'RE STARTING TO SOUND LIKE THE CAPTAIN!
MAGIC SWORD AT THE READY!!
TARGET THE CATERPIL-LARS!
MAKE EVERY SHOT COUNT!! MOST OF ALL—
DON'T STOP FIRING, EVEN IF YOU GET HIT!!

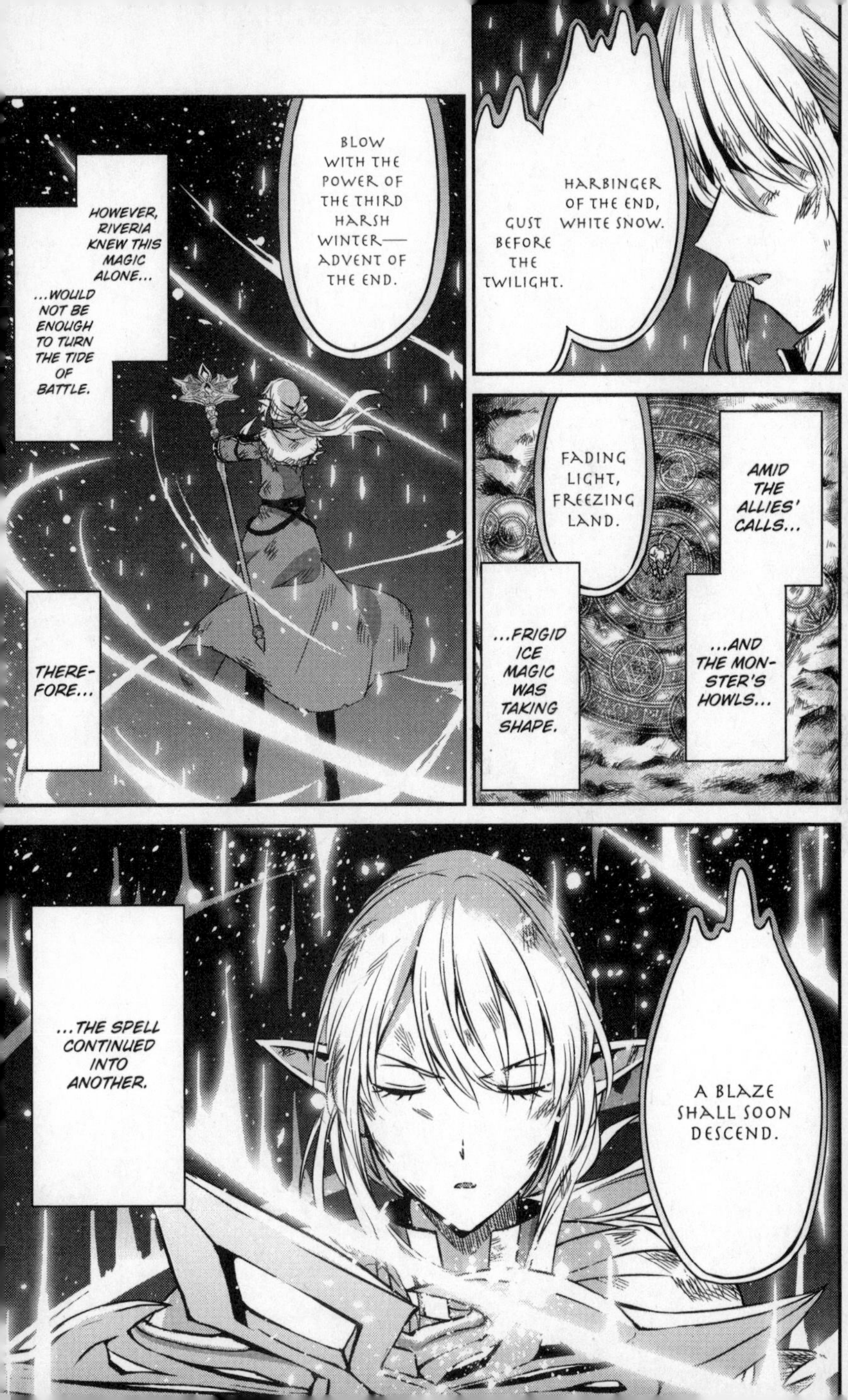
HARBINGER OF THE END, WHITE SNOW.
GUST BEFORE THE TWILIGHT.
AMID THE ALLIES' CALLS...
...AND THE MON-STER'S HOWLS...
FADING LIGHT, FREEZING LAND.
...FRIGID ICE MAGIC WAS TAKING SHAPE.
BLOW WITH THE POWER OF THE THIRD HARSH WINTER— ADVENT OF THE END.
HOWEVER, RIVERIA KNEW THIS MAGIC ALONE...
...WOULD NOT BE ENOUGH TO TURN THE TIDE OF BATTLE.
THERE-FORE...
A BLAZE SHALL SOON DESCEND.
...THE SPELL CONTINUED INTO ANOTHER.

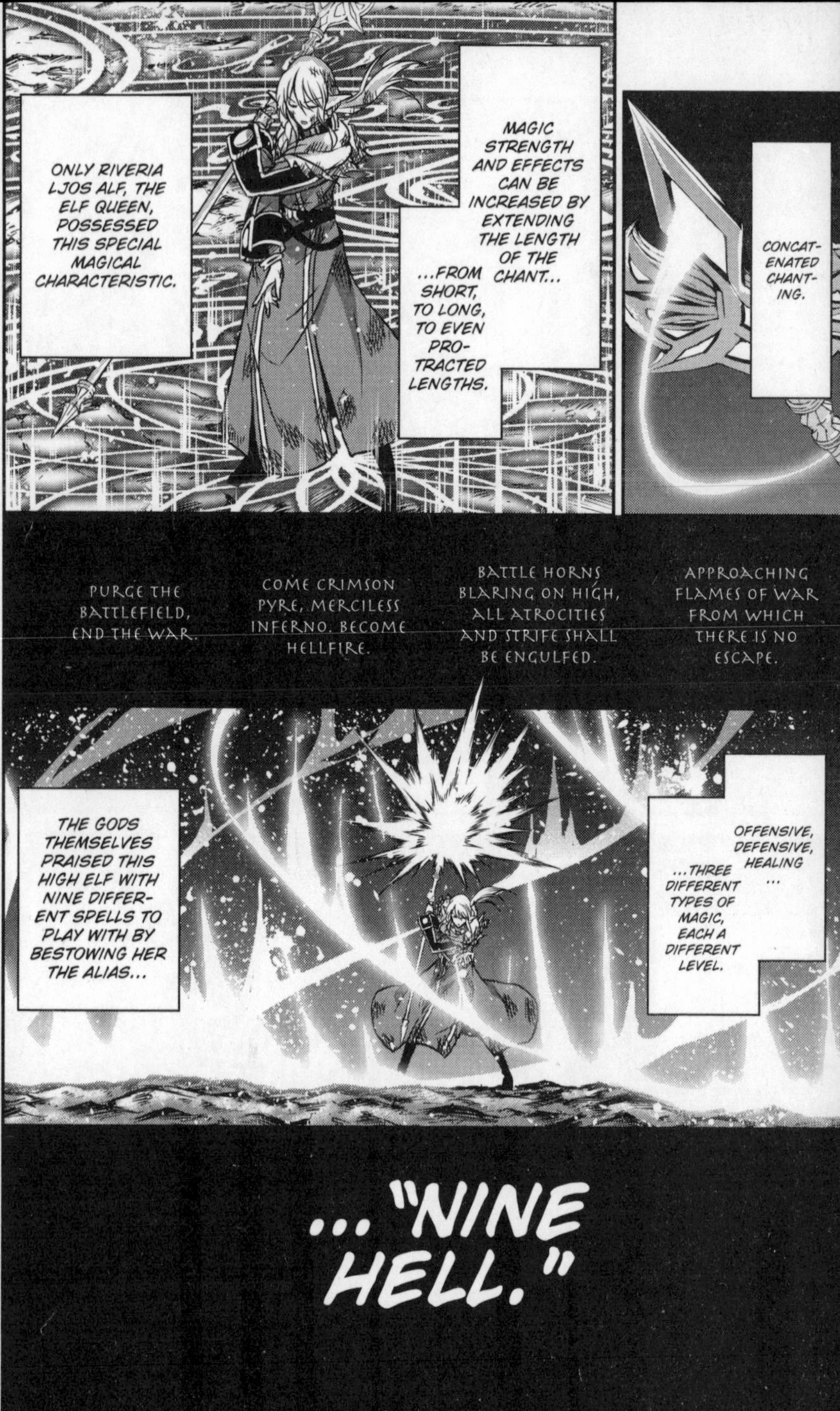
CONCAT-ENATED CHANT-ING.
MAGIC STRENGTH AND EFFECTS CAN BE INCREASED BY EXTENDING THE LENGTH OF THE CHANT...
...FROM SHORT, TO LONG, TO EVEN PRO-TRACTED LENGTHS.
ONLY RIVERIA LJOS ALF, THE ELF QUEEN, POSSESSED THIS SPECIAL MAGICAL CHARACTERISTIC.
APPROACHING FLAMES OF WAR FROM WHICH THERE IS NO ESCAPE.
BATTLE HORNS BLARING ON HIGH, ALL ATROCITIES AND STRIFE SHALL BE ENGULFED.
COME CRIMSON PYRE, MERCILESS INFERNO. BECOME HELLFIRE.
PURGE THE BATTLEFIELD, END THE WAR.
OFFENSIVE, DEFENSIVE, HEALING ...
...THREE DIFFERENT TYPES OF MAGIC, EACH A DIFFERENT LEVEL.
THE GODS THEMSELVES PRAISED THIS HIGH ELF WITH NINE DIFFER-ENT SPELLS TO PLAY WITH BY BESTOWING HER THE ALIAS...
..."NINE HELL."

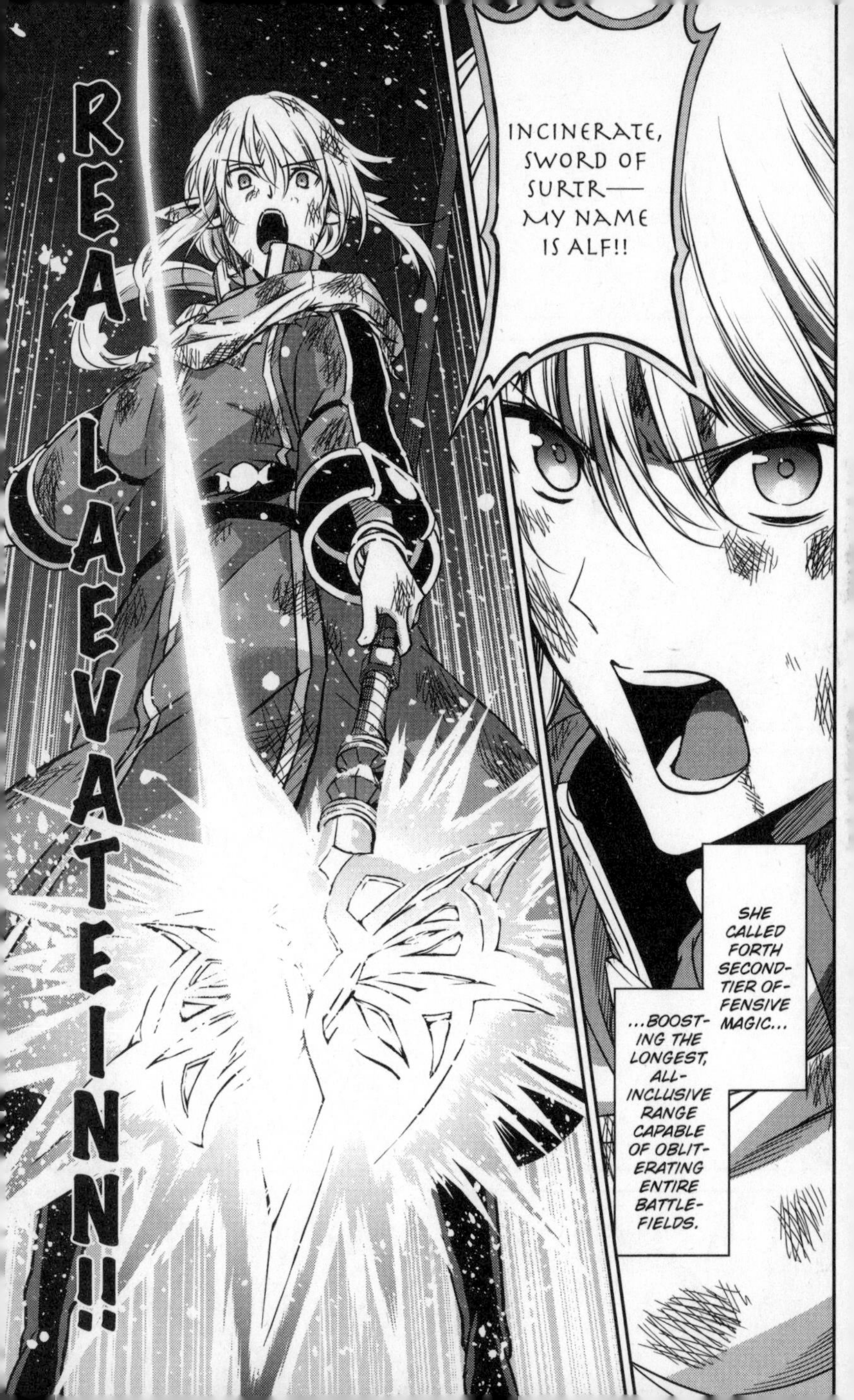

INCINERATE, SWORD OF SURTR—MY NAME IS ALF!!
SHE CALLED FORTH SECOND-TIER OFFENSIVE MAGIC...
...BOOSTING THE LONGEST, ALL-INCLUSIVE RANGE CAPABLE OF OBLITERATING ENTIRE BATTLEFIELDS.
REA LAEVATEINN!!

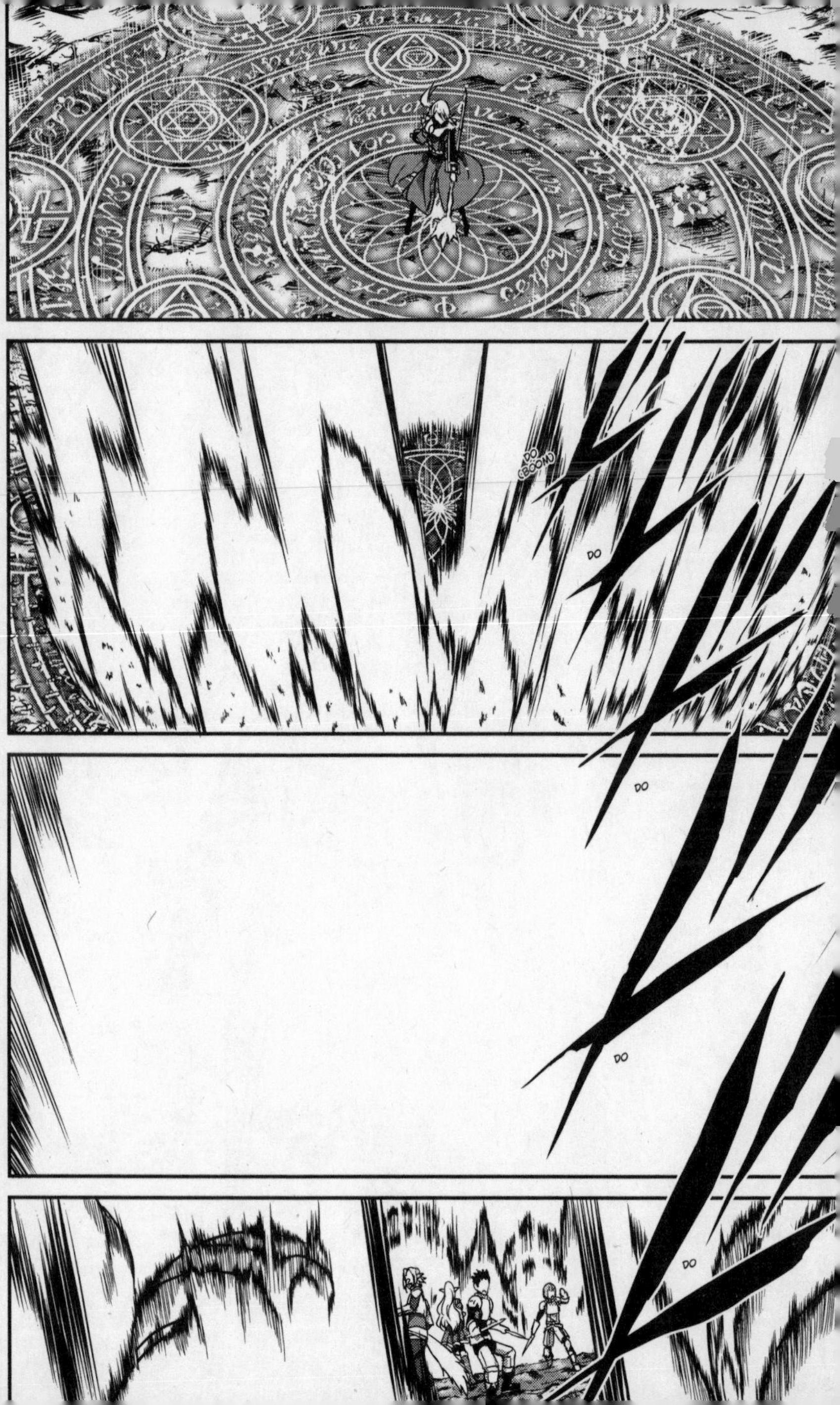
DO (BOOM)
DO
DO
DO
DO

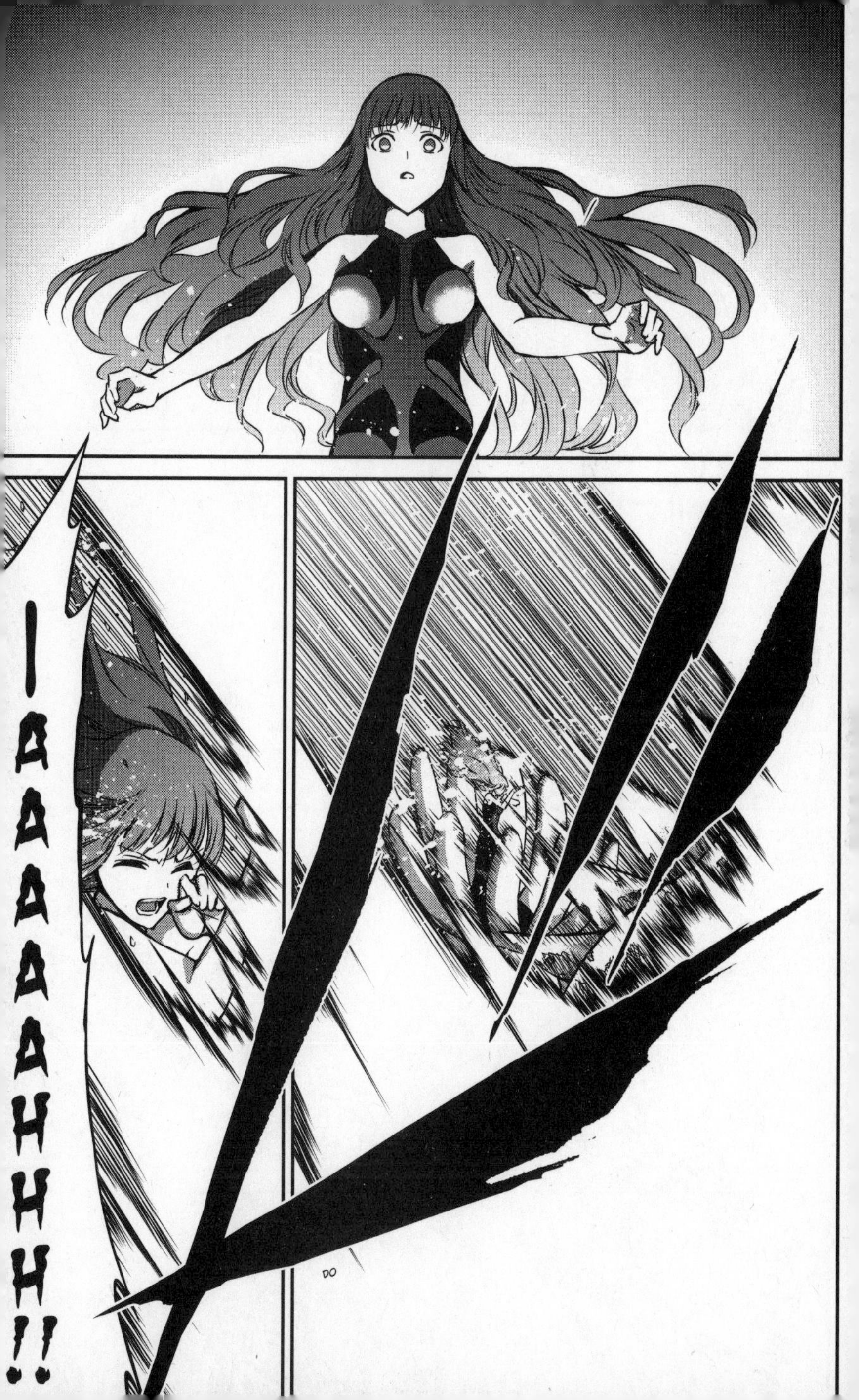

DO
AAAAAAHHHH!!

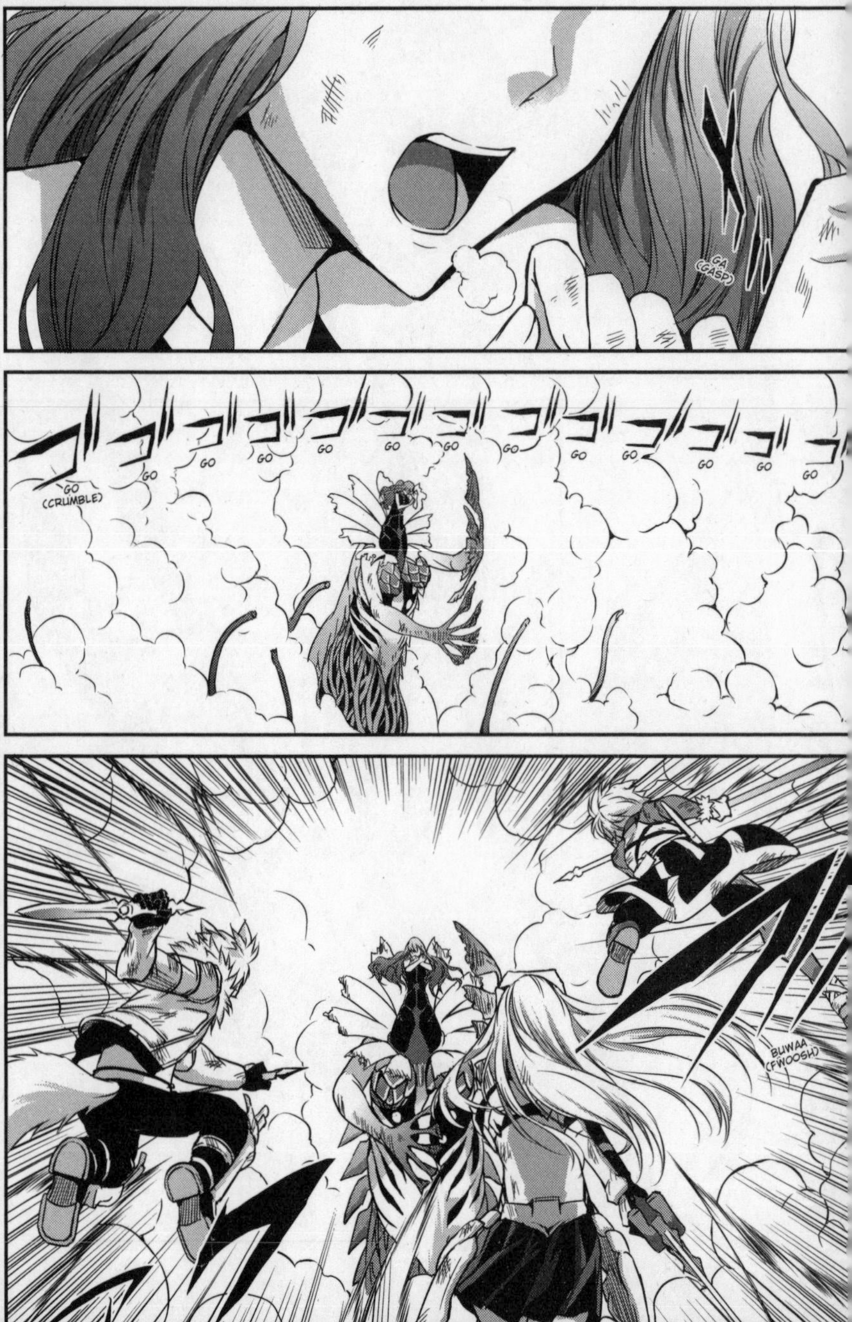
GA (GASP)
GO GO GO GO GO GO GO GO GO GO GO GO
GO (CRUMBLE)
BUWAA (FWOOSH)

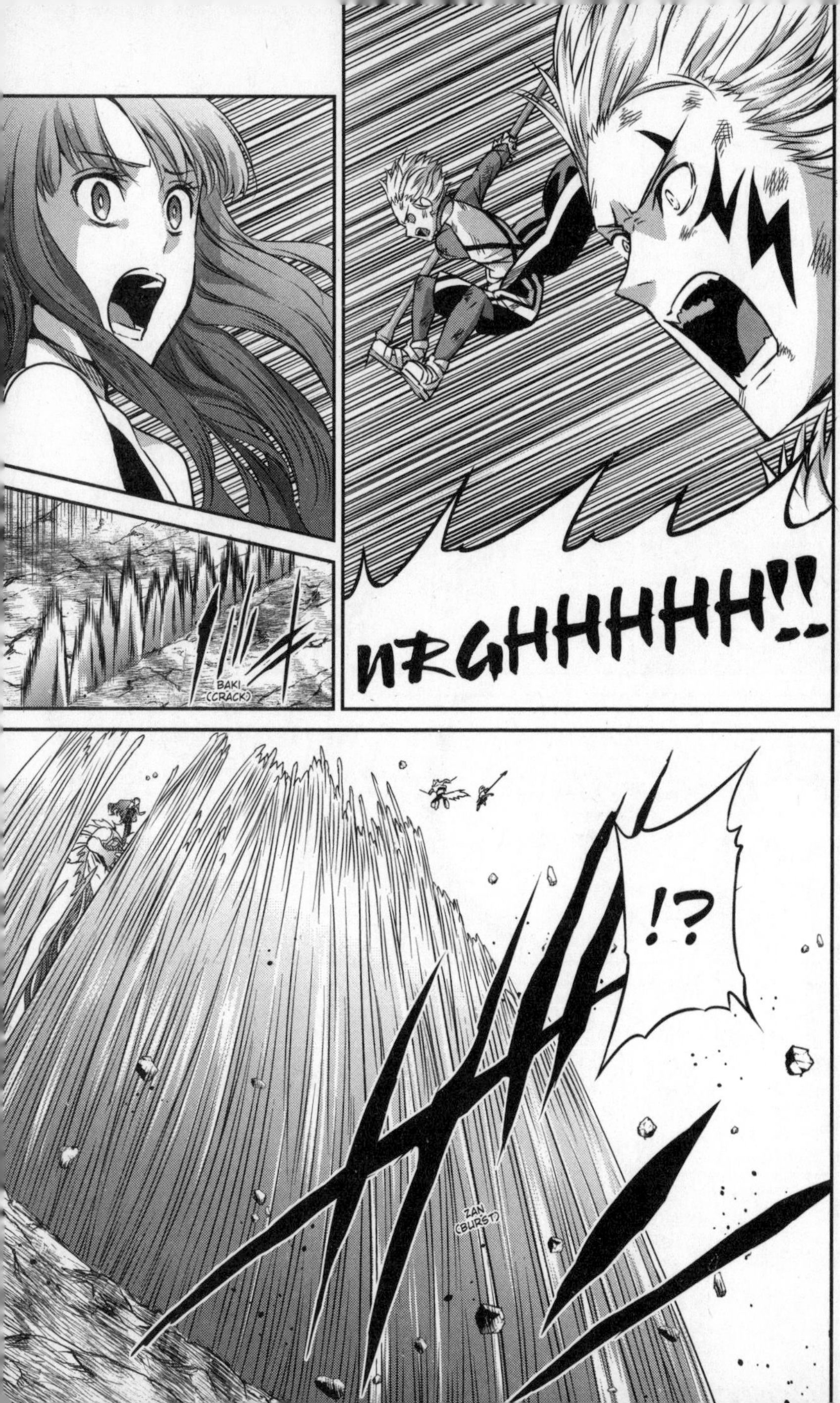
NRGHHHHH!!
BAKI (CRACK)
!?
ZAN (BURST)

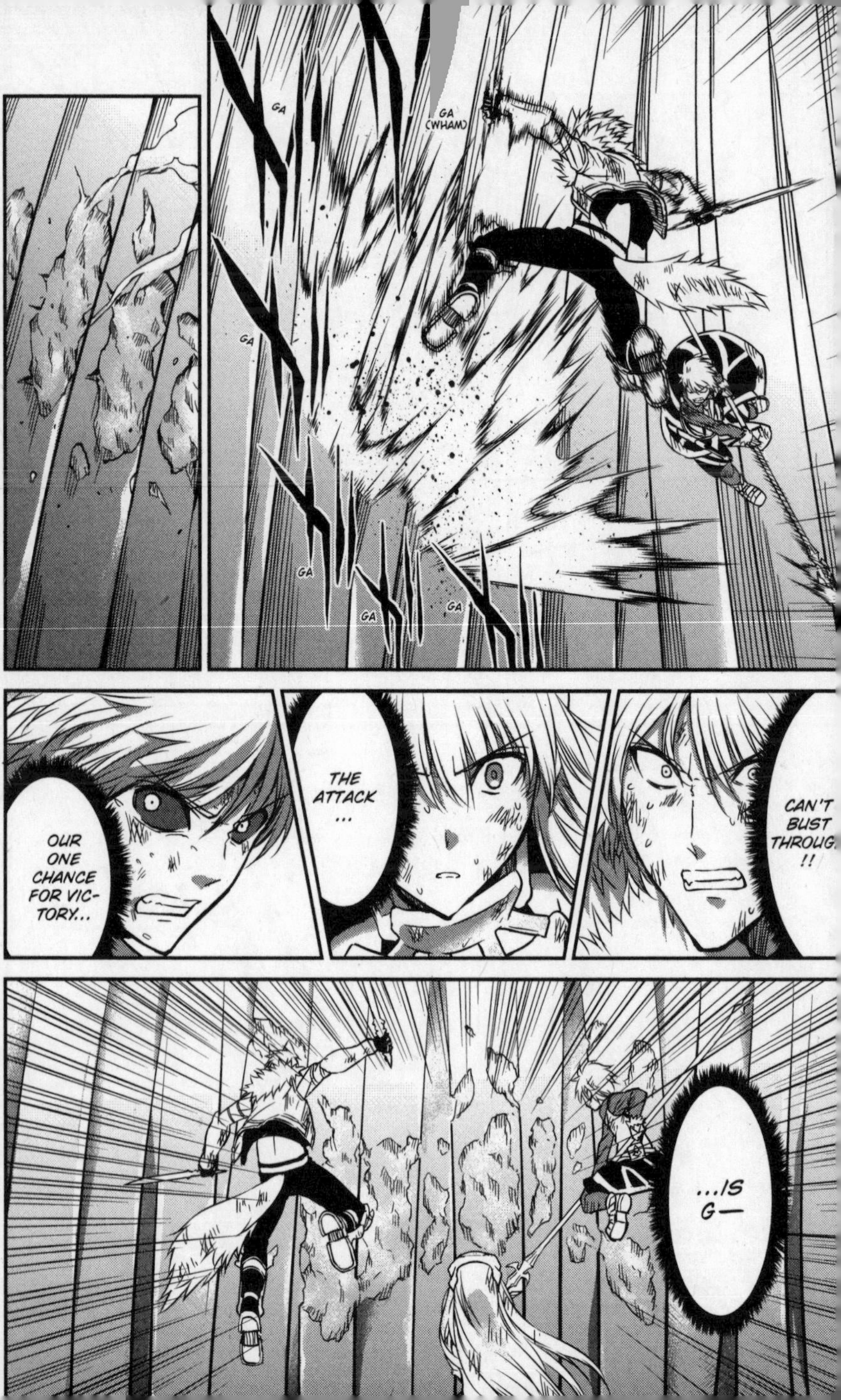
GA (WHAM)
GA
GA
GA
GA
GA
CAN'T BUST THROUG !!
THE ATTACK ...
OUR ONE CHANCE FOR VIC-TORY...
...IS G—

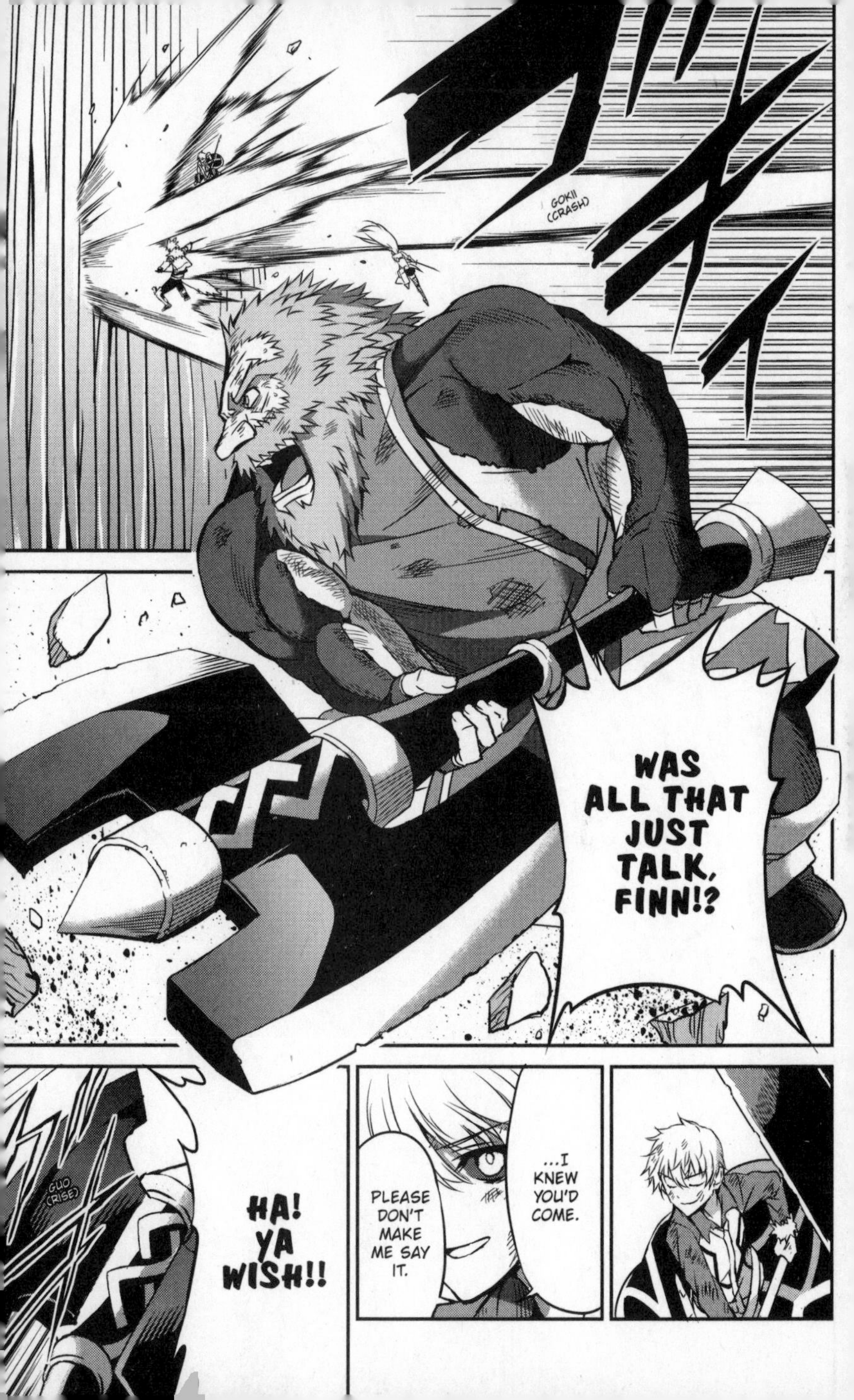
GOKII (CRASH)
WAS ALL THAT JUST TALK, FINN!?
...I KNEW YOU'D COME.
PLEASE DON'T MAKE ME SAY IT.
HA! YA WISH!!
GUO (RISE)

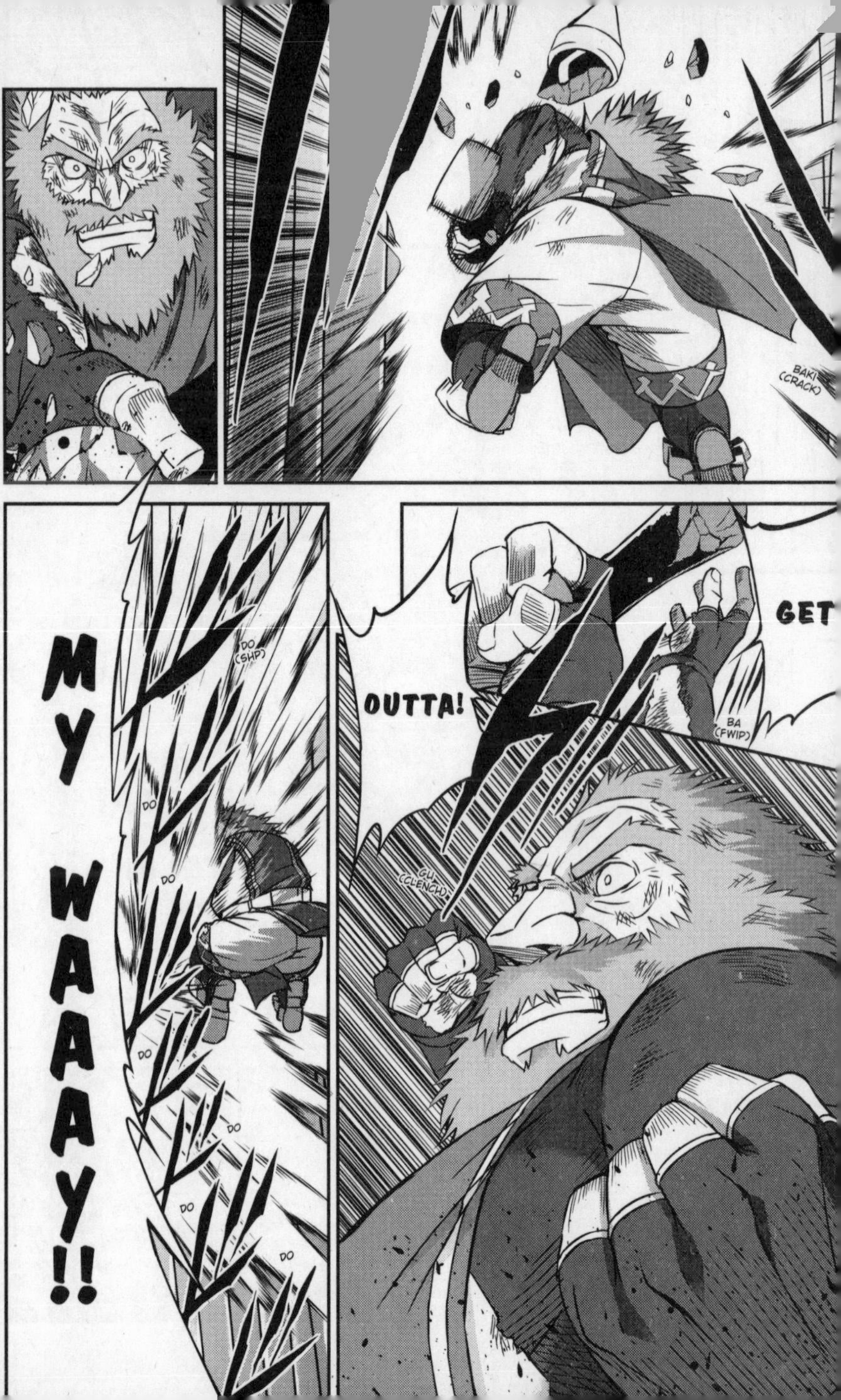
BAKI (CRACK)
GET
BA (FWIP)
OUTTA!
GU (CLENCH)
DO (SHP)
MY WAAAY!!
DO
DO
DO
DO
DO
DO

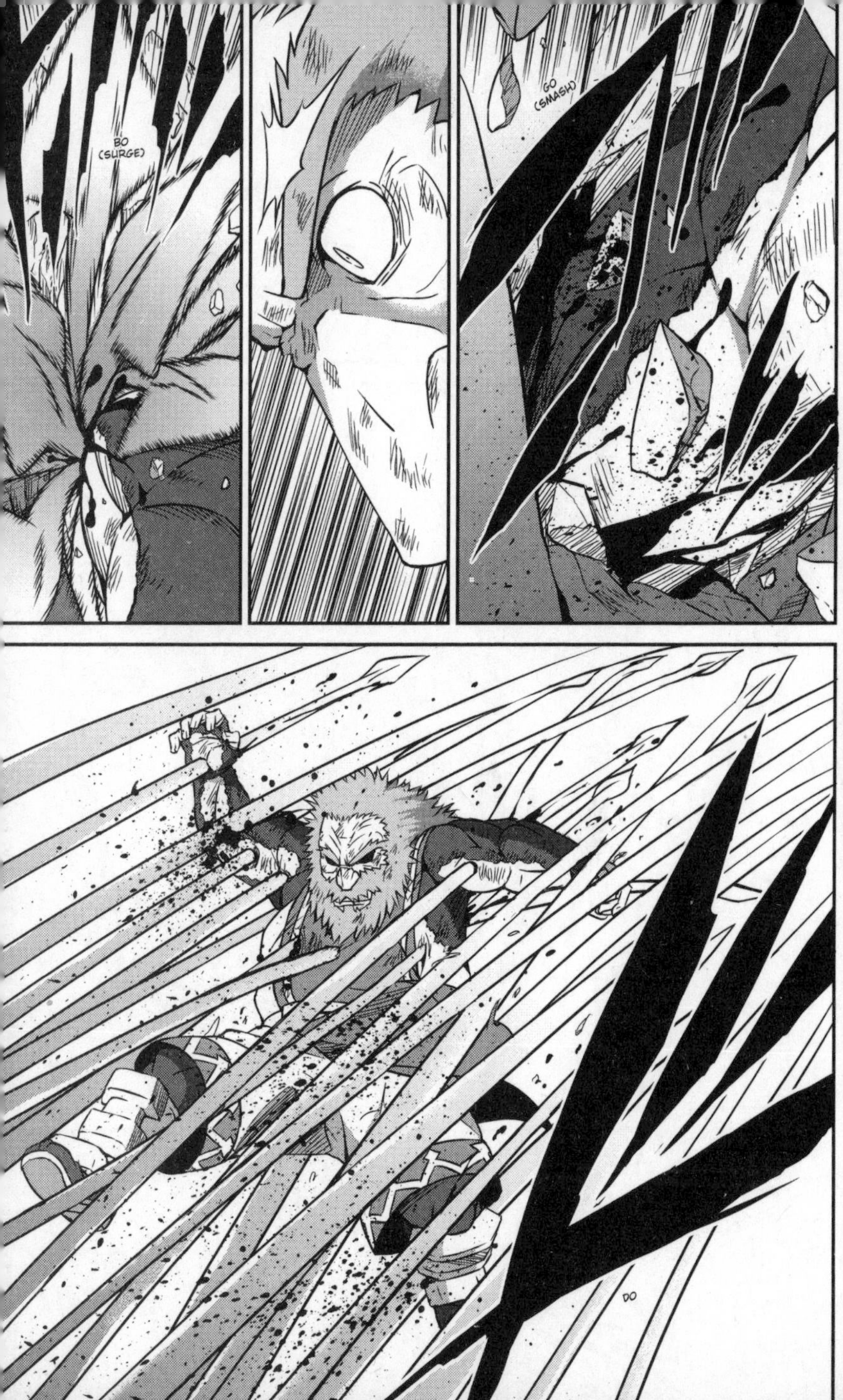
GO
(SMASH)
BO
(SURGE)
DO

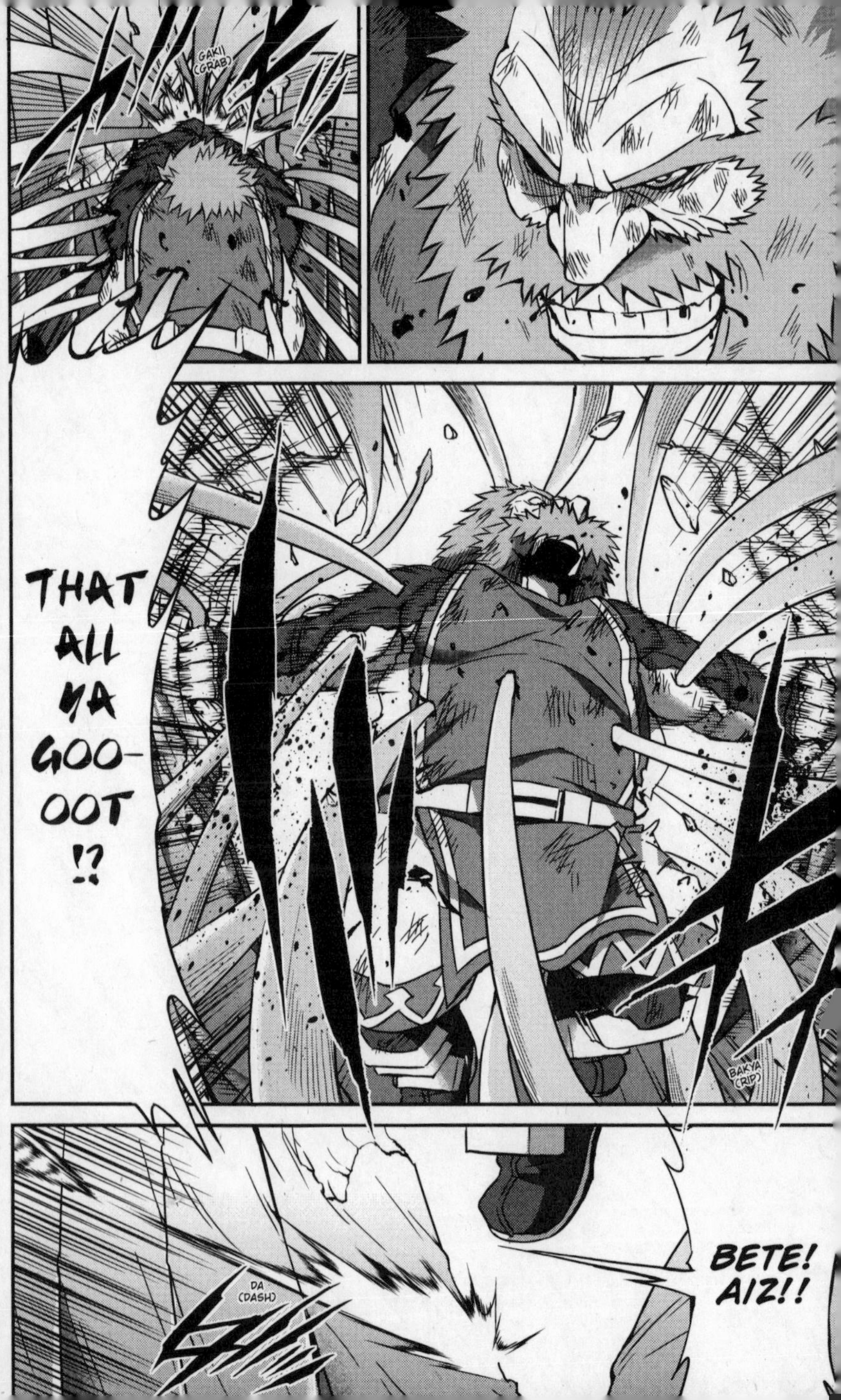
GAKI (GRAB)
THAT ALL YA GOO-OOT!?
BAKYA (RIP)
BETE! AIZ!!
DA (DASH)

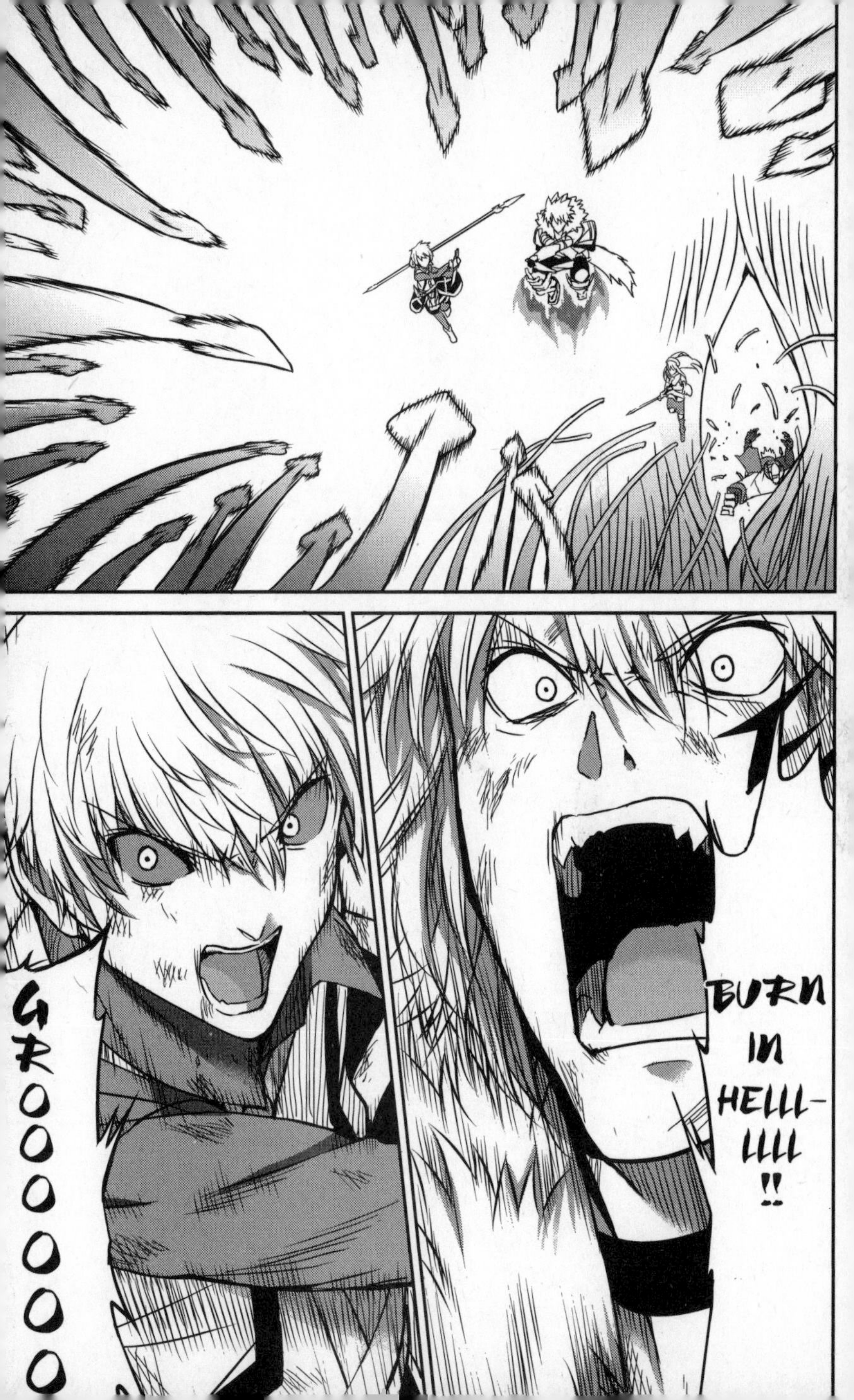
BURN IN HELLL-LLLL!!
GROOOOOO

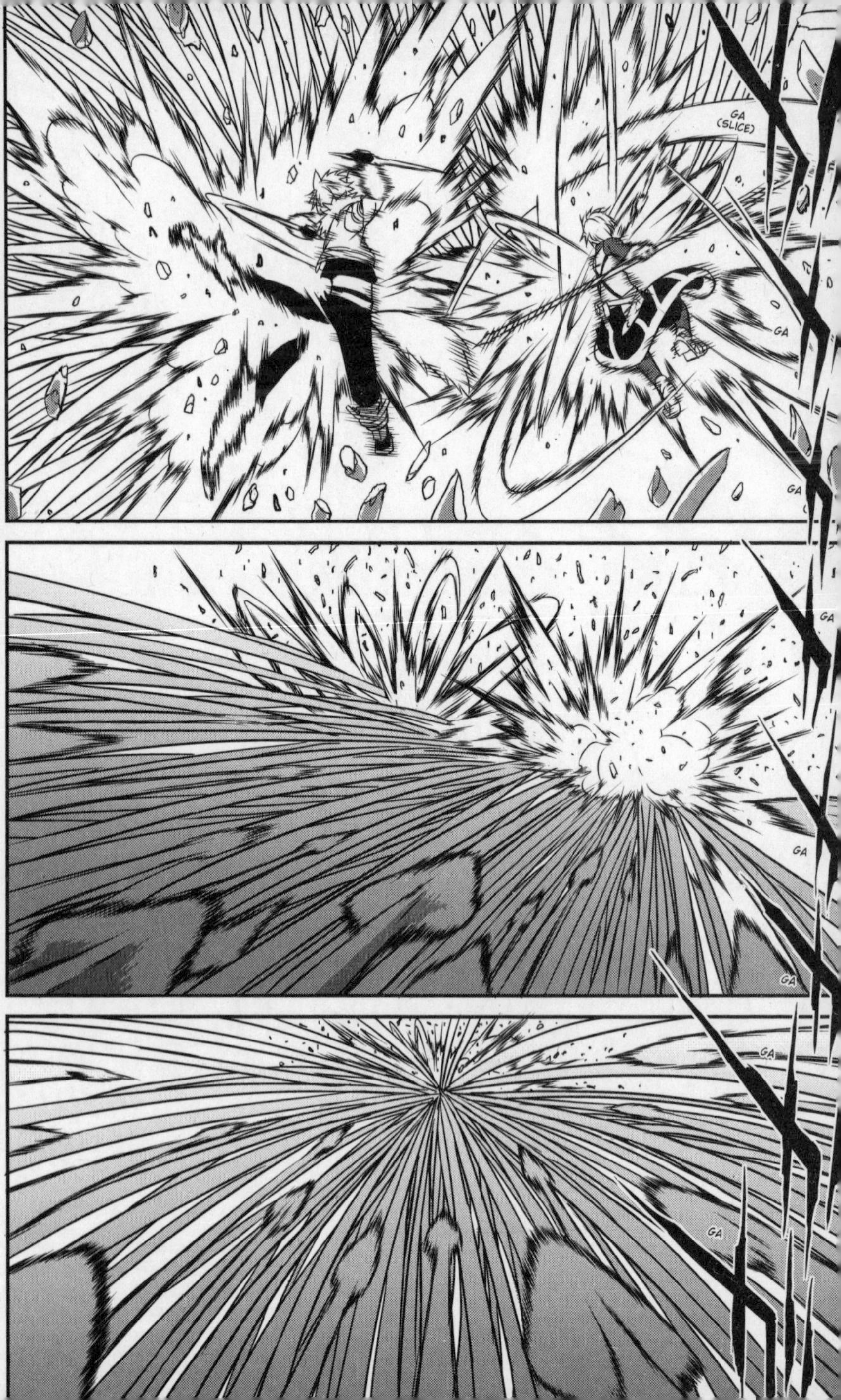
GA (SLICE)
GA
GA
GA
GA
GA
GA
GA

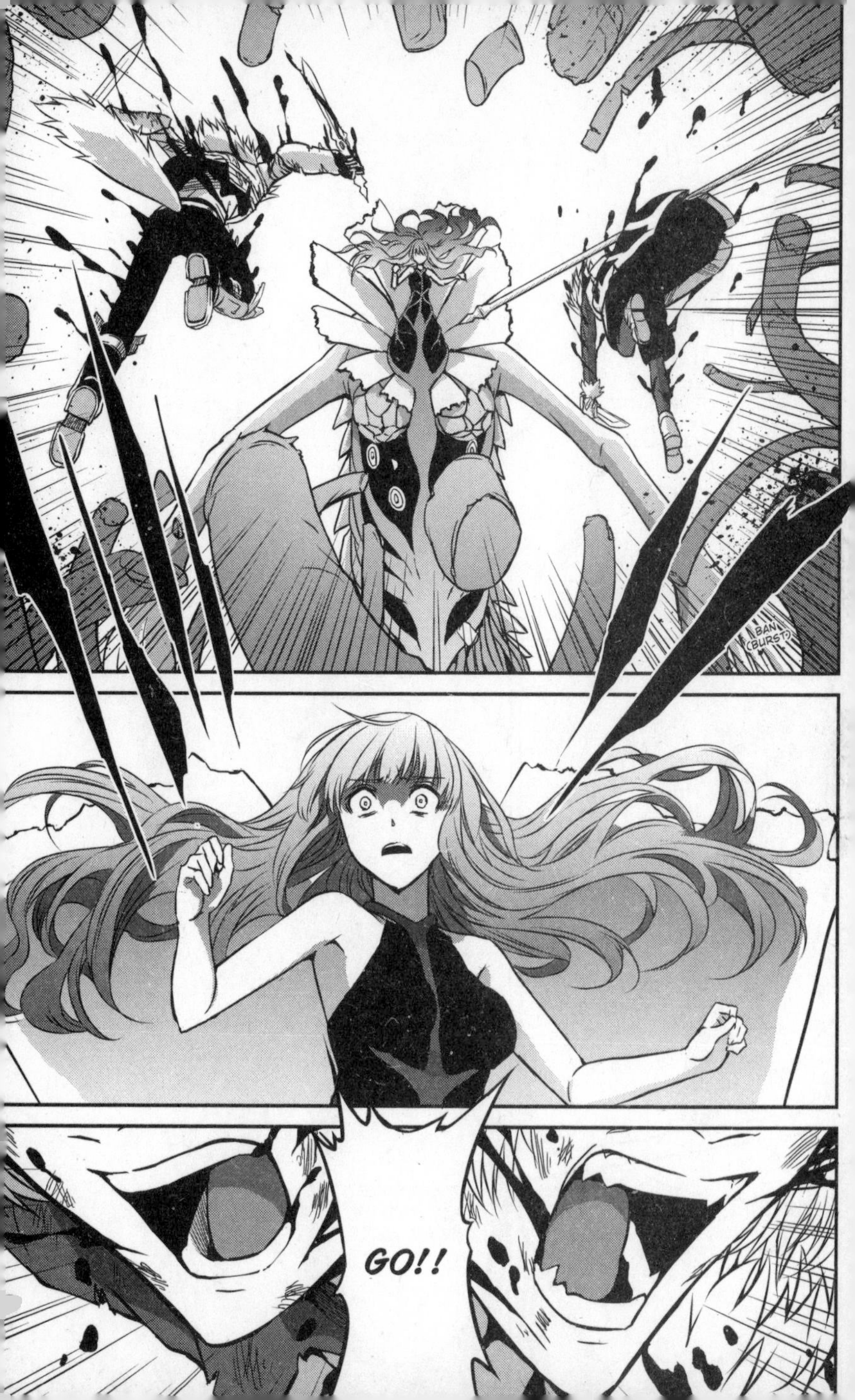
BAN
(BURST)
GO!!

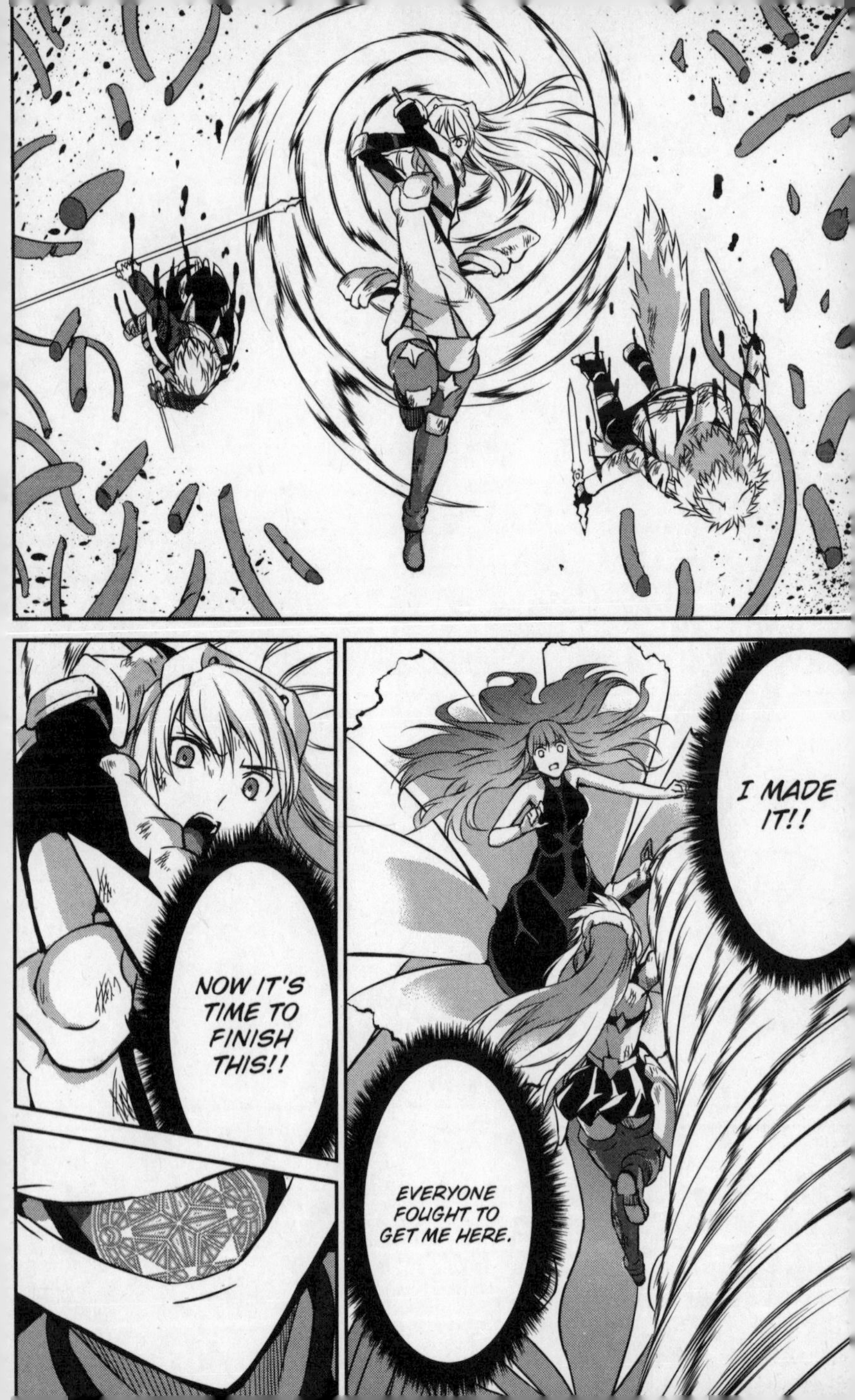
I MADE IT!!
EVERYONE FOUGHT TO GET ME HERE.
NOW IT'S TIME TO FINISH THIS!!

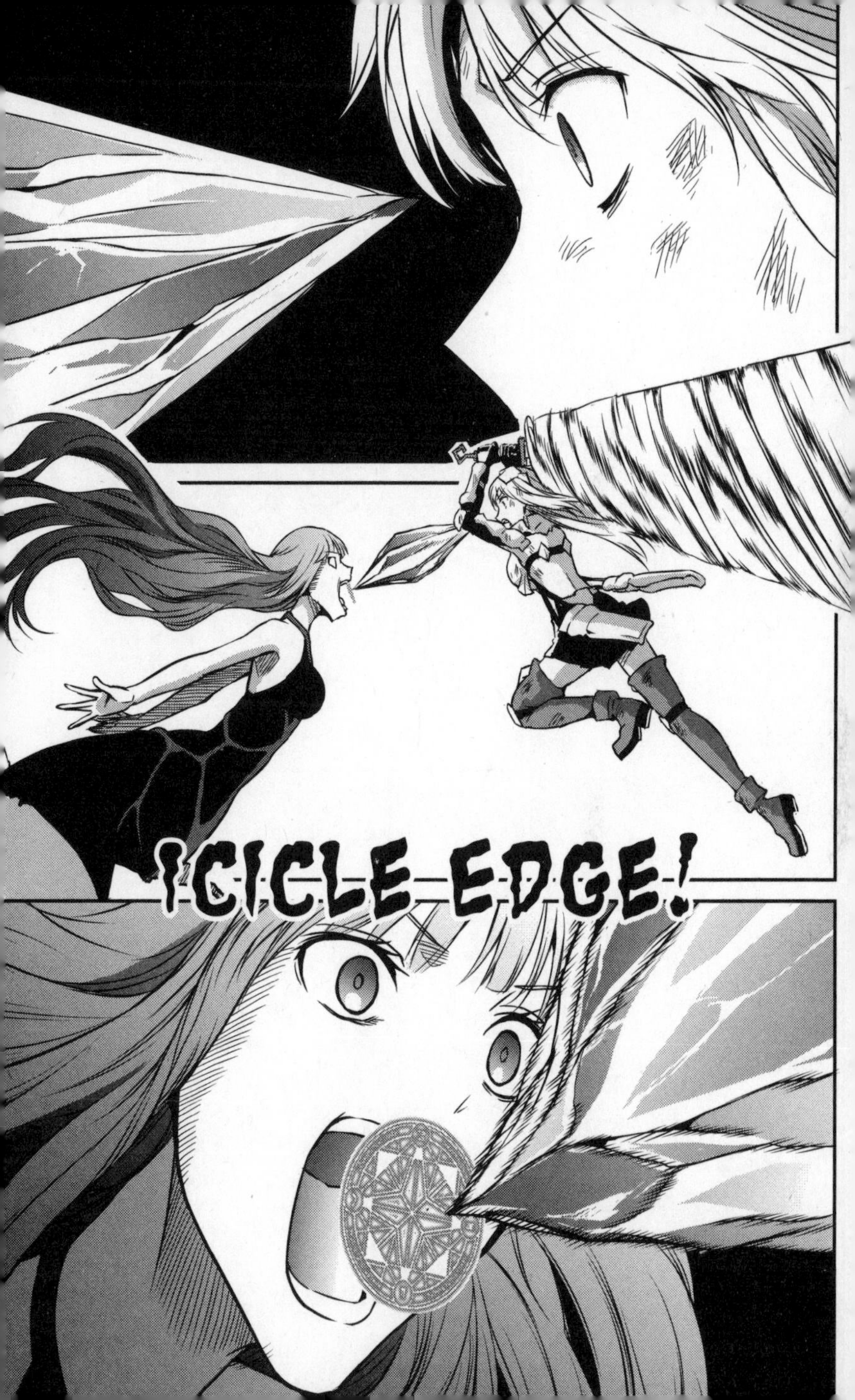
ICICLE EDGE!

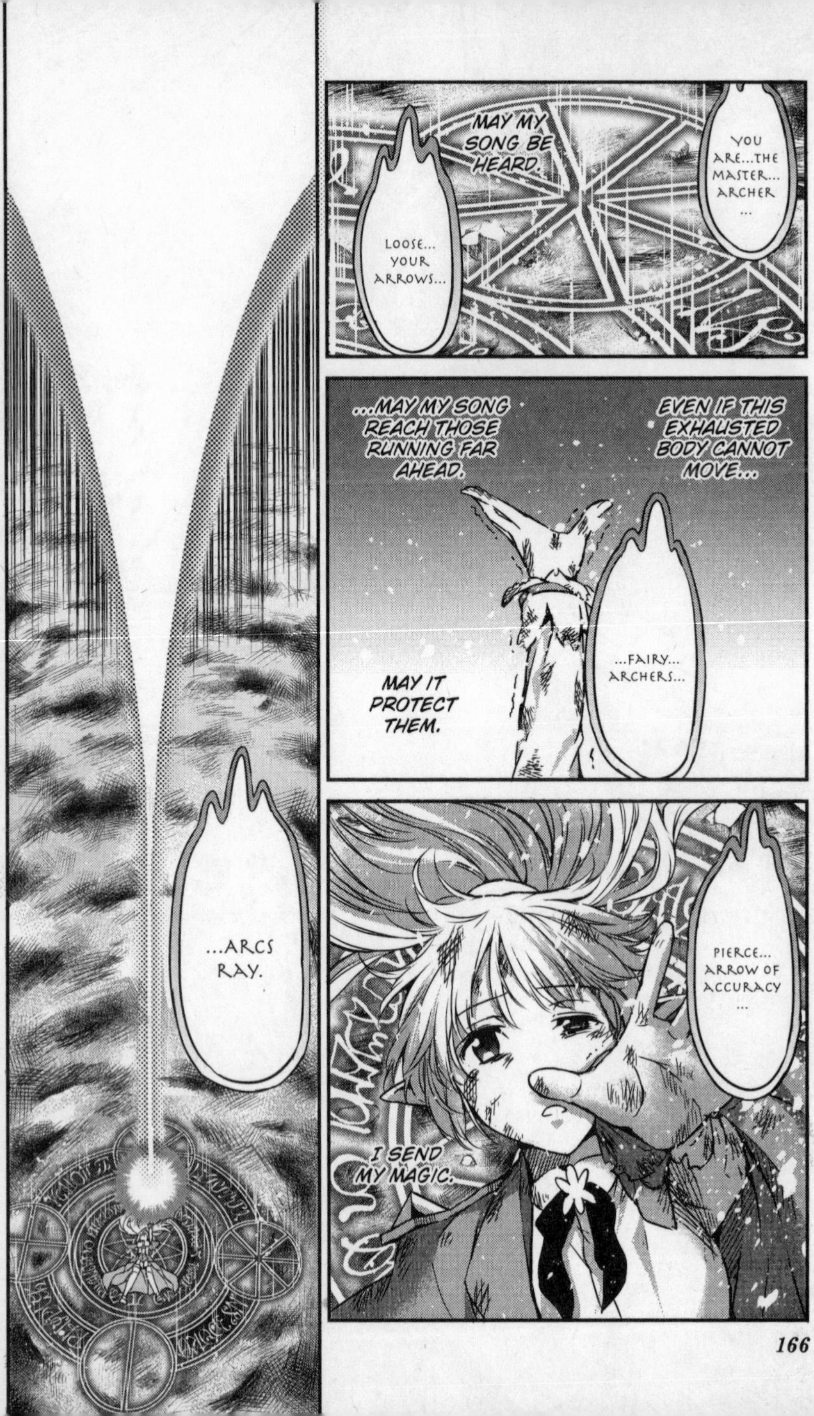
YOU ARE...THE MASTER... ARCHER ...
MAY MY SONG BE HEARD.
LOOSE... YOUR ARROWS...
EVEN IF THIS EXHAUSTED BODY CANNOT MOVE...
...FAIRY... ARCHERS...
...MAY MY SONG REACH THOSE RUNNING FAR AHEAD.
MAY IT PROTECT THEM.
PIERCE... ARROW OF ACCURACY ...
I SEND MY MAGIC.
...ARCS RAY.

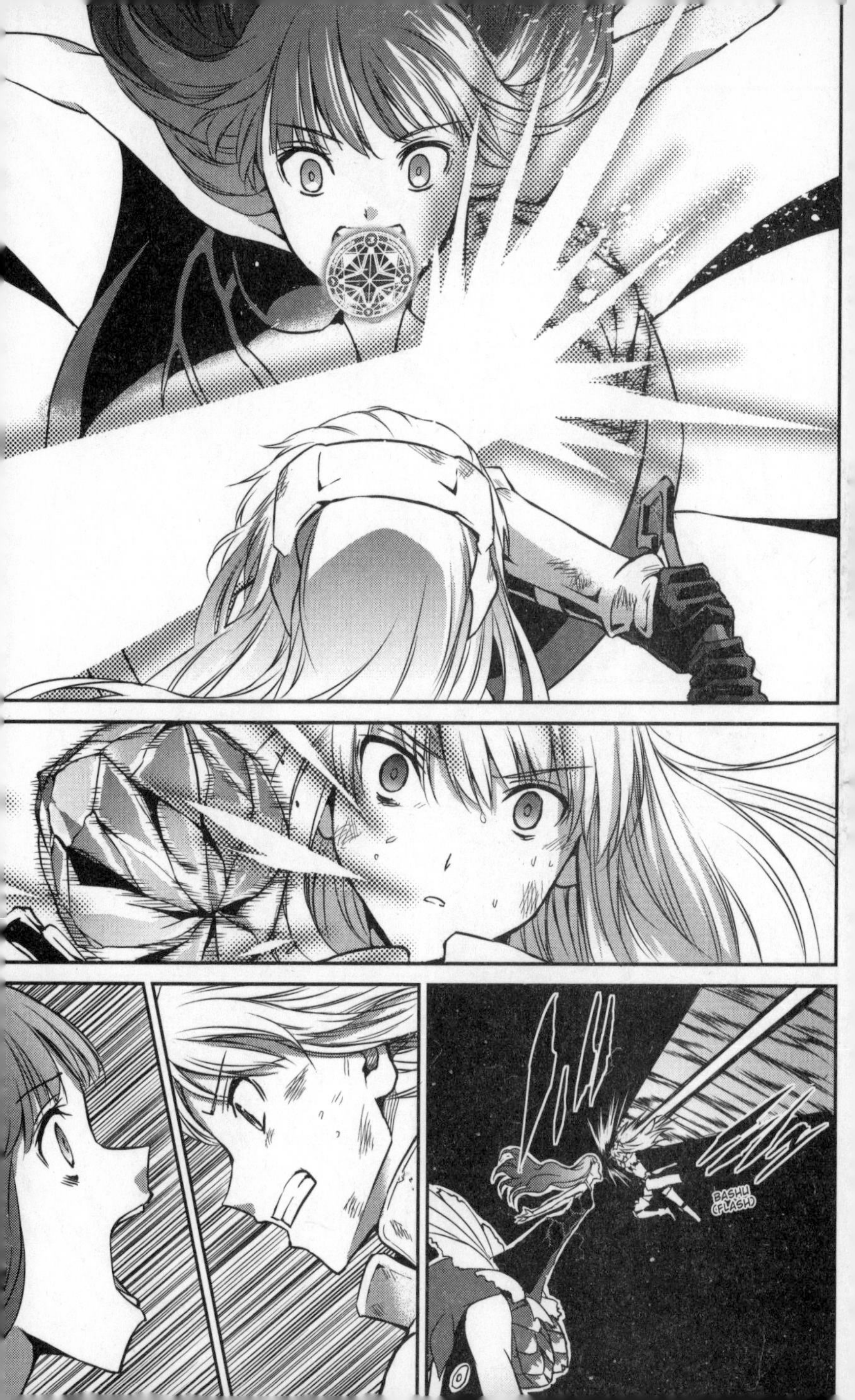
BASHU
(FLASH)

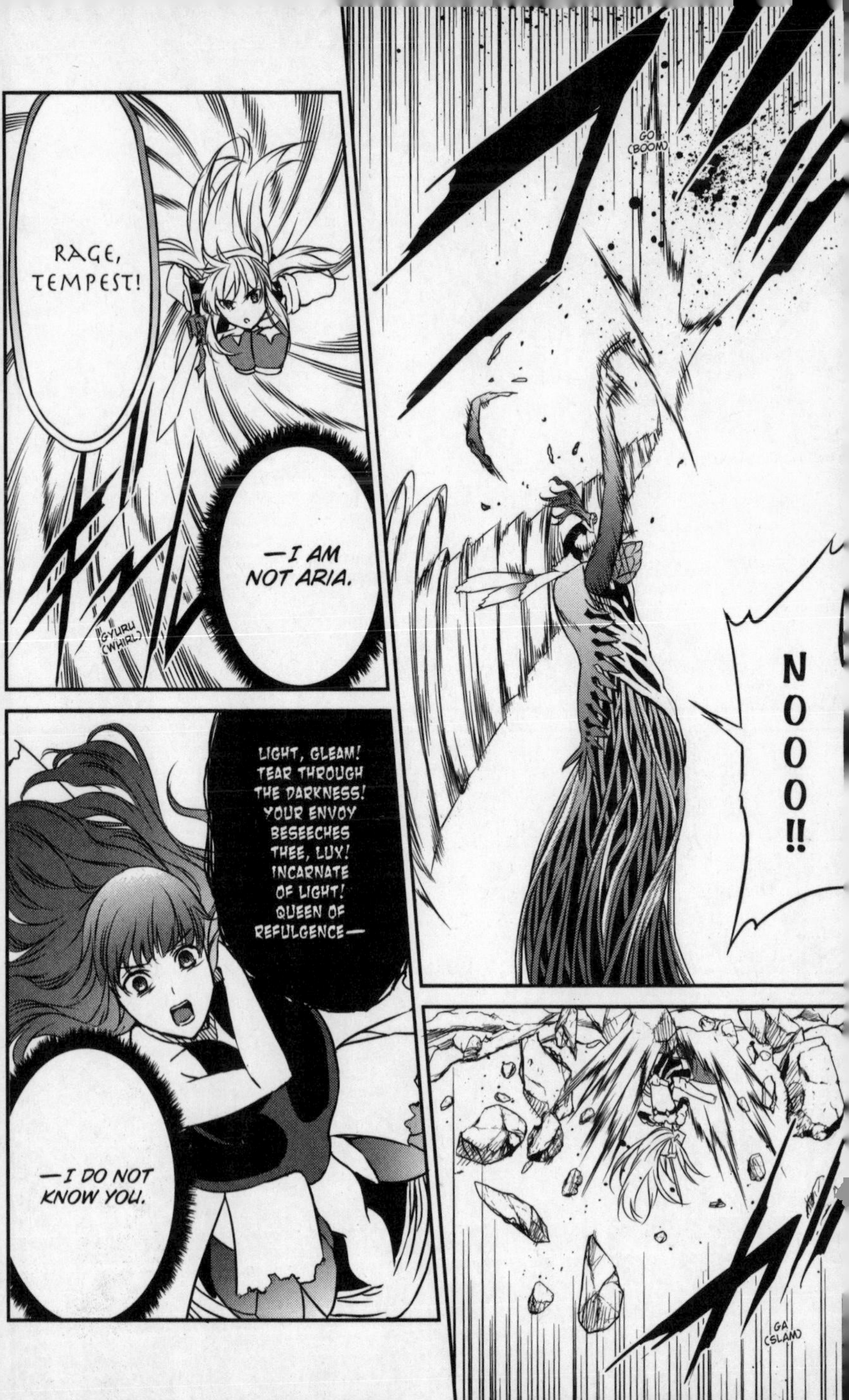
GO (BOOM)
NOOOO!!
GA (SLAM)
RAGE, TEMPEST!
—I AM NOT ARIA.
GYURU (WHIRL)
LIGHT, GLEAM! TEAR THROUGH THE DARKNESS! YOUR ENVOY BESEECHES THEE, LUX! INCARNATE OF LIGHT! QUEEN OF REFULGENCE—
—I DO NOT KNOW YOU.

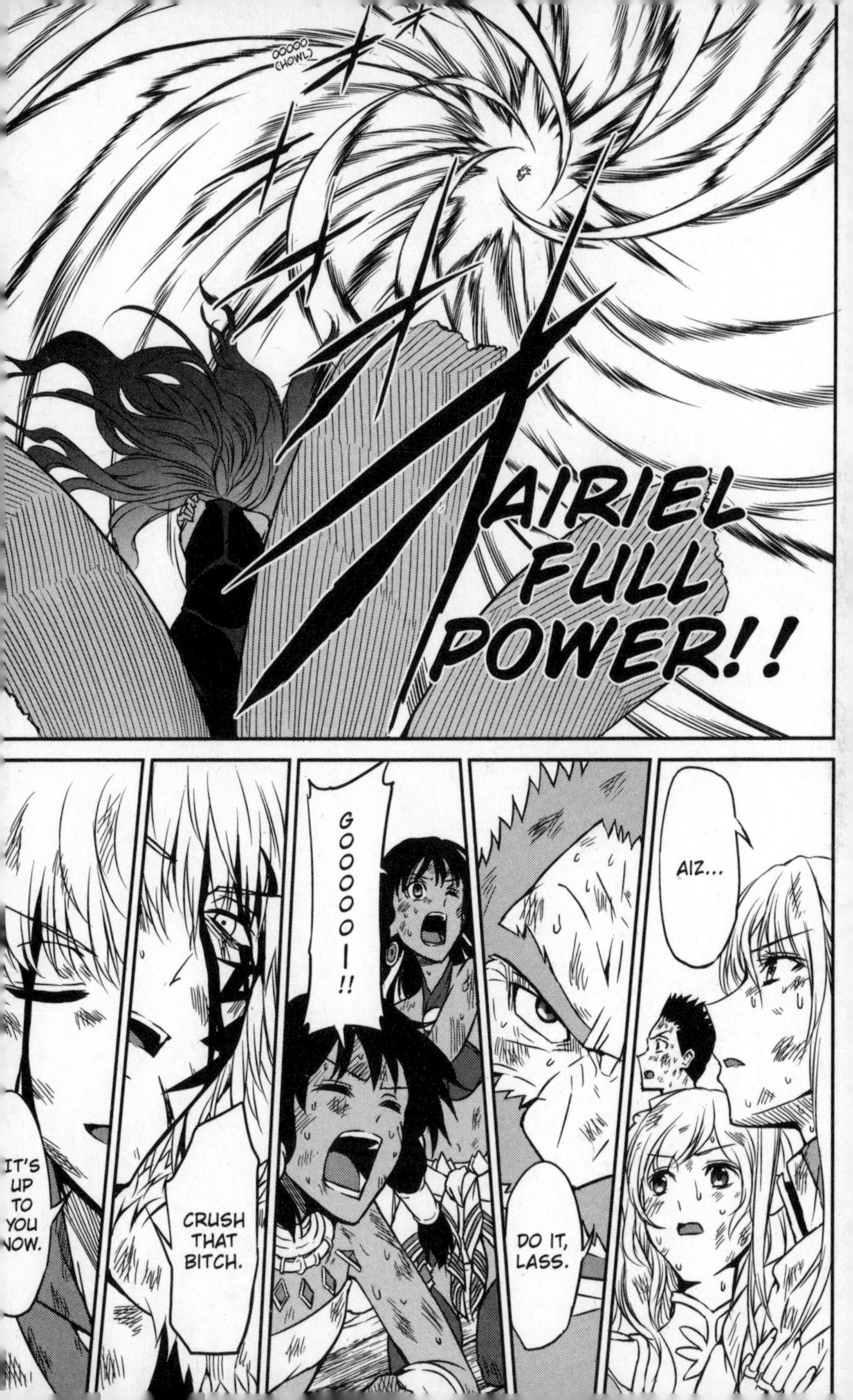
AIRIEL FULL POWER!!
OOOOO (HOWL)
AIZ...
DO IT, LASS.
GOOOOOO—!!
CRUSH THAT BITCH.
IT'S UP TO YOU NOW.

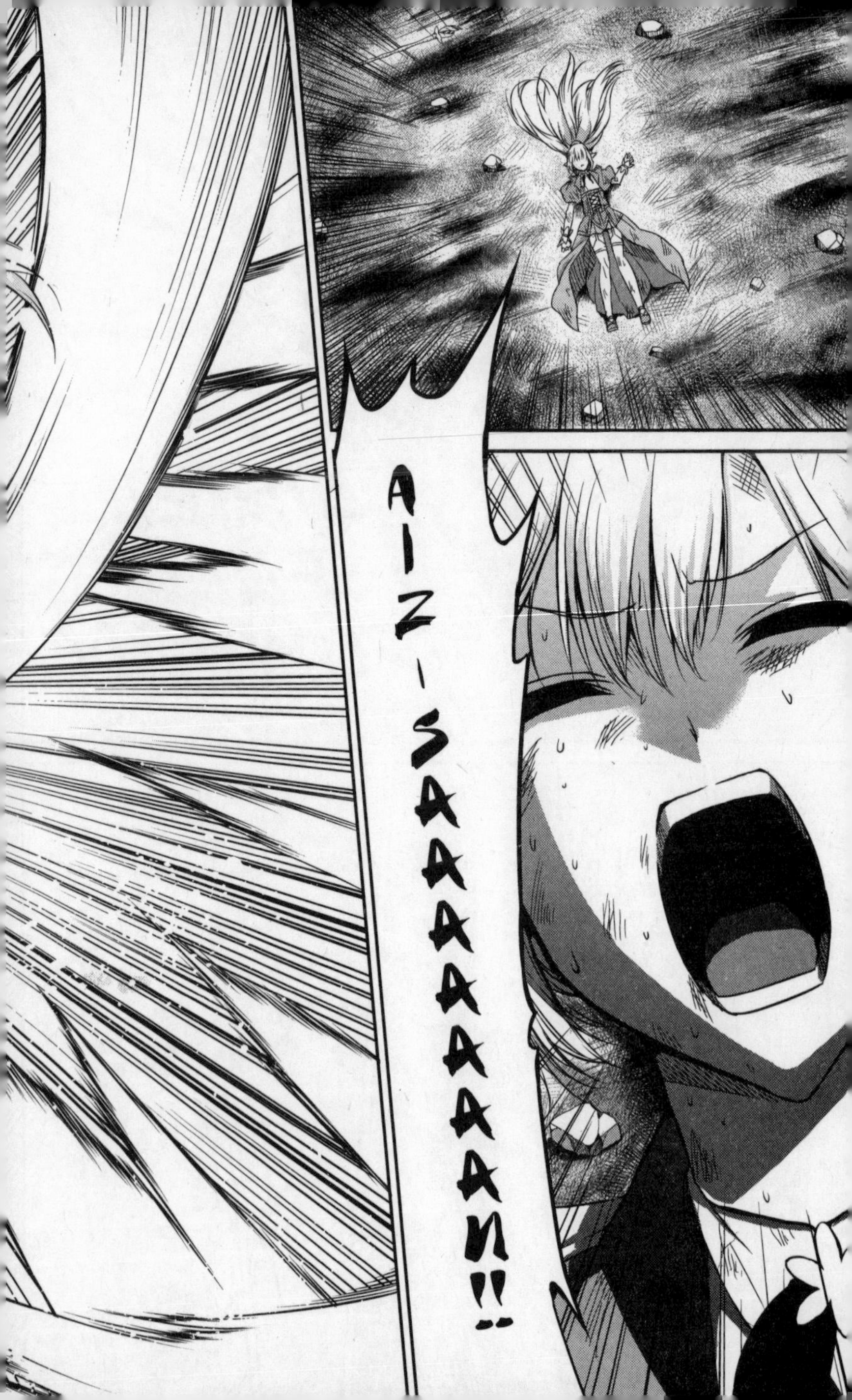
AIZ-SAAAAAAAN!!

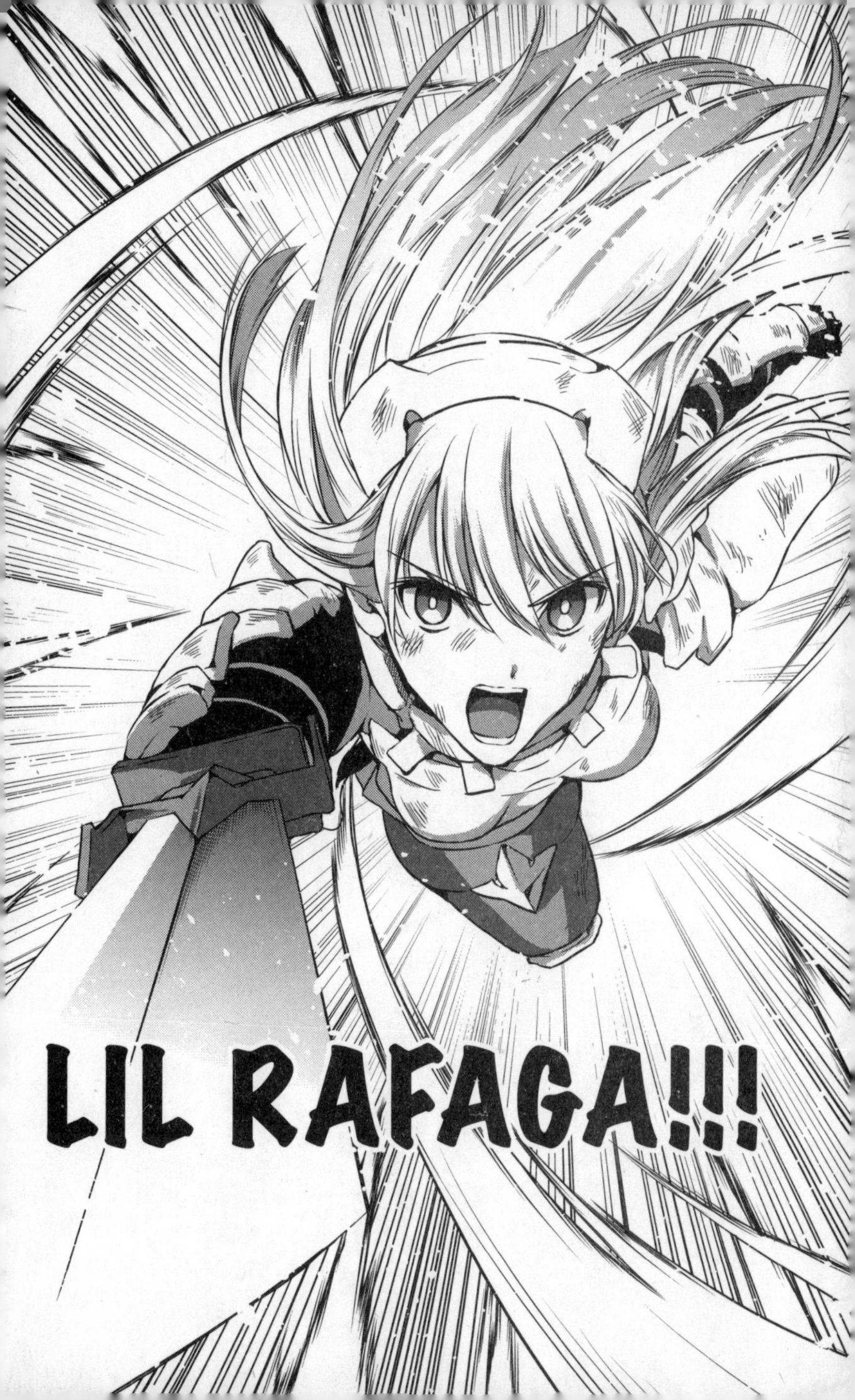
LIL RAFAGA!!!

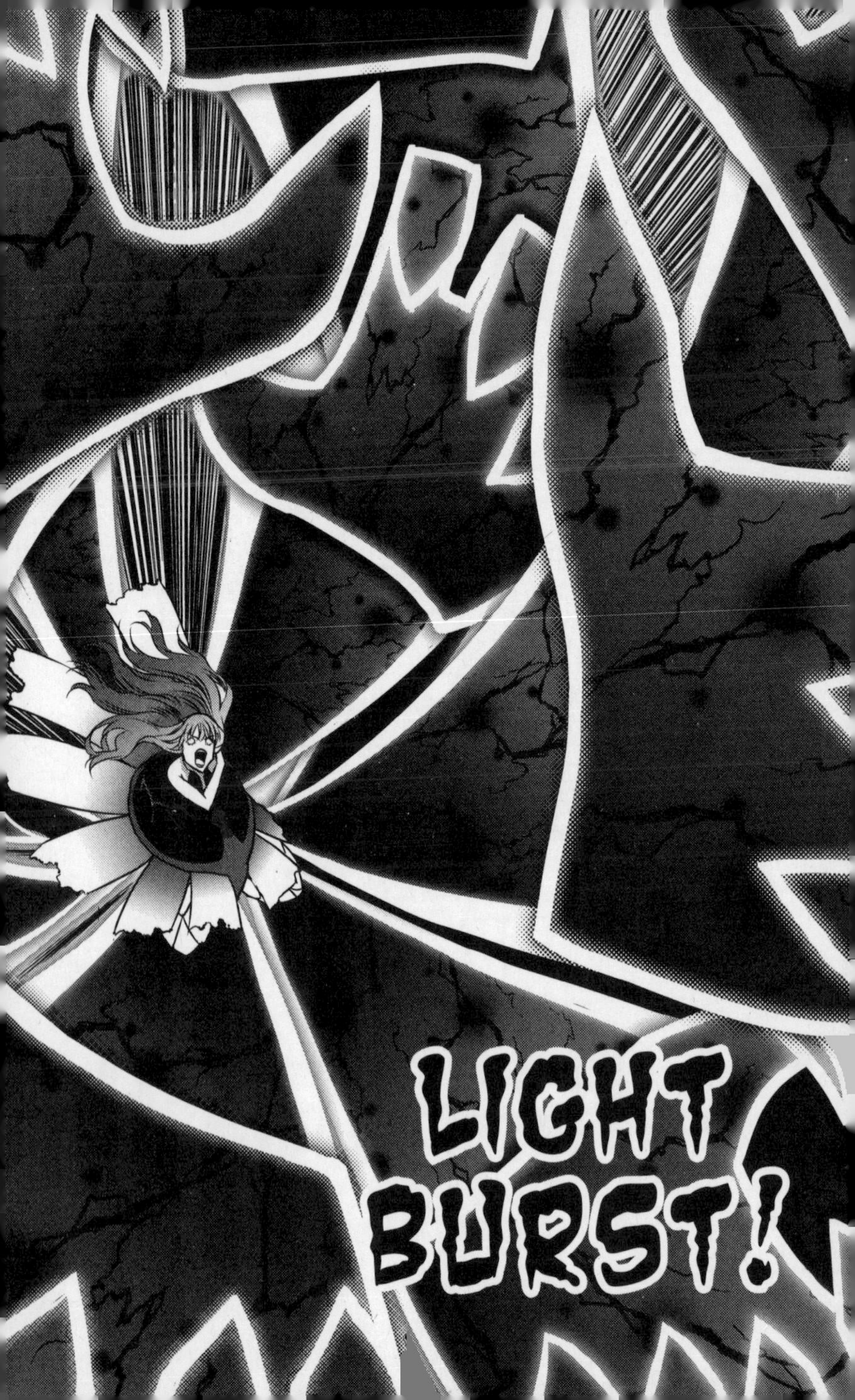
LIGHT BURST!

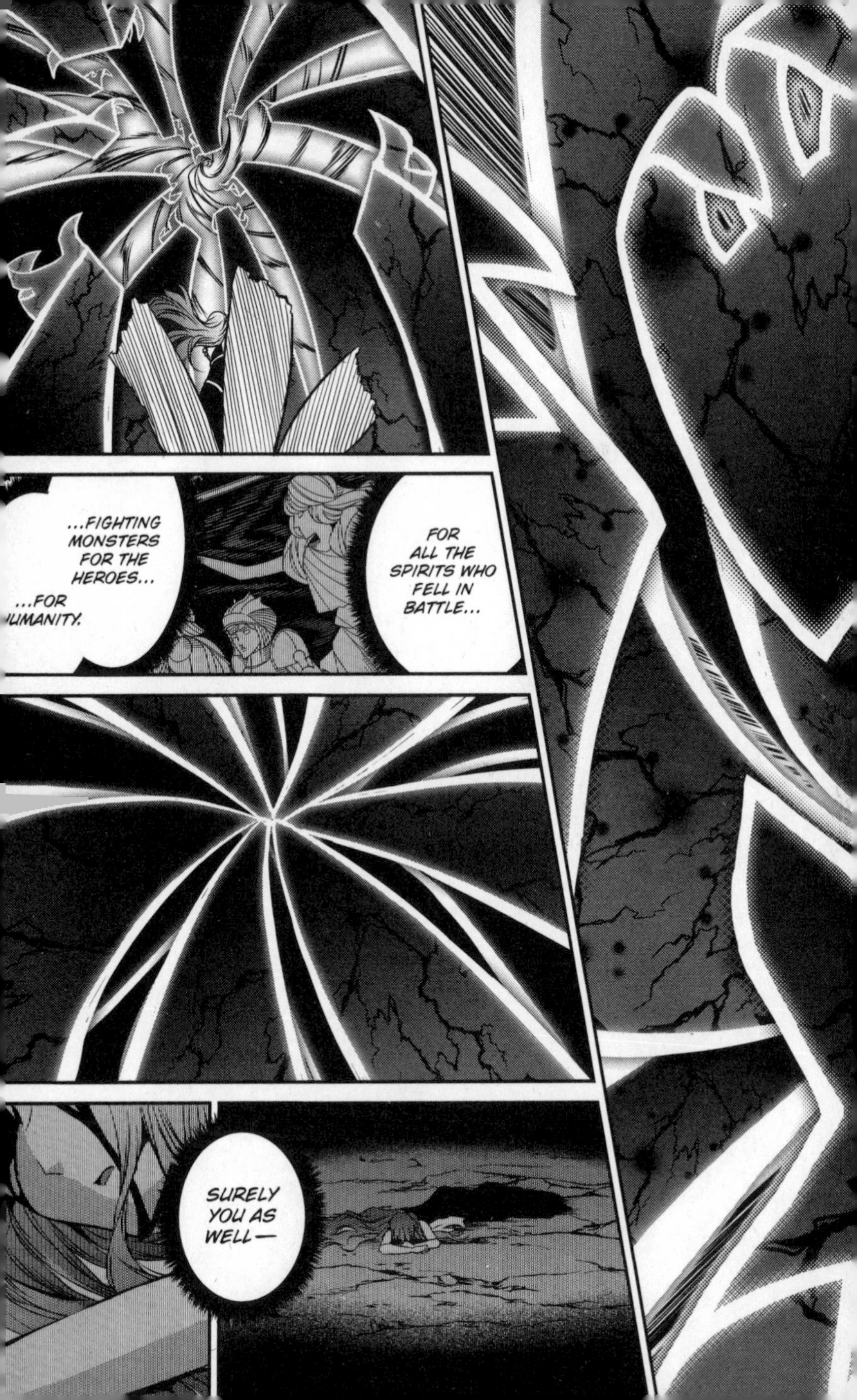
FOR ALL THE SPIRITS WHO FELL IN BATTLE...
...FIGHTING MONSTERS FOR THE HEROES... ...FOR HUMANITY.
SURELY YOU AS WELL—

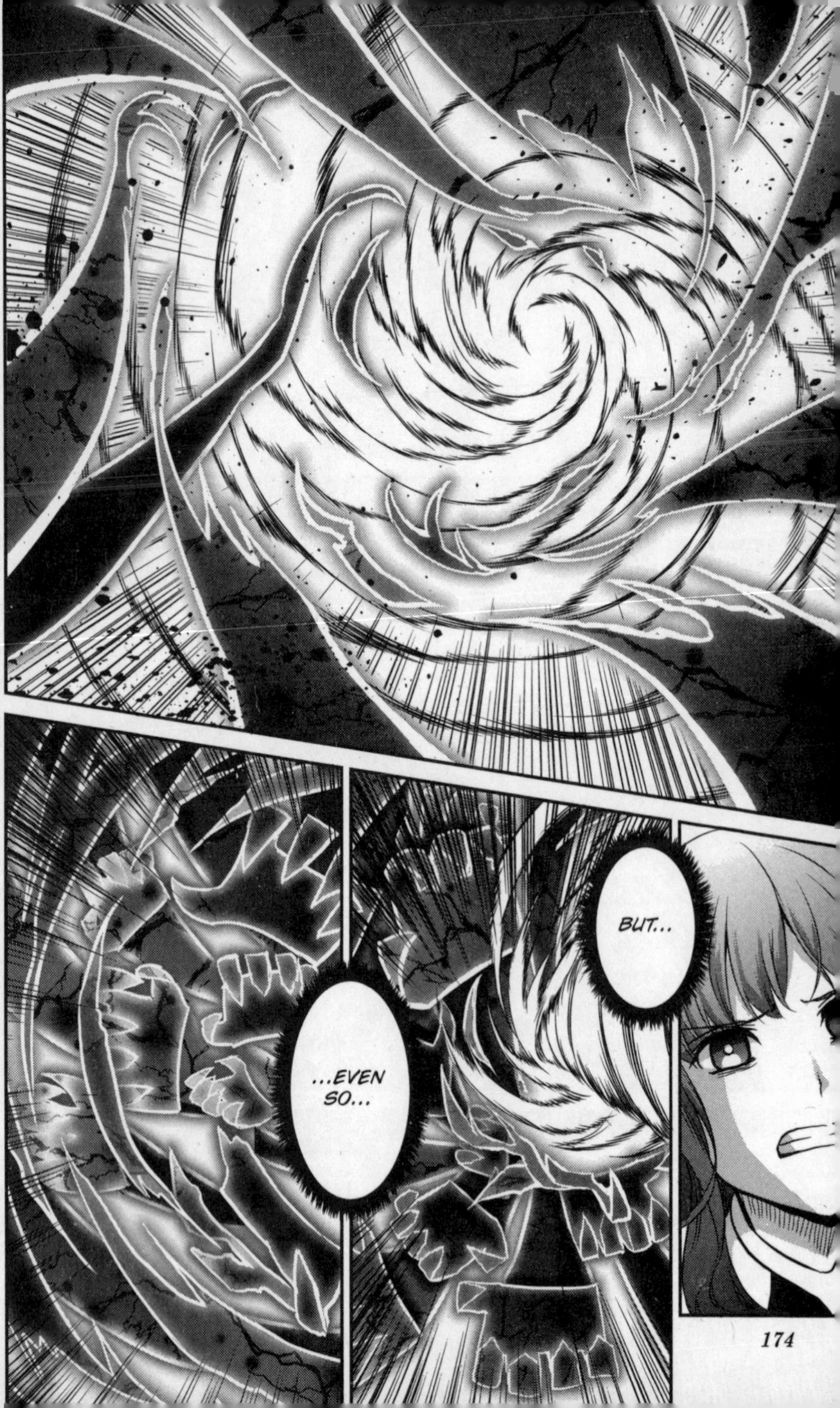
BUT...
...EVEN SO...

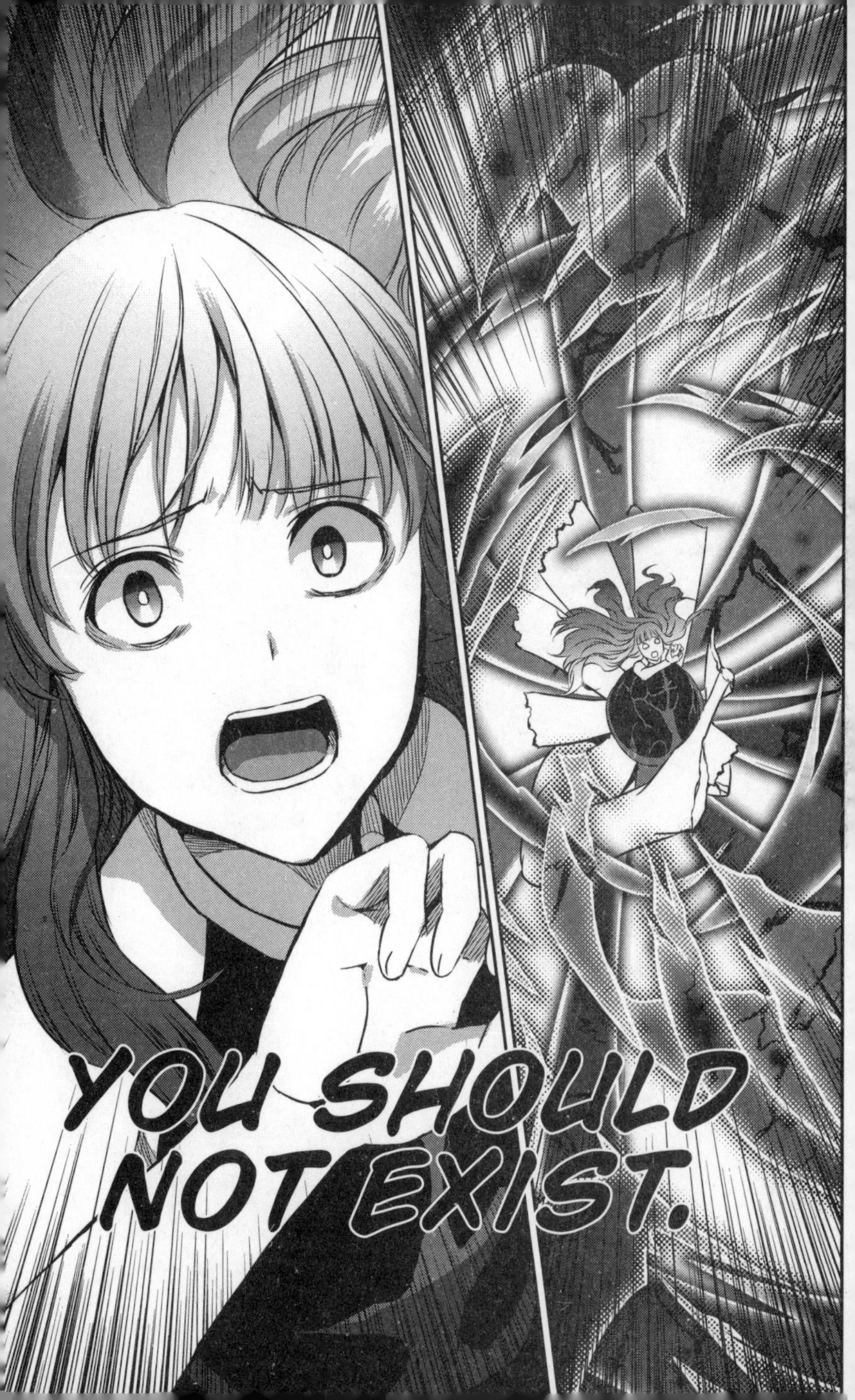
YOU SHOULD NOT EXIST.

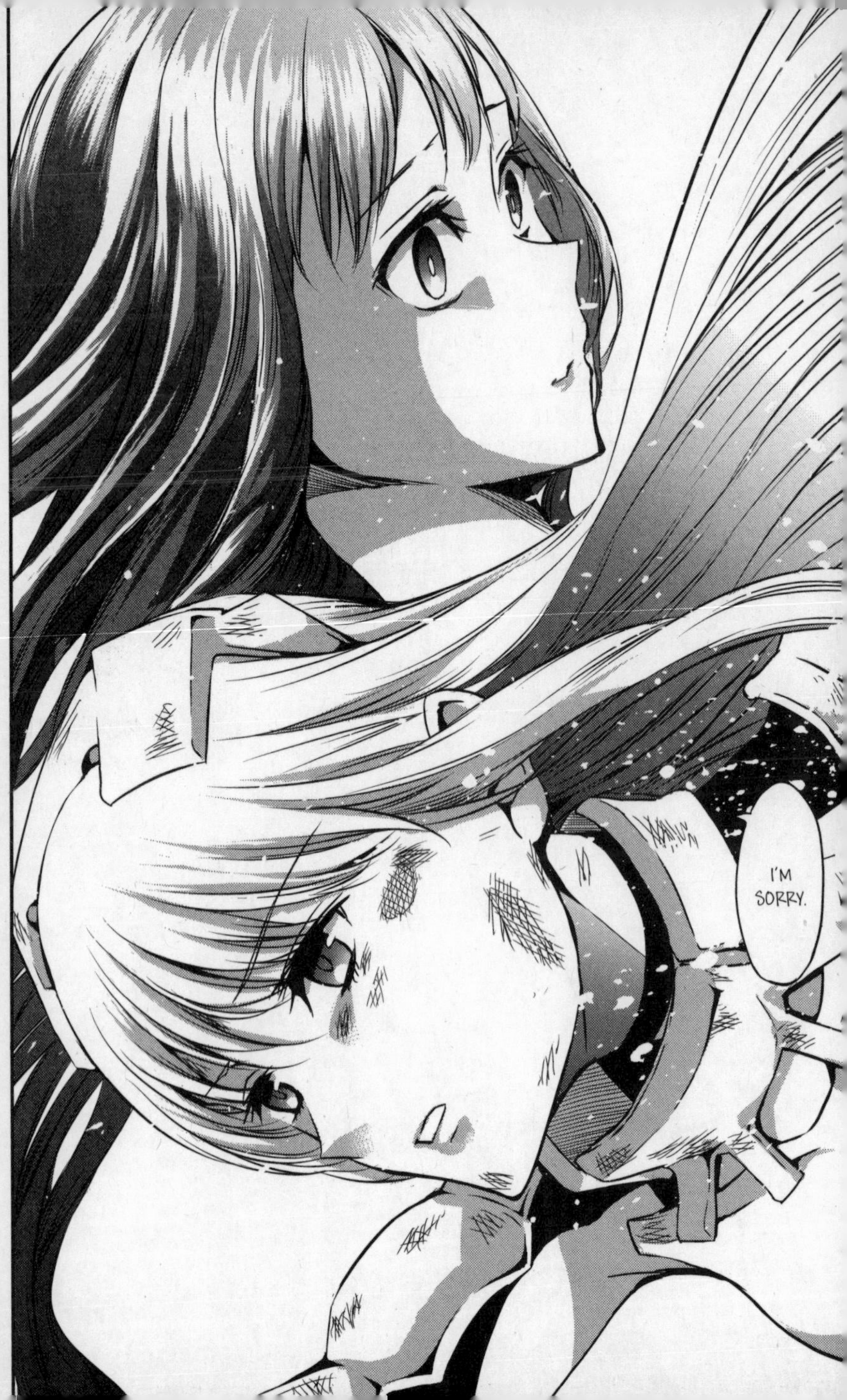
I'M SORRY.

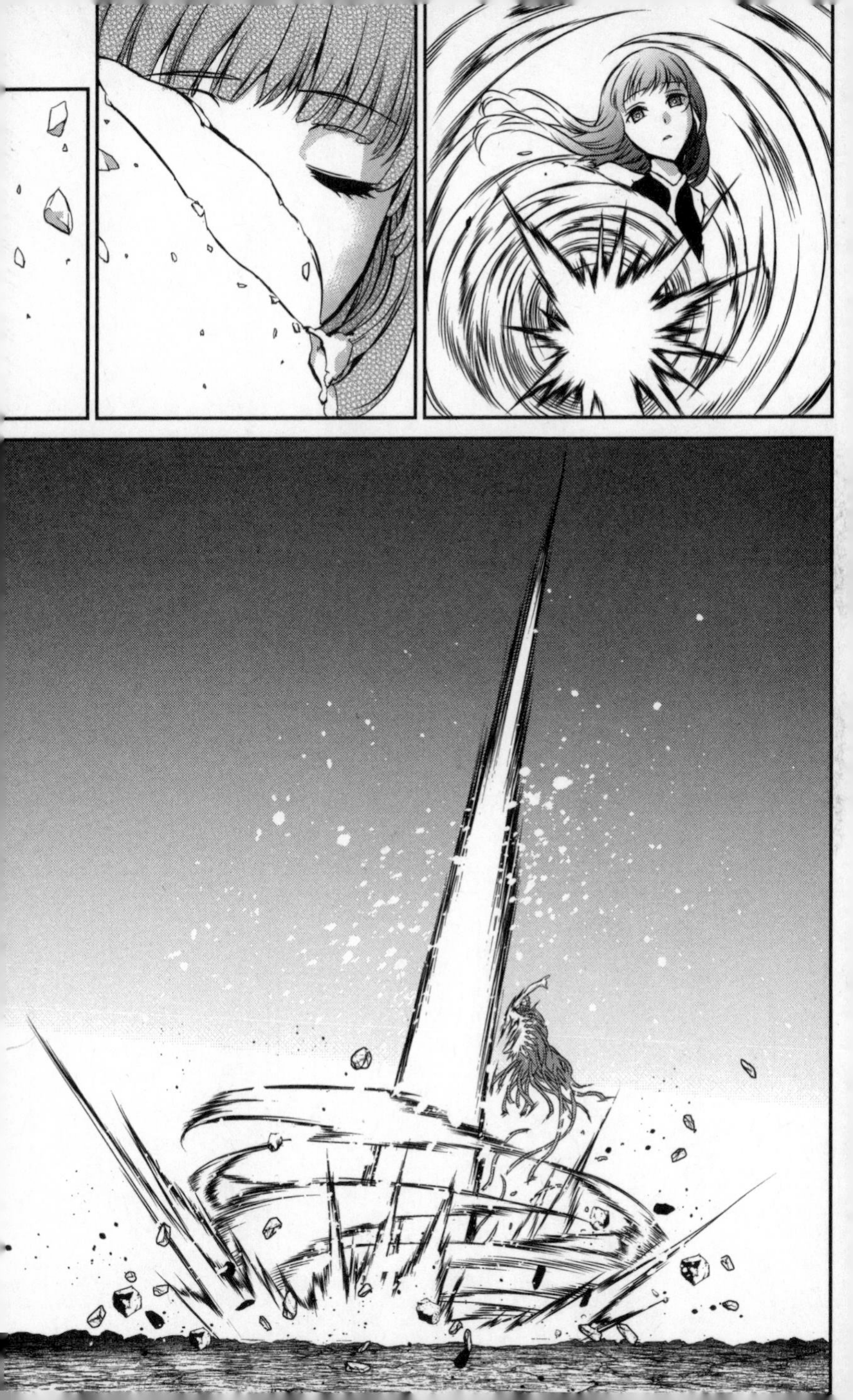

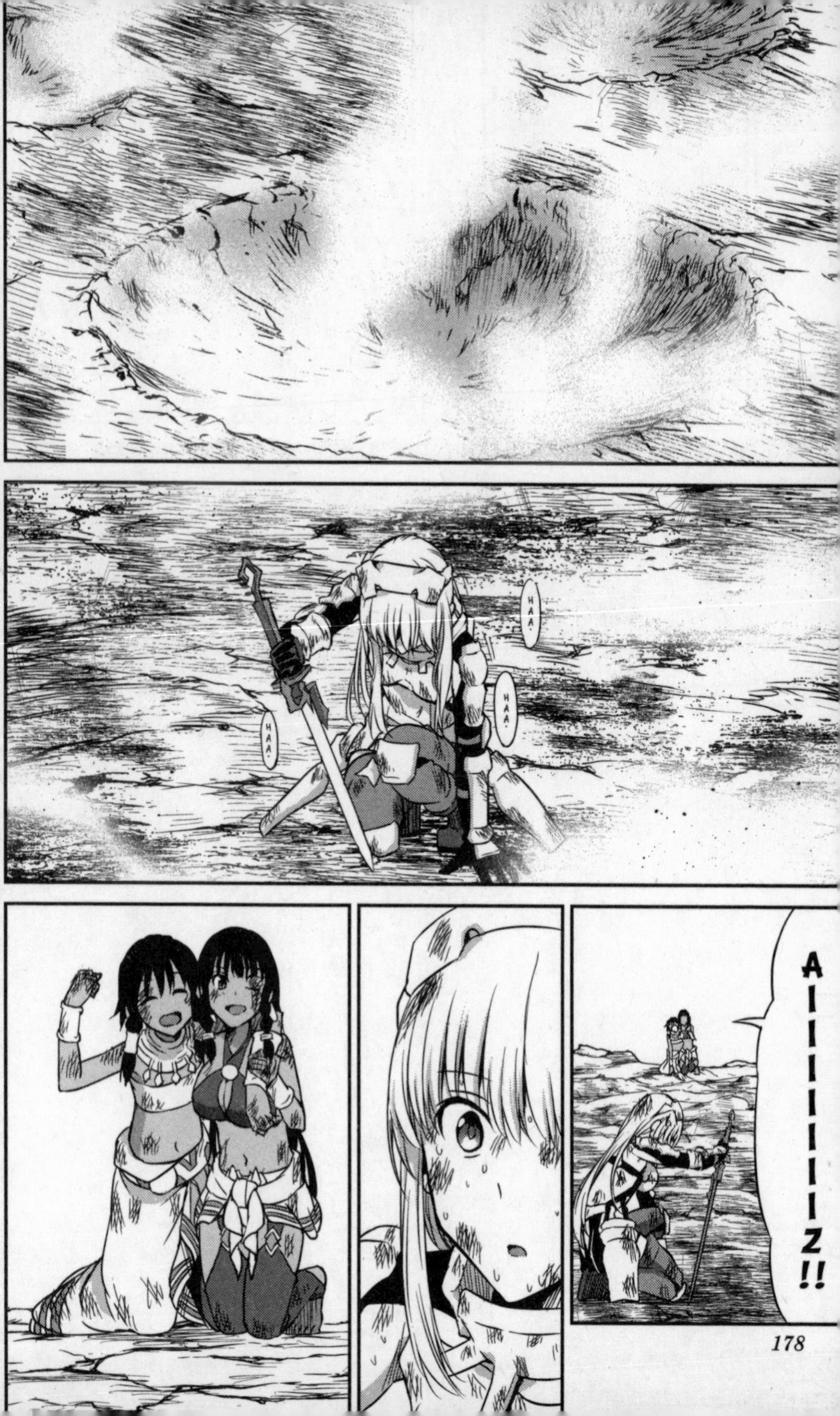
HAA.
HAA.
HAA.
A-IIIIIIIZ!!

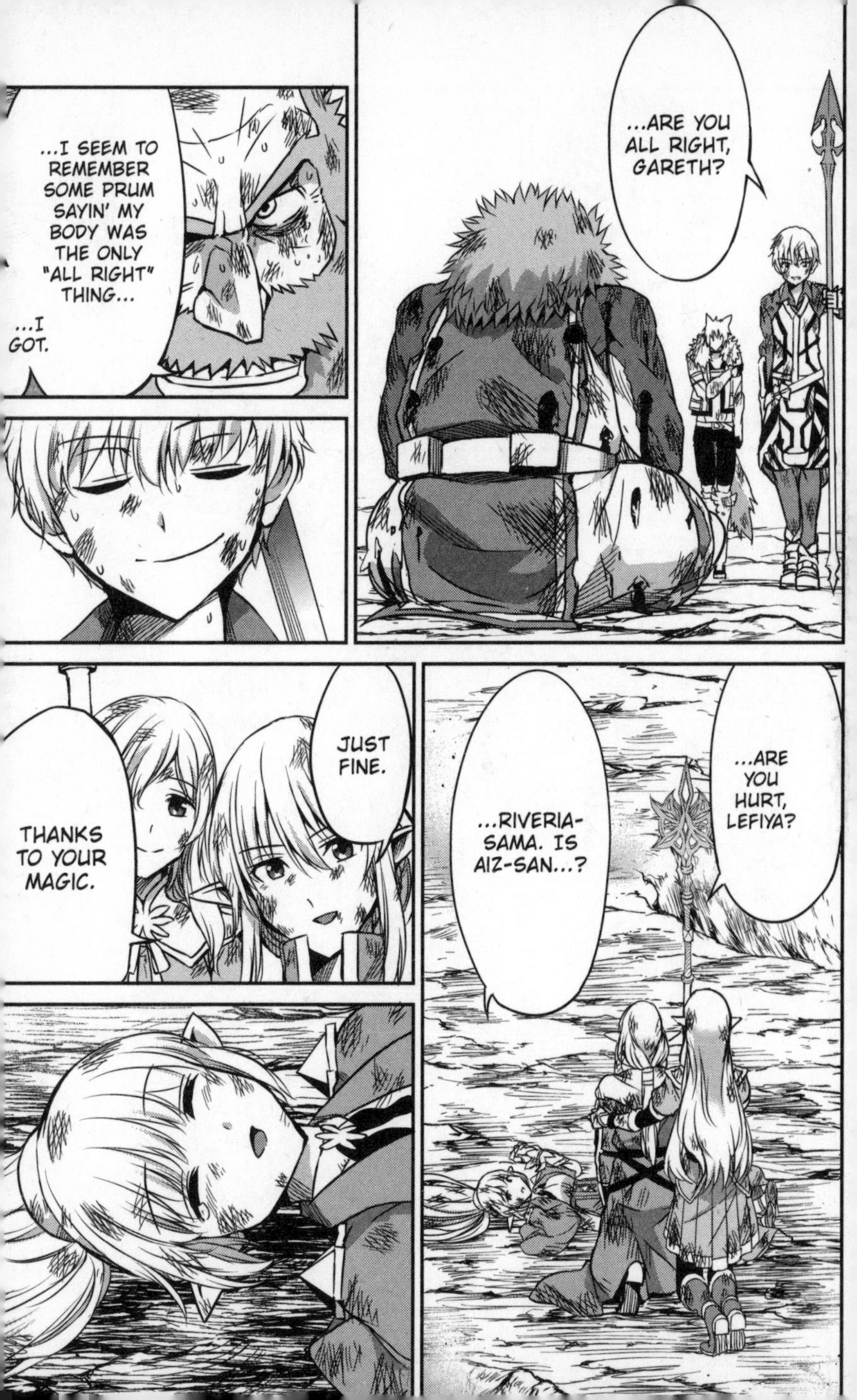
...ARE YOU ALL RIGHT, GARETH?
...I SEEM TO REMEMBER SOME PRUM SAYIN' MY BODY WAS THE ONLY "ALL RIGHT" THING...
...I GOT.
...ARE YOU HURT, LEFIYA?
...RIVERIA-SAMA. IS AIZ-SAN...?
JUST FINE.
THANKS TO YOUR MAGIC.

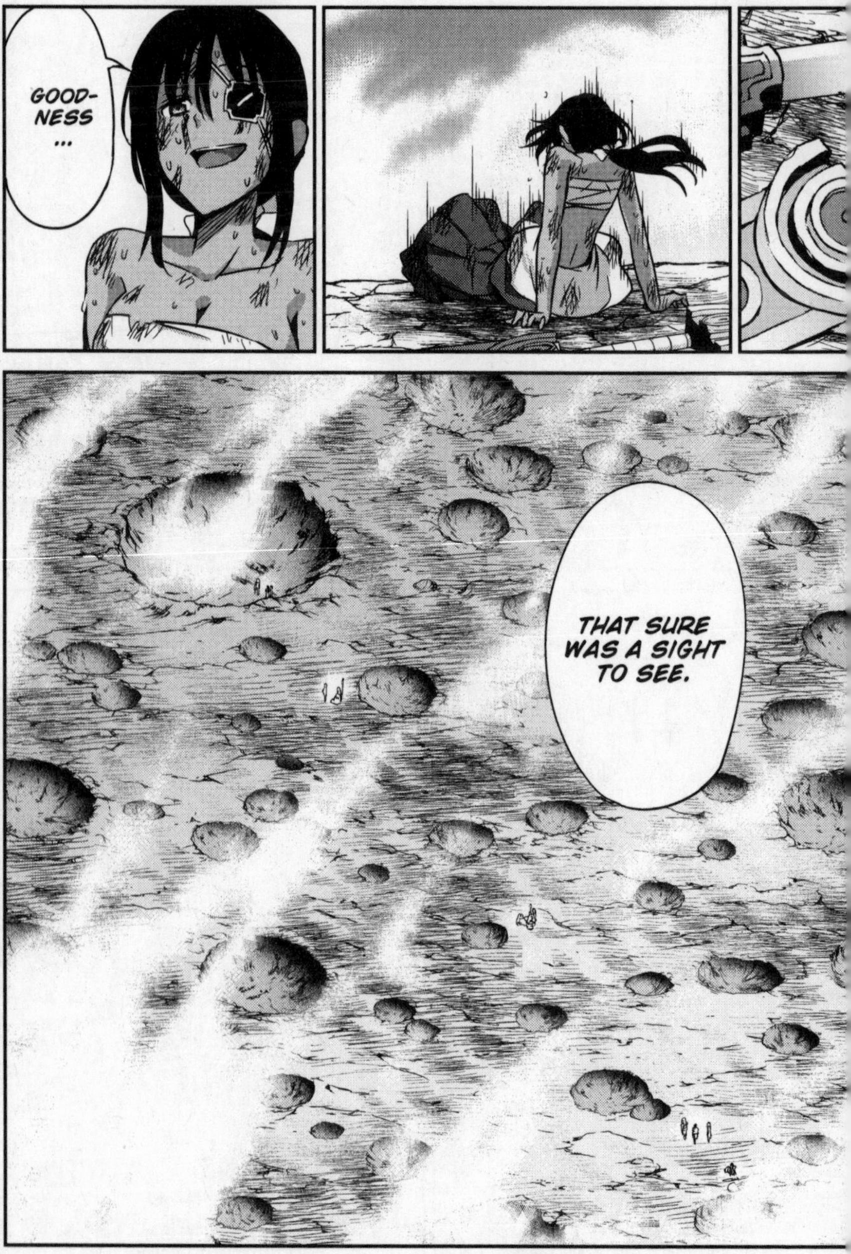
GOOD-NESS ...
THAT SURE WAS A SIGHT TO SEE.

Sword Oratoria 10 End

Is it WRONG to try to PICK UP GIRLS IN A DUNGEON? ON THE SID

Sword Oratoria

bonus. Girl Talk on the Fiftieth Floor

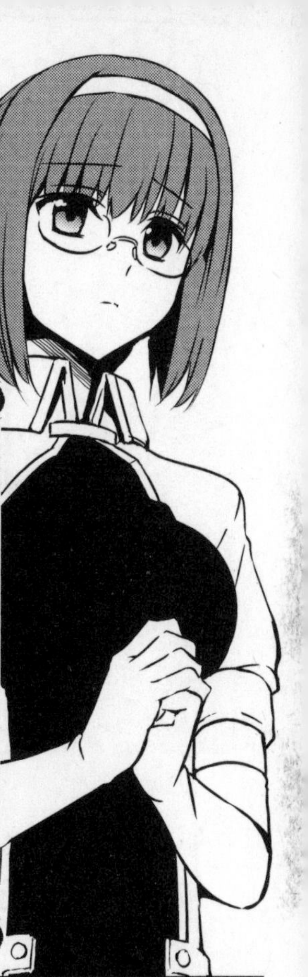

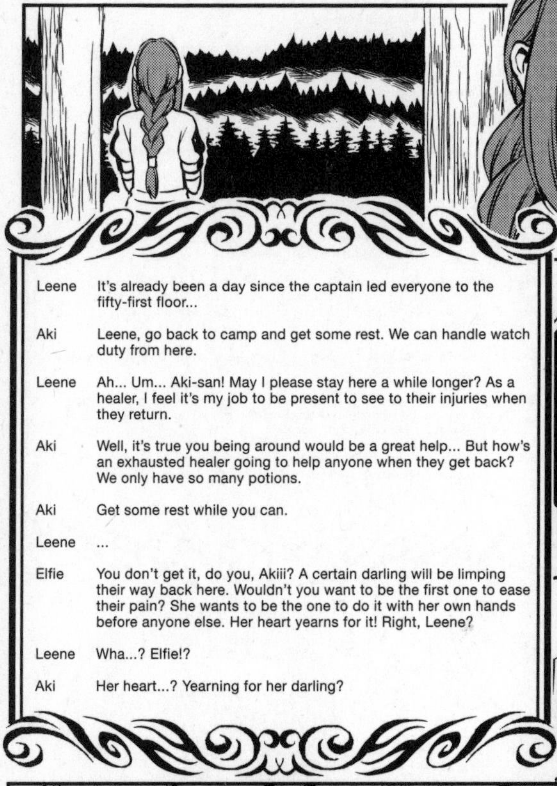

Leene — It's already been a day since the captain led everyone to the fifty-first floor...

Aki — Leene, go back to camp and get some rest. We can handle watch duty from here.

Leene — Ah... Um... Aki-san! May I please stay here a while longer? As a healer, I feel it's my job to be present to see to their injuries when they return.

Aki — Well, it's true you being around would be a great help... But how's an exhausted healer going to help anyone when they get back? We only have so many potions.

Aki — Get some rest while you can.

Leene — ...

Elfie — You don't get it, do you, Akiii? A certain darling will be limping their way back here. Wouldn't you want to be the first one to ease their pain? She wants to be the one to do it with her own hands before anyone else. Her heart yearns for it! Right, Leene?

Leene — Wha...? Elfie!?

Aki — Her heart...? Yearning for her darling?

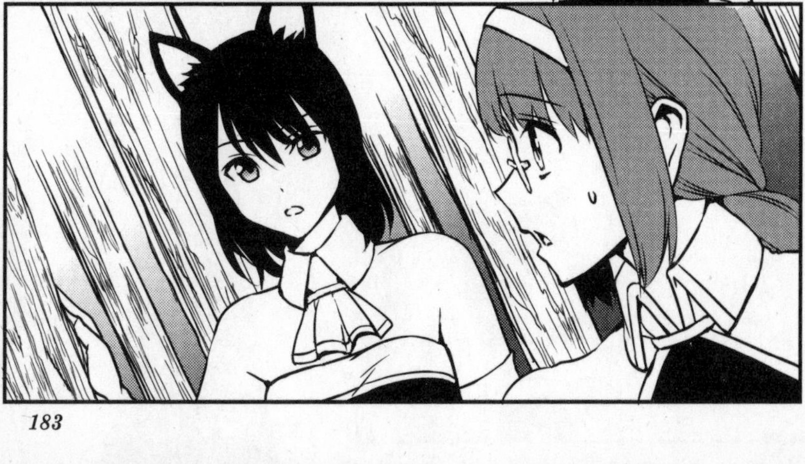

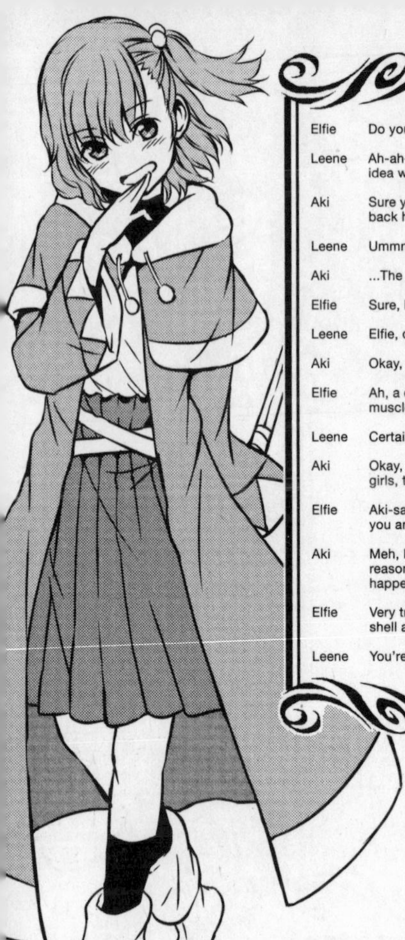

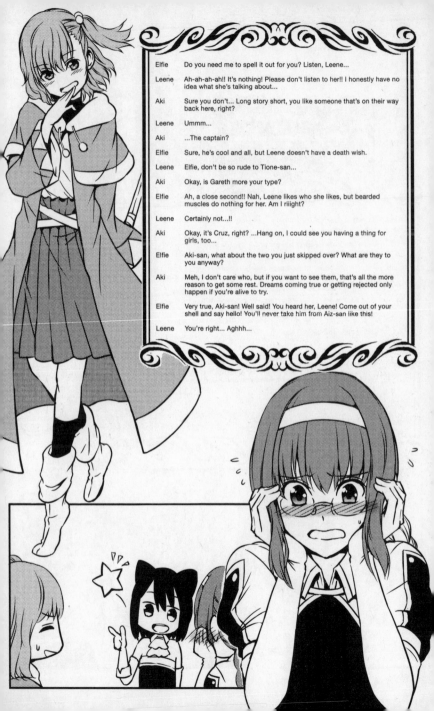

Elfie	Do you need me to spell it out for you? Listen, Leene...
Leene	Ah-ah-ah-ah!! It's nothing! Please don't listen to her!! I honestly have no idea what she's talking about...
Aki	Sure you don't... Long story short, you like someone that's on their way back here, right?
Leene	Ummm...
Aki	...The captain?
Elfie	Sure, he's cool and all, but Leene doesn't have a death wish.
Leene	Elfie, don't be so rude to Tione-san...
Aki	Okay, is Gareth more your type?
Elfie	Ah, a close second!! Nah, Leene likes who she likes, but bearded muscles do nothing for her. Am I riiight?
Leene	Certainly not...!!
Aki	Okay, it's Cruz, right? ...Hang on, I could see you having a thing for girls, too...
Elfie	Aki-san, what about the two you just skipped over? What are they to you anyway?
Aki	Meh, I don't care who, but if you want to see them, that's all the more reason to get some rest. Dreams coming true or getting rejected only happen if you're alive to try.
Elfie	Very true, Aki-san! Well said! You heard her, Leene! Come out of your shell and say hello! You'll never take him from Aiz-san like this!
Leene	You're right... Aghhh...

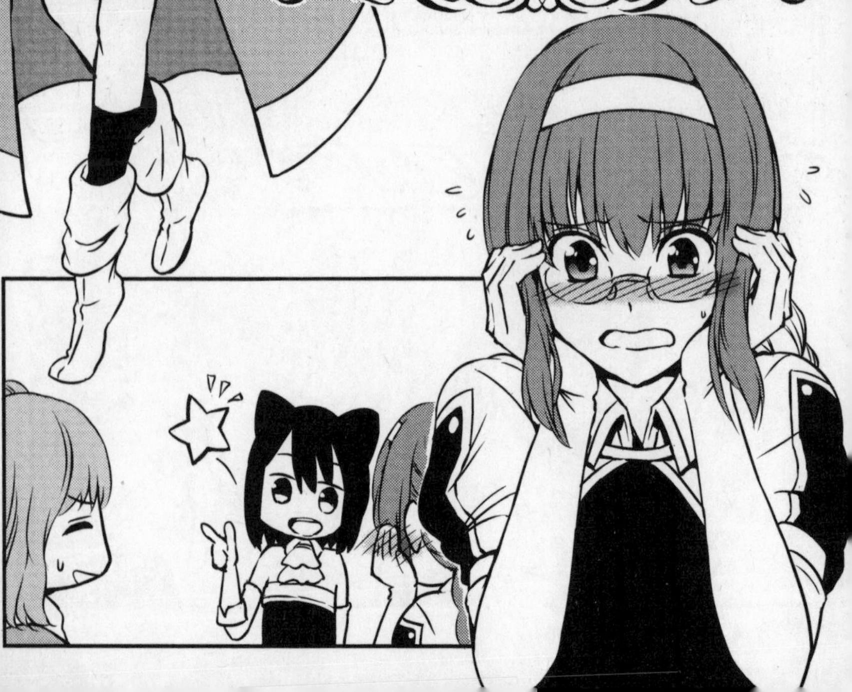

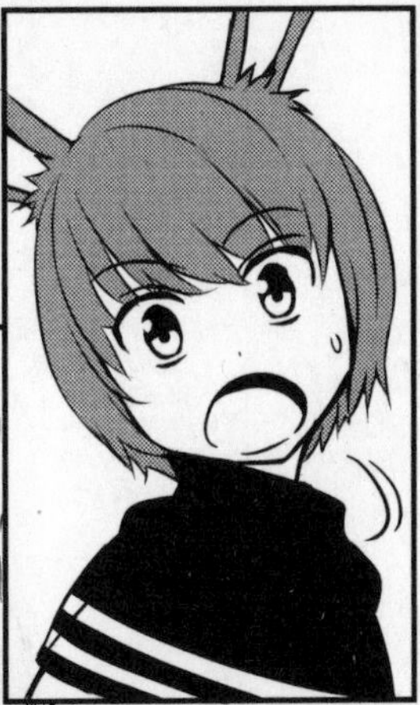

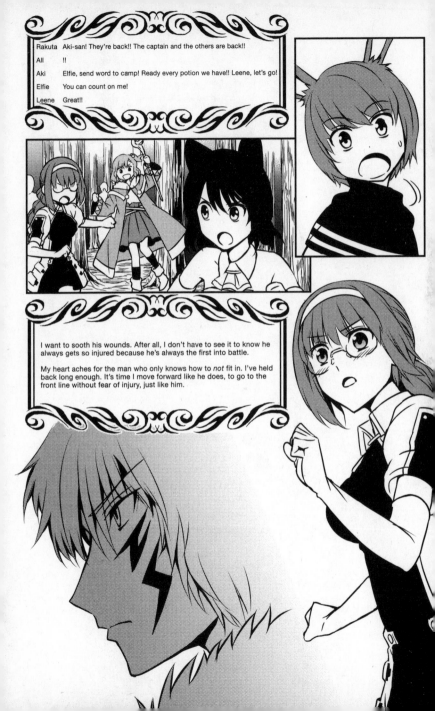

Rakuta	Aki-san! They're back!! The captain and the others are back!!
All	!!
Aki	Elfie, send word to camp! Ready every potion we have!! Leene, let's go!
Elfie	You can count on me!
Leene	Great!!

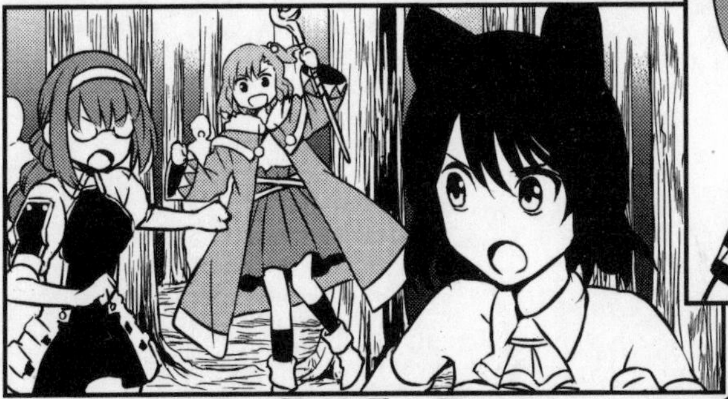

I want to sooth his wounds. After all, I don't have to see it to know he always gets so injured because he's always the first into battle.

My heart aches for the man who only knows how to *not* fit in. I've held back long enough. It's time I move forward like he does, to go to the front line without fear of injury, just like him.

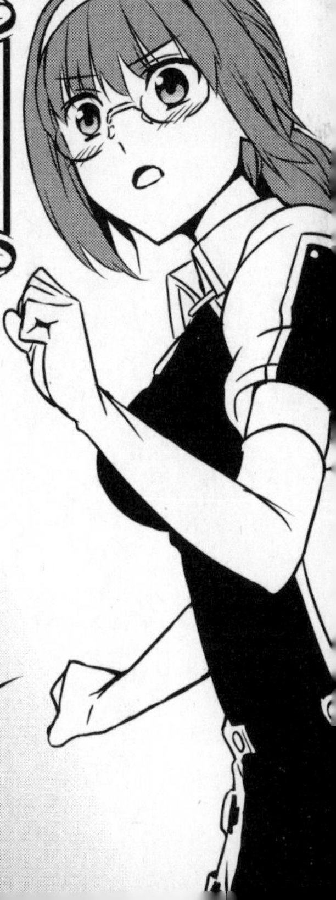

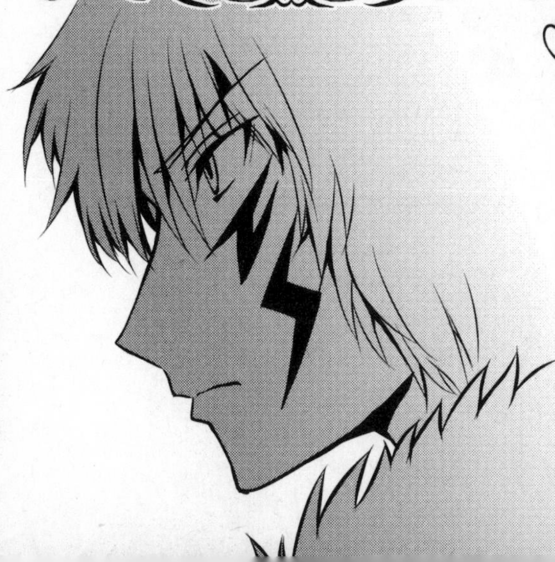

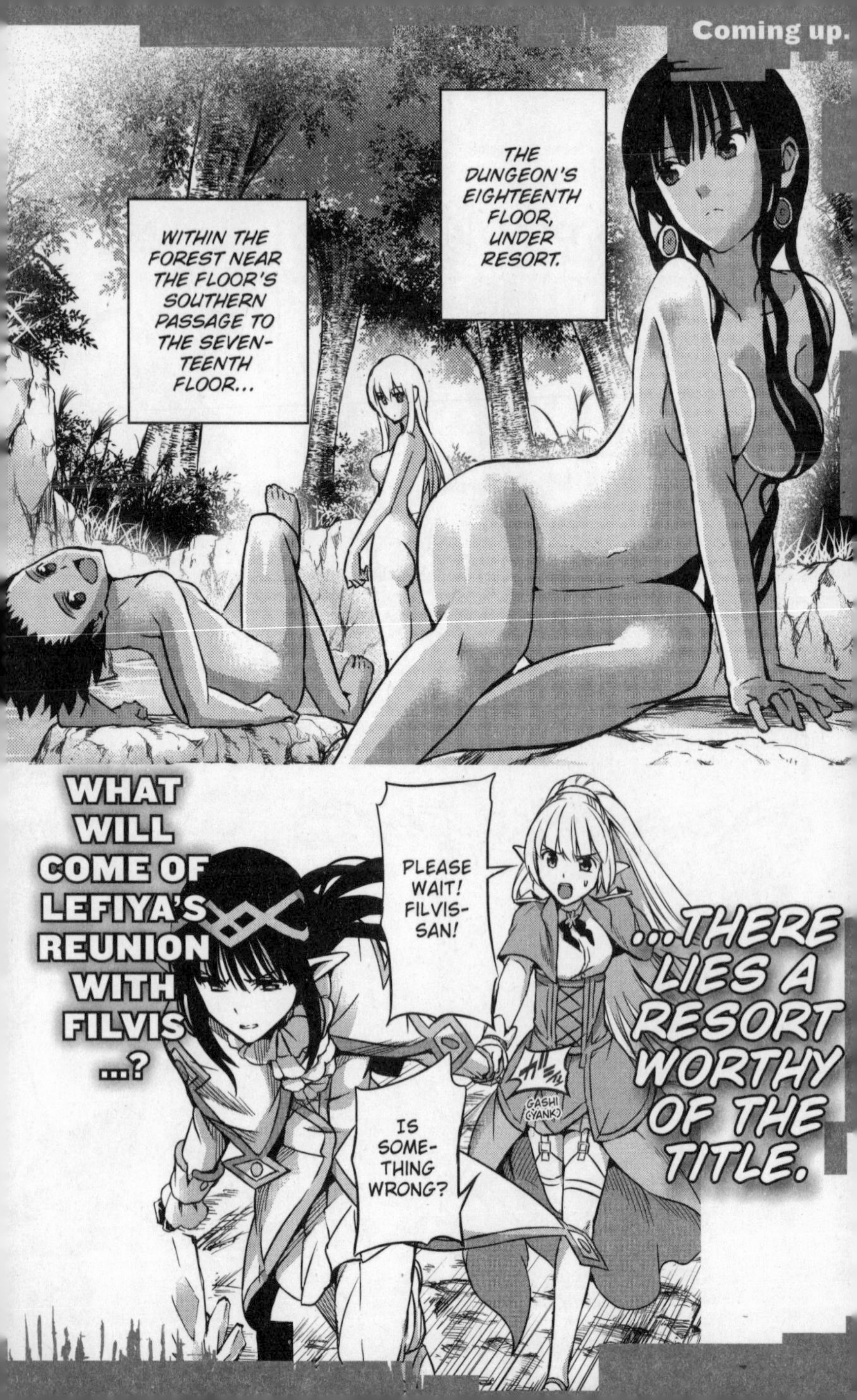
Coming up.
THE DUNGEON'S EIGHTEENTH FLOOR, UNDER RESORT.
WITHIN THE FOREST NEAR THE FLOOR'S SOUTHERN PASSAGE TO THE SEVENTEENTH FLOOR...
...THERE LIES A RESORT WORTHY OF THE TITLE.
PLEASE WAIT! FILVIS-SAN!
GASHI (YANK)
IS SOMETHING WRONG?
WHAT WILL COME OF LEFIYA'S REUNION WITH FILVIS...?

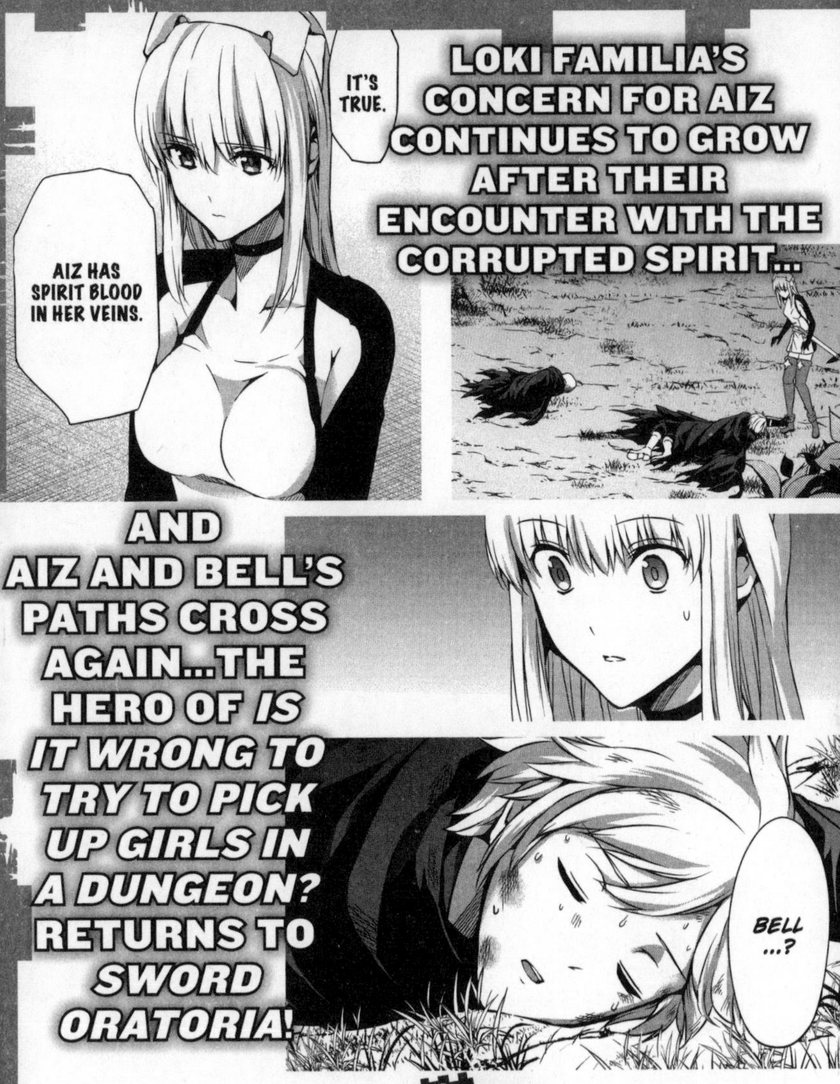
LOKI FAMILIA'S CONCERN FOR AIZ CONTINUES TO GROW AFTER THEIR ENCOUNTER WITH THE CORRUPTED SPIRIT...
IT'S TRUE.
AIZ HAS SPIRIT BLOOD IN HER VEINS.
BELL ...?
AND AIZ AND BELL'S PATHS CROSS AGAIN...THE HERO OF *IS IT WRONG TO TRY TO PICK UP GIRLS IN A DUNGEON?* RETURNS TO *SWORD ORATORIA*!

Is it WRONG to TRY to PICK UP GIRLS IN A DUNGEON? ON THE SIDE

Sword Oratoria 11

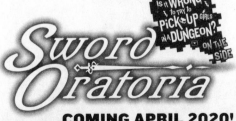

COMING APRIL 2020!

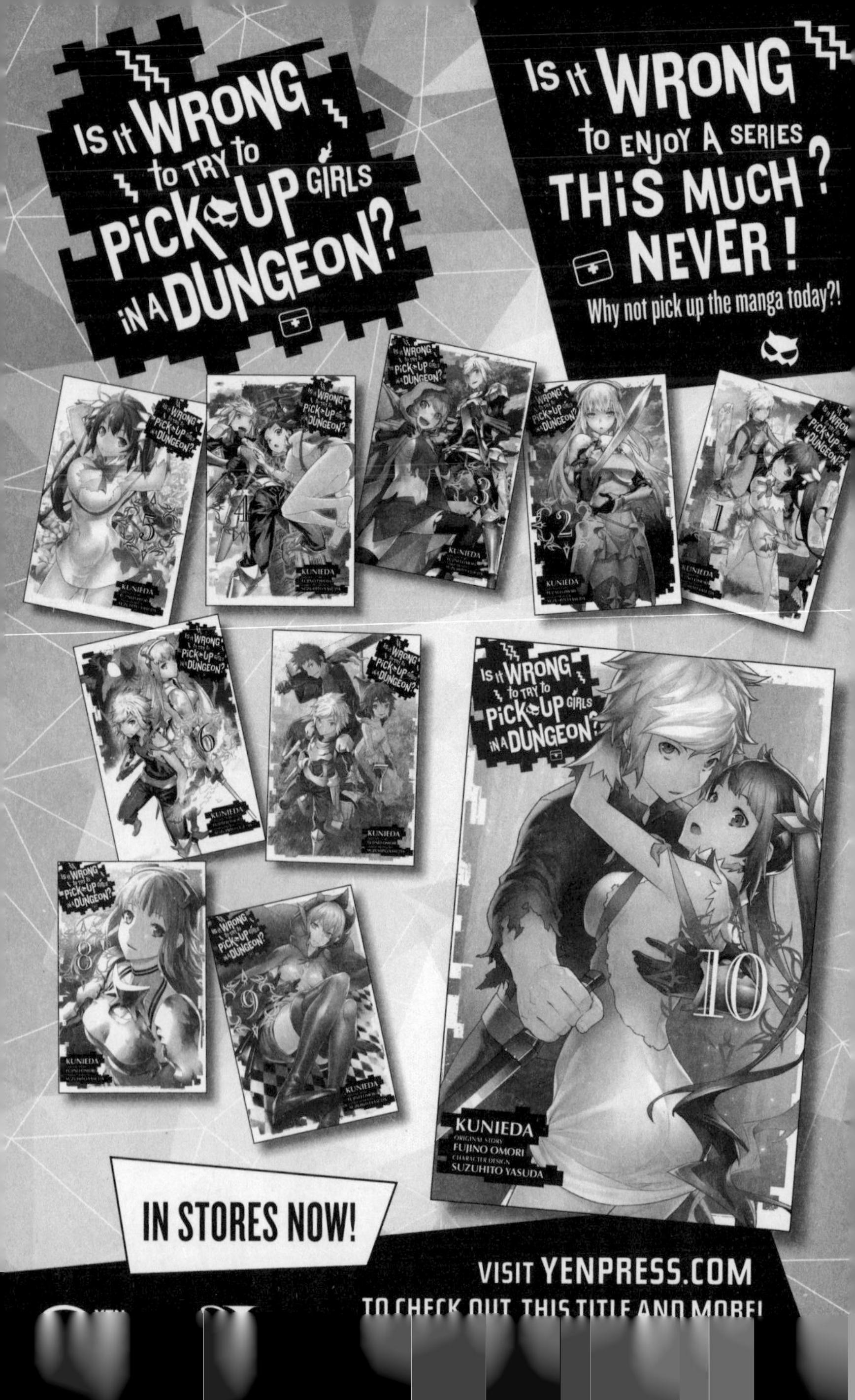
Is it WRONG to TRY to PiCK-UP GIRLS iN A DUNGEON?
Is it WRONG to ENJOY A SERIES THIS MUCH?
NEVER!
Why not pick up the manga today?!
KUNIEDA
ORIGINAL STORY
FUJINO OMORI
CHARACTER DESIGN
SUZUHITO YASUDA
IN STORES NOW!
VISIT YENPRESS.COM
TO CHECK OUT THIS TITLE AND MORE!

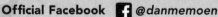

Now read the latest chapters of BLACK BUTLER digitally at the same time as Japan and support the creator!

The Phantomhive family has a butler who's almost too good to be true...

...or maybe he's just too good to be human.

Black Butler

YANA TOBOSO

VOLUMES 1-28 IN STORES NOW!

Yen Press
www.yenpress.com

OLDER TEEN
OT

HE DOES NOT LET ANYONE ROLL THE DICE.

A young Priestess joins her first adventuring party, but blind to the dangers, they almost immediately find themselves in trouble. It's Goblin Slayer who comes to their rescue—a man who has dedicated his life to the extermination of all goblins by any means necessary. A dangerous, dirty, and thankless job, but he does it better than anyone. And when rumors of his feats begin to circulate, there's no telling who might be coming calling next...

Light Novel V. 1-9 Available Now!

Check out the simul-pub manga chapters every month!

FINAL FANTASY®

ファイナルファンタジー ロスト・ストレンジャー

LOST STRANGER

Keep up with the latest chapters in the simul-pub version! Available now worldwide wherever e-books are sold!

For more information, visit www.yenpress.com

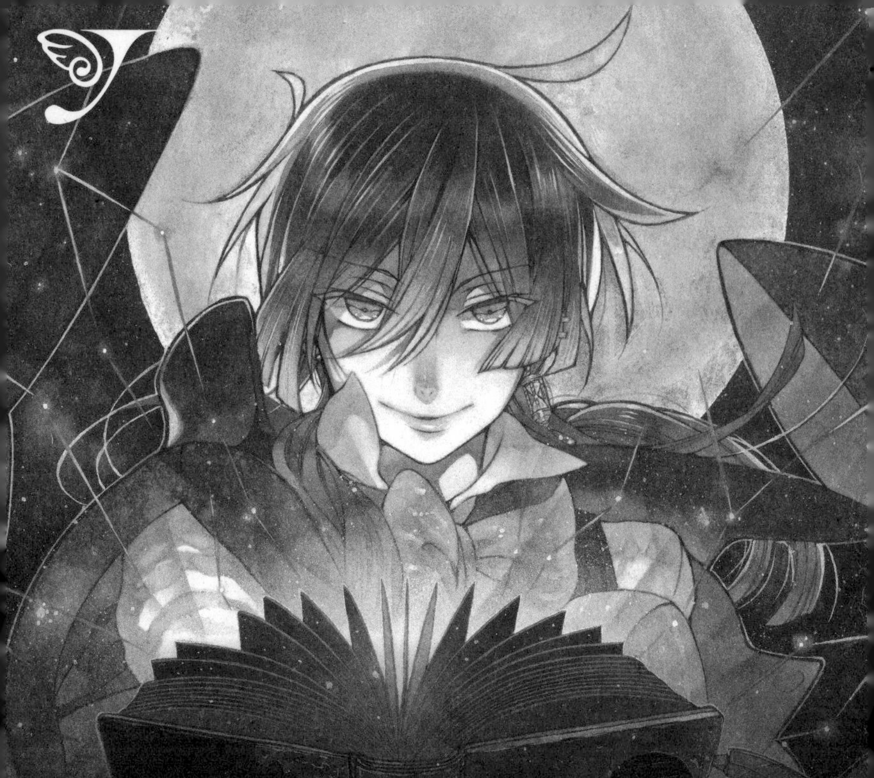

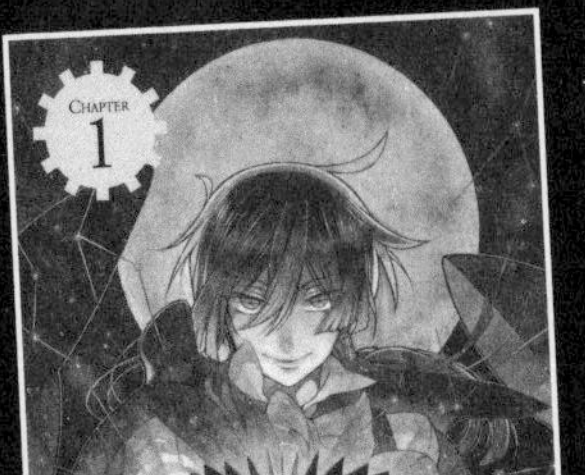
CHAPTER
1
JUN MOCHIZUKI
THE CASE STUDY OF
VANITAS

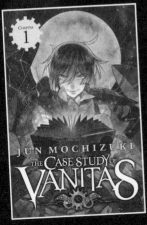

IS IT WRONG TO TRY TO PICK GIRLS IN A DUNGEON? ON TH SIDE: SWORD ORATORIA ⑩

02/20

Fujino Omori
Takashi Yagi
Haimura Kiyotaka, Yasuda Suzuhito

Translation: Andrew Gaippe • Lettering: Barri Shrager

DUNGEON NI DEAI WO MOTOMERU NO WA MACHIGATTEIRUDAROUKA GAIDEN SWORD ORATORIA vol. 10
© Fujino Omori / SB Creative Corp. Character design: Haimura Kiyotaka, Yasuda Suzuhito
© 2018 Takashi Yagi / SQUARE ENIX CO., LTD.
First published in Japan in 2018 by SQUARE ENIX CO., LTD.
English translation rights arranged with SQUARE ENIX CO., LTD. and Yen Press, LLC through Tuttle-Mori Agency, Inc.

English translation © 2020 by SQUARE ENIX CO., LTD.

Yen Press
150 West 30th Street, 19th Floor
New York, NY 10001

Visit us at yenpress.com
facebook.com/yenpress
twitter.com/yenpress
yenpress.tumblr.com
instagram.com/yenpress

First Yen Press Edition: January 2020

Yen Press is an imprint of Yen Press, LLC.
The Yen Press name and logo are trademarks of Yen Press, LLC.

The publisher is not responsible for websites (or their content) that are not owned by the publisher.

Library of Congress Control Number: 2016946068

ISBNs: 978-1-9753-3212-9 (paperback)
       978-1-9753-3213-6 (ebook)

10 9 8 7 6 5 4 3 2 1

WOR

Printed in the United States of America